COMMON POSTSCRIPT OPERATORS

Array and String Operators	
int **array** array	creates *array* that initially contains *int* null objects as entries.
array **aload** $a_0..a_n$ array	successively pushes all *n* elements of *array* onto the operand stack, where *n* is the number of elements in *array*, and finally pushes *array* itself.
int **string** string	creates *string* that initially contains *int* null objects as entries. *int* must be a non- negative integer less than the device-dependent maximum string length.
array index string index **get** any	looks up the *index* in *array* or *string* and returns the element identified by *index* (counting from zero).
array index value string index value **put** —	stores *value* into *array* or *string* at the position identified by *index* (counting from zero).
array string **length** int	returns *int* as the number array of elements that make up the value of *array* or *string*.
any string **cvs** substring	converts object *any* to a string. *any* is changed from its current form to an appropriate string representation, and stored in the first section of *string*, which is overwritten.

Dictionary Operators	
int **dict** dict	creates a dictionary *dict* with the initial capacity for *int* value pairs. (In Level 1, also the maximum number of pairs that can be contained in the dictionary.)
dict **begin** —	pushes *dict* onto the dictionary stack and makes it the current dictionary.
— **end** —	pops the current dictionary from the dictionary stack.
key value **def** —	associates *key* and *value* in the current dictionary.
dict **length** int	returns *int* as the current number of key-value pairs in *dict*.
dict **maxlength** int	returns *int* as the maximum number of key-value pairs that *dict* can hold using the current amount of memory allocated to it.
dict key **get** any	looks up the *key* in *dict* and returns the associated value.
dict key value **put** —	uses *key* and *value* and stores them as a key,value pair into *dict*.
dict1 dict2 **copy** dict2	copies all elements of *dict1* into *dict2*.

(Continued on inside back cover)

Computer users are not all alike.
Neither are SYBEX books.

We know our customers have a variety of needs. They've told us so. And because we've listened, we've developed several distinct types of books to meet the needs of each of our customers. What are you looking for in computer help?

If you're looking for the basics, try the **ABC's** series. You'll find short, unintimidating tutorials and helpful illustrations. For a more visual approach, select **Teach Yourself**, featuring screen-by-screen illustrations of how to use your latest software purchase.

Mastering and **Understanding** titles offer you a step-by-step introduction, plus an in-depth examination of intermediate-level features, to use as you progress.

Our **Up & Running** series is designed for computer-literate consumers who want a no-nonsense overview of new programs. Just 20 basic lessons, and you're on your way.

We also publish two types of reference books. Our **Instant References** provide quick access to each of a program's commands and functions. SYBEX **Encyclopedias** and **Desktop References** provide a *comprehensive reference* and explanation of all of the commands, features and functions of the subject software.

Sometimes a subject requires a special treatment that our standard series don't provide. So you'll find we have titles like **Advanced Techniques, Handbooks, Tips & Tricks,** and others that are specifically tailored to satisfy a unique need.

We carefully select our authors for their in-depth understanding of the software they're writing about, as well as their ability to write clearly and communicate effectively. Each manuscript is thoroughly reviewed by our technical staff to ensure its complete accuracy. Our production department makes sure it's easy to use. All of this adds up to the highest quality books available, consistently appearing on best-seller charts worldwide.

You'll find SYBEX publishes a variety of books on every popular software package. Looking for computer help? Help Yourself to SYBEX.

For a complete catalog of our publications:

SYBEX Inc.
2021 Challenger Drive, Alameda, CA 94501
Tel: (510) 523-8233/(800) 227-2346 Telex: 336311
Fax: (510) 523-2373

SYBEX is committed to using natural resources wisely to preserve and improve our environment. As a leader in the computer book publishing industry, we are aware that over 40% of America's solid waste is paper. This is why we have been printing the text of books like this one on recycled paper since 1982.

This year our use of recycled paper will result in the saving of more than 15,300 trees. We will lower air pollution effluents by 54,000 pounds, save 6,300,000 gallons of water, and reduce landfill by 2,700 cubic yards.

In choosing a SYBEX book you are not only making a choice for the best in skills and information, you are also choosing to enhance the quality of life for all of us.

Understanding PostScript

Understanding PostScript®

Third Edition

David A. Holzgang

SYBEX®

San Francisco • Paris • Düsseldorf • Soest

Acquisitions Editor: Dianne King
Developmental Editor: Kenyon Brown
Copy Editor: Peter Weverka
Project Editor: Kathleen Lattinville
Technical Editor: Sheldon M. Dunn
Word Processors: Ann Dunn, Susan Trybull
Book Designer: Eleanor Ramos
Production Arist: Lisa Jaffe
Chapter Illustrations and Art: Alissa Feinberg
Technical Art: Delia Brown
Screen Graphics: Cuong Le
Typesetter: Stephanie Hollier
Proofreader: Arno Harris, Janet Boone
Indexer: Anne Leach
Cover Designer: Ingalls + Associates
Cover Illustration in Photo: Len Gilbert
Cover Photographer: Michael Lamotte

SYBEX is a registered trademark of SYBEX Inc.

Library of Congress Card Number: 92-80098
ISBN: 0-7821-1059-2

Manufactured in the United States of America
10 9 8 7 6 5 4 3 2 1

ACKNOWLEDGMENTS

Although nothing is more solitary than the practice of writing, turning an idea into a book requires both personal and professional support and assistance, and I have been lucky enough to have both.

On the professional side, I would like to thank Bill Gladstone for encouraging me to turn my ideas into a proposal and for his guidance on the most effective format for doing it. I would also like to thank Chuck Ackerman at SYBEX for believing in the proposal and building it into a project. And I would like to thank Yvonne Perry at Adobe Systems for her help and advice.

Once the project was under way, I was particularly helped by the constructive and supportive editorial staff at SYBEX. David Kolodney gave invaluable advice on organization and approach. Jim Compton organized the work, clarified my prose, and generally put up with the first-time author's crises and traumas with good humor and consistently constructive advice. Elizabeth Forsaith scrupulously edited the manuscript, and Jeremy Elliot worked through the examples and critically reviewed the technical information.

For the second edition, I would like to extend additional thanks to those who have helped me review and revise the book. At SYBEX, Marilyn Smith provided the detailed editorial support and Barbara Gordon provided the overall editorial direction, both with their usual combination of patience, precision, persistence, and good humor. I would also like to thank Glenn Reid of Adobe Systems for his continued willingness to answer my questions and share his outstanding technical expertise.

The third time is, indeed, a charm. For this third edition I would like to once again extend additional thanks to those who have helped revise the book and keep it relevant and useful. On the professional side, thanks to Ross Smith for his help and comments on PostScript Level 2. Thanks also to the very enthusiastic editorial supports, including Ken Brown at SYBEX, who helped steer this through the revisionary shoals; Peter Weverka, who edited the manuscript with dedication; and Mac Dunn, who persistently and ably worked through all the examples, both old and new, to see that I got it right. Many thanks also to the dedicated support personnel at SYBEX: Kathleen Lattinville, project editor; Susan Trybull and Ann Dunn, word processors; Stephanie Hollier, typesetter;

Alissa Feinberg and Lisa Jaffe, artists; Arno Harris and Janet Boone, proofreaders; and Anne Leach, indexer. Also thanks to Richard Mills for being such a superb courier.

On the personal side, I would like to thank Frank for getting me into this and Colman for advice and for not laughing when I told him. And I would like to thank Shirley for setting the alarm every morning and not minding.

Contents at a Glance

Table of Contents

3

Introducing Fonts and Graphics
127

4

Creating and Modifying Fonts
203

5

Building a Basic Document
265

6

Working with Advanced Text
355

7

Working with Advanced Graphics
399

A

Summary of PostScript Operators
443

INTRODUCTION

This book is a guide to understanding and using the PostScript page-description language. PostScript was designed and developed by Adobe Systems, Inc., as a general-purpose programming language that also contains a large number of graphics operations defined within it. The entire concept of programming in PostScript, as you will learn from this book, is to combine the basic PostScript operations into powerful procedures that you can use to create and print complex pages of text and graphics.

WHAT IS POSTSCRIPT?

PostScript is a *page-description* language. That means that it was designed specifically to communicate a description of a printable document from a computer-based composition system to a raster-output printing system. This description is a *high-level* description, because it describes pages as a series of abstract graphic objects rather than describing them at a detailed, device-limited level.

PostScript is embedded in an interpreter program that generally runs in an independent device, such as a laser printer. The interpreter program (or just the *interpreter*) translates PostScript operations and data into device-specific codes and controls the output device to generate the graphics being described on the page. The interpreter processes each element—a name, string, array, number, or whatever—that is presented to it completely before it proceeds onto the next element. You will learn all about these *syntactic objects* in the following chapters as we discuss PostScript programming and its requirements.

This introduction and overview will help you understand how to use this book and how the book was set up to help you learn PostScript. The first section introduces you to the PostScript language and discusses how to "think" in PostScript. Because PostScript embodies many new concepts, particularly those oriented toward graphics and page structure, you will want to understand some of the unique characteristics that give PostScript its distinct flavor before you start learning the language itself. Although all of these characteristics are more fully explained in the body of the book, you will find the work easier and more understandable if you have a survey of the language before you get caught up in the specifics.

The second section of this introduction deals with the purpose of the book and the structure that has been used to support that purpose. Post-Script is a rich and complex language, and, like any such language, there is more to be said about it than can be reasonably contained in a single book. This section sets out in some detail the objectives that this book is designed to meet and relates those to the reader's expected needs and background.

This book is heavily oriented toward examples and illustrations; it adopts a "learn by doing" approach. Because of this approach, the second section of this introduction also contains information about the setup of hardware and software that will enable you to run the examples.

THINKING IN POSTSCRIPT

PostScript represents a new and exciting way of creating complex pages of output, including both graphics and text. In many ways, PostScript seems to me to return to a time of artistry and craftsmanship when creating a page of output was not a purely mechanical operation performed by high-speed presses, but was an interaction between a human hand and mind and the physical output. Although PostScript provides links to high-speed output, the basic language and approach has much more in common with letter-ing and calligraphy than with mechanical presses and typewriters.

By design, PostScript treats letters as graphic objects, or as shapes to be painted onto the output page. Moreover, PostScript provides features and oper-ations that will allow you to control the precise rendering of text and graphics in ways that are not easily possible with older typesetting and printing technol-ogies. You can stretch, bend, shade, and clip letters, using their shapes as graphic elements to create interesting (and sometimes even bizarre) effects. The net result of these possible controls is to create an environment where you can design pages in ways that are more reminiscent of a medieval manuscript than a newspaper front page.

One of the driving forces behind the increased use of PostScript is the need to be able to represent the potential range of output on raster devices in some high-level, device-independent way. Graphic artists have come to realize that there is a new, effective tool available to them, one that can both do the old tasks well, reducing the repetitive portion to a minimum, and also provide scope for new, innovative approaches that were not feasible before. This feeling has been enhanced by the development and acceptance of electronic page-composition systems that use PostScript as their link to the individual devices, thus greatly expanding the potential for high-quality output. To appreciate the potential range of opportunities embodied in these applications, you need to understand PostScript's unusual capabilities as a computer language.

PREVIEW OF THE POSTSCRIPT LANGUAGE

The PostScript language has several distinctive characteristics that are important from the viewpoint of the PostScript user and programmer alike. It is both a programming language and a page-description language, and its special characteristics derive directly from this dual nature. It is

- Interpreted
- Device-independent
- Graphically powerful
- Page-oriented

These characteristics are important qualities for you to understand before you begin working in PostScript.

Interpreted

PostScript is an interpreted language, like BASIC or APL. This means that PostScript operators are understood and acted upon by another program, the interpreter, which generally resides in the controller of the output device (the laser printer, typesetter, etc.). Use of an interpreter provides both advantages and disadvantages to the programmer. On the plus side, it allows the definition of many program requirements as the commands are being executed, which provides both flexibility and sensitivity to the current state of the output and the output device. It also allows for immediate feedback, error recognition, and command execution, which makes interpreted languages easier to debug and correct. Finally, an interpreter may use specialized hardware to speed up common tasks and so enhance efficiency and throughput.

However, there are some negatives to an interpreted language as well. In particular, because the interpreter is itself a program, there is an additional layer of software being executed. This can slow things down. In PostScript's case, this loss is usually not great, since the interpreter is running by itself in the output device and therefore doesn't take up the resources of your computer.

Interpreted languages do not, in themselves, impose any specific structure on a program. So PostScript does not place any required structure on a document description—which is the PostScript equivalent of a program. This can be a negative point if the programmer doesn't impose a clear structure on him- or herself. Generally, attention to such requirements and the self-discipline to enforce them comes only with some experience in the language. There is both discussion and practice of certain recommended formats and conventions in the following chapters precisely because this kind of self-discipline is essential in an interpreted environment.

PostScript has already established a recommended structure and approach that we will discuss more fully in Chapter 2. Use of these conventions is not required for creation of successful PostScript page descriptions (programs), but following them makes clear to yourself and others what each part of the program is doing so programs can be easily compared and modified.

Dynamic

Because PostScript is an interpreted language, it is able to provide feedback to the programmer or the PostScript application. This is particularly valuable in determining the current state of the execution environment; such as, for example, whether a certain font is currently loaded and available. This is one sense in which the PostScript language is dynamic.

Another sense is that PostScript page descriptions can be defined and modified as they are created by definition of new operations from the basic set of graphic and procedural operators. This dynamic process, which also is a function of the interpreter, makes PostScript significantly more powerful than traditional page-description mechanisms.

Device Independent

One of PostScript's great strengths is that it is independent of any specific output device. The basic set of PostScript operators is designed to be appropriate to the general class of raster-output devices upon which the language can be implemented. It is the interpreter's problem to adjust and convert PostScript commands to the specific device's requirements. On the other hand, where there is a need for specific, device-dependent information in order to construct a page or an image, PostScript has the capability to do that as well.

This freedom from the constraints of a specific output engine provides two major benefits to the PostScript programmer. First, you can generally remain unaware of the specific requirement of the output device. Second, a page described in PostScript can be proofed on one device and then produced on another with no modification of commands or operators. This means that pages can be proofed, corrected, and reset very quickly by use of a convenient, relatively inexpensive output device, such as a laser printer. It also means they can be generated for final printing output on a typesetting machine once the proof and correction cycles have been completed. In this way, you gain the benefits of automated processing and quick turnaround while still having the quality of output only available from high dot-density devices. It is this benefit that has created much of the excitement about "desktop publishing" in the business community.

Graphic Power

PostScript is especially designed for the creation and manipulation of graphic objects on a raster-output device. This orientation towards graphics is such a major component of the language that I believe that the best way to think of PostScript is as a method of drawing electronically. It is, in a sense, electronic calligraphy. Almost 30 percent of the operators deal with graphics; and many of these operators are intuitively similar to the actions of a skilled calligrapher handling a pen—raising it, positioning it on the paper, inking it, and then stroking each character onto the page. And PostScript provides powerful primitive operators, such as **scale** and **rotate**, which, as mentioned above, can be combined in many ways to produce dramatic and surprising output. A number of examples in later chapters demonstrate this power.

This flexibility makes PostScript the language of choice for serious work, particularly work that combines text and graphics on a page. Where other languages or mechanisms are impediments to combining text and graphics, PostScript makes it easy and natural. This facility in combining the two modes derives in a large measure from PostScript's approach to text.

Within PostScript, text elements—individual characters—are themselves graphic objects that can be positioned, scaled, and rotated as required.

Page Description

Finally, PostScript is a page-description language. A raster-output device essentially prepares graphic output as a unit, all at one time. For convenience, we generally call this output unit a "page," since it most often represents a physical page; however, the actual output might be a roll of output film or paper, a computer screen, or any other appropriate output mechanism. Raster devices work by setting each point on the page to a precise value. For black-and-white output, these points, or pixels, are set to either 0 or 1, representing either black or white. The page description is therefore a complete map of these values for the entire surface to be output—usually a full page, but sometimes less.

There are fundamental drawbacks to the pixel-by-pixel method of page description. Three of these issues stand out as particularly undesirable from the user's viewpoint:

- The description is particular to a specific device. It can only represent one array of values for a given page, even though different devices (of differing resolution or format) may require different values to represent the same page.

- The full description of a page is inevitably large. It requires one value for every addressable point on the page. For a typical laser output device, for example, this comes to more than 90,000 values per square inch.

- The mathematical process of deciding which points get what values for representation of a given image (called scan conversion) requires a substantial amount of computation and may not be possible to do at an acceptable speed on a small machine like a personal computer.

PostScript provides a mechanism for describing a page of graphic objects rather than a page of pixels. It does this by using powerful primitive operators that correspond in a relatively natural way to how you ordinarily handle graphics. These operators can be combined to produce a wide range of complex output.

PostScript Language Levels

Over time, the PostScript language has grown and changed in several ways. It has become more flexible and added additional features as it has become more popular. As a result, Adobe Systems, the creator of the PostScript language, has consolidated all these advances into a single, new language level, called Level 2. Level 2 consolidates many features of PostScript that were not uniformly provided in earlier devices, and adds some important new features as well, such as file filters and device-independent color. At the time that this book is being written, the available Level 2 devices are the Apple LaserWriter IIf and IIg printers, the Data Products 960 printer, and the Tektronix Phaser 2PXi color printer. However, more and more Level 2 devices are being announced and distributed every day, and, in the long run, all PostScript devices will migrate to Level 2 functionality.

All PostScript devices that are not Level 2 devices are called Level 1 devices. Typical Level 1 devices are the Apple LaserWriter IINT and IINTX, the Hewlett-Packard LaserJet family of printers when equipped with a PostScript cartridge, the Linotronic family of image-setters, and many others. All PostScript devices, both Level 1 and Level 2, support the same core features. Some Level 1 devices incorporate additional features, such as additional color operators, packed arrays, or composite fonts, that are now included in all Level 2 devices.

In this book, you will learn primarily these core operations that are part of every PostScript device. In addition, we will discuss some of the advanced features that are available in Level 2. In coding, the emphasis will be on creating code that is compatible with both Level 1 and Level 2 devices. As you will see, if you create compatible code, you generally will be using the most efficient techniques for coding, regardless of the actual output device.

PostScript Operators

One of the strengths of PostScript is its extensive set of basic operators; they cover both ordinary program tasks and graphic operations. The library of PostScript operators can be divided for this work into five major groups:

- Stack and mathematical operators. This group covers stack-handling operations, array and dictionary processing, and all mathematical operations.

- Graphics operators. This group consists of all operators that handle graphics on the user page except those operators specifically related to font definition and handling. This includes operators to handle path construction and painting, as well as those that control PostScript's internal graphics memory.

- Font operators. This includes all operators to define and control fonts.

- Program control operators. This set includes operators to handle relation tests of various types and file operations as well as altering or controlling the sequence of execution.

- Device control and status operators. This group of operators contains all the operators that set or report the current state of the output device being used.

Do not confuse this grouping of operators with the standard groups presented in the *PostScript Language Reference Manual, Second Edition*. Even when the names are similar, the above groups are generally more inclusive and are presented and used here for conceptual organization and discussion purposes.

This represents a rich set of possible operations; and each has a specific, useful place in a programmer's PostScript lexicon. However, similar to English itself, you will probably be able to accomplish 90 percent of your work (or more) with 15 percent of the operators (or less). Because this book is directed toward understanding the basics of the language, it will concentrate its examples and discussions on the most useful 15 or 20 percent of these operators.

This is a reasonable and effective method for mastering a new programming language. It is in many ways analogous to learning a foreign language. You want to learn the structure and flow of the language—the "grammar" if you will—and then a useful "vocabulary" of frequently used operations. Once that is done, you should try to add one or two new operators to your repertoire with every new programming opportunity. This will help you grow in confidence and competence and master the full range of PostScript's possibilities.

BOOK PURPOSE AND STRUCTURE

The purpose of this book is to teach you to understand and use Post-Script. PostScript is, as has been said repeatedly, an extremely powerful language. Unfortunately, the power of a computer language is generally directly related to its complexity, and PostScript is no exception to this relationship. PostScript is not inherently difficult to use; it is only unfamiliar and complex. This book is structured to minimize the complexity by introducing you to PostScript operations step by step, which helps you become familiar and comfortable with PostScript through practice and discussion of many examples, and thus opens up to you the range of power in PostScript procedures.

The structure of this book has developed out of long experience in using and teaching interpreted programming languages. PostScript, like most interpreted languages, provides an interactive mode of operation. In this mode, the interpreter holds a dialogue with the user, immediately performing each operation and reporting back any results or errors. This mode of operation is an advantage for learning a language because it allows you to see the effect of each command as it is executed. In this way it pinpoints the place where a program has gone wrong or done something you didn't expect it to do. This mode also allows you to stop at any point, try out alternative commands, and see how the page looks as a result. Thus, you can see the changing page as you reshape its description. The book takes advantage of this by providing exercises that are designed to allow you to develop and test them interactively.

There is one point of caution for readers who are running on an Apple-Talk network. You will need some special help to get interactive access (or as close to interactive access as AppleTalk will allow). Please read Appendix C, ''Configuration Data and Setup,'' which contains some specific instructions on how you should set up and run the exercises.

The book also includes in its structure three proven techniques that can help you build your understanding of PostScript. First, the book follows a course of study that is designed to present the various operations in Post-Script in a natural way. The book also proceeds in a cumulative manner, with each topic and exercise building on the previous ones. Finally, the book provides ample exercises and examples to help you practice the concepts presented in a concrete setting and allow you sufficient drill to make these concepts and operations really familiar.

OBJECTIVES OF THE BOOK

As stated previously, no single book can adequately explore and discuss the complete range of PostScript operations. Therefore, objectives that are discussed here represent the primary criteria that were used to determine what materials were included and in what order and depth those subjects were covered.

At the broadest possible level, the goal of this book has already been stated: to help you understand and use PostScript. This statement, however, is too expansive to provide much guidance for the construction of a satisfactory work. Therefore, three more specific objectives have been defined and arranged in a priority ordering.

The first objective is to teach you to read PostScript code. This means more than just looking up the operators in a manual. Sometimes that kind of reading is necessary, but it is not the kind of fluency that we want to develop here. This objective means that you should be able to understand PostScript concepts and operations with depth and accuracy. You will learn the basic PostScript vocabulary and structure, so that you can follow most PostScript code without recourse to a reference guide (either this book or any other). By the end of the book, you should be able to follow most PostScript programs, especially ones that you have not written yourself, and comprehend at a general level what the program does and how it does it. In other words, you should be able to read PostScript pretty much the same way you read English—sometimes by referring to a dictionary or grammar, but mostly by following ordinary constructions without difficulty.

The second objective is to teach you to work with PostScript. This means that you will be able to set up PostScript in its various modes of operation and, particularly, be able to invoke and use the interactive mode for debugging and testing. From the exercises, you will be familiar with defining PostScript operations and analyzing PostScript problems. Overall, you should have a good grasp of how PostScript works and what facilities it has available.

The last objective, but by no means the least important one, is to teach you to write PostScript programs. You will learn to analyze and set up page output. You will use these setups to generate the necessary procedure definitions, and you will then program those procedures to generate the pages that you have analyzed. This process of structuring pages, designing solutions to create the pages, and then implementing them in PostScript is at least as important a component of learning to write the language as is the use of the various operators.

Obviously these objectives are intertwined so closely that each supports and makes use of both of the others. Like any good text, the book does not distinguish each objective, but tries to teach all three of them with each exercise or lesson. In this way, you will learn both the individual PostScript operators and the process of combining those operators into PostScript procedures in a unified way.

Requirements

What do you need to get the most out of this book? To begin with, you should be willing to work through the examples. PostScript is like any other language, in that ease and proficiency come from practice. So you should do the exercises and examples, perhaps even more than once. I would encourage you to try alternative approaches, and print out your variations to see how you are progressing. One of the most interesting things about PostScript, in my experience, has been how much fun it is to play with. You can generate an amazing variety of graphics just by trying options and operators. Please enjoy this experience; it will make the whole process more satisfying for you.

General computer concepts are not covered here. Although I try to define precisely all terms that are intrinsic or even related to PostScript, a number of concepts that apply to computer operations and computer languages generally are not defined. Things like what a file is and what a computer language does are taken more or less for granted. If you find yourself having trouble with these kinds of things, look in the computer books section of your local bookstore for some recommended books on basic computer concepts.

The general matter of computer operations also is not covered here. I'm not going to tell you how to turn on the computer or the printer, or how to start up your programs (other than PostScript). The issue of computer operations is particularly sticky with PostScript, since it can be run on any computer onto which you can hook an RS232 port and connect a PostScript-equipped device. In particular, PostScript is widely used on both the Apple Macintosh and IBM-PC lines of computers, both of which (to make a vast understatement) are quite different. The general tendency in this book has been to avoid device- or operating-system-dependent text and examples, and allow you to work out how to talk to the PostScript device on your own. This presumes, of course, that you are familiar with the computer you're using. If you have trouble, look first at the operations manual (or manuals) that came with the computer, then try the device manual for your specific output device, and finally try this book.

You will want to know what resources, besides this book, you might want to have handy. To begin with, you will almost certainly require a PostScript output device. Although it is possible to follow the examples in the book without actually doing them yourself, the learning experience will be immeasurably improved if you can input and execute these examples. The book expects you to do so, and meeting the second objective above can only be accomplished through a "hands on" approach. If you don't have a PostScript device available for your own use, a number of places (at least in Northern and Southern California) rent time on their PostScript-equipped Apple LaserWriters for reasonable fees. It would certainly be valuable for you, under these circumstances, to rent a little time and try at least the larger exercises on a PostScript device.

If you are going to do much PostScript work, you will also want to own the book mentioned earlier, the *PostScript Language Reference Manual, Second Edition*. It is written by Adobe Systems, the creator of PostScript, and is the definitive source for all PostScript operators and operations. The *Second Edition* covers all the new and improved features in Level 2. It has been reorganized and presents some additional information on the language. You don't need it to use this book; all the required definitions are provided here for your use and reference. Even if you have other references, you don't want to be flipping back and forth between several books while you are trying to learn the material. But as you grow beyond what you have learned here, you will need precise and complete definitions for every possible PostScript operator. That is what is provided in the *PostScript Language Reference Manual*; it is the ultimate reference and referee for all PostScript operations. There are several places throughout the book where you are referred to the *Language Reference Manual* for further detail or explanations of various operations.

STRUCTURE

The book follows a regular pattern that grows naturally out of the objectives discussed above. It is organized in a sort of spiral, in that certain topics recur in regular succession but with increasing depth and complexity. Thus you will first encounter simple text output, using the most basic operations and relying, as much as possible, on default parameters in the language. Then you will explore PostScript procedures and dictionaries, followed by basic graphics. Then you return to text processing again, this time using the procedures and graphics techniques already developed to help you build more complex text output. And so on, through advanced fonts and dictionaries, more text and, finally, very advanced graphic concepts.

Task Orientation

The basic orientation of the book is to do first and talk after. The idea is that you will have a much better appreciation of the discussion of what the program means after you have executed it, instead of analyzing it to death before running it. This is an excellent basic approach to language instruction generally, whether natural or computer languages—just ask Berlitz.

However, this approach cannot be followed entirely. Page composition is inherently a process that depends on some analysis and planning to work correctly. Moreover, some choices have to be dealt with before you start programming, otherwise the program and the associated procedures will look entirely arbitrary and capricious. To this extent, the exercises include preliminary setup and analysis. Beyond what is required for that reason, no preliminary programming is undertaken. Instead, the exercises and examples all have extensive discussions, usually line-by-line, after the program is presented and run. The intention is to provide you with the concepts necessary for the program before you write it, to use the actual program as an example, and then to discuss the specific use and results of these concepts as embodied in the program after the exercise is completed.

Exercises and Examples

The programs included in this text are broken down into two informal groups: examples and exercises. The examples are short, usually quite simple, and designed to illustrate one or two specific points from the text. The exercises are longer and more complex, and generally combine several previous techniques into one major program.

Both the exercises and examples are to some extent cumulative. Because of the structure of the PostScript language, it is both appropriate and useful to create procedures that do certain tasks and reuse these procedures over and over, occasionally reworking them in small ways to fit the current need. That is not to say that you need to work the examples in order; most of them are complete programs in themselves, and can be entered and executed on their own without error. However, the explanations that accompanied them initially are not repeated in the text when the procedure is reused. Therefore, if you are skipping around and you need to look up a specific procedure to understand some point, you will have to look back at the first instance of its use in the book to find a complete discussion.

The concepts used in the book are also cumulative. As you might have guessed from the earlier discussion of the spiral nature of the material, much use is made of previous concepts and techniques as you proceed further into the book. Indeed, some of the material in the later chapters will be almost incomprehensible if you are not fully familiar with certain PostScript operations and ideas that have been explained, discussed, and illustrated in earlier portions of the book. This is, to some extent, a process of developing vocabulary to enable further discussions to proceed quickly and precisely.

If you do want to skip around in the book, I would recommend that you use the "Operator Review" sections at the ends of the chapters as a quick guide to the material covered in the chapter. I would also suggest that you at least read through the exercises before you skip the chapter. If the exercise is clear, well and good; you can proceed with the assurance that you understand the work done so far in the book. If the exercise is not clear, however, you should read the explanations and discussions before proceeding.

Device Use

All of the work in this book, both text and examples, relies on generic PostScript features and is not tied to any specific implementation of Post-Script in any specific device. Any exercise or example should execute correctly on any PostScript-equipped device and at any language level, and the concepts and techniques that you will learn are as applicable to a typesetter as they are to a laser printer.

The work in the book is based solely on PostScript; there is no use of any language or program other than PostScript in this book. That means that you can complete all of the examples using only a PostScript-equipped device and a terminal, if necessary. Note that this would be an impossible request if it were not the case that PostScript is a perfectly good general-purpose language as well as a specialized one.

Obviously, each reader will have a specific configuration of hardware and software. The book is structured for use by everyone; but what do you do if you have a specific problem? Unfortunately, we are not able to provide detailed information on every possible configuration. However, Appendix C, "Configuration Data and Setup," contains specific information for two common configurations, one for an IBM-PC and the other for an Apple Macintosh. Even if your specific setup is not included, you may want to read whichever of these is most similar to your configuration if you have a problem. It may give you some ideas or information that will help you out.

Chapter Summaries

This book contains seven chapters (besides this Introduction). These illustrate the spiral or recurring nature of the topics that we discussed above. The general contents of the chapters are outlined below.

Chapter 1: Getting Started

This chapter covers the basic functions of PostScript and starts you working in the interactive mode. It also introduces certain PostScript concepts that are essential to understanding and working with PostScript operators. The chapter includes a number of exercises to illustrate these basic functions. The examples and exercises all produce a variety of text output onto a simple page.

Chapter 2: Definitions and Dictionaries

This chapter covers two important PostScript facilities. The first is the PostScript dictionaries. PostScript uses dictionaries heavily for a variety of processes. Here is your first encounter with these vital objects, and with an associated set of examples to help you use their basic operators. The second is the facility within PostScript to define procedures. This is at the heart of PostScript programming, and the exercise here provides a good illustration of how to use procedures in PostScript. The chapter ends with a section on naming and structural conventions, which are extremely important in PostScript.

Chapter 3: Introducing Fonts and Graphics

With these basic concepts under control, this chapter introduces the first use of graphics in the book, and shows the connection between the creation of characters in fonts and general graphics operations. The chapter starts with a number of small examples that illustrate the basic graphics operations: creating a line, creating closed figures, and shading or filling an area on the page. Then the chapter discusses basic font mechanisms, including how you establish and use the PostScript fonts. Finally, the chapter returns to the use of graphics and discusses curves and coordinate transformations. Again, there are a number of examples, culminating in an exercise that links many of the preceding functions to create a logo for an imaginary company.

Chapter 4: Creating and Modifying Fonts

This chapter returns to our discussion of the PostScript font machinery and how it works in actual use. The chapter covers typical operations of the font mechanism in some detail, and then begins to review the possible changes that the programmer can make to a font. These are categorized into two simple sets: the modification of all characters in the font simultaneously, and the modification of characters individually to achieve certain effects. A general discussion of adding fonts to PostScript either by creating new ones or downloading them is included. The chapter contains a variety of examples that illuminate the techniques involved.

Chapter 5: Building a Basic Document

This chapter discusses Level 2 enhancements in the language in general terms, and then turns to a large and complex exercise. The chapter discusses basic types of documents, and then proceeds to the creation of a simple order form using PostScript exclusively. Because form processing is supported directly in Level 2, this offers the opportunity to discuss and illustrate how to test for and use Level 2 features in a compatible way. The form is designed to be filled in by data output from a simple data-handling application. The chapter concludes by taking the application data and inserting it onto the form, so that the complete document prints out with all the data inserted as required.

Chapter 6: Working with Advanced Text

This chapter builds upon the concepts discussed in the previous chapters to develop advanced techniques for handling and displaying text. The chapter has only a few examples because of the complexity of the issues, but there is a full discussion of string handling and manipulation along with discussion of word and character justification. An exercise on text justification is included as an example and an inspiration. Next, the chapter discusses joining application output with PostScript programs. This is an important topic, and includes information on how to read and interpret the PostScript code generated by several typical applications.

Chapter 7: Working with Advanced Graphics

This last chapter deals primarily with specialized graphic processing. The first section of the chapter discusses the PostScript advanced graphics controls and operations. The first of these is the concept of stroke adjustment for precise line alignment and control. Because Level 2 devices offer automatic stroke adjustment, this is also used to illustrate again how to test for and use Level 2 features. The next concept is clipping, and some examples of its use in typical situations are provided. This is an important topic for PostScript programmers because it is a powerful tool to aid them in producing some of the most typical PostScript effects. Additional advanced graphics controls cover line handling, arbitrary curves, and various transformations. The second part of the chapter covers image processing, a complex and very demanding process. You will read all about the basic concepts and parameters that are necessary for processing both sampled and synthetic images.

Appendix A: Summary of PostScript Operators

This appendix presents all the operators that you have learned throughout the book in one place and in a common format.

Appendix B: Encapsulated PostScript

This appendix describes the use of Encapsulated PostScript (EPS) files, which are primarily used to produce illustrations.

Appendix C: Configuration Data and Setup

This appendix contains two subsections. The first discusses a typical IBM-PC setup (hardware and software) as required to run an Apple LaserWriter, the second section presents a similar configuration for an Apple Macintosh.

Appendix D: Bibliography

This appendix offers a short list of books related to PostScript programming and other topics discussed in the body of the book, including advanced graphics computations. It also lists some useful PostScript tools for the PostScript programmer.

1

Getting Started

IN THIS CHAPTER YOU WILL BEGIN to examine PostScript operations and operators in depth. This chapter, together with the next, "Definitions and Dictionaries," is intended to give you a clear understanding of how PostScript operates and of how you read and write PostScript code. You will be introduced to a variety of PostScript operators, which command the PostScript interpreter to take various actions. These operators form the basic building blocks of PostScript procedures and programs.

The chapter is centered around two exercises, which are intended to get you acquainted with some actual PostScript coding without becoming too complex and bewildering. Because PostScript is a relatively complex language, these first exercises will be kept simple, thereby avoiding an excessive—and tedious—amount of explanation before you can see any output.

Before you can start the exercises, however, you must understand how PostScript describes a page of output and how to use these page-description concepts in your work. So the chapter begins with a section on PostScript page structure and concepts.

In addition, you need to understand issues relating to starting and operating your system, such as communicating with the PostScript interpreter, typical screen presentation, and possible error conditions. You also need to understand the basic functions that need to be performed within your program in order to print even one line of text. So you will read about the basic start-up issues and about text initialization and positioning.

After these necessary preliminaries, you will execute the two programs that constitute the first exercise, each of which outputs a line or two of text onto the printer. The simplicity of these programs allows you to start working in PostScript and to become familiar with the interactive mode of the interpreter without being too concerned with program errors. Each program is given in detail and includes a complete discussion of what each line is intended to accomplish.

With the successful completion of the first exercise to motivate you, you continue the chapter with a section on PostScript programming in general. After your first excursion into the world of PostScript, you will naturally have questions and will have observed some unusual qualities in the PostScript code. These points, including PostScript stack operations, notation for PostScript examples, and a short discussion of how PostScript handles strings of characters and comments, are covered in this section.

The next section of the chapter consists of a longer program as a second exercise. This program sets several paragraphs in a text-and-commentary, two-column format. This exercise will show you how you can easily use PostScript to accomplish things that may look quite difficult. As before, the actual program is preceded by a discussion of page-setup issues and requirements and is followed by line-by-line analysis of the program so you will understand exactly what was done and, more importantly, why it was done.

The chapter ends with a brief review of the basic PostScript operators that you have encountered so far. This final section is intended as a review and a reference, and it provides in one place and one standard format all the operators that have been previously discussed.

WORKING WITH POSTSCRIPT

The original definition of the PostScript language contained more than 240 *primitive operators* to perform various functions. Over time, that set has been extended, so that Level 2 of the PostScript language includes almost 400 operators (not including the specialized operators which are used only in Display PostScript), which now encompass color printing, image compression, file handling, additional font processing, patterns and forms, and more. These are the operators that are defined in the *PostScript Language Reference Manual, Second Edition*, and are implemented within the PostScript interpreter. They are called ''primitive'' operators because they define the specific functions that the interpreter knows how to perform. These operators form the basic building blocks that make up the PostScript language.

Before you begin writing or modifying PostScript code, you need to acquaint yourself with a basic subset of those operators and become familiar with the unusual structure of PostScript itself. While PostScript is by no means unique in its format and structure, it is distinctive; and a little time spent on understanding and appreciating this will pay off in quicker comprehension and easier handling of PostScript programs.

The PostScript interpreter processes a series of entities, called *objects*. This is a convenient name to describe all the different things that the PostScript interpreter can work with and understand. For our purposes they can be grouped into several intuitive categories: literals, names, and procedures. *Literals* are just what you would expect from the name—numbers, characters, strings, and so forth. *Names* are basically labels for other objects—literals and procedures—that are entries into the various dictionaries. *Procedures* are groups of other objects, meant to be executed in sequence, that are treated as a unit and stored in PostScript memory. All of this sounds more complex than it is, as you will see when we get to the examples further on.

MODES OF OPERATION

There are two basic modes of operation: batch and interactive. These two modes are much the same in that the interpreter behaves the same way in both of them; they differ in the source of the PostScript objects that are being processed by the interpreter and in how error messages and status information are reported.

In the *batch mode*, the PostScript interpreter is presented with a series of objects, usually from a file which it processes sequentially. Generally, of course, such a file is generated by an application program or by a programmer and is intended to create a description of a page or pages. That description is then used to generate output onto the raster device controlled by the interpreter. Most of the interpreter's work is in the batch mode.

Interactive Mode

It is also possible to interact directly with the interpreter when it is implemented in a dedicated device (such as the Apple LaserWriter family of printers). In this *interactive mode*, each PostScript object is sent by the user directly to the interpreter using a terminal and a communication link, or an equivalent mechanism. The PostScript interpreter acts on each object as it is presented, carries out the requested action, and returns any error or status messages back through the terminal. This mode then becomes a kind of "dialogue" with the interpreter, which is particularly useful for learning Postscript and for debugging PostScript programs. For this reason, the interactive mode will be used in our examples almost exclusively.

As we proceed through the examples, we will display the entire contents of the screen so you can see what is going on. Since we are using the interactive mode, you will see both the input and the interpreter response, which will help you see what the PostScript commands are doing.

Operation Overview

There are a few points that you need to know before proceeding. All of these points will be discussed in depth later.

The first key concept is that PostScript works through a *stack* mechanism. This is a place where PostScript operators look for data and return results. For now, you can think of it as a temporary storage area within the interpreter.

As you know, PostScript is a language of *operators* and each operator performs a single function, although sometimes that function can be complex. Most operators require some type of information to work with; this required data is called *operands*. Our second key point is that in PostScript, unlike most other computer languages, the operands must come before the operator. This makes life easy for the interpreter, but hard for the programmer. It means, for example, that you must enter the coordinates for where you want to go on a page before you can tell PostScript to move there. This is a little disconcerting at first, but you'll soon get used to it.

PAGE STRUCTURE

A unique and powerful characteristic of PostScript is its design as a page-description language. A page is the natural unit of output on a raster output device and PostScript operates within that unit in an easily comprehensible way by means of its operators. In this section, you will examine more closely what is meant by a ''page'' and how PostScript's operators work within it.

CONCEPTS

To begin with, remember that when we discuss a ''page'' here, we are not specifically referring to any particular shape or size of output. A PostScript page is simply a unit of output, not a physical description of that output. It may be very large or very small; it may take up all or only some of an actual unit of output; it may even be one physical output page or several. This is particularly important because PostScript provides, by design, device- and media-independent descriptions for pages. This allows one "page" to be embedded onto another for final output, and it allows a wide variety of processing options that are at the heart of what has made the Post-Script language so widely used and admired.

PostScript maintains a simple conceptual model of a "page" as a two-dimensional space. Images are "built" on the page by placing "paint" in selected areas. The paint may be put on the page in the form of letters, lines, general filled shapes, or halftone representations of photographs. The paint may be in black or white, in any shade of gray, or in any color. It is always opaque, so that the last mark on the page completely overlays any previous marks. Any element may be cropped, as it is painted onto the page, to fit within a desired shape or border. Finally, once a page is built up into the desired form, it may be rendered onto an output device.

In all these things, PostScript follows a simple, intuitive, and natural model of moving a pen or brush across a page of paper. Even though the "page" may be a metal drum, and the "paint" electrons, the concepts remain the same. The major conceptual change follows from PostScript's ability to generate a path and then fill it in. This is similar to an artist lightly penciling in a letter or figure, filling in the outline with ink or paint, and then erasing the original line to render the final object—except, of course, that PostScript's "pencil lines" are invisible. Nevertheless, both the power of PostScript page descriptions and the natural way they behave, particularly for the graphic artist, can be readily understood.

Current Page

The PostScript artist (or programmer) begins work on an "ideal page," which is independent of any specific output device. PostScript calls this the *current page* and this is the two-dimensional space where PostScript makes its marks. When PostScript begins, the current page is blank. Painting operators, which form a subset of the complete set of graphic operators, place marks on the page. The principal painting operators are as follows:

OPERATOR	FUNCTION
fill	fills in an area on a page.
stroke	marks lines on a page.
image	paints an image, such as would come from a scanner or similar device.
show	paints character shapes onto a page.

Each of these operators (and the other graphic operators) have various operands, both explicit and implicit. We will fully discuss them in Chapter 3.

Current Path

Most of the painting operators (**fill**, **stroke**, and **show**) have one common and important implicit operand, which is called the *current path*. This is the invisible "pencil line" we discussed before. It marks for the Post-Script interpreter where to apply paint on the current page. The current path is an arbitrary sequence of points, which may be both connected (as in a line or curve) and disconnected (as a separate point). Taken together, this sequence of points describes shapes on the page and further describes the position and orientation of the shapes with respect to the overall page. The last point on the existing current path is the *current point*.

You can construct more than one path on a page. There is no requirement that a page be output before you start a new path. Of course, only one current path can be on a page at one time.

Path Construction Operators

The current path is built by means of PostScript path construction operators. Each of these operators alters the current path in some way, generally by adding a new segment to the existing path. Typical path construction operators are the following:

OPERATOR	FUNCTION
newpath	starts a new path.
moveto	moves from the current point to a defined point.
lineto	creates a line from the current point to a defined point.
rlineto	creates a line from the current point to a new point defined by its relation to the current point; also known as **relative lineto**.

Remember that all these operators only move the current path; they do not mark the page. All marking is done by use of the painting operators.

MEASUREMENT AND COORDINATES

As you might expect, we specify paths and points on a PostScript page in terms of coordinates. Since PostScript uses a two-dimensional page, we require two coordinates: x and y. With this method, every point on a PostScript page can be described by a pair of numbers (x,y) which conceptually define its location on the page. You must understand that, at this point, these coordinates have no relationship to the actual output device. They are ideal coordinates that always maintain a fixed relationship to the current page. This coordinate system is called the *user space*.

Default User Space

In order to understand precisely where a specific pair of (x,y) values puts us on a page, we have to define three things:

1. Location of the origin: point (0,0). The point (0,0) or the *origin* on a PostScript page is at the *bottom-left corner* of the page.

2. Direction of the x-axis and the y-axis. The *positive* direction on the x-axis extends *horizontally to the right* across a PostScript page. The *positive* direction on the y-axis extends *vertically upwards* on a PostScript page.

3. The scale, or unit of measure, on the x-axis and the y-axis. The length of *one* unit along both the x-axis and the y-axis is $1/72$ *of an inch*.   .

If you are not familiar with printing, the choice of $1/72$ of an inch may seem like a strange value to use; in fact, this is almost precisely a printer's *point* (which is fractionally larger than $1/72$ of an inch). In this way, the default x and y values become the equivalent of point values as you move around the page. You will find this a very useful feature as you begin page composition. You should also notice that by this choice of the origin and orientation, every point on the page is described by a positive value of x and y.

This entire set of conventions now precisely defines every point on an ideal page in units which are easy and natural to use from a printing and graphics standpoint. This set of conventions defines what is called the *default user space*.

Like many PostScript conventions, this set of coordinates, although perfectly logical, is a bit difficult to get used to. The natural coordinate system, particularly for anyone familiar with programming for graphics displays, would start at the top-left corner of the page rather than the bottom, and a positive value of y would move down the page rather than up. The PostScript convention is more traditional, as it conforms to the standard mathematical notation, but it does require a change in thought patterns as you work on a page of output.

FIRST EXERCISE: PRODUCING LINES OF TEXT

For the first exercise, there will be several examples displaying a line of text in various positions. Each of the examples has a specific purpose, and each will help you understand how PostScript handles a page of output. Each of the examples displays a slightly different line of text (for identification purposes), and each line is displayed at a different place on the page.

SETUP

In the best epic tradition, we are going to start "in the middle of the action" in order to provide some concrete examples of PostScript output. This has a very real benefit, in that it helps structure and motivate the learning process; computer languages generally—and PostScript in particular—are sufficiently complex that they can best be assimilated and understood by means of practical, explicit examples rather than abstract discussion. However, PostScript has almost no default options or structure, and therefore we need to do some setup work before you can do the exercises.

The requirements for setup and the concepts behind the setup functions that have not already been explained will be covered in some detail. However, in these initial exercises, you will have to enter each line of the examples exactly as shown. Because PostScript is an interpreted language and we are working in the interactive mode, you will get appropriate error messages if you make a mistake. Don't worry if that happens; just reenter the statement with any necessary corrections. But do be aware that Post-Script, like most computer languages, is particular about format and syntax. Later in the chapter we will cover this subject in detail; for now, you only need to copy the exercises exactly.

In entering each line, there are two points that you should know about PostScript syntax. First, PostScript requires at least one space between words or data, but won't mind if you use more than one. If you have any doubt whether there is a space in a line, put one in; generally, it won't hurt anything. Second, PostScript distinguishes between uppercase and lower-case letters; you must use the same letters as the examples do, both upper- and lowercase. Sometimes this may look strange, but it is important. We will discuss the issue of names and naming conventions (which is what this relates to) in the next chapter.

Communications Setup

This section discusses the setup of the examples in general terms. Specific details on how to set up your personal computer and interact with the output device are contained in Appendix C. Since the Apple LaserWriter is the most common—and a relatively inexpensive—PostScript-equipped output device, we will assume for example purposes that this is the output device. Nevertheless, all the example programs will work on any standard PostScript interpreter. The examples all presume that you are running in the interactive mode, using either an IBM-PC (or compatible) or an Apple Macintosh in terminal mode as input into a LaserWriter. In order to run your personal computer as a terminal, you will have to run a communication program. There is a discussion of this point, with specific recommendations of programs for this purpose, in Appendix C.

Since the interactive mode requires a dialogue between you and the printer, it is essential that the method you use for communication be bi-directional so that the printer can talk back to you. For the LaserWriter this is not a problem, since it only allows network or serial connections, both of which are naturally bidirectional. However, in the IBM-PC world, many users of other types of PostScript-equipped printers connect them using the parallel port. This is the recommended method to increase printing speed and simplify connections for the PC user. (In fact, it does neither; and it is a foolish recommendation made, in my opinion, by people who have no experience in either PostScript or in practical use of a PostScript output device.) However, the parallel port is a one-way street; it transmits data to the printer but never lets any come back to you. Therefore, to use the exercises in this book, you must be connected to your printer either by a network or by the serial port. We will assume that you are using the serial port for the discussion here. If you are using a network connection, such as AppleTalk, read the information in Appendix C for guidance on how to set up an interactive connection.

In order to communicate with the LaserWriter, you must set the serial port to either the 1200 baud or the 9600 baud setting. How you do this varies from printer to printer; generally, you can either set a physical switch on the device or set the communication parameters from the front panel display. Review your printer documentation for advice on how to do this. I recommend the 9600 baud setting unless you are having difficulty in communications or unless the printer is located some distance away—more than 50 feet of cable, say. After setting the communication parameters, turn on the printer. You should receive the standard start-up sheet, indicating the correct operation of the printer.

Next, start up your communication program, using the following settings:

- baud rate set to 1200 or 9600 (depending on what you set on the printer)
- 8 data bits
- no parity
- 1 stop bit

Open a direct communication link with the printer. This is done by not using any telephone number or modem commands when you establish the connection. Some communication software has a direct-link option which you can use. Set up your communication program to *not* echo your input; the printer will automatically echo once you have started PostScript in the interactive mode.

Most PostScript printers support one or both of two communications protocols. A *communication protocol* is a way for the printer and the computer to exchange information about when the computer can start to send data and when it must stop, usually because the printer cannot handle any more data. There are two basic methods of doing this, one using hardware signals, called DTR/CTS, and another using software controls, called XON/XOFF. Many PostScript printers will allow you to use both of these methods; this means that you don't have to worry about what method your computer uses. If you can set your printer to accept both methods, do that. Otherwise I recommend that you should set up to use the XON/XOFF protocol, unless you know that your computer supports the hardware alternative.

If you have to set XON/XOFF, you should also set the same protocol in your personal computer. If your communication program or system software has this feature, it will be a menu or a command option. Check your software manual for details. If you don't have the option, or can't find it, don't worry about it. Since you will be typing in your commands in the interactive mode, you are not likely to cause a data overrun in any case. The protocol is most necessary when you are sending large amounts of data (or a large and complex program) to the printer, such as you might do with a long batch file.

Typical Presentation

Once your communication software tells you that you are connected to the printer, type in the word "executive." At this point you will not see anything on the screen, since you set "echo off" in the communications program and you have not yet started the interactive mode with the Post-Script interpreter. The command "executive" is the command that starts the interactive mode.

You should receive the following response after you enter "executive":

PostScript(r) Version 47.0

Copyright(c) 1985, '86, '87, '88 Adobe Systems Inc.

All Rights Reserved.

PS>

The exact wording and the version number may differ depending on when you got your printer, and there may be more lines in the heading. The prompt PS> means that the interpreter is ready for you to enter a command.

At this point, there are several possible problems you might encounter. These usually arise because of some problem in the communications link between the personal computer and the printer. Although we can't cover all the possible problems, let's discuss one or two of the more common glitches. Even if something goes wrong that isn't covered, this discussion may help you diagnose what is happening.

In the first typical problem, your screen shows one or two lines that look like comic-book curses. It may look something like the following:

%@&1'1%$$#&^%$&*&%^%%&#&$^^%$

Actually, this is not as bad as it might seem; at least you're talking to the printer. Generally, this kind of display is caused by incompatible communication parameters between the terminal and the printer. Check the baud rate settings on the printer and in the communications software. If these are set correctly, check the settings for data bits and stop bits (8 and 1, respectively), and check for correct parity (none).

A second typical problem is more difficult to diagnose. In this case your communication software tells you that you are connected, you type in "executive" (which you can't see), and nothing happens. Basically, this occurs because you are not communicating with the PostScript interpreter in a way it can understand; unfortunately, there can be many reasons for this.

The first thing to do is to check all physical connections between the devices. Review Appendix C and the hardware manuals of the personal computer and the printer for specific advice and directions. If the physical connections and switches all appear correct and firmly in place and you still have a problem, turn off the printer for a minute and then turn it on again. After the test page is produced, re-initialize the communications software on the PC. Make sure all the communications parameters are set correctly, then type the "executive" command again. This should resolve most of these problems.

Finally, you may get an error response from PostScript when you start up, as in the following:

= = = DIALING LaserWriter II NT

%%[Error: undefined, Offending Command: ATDT]%%

%%[Flushing: rest of job (to end-of-file) will be ignored]%%

This is caused by the communication program, which has sent something—in this case a modem command to dial (ATDT)—to the PostScript interpreter before you entered the "executive" command. This generally occurs because the communications software expects to talk over a dial-up telephone line, through a modem, rather than to talk over a direct communication link. Therefore, the program sends modem-control signals such as ATDT to direct the modem it thinks is attached. Any such automatic dialing or other modem commands should be deleted from your communications software or be disabled while you are accessing the LaserWriter. If this problem does occur, you will have to send an end-of-file command to the PostScript interpreter before it will recognize your "executive" command. As you can see from the message, PostScript says it is going to skip all commands until it receives an end-of-file character. To send an end-of-file command, press Ctrl-D(ASCII 4) on the IBM, or Command-D on the Macintosh. Then enter the "executive" command as before. The result looks like this:

= = = DIALING LaserWriterII NT

%%[Error: undefined, Offending Command: ATDT]%%

%%[Flushing: rest of job (to end-of-file) will be ignored]%%

◆

PostScript(r) Version 47.0

Copyright (c) 1985, '85, '86, '87 Adobe Systems Inc.

All Rights Reserved.

PS>

Text Setup

This first exercise will produce text output on your printer. Since almost every page that is created for output on a PostScript system contains text, this seems like an excellent place to start.

Text is presented and manipulated in PostScript as *strings*. A string is just a line of characters, enclosed in parentheses, like this:

(This is sample string number 1)

In fact, this will be the string you will use for display in the first example. Of course, strings may contain other characters, and later in the book we will discuss all the varieties of strings.

PostScript displays strings by use of the **show** operator. This is one of the PostScript painting operators which places marks on the current page. In this case, the marks are in the form of letters, as described by the currently active font. Each font contains a description of letters and symbols which defines for **show** how to mark them on the page.

With few exceptions, PostScript devices contain built-in descriptions of a number of common fonts. The most basic set of these include two character fonts, Times-Roman and Helvetica, along with a Symbol font that provides mathematical and other special characters and a typewriter-like font, Courier. There are a number of additional fonts available for PostScript, including Palatino, Avant-Garde, Bookman, and a wide variety of other text and decorative fonts. Any or all of these additional fonts may be loaded into the PostScript interpreter and used in normal PostScript operations. The examples in this book will only use a minimal number of built-in fonts to insure that any setup will be able to run the exercises as they are shown. You can easily substitute other fonts if you have them installed; it won't affect the exercises at all—although, of course, it would change the output to the selected font.

There are three essential font operations which must be done before the **show** operator can do its work. First, you have to tell PostScript what font you want to use. This is done by supplying the name of the font to the **findfont** operator. Second, you must tell PostScript what size you want the letters to print. This is done by giving a size number, in user units, to the **scalefont** operator. Since you will be using the default units, this size will be in points—which is a natural and convenient measurement for text. Finally, after having done both of the above steps, you have to tell PostScript to make your selected, scaled font into the currently active font. This is done by the **setfont** operator. The whole process can be done in one line of PostScript, and looks like this:

/Times-Roman **findfont** 12 **scalefont setfont**

This sequence of operators finds the Times-Roman font, sets it to 12-point size, and makes it the current font. Now, when you issue a **show**, PostScript knows what font you want and what size you want the letters to be.

This sequence of operations is so common in PostScript programs, that Level 2 has an alternative version using only the single operator **selectfont**. If you have a Level 2 device, you can replace the line above (which still works, however) with the following:

/Times-Roman 12 **selectfont**

Positioning

There is one more thing that must be set before you can use **show** to paint a string of text. You must set the current point so that **show** knows where on the page to paint the desired string of text. Anytime you start a new page, the current point is undefined—remember, there are almost no defaults in Post-Script. The **show** operator paints a string of text beginning at the current point, and it resets the current point to the end of the string when it's done. In this way, successive **show**s will place strings one after another, as you would expect and want. However, the operators will not sense when the text goes off the side of the page (or top or bottom, for that matter); you will lose the part of the string that exceeds the page margins, and you will get a current point that is off the visible area of the page. It is up to the programmer, or the application program, to keep track of the current point and break the string when it is too long to fit across the remainder of a line.

Going back to our initial problem of setting the current point, for this example you will display the line of text 5.5 inches from the bottom of the page and 1.5 inches from the left side of the page. This assumes that you are printing on a standard, letter (8½ by 11 inch) page. Recall that PostScript coordinates are in points ($1/72$ of an inch) and that you need a pair of coordinates (x,y) to define the desired point. Therefore the desired point on the page has coordinates (108, 396).

The current point is set by the **moveto** operator. This operator takes a pair of numbers—the x,y coordinates—and sets the current point to them. The command looks like this:

    108 396 **moveto**

FIRST EXAMPLE

Now you understand what needs to be done before a **show** will execute correctly. You have to set the following items:

- define the font you intend to use,
- set the point size of the font,
- set that font and size as the current font, and
- establish the current point where you want the text to print.

The entire sequence can be done in two lines of PostScript commands: one to set the font information and a second to set the current point, as shown here:

```
/Times-Roman findfont 12 scalefont setfont                    %1

108 396 moveto                                                %2
```

Now you can issue a set of commands to print a string of text onto a page. This will require two more lines of PostScript commands, as follows:

```
(This is sample string number 1) show                        %3

copypage                                                      %4
```

This sequence introduces two new elements. The first is the sequence of numbers %1, %2, and so on off to the right of each line. In PostScript, the percent sign (%) indicates the beginning of a comment and everything beyond the % is treated as a comment by the interpreter. For these exercises, numbers will be used in the comments as line references. So there are four numbered lines in the first exercise. You can include these in your work or not, as you choose; their presence or absence will not affect the output.

The second new element is line %4, which consists of the operator **copypage**. The PostScript interpreter builds pages in memory according to the commands it receives, but it doesn't actually print any output until it gets a specific command to do so. The **copypage** operator is such a command; it causes the interpreter to print the current page and to retain an image of the current page internally so we can continue to work on it. You will discover how important and valuable it is to be able to explicitly control when a page gets produced on the output device.

Figure 1.1 shows the four lines of PostScript code as they might look on the screen, and Figure 1.2 shows the page of output that they produce. That completes our first program example—simple, but effective.

```
PS>/Times-Roman findfont 12 scalefont setfont
PS>108 396 moveto
PS>(This is sample string number 1) show
PS>copypage
```

Figure 1.1: First program example

Figure 1.2: First (partial) output from the first exercise

Example Structure

Let's look over this example. Even though it consists of only four lines of PostScript code, it provides some important points for discussion regarding PostScript structure and control.

You have already covered the requirements of the **show** operator. Obviously, from this previous discussion, lines %1 and %2 had to be executed before line %3. In the same way, you had to paint the characters onto the page before you printed it; therefore, line %3 must come before line %4. You can think of this as inking the press before printing; if you set the type but don't ink it, nothing will be printed. Similarly, you need to paint characters, lines, or shapes using the appropriate PostScript operators before you output the page.

This still leaves the issue of sequence for lines %1 and %2. You may think this order was arbitrary; and indeed, from the point of view of the interpreter, either line could come first. All that is necessary is for both operations to be completed by the time the interpreter reaches line %3 (the **show**). But to you as a programmer, the order is important. Font changes and scaling take time and consume resources; for efficient PostScript programs, you want to minimize how often they occur. In addition, all of the text in a given portion of the document will likely be in the same font and point size. Movement around the page, however, occurs all the time; it's one of the most frequent actions you will need to take. If you were going to print multiple lines of text, you would probably have to move on every line. For these reasons, you should habitually set the font first, followed by the **moveto**, which is how it was done in the example.

SECOND EXAMPLE

While you are still in PostScript and in the interactive mode, let's do a second page. Here again, the output will be two simple lines of text, with some small variations. This example assumes that you have successfully completed the previous example and are still in the interpreter; that is, you still have the PS> prompt on your screen.

Here is the code for the second example:

(! This is sample string #2.) **show**	%5
108 432 **moveto**	%6
(And this is sample string #3.) **show**	%7
showpage	%8

If you have done this example immediately after the first example, your screen will look like Figure 1.3 and you will get output that looks like Figure 1.4.

There are several distinctive points that you have probably already noticed about this example. The first and most obvious one is that the previous text is still on the page where it was in the first example. This happened because you used the **copypage** operator, which saved a copy of the page being output, to print the first page. In this second example, you have used the **showpage** operator (on line %8) to print the page instead of **copypage**. Because you used **showpage**, the page is now blank and all the previous data is gone; if you issued a new string and printed it, only the new string would show on the page.

The **showpage** operator is the usual method for your output. The **copypage** operator is useful for testing or (as in this exercise) as a learning tool to aid you in seeing what you've already placed on a page.

The second point that you probably noticed is that you didn't have to set or scale the font anywhere in this program. Since you performed these operations once before, the interpreter will continue to use those settings until you end the program, by using the **quit** operator (which we will discuss shortly) or by turning the printer off, or until you explicitly change one of the settings by issuing new font operators.

Example Analysis

Keeping these two observations in mind, let's discuss this second example, line by line. In line %5, you again give the interpreter a **show** command. You remember that there are certain requirements for **show**: a current font must be active and there must be a current point. The **copypage** operator, as we discussed above, has left both of these unchanged

```
PS>/Times-Roman findfont 12 scalefont setfont
PS>108 396 moveto
PS>(This is sample string number 1) show
PS>copypage
PS>(!  This is sample string #2.) show
PS>108 432 moveto
PS>(And this is sample string #3.) show
PS>showpage
```

Figure 1.3: Second program example

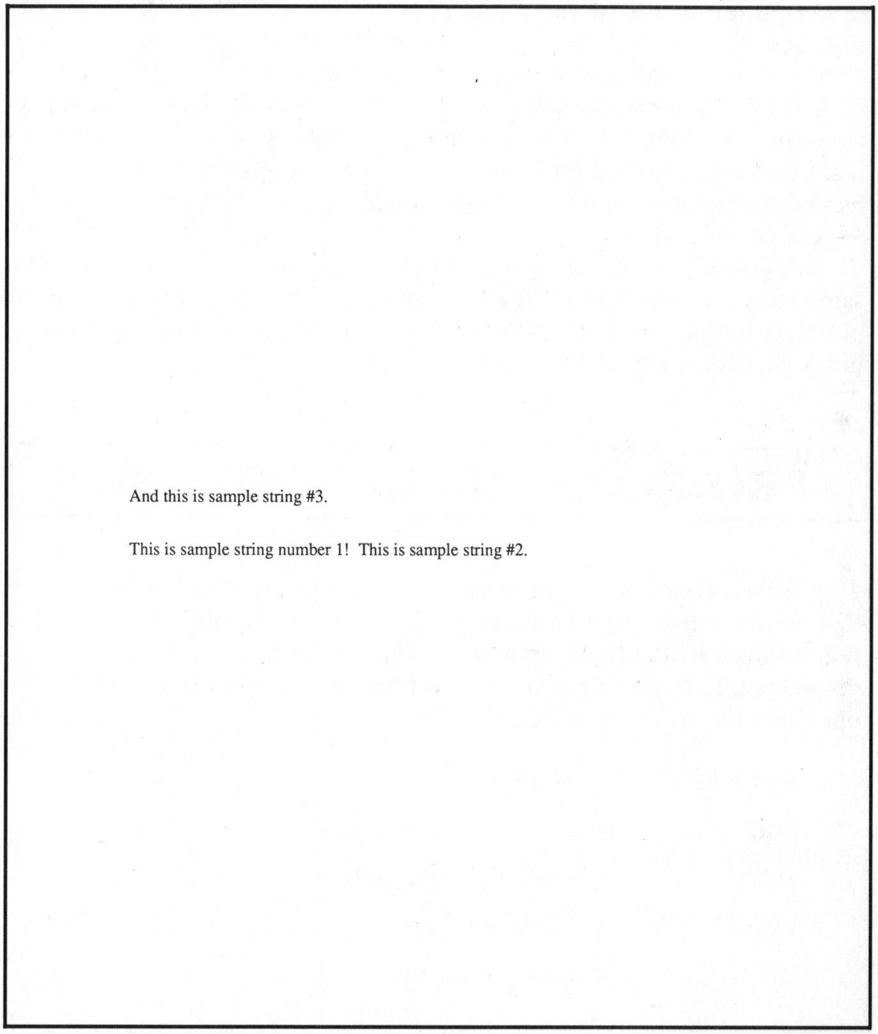

And this is sample string #3.

This is sample string number 1! This is sample string #2.

Figure 1.4: Final output from the first exercise

from the first example. This is illustrated graphically by the placement of the
! as the first character in the second string (on line %5), which shows up
right behind the first string (see Figure 1.4). This also illustrates the point
made earlier, that the **show** operator adjusts the current point to the end of
the string when it paints the string; the next **show** will begin where the previous one ended.

In line %6 you deliberately reset the current point by means of **moveto**. The x-coordinate is reset to 108, where it was for the first string. This will line up the beginning of the new string with the beginning of the first string. The y-coordinate is reset to 432, which is ½ inch up the page from the first string, which was positioned at 396. Remember that the positive direction for y is up the page; if you wanted to position the third string below the first one, you would have to subtract 36 (or ½ inch) from 396 instead of adding it.

In line %7 you paint the third string on the page, which appears in the same font as the two previous strings but is positioned at the new current point set in line %6. Line %8 prints the page on the printer and creates a blank page for the next operation.

PROGRAMMING IN POSTSCRIPT

As you continue on in this chapter, text examples will be provided so that you may gain a clearer understanding of the concepts. These examples will be given in addition to practical exercises such as the ones you've just completed. To facilitate this process, we will define here a few mathematical operators for use in these examples.

OPERATOR	FUNCTION
add	adds two operands together
sub	subtracts two operands
mul	multiplies two operands
div	divides two operands

Each of these operators requires certain items of information in order to execute; you may recall that we named these operands. All of the mathematical operators are presented and discussed in a later section of this chapter.

These are probably the most intuitive operators to use; you should not find the examples difficult to follow. Where the operands come from and where the results go to are the subject of the next section.

STACK OPERATIONS

One of the important characteristics of PostScript is that it works through a series of stacks. You have already been introduced informally to the work of the stack in the previous examples. Now you need to know more about PostScript stacks.

Physically, a stack is an area of memory that holds items to be referenced by the PostScript interpreter. PostScript uses four distinct stacks, as follows:

- execution stack

- dictionary stack

- graphics state stack

- operand stack

All of these stacks are independent of one another; what happens to one doesn't have any direct effect on the others. Each stack has its own method of access, but all of them are similar in concept and operation. If you understand how one of the stacks works, you will understand how they all work.

The first of these, the *execution stack*, sometimes also referred to as the *call stack*, is directly under the control of the interpreter and can be interrogated by the PostScript program but not modified. It is used by the interpreter to store the current state of the program. For our purposes, we can treat it as a black box. The second and third stacks, the *dictionary stack* and the *graphics state stack*, are special stacks controlled by specific operators. We will examine the most useful of these operators later in the book. They have particular importance in program structure and control.

The last stack, the *operand stack*, is the most important stack for our purposes. This stack contains the operands for PostScript and receives the results as operators are executed. The majority of PostScript operators either get their data to operate on from this stack, or return the results of their execution to this stack, or both. This is the stack that we mean when we refer to "the stack," and it is this stack that we will now discuss in detail. Remember that all the other PostScript stacks operate in essentially the same way.

The operand stack (like all PostScript stacks) is a push-down, pop-up stack. It can also be described as a last-in, first-out (LIFO) stack, but the push-down, pop-up terminology is easier to visualize. You may have seen a plate stacker in a restaurant. That's a spring-loaded hole in a counter where a pile of clean plates is loaded. As needed, a plate is taken off the top of the pile, and the plate underneath pops up, ready to be used. As fresh, clean plates come out of the kitchen, they are loaded on top of the stack of plates already there, pushing down the old ones. And that's how you can visualize a push-down, pop-up stack. Not exactly high-tech, but it works.

Let us visualize how this stack might appear in operation. Suppose we present the number 25 to the PostScript interpreter—for the moment, let's not worry about how the number got to the interpreter. The interpreter will take the number (the first "plate") and put it on the operand stack, which then can be visualized like this:

25
—

This would be a cutaway view of the plate stacker from the side of the counter, if you're following the visualization process. Next the interpreter gets the number 60. Now the stack looks like this:

60
—
25
—

Finally, the interpreter gets the number 10. The final state of the stack is shown here:

10
—
60
—
25
—

Whatever image or analogy you choose to help you understand the stack mechanism, there are three points to keep in mind. First, the next item available is always the one on the top of the stack; nothing beneath it can be reached without moving the top item. Second, the next item down becomes the top item automatically when the top item is used or otherwise removed. Third, as you begin to construct reasonably complex procedures, you must remember to think ahead about the desired sequence of operands and results on the stack. These points will be made clear in the following examples.

Let us consider the following series of actions as an example of stack operations. Consider this series a dialogue between us and the PostScript interpreter; this is an example of the interactive mode of operation, which was described earlier in the chapter.

a.

20	60	**add**	80
	20		

b.

20	60	**sub**	– 40
	20		

c.

2	6	**mul**	12
	2		

Note that, in series *b*, the number on top of the stack, which is the last number presented to the interpreter, is subtracted from the number below it on the stack, which was the first number presented to the interpreter. The sequence of presentation is of major importance.

The issue of sequence can perhaps best be thought of as an extension of the problems of order of operation, which are usually solved in mathematical notation by means of parentheses. For example, let's compute the following equation in PostScript:

$$25 - (3 \times 4)$$

This can be accomplished as illustrated in series *a* below. As you see, the whole presentation is different than our intuitive sequence, which is shown in series *b*. Note that, when the sequence of operands is different, we get different results. This illustrates why we must think ahead in planning PostScript programs. This different kind of thought process is inherent in the PostScript language, as you will discover in the next section.

a.

25	3	4	**mul**	12
	25	3		25
		25		

12	**sub**	13
25		

b.

3	4	**mul**	12
	3		

12	25	**sub**	− 13
	12		

NOTATION

Because of PostScript's interpreted nature and stacked operation mechanism, it requires an unusual syntax for execution. Recall that, in the examples above, the interpreter executes an operator when it receives it, taking the necessary operands from the stack. Operands must precede their operators in order to execute properly. This is known as *post-fix notation*. While this is eminently rational, and both easy and practical for the PostScript interpreter, it is not how we usually write operations. We would normally use either "1 plus 2" or "add 1 to 2," where PostScript uses

1 2 **add**

So you need to begin thinking "backwards," in a way, in order to read PostScript. This becomes especially necessary when you start to read procedures (described below), which may contain several nested levels of operation. It is also reflected in the issue of sequence that was illustrated above, in which the operands had to be presented in "reverse" order to get the desired result. PostScript has operands to help with this sequence issue, as we will see.

Example Notation

The examples above were presented graphically, showing the stack during execution, to help you follow how PostScript operates. However, we cannot continue presenting it this way for obvious reasons. We need to establish a standard notation for writing PostScript statements.

We will assume that the PostScript interpreter reads statements from left to right, as we do. That means that the sequence of operations presented in our first stack example would be written as follows:

25 60 10

and our second stack operations example would become

20 60 **add**

20 60 **sub**

2 6 **mul**

So, from now on, I will write examples across the page as illustrated, and you must envision them going onto the stack and being pushed down, or popped up, as required. This may seem foolish, but, as I tried to show you with the examples on sequence, visualization of the current state of the stack is essential to successful PostScript programming.

Also, when we do examples, we will need to show the result, which generally is returned to the top of the stack. Where an explicit result is returned to the top of the stack, we will illustrate that as follows:

20 60 **add** → 80

20 60 **sub** → −40

2 6 **mul** → 12

Operator Notation

We have established how we will write PostScript operands and operators in a program context. Now we must also establish how to write the operators for general reference purposes, since the conventional notation that we established above was specific to a program context. For example,

20 10 **add**

adds two specific numbers and returns the specific result, 30, on the operand stack. Now we need to work out how to write operators so that you will know as you read them how they work, what operands they require, and what results they return.

Let us establish the following conventions for writing operators. On the left of the operator we will show the operands required in the same order as we agreed to write them above: that is, with the last operand (the one on the top of the stack) as the rightmost operand. Where no operands are used, we will use a dash (—). And we will use names that are suggestive of the characteristics of the operands: for example, num (for numbers), int (for integer numbers), proc (for procedures), and so on. Thus we would write

num1 num2 **add**

On the right of the operator we will show the results in the same order as the operands: again, with the rightmost result on the top of the stack. This is similar to the notation we established for writing explicit results above, except that we omit the → before showing the result. Where the operator does not return a result we will show a dash (—). Then our full set of notations will look like this:

SYNTAX	FUNCTION
num1 num2 **add** sum	adds *num1* and *num2*.
num1 num2 **sub** result	subtracts *num2* from *num1*.

These are the same conventions used in the PostScript manuals.

STRINGS AND COMMENTS

You were introduced to the use of strings and comments in PostScript code in the first exercise. There is additional information regarding these objects that you will want before we begin the next exercise. This still does not represent a complete discussion of either object; that discussion will come in the next chapter where you will read about all the types of PostScript objects in one section.

Strings

You saw strings used in the first exercise as the operand of the **show** operator. This is probably the most typical use of strings in PostScript, since strings are the natural and usual method for representing and handling textual material.

A string usually consists of a collection of characters which is bounded by left and right parentheses. The string begins at the initial left parenthesis, (, and is terminated by the matching right parenthesis,). PostScript strings are extremely flexible, and have no restrictions on what characters can be placed within the string delimiters. Even the characters (and) can be put within the string, as long as each is part of a matched set. You will see an example of this useful feature in our next exercise.

Comments

Every programming language must provide some method to allow a programmer to annotate the code being generated, for self-preservation, if no other reason. PostScript is no exception. Such annotations are called *comments*, and they are markers for the interpreter that indicate the end of the PostScript-readable material and the beginning of a line of code ''for your eyes only.''

A PostScript comment, as you have already learned, begins with the character % and ends at the end of the line. The PostScript interpreter ignores all information after the % and only starts processing again on the next line. This means, in particular, that once you have begun a comment with the %, you can continue with any characters or words you want, including more %'s, operators, strings, or whatever. The PostScript interpreter will ignore everything until a new line begins. There is no method of continuing a PostScript comment onto a second line; each line of comments must begin with its own %. The only exception to this rule is that the character % can be used within a string without starting a comment; in this case the interpreter will not recognize the % and will continue to process the string (and the rest of the line) normally.

The exercises use comments within the PostScript code itself for two purposes: first, to number the lines for reference purposes, and second, to point out important issues within the code itself. You will find examples of both uses in the second exercise.

SECOND EXERCISE: PRODUCING MULTILINE TEXT

The second exercise consists of a single program designed to show you how you (or an application program) might set multiline text. To make the full exercise easier and more understandable, however, we need to review the PostScript operators and do some additional work with program fragments before we move on to the program example.

This section provides a review all of the previous PostScript operators, presented in a standard format. You will also find some new mathematical operators that will be useful. In addition, this section contains a number of program fragments using these operators. Working with these tools, including the operator summary, should give you a good understanding of the basic structure of PostScript before you proceed into the next chapter.

SAMPLE PROGRAM SEGMENTS

Having seen all of these operators in the abstract, you will now work with them in some program fragments.

Let us begin by reviewing some of the earlier exercises in the chapter, where we were developing this notation.

20 60 **add** → 80

20 60 **sub** → −40

2 6 **mul** → 12

You may also recall the problem presented in the discussion of sequence

$25 - (3 \times 4)$

You saw that, to derive the correct result from this equation in PostScript, you had to write the following:

25 3 4 **mul sub** → 13

The more natural sequence

3 4 **mul** 25 **sub** → − 13

gives an incorrect result because the operands for the **sub** operator are not in the correct order. Using one of the new stack operators, **exch**, you can also obtain the correct result by writing the sequence as follows:

3 4 **mul** 25 **exch sub** → 13

This sequence obtains the correct result by exchanging the 12 result of the **mul** and the 25 on the stack. The **exch** operator works by swapping the first two items on the stack, and this illustrates its use.

Note that you can also combine arithmetic operators with other operators on the same line of code. For example, the three statements below move the current point to exactly the same location:

108 648 **moveto**

108 612 36 **add moveto**

108 684 36 **sub moveto**

We also have the other mathematical operators, such as:

2 3 **div** → .666 . . .

and

2 3 **div round** → 1

The **round** operator has one result that you might not expect until you think about it:

− 5.5 **round** → − 5

(since − 5 is mathematically greater than − 6).

All in all, I think you will find the mathematical operators straightforward.

Text Handling Segments

You have already seen how to use the **show** operator to display a single line of text. As we discussed during the first exercise, the **show** operator positions the current point to the end of the string when it paints the string on the page. However, it can't move down to the next line automatically. You, as the programmer (or the application program), must provide the necessary up or down movement. This is generally done by issuing a **moveto** operator with appropriate new coordinates.

The next, obvious question is how to determine the new coordinates. Remember that you scaled the type you were using to a particular size by use of the **scalefont** operator. This size, the point size, governs the height of the characters; since you are using proportional fonts, the width of each character is scaled to the height but varies also in proportion to the nature of the character—the letter *w*, for example, is wider than the letter *i*. In this case, the minimum distance between two lines of type must be the point size; otherwise letters would start to run into the type on the lines above and below them.

Generally, setting successive lines of type only the minimum distance apart makes a page look crowded and makes it difficult to read if there is much text on it. For this reason, typesetters usually space lines slightly farther apart than the point size of the type. This spacing is called *leading*. Leading is proportional to the size of the type being used; as a guide, for type in the 10- to 12-point range, leading would be one or two points. Therefore, if the type is 12-point (as in our example), the line spacing would be 13 or 14 points. This means that the y-coordinate would have to decrease (if you're moving down the page) by 13 or 14. To illustrate the effect of leading, and to keep computation easy, the program example will use 12-point type with 14-point leading.

Like so many other elements of page design and makeup, the choice of type size and leading are essentially aesthetic decisions. The object, as always, is to have a page that is beautiful because it is clean in layout, easily legible, and pleasant to the eye. Factors that influence choice of point size and leading include the amount of text that needs to be set, the position and dimensions of the text block on the page, and so on.

Some of the books listed in Appendix D contain valuable discussions of these and other issues of design and typography. You can also learn a great deal by carefully studying examples of work that you consider particularly good (effective and attractive) or bad (ineffective and unattractive). Once you start looking, you'll find these examples everywhere: books, newspapers, posters, advertisements, even restaurant menus. As you become more experienced (and start looking critically at your own work), you may find yourself developing an almost intuitive "sense of design."

PROGRAM EXAMPLE

Now you're ready to begin your third PostScript program. Once again, the program will display lines of text on the page, but this time the text will be set in two columns, as text and commentary might be in a textbook or in a translation. This is just a convenient format to illustrate two-column text being typeset without having to fill one column completely before starting the next. (After a few of these exercises, you will quickly understand why having a word-processing program that can produce PostScript output is so useful.)

Both columns will have sentences of several lines each to show you how multi-line text might be set and to use some of the arithmetic operators you have learned in a more typical situation. In addition, you will set two different type fonts: one for the body of the text and another for the commentary.

Setup

Before you can begin the program, you must make some decisions regarding the layout of the output page. This page is relatively simple, and the layout parameters will be given in complete detail here. You should calculate each of the coordinates as we go through the setup; this will help you when you come to the program itself.

In this example, the output consists of a two-column page. Since it often helps to make a sketch of the page layout, Figure 1.5 shows a sketch of our example page.

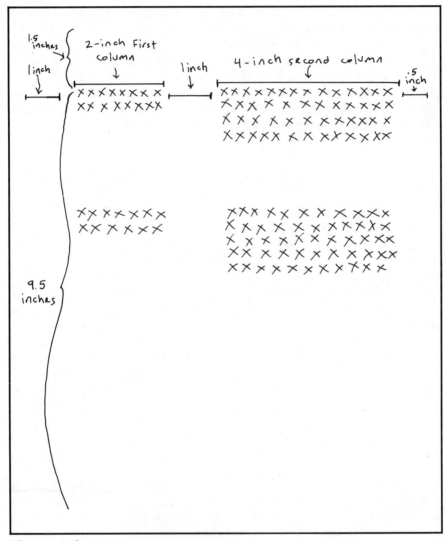

Figure 1.5: Sketch of the page layout

The first column on this page will be the commentary. (Note that you may want to reverse the columns on facing pages, although we're not going to do that here; it would make the example too complex for now.) This column will be 2 inches wide with a 1-inch margin. There will be 1 inch between the first and the second column, to set the commentary well away from the body text. We will plan to leave half an inch for the right margin; this leaves 4 inches for the body-text column.

The example will be set in 12-point type with 14-point leading, as discussed above. The body text will be in Times-Roman again, but the commentary will be set in Times-Italic (the italic version of Times-Roman) to set it apart but keep it in the same type family. In addition, to enhance legibility and to make the start of each paragraph quite evident, there will be 28-point spacing (two lines) between the paragraphs.

The text will begin 1.5 inches from the top of the page, which is 9.5 inches from the bottom of the page. This may sound foolish, but remember that PostScript is measuring from the bottom, left-corner of the page in units of $\frac{1}{72}$ of an inch. As a final touch, we will align the commentary paragraphs to begin at the same vertical point as the corresponding body text paragraphs. In order to do that, you have to know where the body text paragraphs begin, which means that the body text column (the second column physically) must be set first. The commentary column (the first physical column) can then be set to match, aligning each paragraph with the body text. In the example, there are only two paragraphs, but the principle is the same for multiple alignment points.

Multiline Text

Figure 1.6 is the text of the complete program. As you can see, it is a rather long, but not very complex, program. When complete, the program produces a page of output that looks just as you might have visualized it, as shown in Figure 1.7

This example provides several instructive points for your review. Let's go over it, line by line. The first three lines should be familiar from the first exercise. These lines set the font, establish the initial current point, and **show** the first line of text. You note that the x-coordinate of the **moveto** operator is 288, which is 4 inches from the left margin, while the y-coordinate is 684, which is 9.5 inches from the bottom edge of the paper. So far, so good.

Now look at lines %4 through %6. You have completed the output of your first line of text in the second column; now you must move down one line. Since positive y is up, you have to subtract; and since you have decided on 14 point leading, you want to subtract 14 from the original y value. First, you set the x-coordinate for the **moveto** at the same 288 that began the previous line. Then you subtract 14 from 684, leaving the result (670) on the stack. Then you issue the **moveto** command. Since you had the foresight to

```
/Times-Roman findfont 12 scalefont setfont              %1
288 684 moveto                                          %2
(The quick brown fox jumps over the lazy black) show    %3
288                                                     %4
684 14 sub                                              %5
moveto                                                  %6
(dog and then the quick brown fox jumps over that) show %7
288 684 28 sub moveto                                   %8
(lazy dog again and again and again ...... but the) show %9
288 684 42 sub moveto                                   %10
(dog just doesn't pay any attention.) show              %11
%Now begin the second paragraph of the body text        %12
%Note the computation for use in the commentary section  %13
288 684 70 sub moveto                                   %14
(Here is the quick brown fox playing the same) show     %15
288 684 84 sub moveto                                   %16
(games again in a second text paragraph.  You) show     %17
288 684 98 sub moveto                                   %18
(can easily see how this could go on and on and ......) show %19
%
%
%Now we can set the commentary column                   %20
%
%
/Times-Italic findfont 12 scalefont setfont             %21
72 684 moveto                                           %22
(This is a classic text) show                           %23
72 684 14 sub moveto                                    %24
(and commentary layout;) show                           %25
%Now set the second commentary item
%  to match the second body paragraph
72 684 70 sub moveto                                    %26
(using two fonts: ) show                                %27
72 684 84 sub moveto                                    %28
(Times Roman and Times Italic) show                     %29
showpage                                                %30
quit                                                    %31
```

Figure 1.6: Second exercise: text-and-commentary format

put the x-coordinate on the stack before your calculations, the two required operands are on the stack for the operator.

Having reset the current point, you are now ready to **show** the next line of text. In line %8, you repeat the previous calculation—this time subtracting 28 (2 × 14, since you're on the second line) from the initial value of 684. As you remember from our earlier discussion, all of these calculations can be placed on one line. That is easier to understand, since the **sub** simply replaces the y-coordinate. You follow this pattern for two more lines, down to line %12.

Now you have to set up to **show** the second text paragraph. This is really no different than the previous calculations, except that the value for subtraction must be increased by 28, as discussed earlier, in order to provide double-line spacing between paragraphs. The second paragraph continues, following the same sequence, down to line %19.

This is a classic text
and commentary layout;

The quick brown fox jumps over the lazy black
dog and then the quick brown fox jumps over that
lazy dog again and again and again ... but the
dog just doesn't pay any attention.

using two fonts:
(Times Roman and Times Italic)

Here is the quick brown fox playing the same
games again in a second text paragraph. You
can easily see how this could go on and on and ...

Figure 1.7: Output from the second exercise

At this point, line %20, there is a block of comment lines to set off the
work on the commentary column from the work on the body text. The commentary section begins by establishing a new current font, Times-Italic, on
line %21. Then there is the expected **moveto**. In this case, the x-coordinate
value has been changed to 72 to reflect the 1-inch margin that was designated for the left edge of the paper. The y-coordinate, however, is set to the

previously established value of 684; this will set the first line of the commentary at the same height as the first line of the text, as we wished.

The program proceeds to print two lines of commentary, using the same mechanisms as were used earlier in the program. At line %26, the second paragraph commentary begins by setting the y-coordinate to the same value as the y-coordinate that begins the second text paragraph. You can compare lines %14 and %26 to see how this was done; the essential point is to use the same value to be subtracted from the initial y-value.

Finally, the program concludes its page work by displaying two more lines of commentary. Note the use of parentheses within the string on line %29.

Now that the page is composed, you need to print it. You do this by the use of the **showpage** operator, as in the first exercise. The last line, line %31, introduces you to a new operator: **quit**. This operator ends a PostScript session gracefully. You could end the session just by stopping your input and turning off the printer. That's not a graceful way to exit, but it works and it won't hurt anything if you use it. The preferable method, however, would be to use the **quit** operator, which allows you to leave all the equipment turned on and still terminate the execution of the interpreter. It allows the interpreter to reset all states and clean up anything left over in the stack; the specific actions taken depend on the operating environment. I think it's the best way to end your session.

OPERATOR REVIEW

We will now review the operators which have been presented in this chapter. You will also be given some new operators where they fit in naturally and where use of the operator does not seem to require additional explanation. This same format will be used throughout subsequent chapters to summarize operators that have been used for the first time in that chapter. This will help you to recall the operators in each chapter, and it also forms a kind of informal index for review of the topics covered in the chapter.

BASIC OPERATORS

Not every operator is presented in these reviews. As was noted earlier, the best way to work with a language is to learn the primary functions in the language well, and then to broaden your scope to include the more specialized operators. That is the rule followed here; only the major functions are presented or used. Some related functions or operators will only be noted; some will be omitted altogether. If you want to use these other operators, be sure to consult the *PostScript Language Reference Manual, Second Edition* for full specification of their requirements and results.

Let me emphasize that I am not discouraging you from using these other operators; they have a specific place in your PostScript work. In this book, however, the purpose is to keep to the basic operations. In my experience, you will understand the language better and achieve your objective of writing PostScript code more quickly by staying with a subset of the language that contains the operators most often used.

Mathematical Operators

These are, without doubt, the most straightforward of all the operators. PostScript supports almost every mathematical operation that you may require for page processing; the following operators are those most useful in regular PostScript page descriptions.

The basic mathematical operators are the following:

SYNTAX	FUNCTION
num1 num2 **add** sum	adds *num1* to *num2*.
num1 num2 **sub** result	subtracts *num2* from *num1*.
num1 num2 **mul** product	multiplies *num1* by *num2*.
num1 num2 **div** quotient	divides *num1* by *num2*.

There are operators that affect the signs of results:

SYNTAX	FUNCTION
num **neg** −num	reverses the sign of *num*.

There are operators that make integers of fractional results:

SYNTAX	FUNCTION
num1 **round** num2	rounds *num1* to the nearest integer. If *num1* is equally close to its two nearest integers, the result is the greater of the two.

Graphics Operators

The two following operators were introduced and explained in the examples. They are grouped here for review and convenience.

SYNTAX	FUNCTION
string **show** —	paints the characters of *string* on the page at the current point.
num1 num2 **moveto** —	sets the current point to x-coordinate *num1* and y-coordinate *num2*.

Output Operators

These two operators were used in the examples also:

SYNTAX	FUNCTION
— **copypage** —	prints out the current page onto the output device, and retains a copy of the current page and all current settings.
— **showpage** —	prints a copy of the current page onto the output device and clears the page.

Stack Operators

The following operators directly access or manipulate the stack:

SYNTAX	FUNCTION
any1 any2 **exch** any2 any1	exchanges the top two elements on the stack.
any **pop** —	discards the top element.
any **dup** any any	duplicates the top element, and adds a copy to top of the stack.
⊢ ... anyn **clear** ⊢	empties the stack.

This last operator introduces a new conventional symbol, $\vdash$, which represents the bottom of the stack.

Interactive Operators

This is the final group of operators to be discussed in this chapter; they are put here only because I think you will want to know them, but they really don't fit anywhere. Two of these are operators that only work in the interactive mode; that is, they are inquiries that can be directed to the PostScript interpreter only from a terminal. As such, they can be extremely useful during the interactive work that you will be doing. However, they cannot be used in the batch mode.

SYNTAX	FUNCTION
any = = —	shows the top element of the stack and removes it.
$\vdash$ . . . anyn **pstack** $\vdash$ . . . anyn	shows the entire contents of the stack, but does not remove any element.

The final operator is one you have already met in the examples; it seems appropriate to end the chapter with

SYNTAX	FUNCTION
— **quit** —	ends operation of the PostScript interpreter.

2

Definitions
and Dictionaries

THIS CHAPTER IS CONCERNED with two basic issues. The first issue is how you can associate labels with Post-Script objects by using PostScript dictionaries. The second issue is how to create, name, and use PostScript procedures to build a PostScript program.

These are clearly critical issues in understanding and using any computer language. PostScript has some unique methods and unusual constructs in handling these points. In the preceding chapter you learned the basics of PostScript structure and became familiar with the first group of PostScript operators. In this chapter we will build on this information to fashion programs that begin to take advantage of PostScript's capabilities, by using labels and procedures.

There are two major exercises in this chapter, as there were in Chapter 1. In this chapter, however, the exercises are not the major focus, but are primarily illustrations of the issues discussed in the various sections. For this reason, there is more discussion of page setup and problem analysis associated with these exercises than there has been previously.

The chapter begins with a discussion of PostScript dictionaries and how to use the dictionary facilities to label various PostScript objects. The first section discusses what a PostScript dictionary is, what the various PostScript dictionaries do, and how to create and manipulate them. The second section describes how to use a dictionary and how the interpreter accesses and stores objects in a dictionary.

This discussion is followed by the third exercise. This exercise is a reworking of the last exercise in the preceding chapter, this time using variables and named constants to simplify and clarify the program text. The intention is to illustrate in a strong and clear way why you need to work with and exploit the facilities in the PostScript dictionaries.

The exercise is followed by a rather dry, but necessary, technical discussion, defining and explaining PostScript objects. By now you will have familiarized yourself with many of the PostScript object types in various contexts, and possibly you will have wondered about an exact explanation for them. The discussion is also necessary to allow you to proceed into the next section on the definition and use of procedures in PostScript.

The section on PostScript procedures builds from the explanations of PostScript objects and the use of PostScript dictionaries. This section will allow you to start writing more natural—and more useful—PostScript code, and it introduces a number of new operators and some new syntax to expand your

PostScript vocabulary. The section concludes with a discussion of memory management and error handing in PostScript.

This is followed by the major exercise of the chapter. This exercise is similar in design to the second and third exercises, but is more realistic and produces a moderately complex page as output, with a format (if not content) that might be used in a production setting. There is a discussion to aid you in page setup; and as you work through the exercise, you will see how your PostScript program, with its procedures and variables, grows naturally out of this analytical process. As before, the exercise ends with a detailed analysis of the program so that you can review all the new procedures and techniques that are in the code.

This new exercise begins to exhibit the structure and complexity of any real computer program and so leads into the final major section of the chapter: a discussion of program structure and style in relation to PostScript coding.

The first issue, and one of the most important issues under structure and style, regards use and selection of names. How names are constructed, how they are used, and how naming conventions can aid you in choosing names that will contribute to the clarity and utility of your programs are all discussed. There are some examples, and also some brief comments on the benefits of appropriate names drawn from personal experience.

The next topic describes and discusses an overall structural schema appropriate for a PostScript program. This is based on the very specific and detailed requirements set forth by Adobe Systems as a standard PostScript program structure. This global program structure is neither required by nor enforced by the PostScript interpreter and is not strictly part of the PostScript language. Nevertheless, if you are working with PostScript programs and files in most environments, these issues will be vital. Even if you are using PostScript in the simplest dedicated environment, you should still study and consider these issues and techniques, although you may decide to ignore them in the end.

The final section under structure and style is a brief explanation of programming style in a PostScript context. This includes points on indentation, line-breaking, and similar issues that help make your PostScript code more readable.

The chapter ends in the usual fashion, with a recap of the operators that have been introduced in the chapter. This provides both a reference and a review of the material that has been covered in the chapter.

UNDERSTANDING DICTIONARIES

PostScript uses a dictionary mechanism to implement all of its processing functions. This makes the understanding and use of dictionaries in PostScript important in working with the language. Dictionaries and stack operations are two of the most important concepts in PostScript processing. Neither of these concepts is difficult to understand or to use. Of the two, stack operation, which you read about in the preceding chapter, is probably more difficult; but many computers and computer languages use stacks. The dictionary concept, of course, is familiar to all of us, but it is unusual in the context of a computer language. I think you will find the PostScript dictionaries both conceptually elegant and truly useful. As it does with stacks, PostScript implements multiple dictionaries to perform various functions; once you understand dictionary operations, you will use multiple dictionaries too.

USING DICTIONARIES

A dictionary, in English, French, Japanese, or any other language, is a book that associates words with their definitions. In PostScript, a *dictionary* is a table that associates a name, or *key*, with a *value*. More precisely, a PostScript dictionary associates a pair of PostScript objects: the first object is the key, which is usually a name literal, and the second object is the associated value.

As you probably have guessed, this dictionary mechanism is how we assign names to PostScript objects, particularly variables and procedures. By the end of the last chapter, the handling of program pieces was becoming unwieldy and difficult to follow; in fact, there were several places in the previous exercises which would have been improved by the substitution of variable names for some of the values. Here you will learn how to do this.

Dictionary Stack

PostScript uses its dictionary mechanism in a variety of important functions; for example, fonts are implemented through a series of dictionaries. However, the most important dictionaries are those provided for PostScript operations. PostScript maintains a *dictionary stack* where all

PostScript operations are defined. As you read in the last chapter, all Post-Script stacks work alike, and the dictionary stack works in the same fashion as the operand stack you have become familiar with. There are several operators, which will be described shortly, that specifically access and manipulate the dictionary stack.

Although the dictionary stack works like the operand stack, it is entirely distinct. You will have to keep this in mind as we begin working with user-created dictionaries.

Default Dictionaries

The PostScript system provides a set of default dictionaries on the dictionary stack when it begins processing. In Level 1, there are two default dictionaries: *systemdict* and *userdict*. In Level 2, there are three default dictionaries: *systemdict*, *globaldict* (also called *shareddict*), and *userdict*. These default dictionaries are the bottommost entries on the dictionary stack; they cannot be removed, and the bottom entry is always *systemdict*. For Level 2, *globaldict* is next and *userdict* is on top of that; in Level 1, the entry on top of *systemdict* is *userdict*. These are the only dictionaries on the stack when PostScript begins operation.

In all cases, the topmost entry on the dictionary stack is called the *current dictionary*, and it is referred to by the name *currentdict*. This means that, when PostScript begins operation, the current dictionary is *userdict*, and all references to the current dictionary refer to *userdict*. In fact a substantial amount of work can be done using just the default dictionaries. But creating and using additional dictionaries is easy, and it also adds to your PostScript vocabulary.

Names and Literals

You must be wondering why I keep using the phrase ''name literals'' instead of just ''names.'' The reason is that you have to distinguish between ''names,'' which the PostScript interpreter looks up in the dictionaries, and ''name literals,'' which are the literal values of the names and which the PostScript interpreter places on the stack as it would a string.

If you think about this, you will see that this is an essential distinction. Somehow, the interpreter has to distinguish the use of a name as a reference to an object already in the dictionaries, which is the ordinary use of a name, from the use of the name as a literal to be enrolled into the current dictionary as a key or definition associated with some other object. This distinction is the reason for all the references to "name literal."

A *name* in PostScript can consist of almost any sequence of characters. All alphabetic and numeric characters are acceptable, as are most punctuation characters. There are ten special characters, which will be defined and discussed in the next section, that cannot be used in names. The most important of these is the space; valid names cannot contain spaces.

A *name literal* is any valid name preceded by a slash (/). As you might guess, the character / is one of the ten special characters: it is reserved to distinguish name literals from all other objects.

CREATING A DICTIONARY

There is a good reason why PostScript provides unremovable, default dictionaries on the dictionary stack. Specific PostScript operators, and the interpreter, implicitly reference the current dictionary, which obviously requires that there be a dictionary to reference. However, you may sometimes need to create individual dictionaries that can then be referenced by the various PostScript operators. How you create a new dictionary is the subject of this section.

Before you plunge into dictionary creation, there are two points to be made about notation and capacity. We will use the notation dict to indicate a dictionary in our discussion of operators. This is important because dictionary objects have certain specific characteristics which distinguish them from other PostScript objects. Also, dictionaries are created with a specific capacity to hold pairs of objects. In Level 1, if you try to put more entries into the dictionary than the capacity specified at its creation, you will get an error—and, more importantly, the *key,value* pair will not be entered. In Level 2, however, the interpreter will expand the dictionary to accommodate the new entry and will store it. This ability to expand in Level 2 means that the capacity that you specify when you create the dictionary only represents an initial estimate of the required size of the dictionary; the dictionary will never be smaller than that size, but may grow larger if required.

Dictionaries are created by the use of the **dict** operator. This operator takes one operand, an integer that specifies the initial dictionary capacity. In Level 1, this is also the maximum number of *key,value* pairs that can be placed in the that dictionary. The operator returns an empty dictionary object with the specified capacity. Note that this dictionary object is returned to the operand stack; it is not placed onto the dictionary stack. A dictionary is placed onto the dictionary stack by the operator **begin**, and is removed from the dictionary stack by the operator **end**. The **begin** operator requires a dictionary object on the operand stack, and makes that object the current dictionary. The **end** operator does not affect the operand stack in any way. These operators may be summarized as follows:

SYNTAX	FUNCTION
int **dict** dict	creates a dictionary *dict* with the initial capacity for *int* value pairs. In Level 1 devices, this is also the maximum number of pairs that can be contained in the dictionary.
dict **begin** —	pushes *dict* onto the dictionary stack and makes it the current dictionary.
— **end** —	pops the current dictionary from the dictionary stack.

Now that you know how to create dictionaries and move them on and off the dictionary stack, we need to discuss how to enroll objects into a dictionary and how to get access to them afterward.

HOW THE INTERPRETER REFERENCES DICTIONARIES

In order to understand how to use dictionary entries, you need to understand how the PostScript interpreter uses them. As the PostScript interpreter encounters an object, it takes one of two actions: either it places the object on the operand stack (as it would with a number or a name literal), or it looks the object up in the dictionary stack, using it as the key for the search. This is how the interpreter handles all names that are not name literals; that is, not preceded by a /. Specifically, this is how the interpreter handles operator names, for example.

Operation

Up until now, I have simply described the PostScript interpreter as executing the various operators we have discussed. This is a perfectly reasonable way to describe (and to think about) how the interpreter works; however, it is important for you to understand the overall process in greater detail. Operator names have no special significance to the interpreter; they are not "reserved" in the sense that operator names are in some other languages, such as COBOL and BASIC. Even within MS-DOS, certain names, such as CON and LPT1, are reserved to the operating system. In more ordinary languages, you must use reserved words or names correctly and for particular well-defined purposes; if you do not, you will generally receive an error message, and in any case, the code won't execute properly. In PostScript, however, operator names are simply keys into the *systemdict*, where they are associated with the actual built-in function that performs the action specified by the operator name. This makes PostScript different from other languages, since you could redefine these names if you wanted to. The PostScript interpreter does not prevent you from using operator names for your own functions, although common sense dictates that you avoid such potentially confusing antics except under special circumstances. This also explains why the *systemdict* is always on the dictionary stack and cannot be removed.

As discussed above, when the PostScript interpreter encounters a name that is not preceded by the special character / (which would make it a name literal, to be pushed onto the operand stack), it looks the name up as a key in the dictionary stack. The interpreter begins looking in the current dictionary. If it doesn't find the name as a key in the current dictionary, it continues to look down through the dictionary stack until it either finds a matching key or exhausts the stack. If there is no match, an error status is returned. When a match is found, the interpreter takes the appropriate action. If the value that matches the key is a procedure, the procedure is executed; if the value is not a procedure (in which case it's a string, literal, number, or so on), the value is placed on the operand stack. The interpreter continues on in this way until it has consumed all the PostScript objects presented to it (or until it encounters an error which forces it to stop).

Search Sequence

The sequence used by the interpreter to search for names should be clear from the discussion above. Dictionaries are searched down through the dictionary stack. This process begins with the current dictionary and continues through the *userdict* (which may be the current dictionary), and ends with the *systemdict* at the bottom of the dictionary stack.

There are two exceptions to this default search sequence. These occur with operators that specifically reference a particular dictionary. This may be required for two reasons. First, the operator by its nature may require a dictionary specification; font manipulation operators are a good example of this (recall that fonts reside in a special set of dictionaries). Second, the operator may be defined to provide specific access to dictionary values or operations. Generally, such operators fall outside of the scope of this book. In either case, it is important to remember that, while most PostScript operators deal with the current dictionary, there are operators that can be explicitly directed to work with a specific dictionary.

Accessing a Dictionary

The most frequently used PostScript dictionary operators are naturally the ones which expect to access the current dictionary. Certainly the most common dictionary operation is the act of enrolling a *key, value* pair in the current dictionary. This is done with the **def** operator, which is defined as follows:

SYNTAX	FUNCTION
key value **def** —	associates *key* and *value* in the current dictionary.

Let us consider a few examples that make use of this operator. Consider the example

/abc 123 **def**

This process will associate the name *abc* with the value *123* in the current dictionary. This means that, if you have placed the definition above earlier in a program, the following two statements will produce identical results, as shown:

123 456 **add** → 579

abc 456 **add** → 579

You see what the interpreter did here. In the second instance, the interpreter took the name *abc* and looked it up in the current dictionary, where it

found the value *123*. It then took that value and pushed it onto the stack, just
as it did in the first instance, when it encountered the value directly. Hence
the result of the **add** operator was the same in both cases. In other words,
the dictionary behaves naturally, substituting a name for its associated value,
just as if the value were inserted into the statement in place of the name.

A value is not limited to being a number; it can be any PostScript
object. For example, we may write

/String1 (this is a string) **def**

as a definition in our current dictionary.

In addition to the **def** operator, which always refers to the current dictionary, there are several operators which reference the dictionary stack as a
whole, in a fashion similar to the interpreter. These operators (**load**, **store**,
and **where**) are like **def** in that they do not reference a specific dictionary,
but unlike **def**, they do not stop with the current dictionary. Instead, they
follow the interpreter's search process and search the entire dictionary
stack, beginning with the current dictionary, until they find the key they
have been given.

THIRD EXERCISE: USING VARIABLE NAMES

This seems like an appropriate time for a brief exercise using variable
names in a program. In order to give you a taste of what use of variables does
for a program, we will redo the second exercise, using variables in the program instead of constants. I think you will find this version of the exercise
cleaner and easier to understand.

PROGRAM EXAMPLE

Let's briefly review the structure of this example. This is a program for
displaying multiple lines of text on a page in two columns. The two columns are
set in a text-and-commentary format, with the commentary set in italic type
and the body text in regular type. There have been no alterations in the output,

either in text or in spacing, so that you can compare one with the other to see how different approaches to a program may produce identical results.

As in our previous examples, a complete discussion of the program follows the listing. This discussion will cover the new issues that arise in using variables, and it will indicate some of the new choices facing you as the programmer.

Setup

The page layout remains identical to that of the previous example. The commentary column has a margin of 1 inch and is 2 inches wide. There is 1 inch of space between the first and second columns. The second, or body text, column is 4 inches wide, with a ½-inch right margin. Both columns of text start 1.5 inches from the top of the page. Since PostScript is measuring from the bottom of the page, this is 9.5 inches from the origin.

Each column of text has two paragraphs of several lines each. The text is set in 12-point type on 14-point leading, with double-spacing between paragraphs. The commentary paragraphs are set to align with the text paragraphs, even though the text may be longer than the commentary.

Multiline Text Revisited

Figure 2.1 shows the text of the original program revised to use appropriate variable names in place of constants. The use of variables and named constants makes the program somewhat longer, but it emerges more comprehensible and is still not really complex. Altogether the exercise produces a page of output that looks identical to the previous page output; only the program has been changed. Refer to Figure 1.7 to compare your output with mine.

Review of Example

The first thing you will notice about the revised example is that there are now two sections to the program. The first section begins with the comment line

```
%----Setup Variables----
```

and allows you to keep a particular type of program work in one place. There is a more extensive discussion of these issues of structure and placement later in the chapter, under the heading "Program Structure and Style."

```
%---------------Setup Variables-------------------------
% establish beginning x-coordinates for columns
/FirstColumnStart 72 def                                        %1
/SecondColumnStart 4 72 mul def                                 %2
% establish beginning y-coordinate for text
/VerticalStart 9.5 72 mul def                                   %3
% set up leading and paragraph spacing variables
/LineSpace 14 def                                               %4
/ParaSpace 28 def                                               %5
%---------------Begin Program-------------------------
/Times-Roman findfont 12 scalefont setfont                      %6
/NextLine VerticalStart def                                     %7
SecondColumnStart NextLine moveto                               %8
(The quick brown fox jumps over the lazy black) show            %9
/NextLine NextLine LineSpace sub def                            %10
SecondColumnStart NextLine moveto                               %11
(dog and then the quick brown fox jumps over that) show         %12
/NextLine NextLine LineSpace sub def
SecondColumnStart NextLine moveto
(lazy dog again and again and again ... but the) show           %13
/NextLine NextLine LineSpace sub def
SecondColumnStart NextLine moveto
(dog just doesn't pay any attention.) show
%Now begin the second paragraph of the body text
%Note the changes from the previous example
/NextLine NextLine ParaSpace sub  def                           %14
/SavePara NextLine def                                          %15
SecondColumnStart NextLine moveto                               %16
(Here is the quick brown fox playing the same) show
/NextLine NextLine LineSpace sub def
SecondColumnStart NextLine moveto
(games again in a second text paragraph. You) show
/NextLine NextLine LineSpace sub def
SecondColumnStart NextLine moveto
(can easily see how this could go on and on and ...) show
%
%
%Now we can set the commentary column
%
%
/Times-Italic findfont 12 scalefont setfont                     %20
/NextLine VerticalStart def                                     %21
FirstColumnStart NextLine moveto                                %22
(This is a classic text) show                                   %23
/NextLine NextLine LineSpace sub def
FirstColumnStart NextLine moveto
(and commentary layout;) show
%Now set the second commentary item
%  to match the second body paragraph
/NextLine SavePara def                                          %24
FirstColumnStart NextLine moveto
(using two fonts: ) show                                        %25
/NextLine NextLine LineSpace sub def
FirstColumnStart NextLine moveto
((Times Roman and Times Italic)) show                           %26
showpage                                                        %27
quit                                                            %28
```

Figure 2.1: Third exercise: text output with variables

You should notice, however, that there is a structure, and it has a point and a purpose.

This first program section is where the constants that you are going to use are first given names and initialized. These are constants in the sense that they will not change value within the program, although you might want to change them on a subsequent execution. That facility for change is one of the major reasons to use named constants within a procedure, rather than using straight numeric values as the previous exercises did. It would be easier to adjust a structure like the one shown in this exercise simply by redefining the constant values.

There are five named constants set out in the start of the program. These are listed below with an explanation of what each one represents and how it was calculated.

CONSTANT	FUNCTION
FirstColumnStart	The starting x-coordinate for the first column. The initial position is governed by the desired margin; in this case, 1 inch (72 points).
SecondColumnStart	The same calculation for the second column. In this case, the initial position is 4 inches from the left margin. Note that, unlike the first example, here you can simply insert the desired calculation (4 72 **mul**) within the definition.
VerticalStart	The same mechanism is used to calculate the y-coordinate for the top of the text.
LineSpace	The desired leading value, as discussed previously.
ParaSpace	The desired paragraph spacing. Note that you could have calculated this (by using 2 LineSpace **mul**) if you wanted to make it always a multiple of the line spacing. In this case, the approach was to make it a separate value, not necessarily related to the line-space value.

Now you begin the actual program. Most of this is familiar, so we won't repeat too much of the previous discussion. Line %6 again sets up the necessary font parameters for the **show**. Lines %7 and %8 are new, replacing a simple **moveto** that previously positioned the current point for the show. Line %7 defines and sets a variable, NextLine, to start at the point given by VerticalStart. Line %8 sets the current point to the coordinates given by NextLine and SecondColumnStart. Line %9—and all the subsequent **show** operations—is identical to the previous exercise. Lines %10 and %11 form the core of the change brought into the program by the use of variables. Line %10 resets the variable, NextLine, to its previous value less the LineSpace constant, while line %11 moves the current point to the newly calculated value. This identical operation is performed before each new line of text is output. This couldn't be done without a variable to save and store the current position of the line; and being able to repeat the operation in the identical fashion for each new line makes your programming both easier and clearer. So the program continues until the end of the paragraph.

At the end of the paragraph, line %14, you once again recalculate Next-Line, using the constant ParaSpace to give the correct spacing before the next line of text. Line %15 saves this position in a new variable, SavePara, for use in positioning the next column. The second paragraph of body text continues to be output in the same fashion as the first.

The output of the commentary column begins at line %20. (Don't worry if the numbers aren't in sequence; I restarted at 20 for this section.) Once again, the new font is set for the commentary output. Then line %21 resets NextLine to the beginning of the text position, and line %22 sets the current point to the coordinates given by NextLine and FirstColumnStart. The text output is a repetition of the command structures from the previous column, using FirstColumnStart instead of SecondColumnStart. At line %24, you change NextLine to the value you saved previously at line %15 to position the next line of output to the same vertical location as the beginning of the second paragraph of the body text.

The remainder of the example corresponds to what you have already been familiar with. Once again, you terminate with a **quit** to clear the interpreter.

UNDERSTANDING OBJECTS

Up to this point, we have dealt intuitively with the concept of Post-Script objects. This easy and straightforward approach has worked well for us, primarily because the intuitive concept is fairly accurate. Now, however, you are ready for a complete and precise definition.

A PostScript *object* is any syntactic entity that can be recognized by the PostScript interpreter. All data in a PostScript program, as well as the procedures which form the program itself, consist of PostScript objects. Neither the PostScript language nor the PostScript interpreter makes any formal distinction between data and procedures. Any PostScript object may be either data or program; some objects may be treated as one thing one time and the other the next. This process is most noticeable in the handling of procedures, which are pushed onto the stack when they are first encountered, but are executed when they are subsequently processed.

STATEMENT TYPES

In addition to becoming familiar with PostScript notation, there are a few format conventions you need to become comfortable with in order to read Postscript easily. The PostScript language is designed so that programs can be constructed using only the printable subset of the ASCII character set, plus the characters space, tab, formfeed, linefeed, and carriage return. These five characters, along with the null character ($\emptyset$), are referred to collectively as *white space* characters. These characters serve as separators for other objects, such as names and numbers. Any number of consecutive white space characters are treated as if they were just one. The only exception to this is within strings and comments where each of the white space characters has specific (and different) effects. In addition, there are ten special characters that serve as delimiters or markers for certain objects such as strings, procedures, name literals, and comments. These characters are the following:

CHARACTERS	FUNCTION
{ and }	begin and end a procedure
/	begins a name literal
%	begins a comment
(and)	begin and end a string
< and >	begin and end a hexadecimal or encoded string
[and]	begin and end an array

The more common of these are more fully described below.

Procedures

Procedures are operators and objects grouped together within matched braces ({ }). Procedures are also known as executable arrays in PostScript. Some examples of procedures are:

SYNTAX	FUNCTION
{Xpos 5 add}	Adds 5 to the variable *Xpos*.
{add 5 div}	Adds the top two operands on the stack and divides the result by 5.

Note that the procedures are not executed immediately when the interpreter reads them; they are stored and executed later. This issue is examined and discussed more fully in the next section of this chapter, which covers the creation and use of procedures.

Name Literals

You were introduced to name literals, and their distinction from names, earlier in the chapter. Name literals are just what their name implies, names of objects, usually procedures or variables. All characters except special characters and white space characters can appear in a name literal. A name literal begins with a slash (/). The slash is not part of the name itself, and is not included when reference is made to the name. The special nature of the slash, like that of the braces that enclosed procedures, is to notify the interpreter that what follows is a literal to be placed onto the stack.

Some examples of valid names are:

/name

/NaMe   (note that this is different from **/name**)

/Paragraph_12

/Times-Roman   (a name you have already met)

/$@#&&8*^   (a goofy name, but still valid)

There is no inherent limit on the length of a name, but remember that the newline character is a white space character and invalid within a name literal; therefore a name literal cannot exceed one line in length.

Comments

You have previously read about and used both comments and strings. However, the previous discussion only covered enough information to allow you to work comfortably with the exercises. This section and the next provide complete and precise definitions of comments and strings. As such, they duplicate to some extent information you already know.

Comments begin with the special character % (percent). The comment consists of every character, including special characters, until the next newline character. PostScript treats a comment as if it were a single white space character. There are a few observations to be made about comments. First, since the comment begins with % and extends to the next newline, it will always be the last element on a line or on a line by itself—which is where you would normally code one while programming. Second, in multiple comment lines, each line must start with a %.

The ability to include special characters means that, once you begin a comment, the interpreter will not process anything until the next newline character. This can be extremely valuable in providing documentation within the program itself. Some examples of comments are:

/abc   %this is all comment (including {abc add xyz}

/abc%this is the same effect as the line above

%this is %equally%%%[{] valid

12%is just '12' as far as the PS interpreter sees

%and so on — you get the idea

The single exception to this use of % to introduce a comment is when the character % is included within a pair of string delimiters. In that case, and no other, it is included by the interpreter as part of the string.

Strings

A string in PostScript is a group of characters enclosed within matching parentheses, (and). Within a string, the only special characters are parentheses themselves and the backslash (\) character. The following are examples of valid strings:

(this is a string)

(and so is !@#$%%^&* − = + this)

(and so is 1232 56677 45890)

(white space characters are NOT

excluded from

a valid string)

Parentheses may also be included as long as they are balanced. For example:

(this is ( ) a valid (0) string)

And you can create a null string by entering two () with no intervening space.

The \ character is a signal that there is a special requirement within the string. The character or characters immediately following the \ determines what interpretation is placed on the requirement. The valid combinations are as follows:

CHARACTER	DEFINITION
\n	newline (linefeed)
\r	carriage return
\t	horizontal tab
\b	backspace
\f	form feed
\\	backslash
\(	left parenthesis
\)	right parenthesis
\ddd	character code ddd (octal)
\newline	no character—both are ignored

Any other combination with \ is ignored.

The use of \ddd has a special value in PostScript. Remember that PostScript is designed to be able to use only the printable subset of the ASCII character set for all operations. This enhances both readability and portability, as we have discussed above. Thus the \ddd notation provides a way to incorporate a character outside PostScript's normal range using notation which remains within the recommended subset. The *ddd* should be the octal value that corresponds to the character you want. The actual character represented by any given value may differ from font to font. See "Appendix E: Standard Character Sets and Encoding Vectors" in the *PostScript Language Reference Manual, Second Edition* for the octal values of characters in the standard fonts.

The *newline* provides a method to break a string into a number of lines for legibility or coding purposes without having newline character actually becoming part of the string. This complements the use of \\n to force a new line in the string without adding one in the code. Some examples are as follows:

```
(These three\

lines will be combined\

into one line)


(This string has a newline

character in the middle)


(And so does\n this one)
```

There is a special form of string that is bracketed by < and >. A string within these two delimiters is a *hexadecimal* (base 16) string. The only valid characters are 0 to 9 and *A* (or *a*) to *F* (or *f*), or white space characters. Each pair of hexadecimal digits represents one character. Here are a two examples of hexadecimal strings:

```
<1211a1f3>
<abCDef112290>
```

As you see, both upper- and lowercase letters within the correct range are equally acceptable. Since hexadecimal strings can only contain valid hexadecimal digits, PostScript allows you to place white space characters in these strings without altering their value. For example, these two strings are identical to the two strings shown above:

    <12 11 a1 f3>

    <abCD ef11   2290>

The white space characters in the strings are simply skipped over and ignored.

    We can also illustrate the equivalence of pairs of hexadecimal digits to normal characters. Using the standard ASCII representation of characters, we can form the following example of a hexadecimal string:

    <31355F4e616d65>

which is equivalent to the regular string

    (15_Name)

    Finally, Level 2 has added one additional type of string, bracketed by < ˜ and ˜ >. This type of string is called an *ASCII base-85 encoded* string. Like the hexadecimal string, this provides a method for encoding arbitrary binary data into a printable subset of the ASCII character set. When you use this string, four bytes of binary data are translated into five bytes of ASCII code, using the characters between ! and u. This type of encoding is more compact than the simpler hexadecimal format, since a hexadecimal encoding uses two ASCII characters for each binary byte. If you are encoding a large amount of data, such as a scanned color image, this makes a great difference in size. Because Level 2 provides automatic filtering (that is, encoding and decoding) of this type, this can be a very useful technique when you have a Level 2 device.

OBJECT TYPES

    The PostScript language has seventeen distinct types of objects. These can be split into two groups, as shown in Table 2.1. All syntactic entities recognized by the PostScript interpreter belong to one of these types.

Table 2.1: PostScript Object Types

SIMPLE	COMPOSITE
integer	array
real	packedarray*
name	string
boolean	file
operator	dictionary
save	gstate**
null	lock***
mark	condition***
fontID	

implemented in most Level 1 devices.
** *implemented in PostScript Level 2 devices.*
*** *implemented in Display PostScript devices.*

All PostScript objects have certain common characteristics, which are a type, attributes, and a value. In general, when you deal with a PostScript object, you need only be concerned with its type and value. The attributes of an object are primarily of interest to the interpreter, and, if they interest you, you will find a full discussion in Section 3.3 of the *PostScript Language Reference Manual, Second Edition.*

Table 2.1 divides PostScript objects into two major groups, simple objects and composite objects, because this distinction is probably their most important characteristic from the viewpoint of the PostScript programmer.

Most PostScript objects are *simple* objects. This means that all their characteristics, type, attributes, and value, are inextricably linked together and cannot be individually changed. This is certainly reasonable enough; you would hardly expect that the object 123 was the same as 456. The only way to change the characteristics of a simple object is to copy it to a new object which has the desired characteristics.

Composite objects, on the other hand, are objects such as *array*, *string*, and *dictionary*. This means that each of these types of objects have components and an internal substructure which is both visible and accessible. For these three most common composite objects, the internal structure can be directly accessed and changed; however, other types of composite objects may allow only limited internal access. The individual substructure of each of these three types is discussed more fully later in the chapter.

The major difference between simple and composite objects is what happens when you make a duplicate of the object. Anytime that you store an object or bring it onto the stack, you make a duplicate of the object. If you duplicate a simple object, you automatically get a new object. This means that any changes that you may make to any of the object's characteristics do not affect the original object. When you duplicate a composite object, however, you do not get a completely new object. Instead, the new and the old object share the same internal structure and value. However, it is possible to create new versions of composite objects, if required, by using specific coding techniques. We will discuss this in more detail later in the book.

There are two types of numeric objects in PostScript, *integer* and *real*. Integer objects consist only of integer numbers, between certain limits determined by the implementation. Real objects consist of real numbers within a wider range of limits. Real numbers are generally implemented as floating point numbers, and therefore have specific precision limitations. Numbers of both types may be freely intermixed in PostScript operations, except where an operator specifically requires an integer type (as some operators do). Where that requirement exists, you will find the notation *int* used in our description of the operator, to warn you that only an integer value is allowed.

Although they are not actually numbers, we will also consider *boolean* objects as belonging to the numeric category. Boolean objects have only two possible values, true and false. As you will read later in this chapter, they are produced by the comparison operators and used by the conditional and logical operators. Although boolean objects are equivalent to the binary values, 0 and 1, which are often used in other computer contexts, these are distinct objects in PostScript, and 0 is not false, nor is 1 true. For this reason, the specific objects *true* and *false* exist within PostScript for those occasions when you need a direct reference to these values.

There are three types of PostScript objects that can be thought of as names, or variants of names. These types are: name objects, operator objects, and file objects.

A *name object* is an indivisible symbol uniquely defined by a set of characters. A name is a simple object; although it is referenced and identified by a string of characters, it is not the string of characters. The individual characters that make up the name are not in any sense elements of the name; they must be taken and used as a unit.

There are two important points characteristics you need to notice about names. First, they must be unique. Any specific sequence of characters defines one, and only one, name object. Second, names do not have values in the same sense that they would in other programming languages. Instead, names in PostScript are associated with values through the use of the dictionary mechanism, as you have already seen.

Operator objects represent the built-in PostScript actions; when the operator is encountered, the built-in action is executed. As we already discussed, operator objects are the value half of the pairing in *systemdict* with the key of the operator name. For most purposes, you can simply regard operators as being identical to their names. However, you should know that the operator and its name are not, in fact, precisely identical; and leave it at that.

A *file* is a readable or writable stream of characters, transferring information between PostScript and its environment. A *file object* is a composite object that refers to an associated, underlying file. PostScript always provides two standard files: a standard input file and a standard output file; and may provide other standard files for error reporting and interactive processing as well, depending on the implementation.

The standard input file is where the PostScript interpreter generally receives programs, commands, and data to be worked on; the standard output file is the destination of usual PostScript output, especially error and status messages and certain displays. Most PostScript programs can run very satisfactorily with only the standard files. When these are not sufficient, however, PostScript does provide a full set of file operators, which allow you to open a file (which is the act that creates the file object), and to process the stream of characters in a variety of ways. It is almost never necessary to refer directly to the standard files, but there are names and mechanisms for such reference if required. See the full discussion of file operators in Section 3.8 of the *PostScript Language Reference Manual, Second Edition* regarding these points.

You are already familiar with the construction and use of strings in PostScript. A *string object* is simply a PostScript string. It is, as we said earlier, a composite object. Therefore any operation that duplicates a string, or part of a string, results in a sharing of the string's value. String objects consist of a series of values, stored internally as integers from 0 to 255, and are conventionally used to store character data with one character being represented by each integer. Individual elements within a string can be accessed by use of an integer index.

Dictionaries were also discussed earlier. A *dictionary object* is simply a PostScript dictionary; like a string, it is a composite object. At the risk of sounding like a broken record, copying a dictionary to a new dictionary does not copy the values in the dictionary, it shares the values. That means that, if you change a value in the old dictionary, you will retrieve the changed value in the new one.

An *array object*, or simply an *array*, is an indexed collection of PostScript objects. PostScript arrays differ from arrays in most other computer languages in two respects. First, a PostScript array does not have to be composed of only one type of object. A PostScript array might contain, for example, numbers, strings, names, and even other arrays. The second difference is that PostScript arrays are one-dimensional. That means that access to individual elements in a PostScript array is always provided by a single index. Of course, since elements of a PostScript array may consists of other arrays, you are able to construct the functional equivalent of multi-dimensional arrays if you require them.

The index to a PostScript array must be a non-negative integer. PostScript indices begin at zero, so a PostScript array with n elements would be indexed by values from 0 to $n-1$. Any attempt to access an array with an index that is invalid will result in an error.

A typical PostScript array is created by bounding a collection of PostScript objects with brackets ([ ]). When the PostScript interpreter encounters the [it pushes a mark onto the operand stack and then executes each following object, adding the results to the stack, until it encounters the]. At that point, the interpreter removes everything down to the mark and creates an array out of the objects taken off the stack. Below is an example of a PostScript array.

    [12 34 (abcd) 56 78]

This array consists of five elements: two integers 12 and 34, followed by a string, abcd, followed by two more integers, 56 and 78.

    [/name (name) .125 34]

This array consists of four elements: a name literal, name, a string, name, followed by a real number, .125, and an integer, 34. Remember that the name object, name is not the same thing as the string name. A name object is a simple object and doesn't have component elements as the string does.

Finally, the array

[(div) 6 12 add]

is an interesting and instructive example. This array has only two elements, the string div, and the integer result of adding 6 and 12, 18. You should notice here that the array construction executes operators within it before creating the array itself. This is what distinguishes the square brackets ([ ]) from the curly brackets ({ }) that define a procedure. When the interpreter encounters [, it will continue to execute operators; when it encounters {, it will stop executing operators and instead place them onto the stack.

Most PostScript implementations also allow packed arrays. These are simply standard arrays that are compressed to save storage space. Packed arrays are primarily used to save space when creating and executing procedures.

WORKING WITH PROCEDURES

A *procedure* is an executable array of PostScript objects. As you learned in the preceding section, procedures are enclosed in curly brackets, ({ }). This distinguishes them from other PostScript arrays which are enclosed in square brackets as described above. As you read in the last example, this is an important distinction. You may find the concept of an "executable array" to be somewhat strange; if so, you may find it convenient to think of procedures as a separate type of PostScript object belonging to its own class and having its own properties. The main point to understand here is that procedures are viewed by the interpreter as arrays that can be stored and executed.

The main difference between ordinary PostScript arrays and procedures is how each is handled by the interpreter. In an array, each object is processed by the interpreter in the same way that the object would be in ordinary execution: names are looked up in the dictionary stack and the appropriate value is substituted into the array; operators are executed in the ordinary fashion, taking operands from the stack and returning results that are inserted into the array definition; and so on. When a beginning procedure marker ({) is encountered, however, the interpreter stops executing the following objects and places everything onto the stack until the end-of-procedure marker (}) occurs. At this point, names are not looked up, and operators are not acted on; everything is placed onto the stack as one large object, almost as if it were a string. The actions specified within the procedure will only take place later in the program, when the entire procedure is executed by the interpreter.

Procedures are essentially small segments of PostScript programs. They are ordered collections, or arrays, of PostScript objects that accomplish a given task. These segments can be entered into a PostScript dictionary like any other PostScript object, and referenced by name. In fact, most PostScript program analysis consists of identifying a hierarchy of required procedures.

TRANSFERRING CONTROL

Since PostScript is a programming language, it necessarily provides several mechanisms for changing the order of execution of operations. Some such mechanism is essential for any type of programming. Interestingly, PostScript does not provide a traditional "go to" or branch operator, nor does it have branch labels. In this sense, PostScript is a perfect example of a "structured" language. Since, however, most programmers have grown up with the notion of branching, you may find that you need to rethink your old habits.

Instead of branching, PostScript provides a variety of operators to perform procedures repeatedly or to execute them based on a particular condition. PostScript also provides a set of logical operators for creating, combining, and testing conditions. By using these facilities, a PostScript programmer can create complex procedural variations to accomplish any task. The essential requirement is to think of your task as a series of processes rather than as one complex flow. As we work through the examples in the following sections and chapters, I will try to show you some simple but effective methods for thinking about pages and processes to help generate good PostScript code.

PostScript operators that provide control of procedures can be divided into three groups, as follows:

- operators that execute a procedure repeatedly

- operators that execute a procedure conditionally, based on a test of some external object

- operators used by PostScript itself to control flow

These groups are somewhat arbitrary, and the first two groups, at least, will be common in your work. The first group is distinguished by being a simple, repeated operation. The operators in this group are the following:

SYNTAX	**FUNCTION**
{proc} **exec** —	executes *proc*.
int {proc} **repeat** —	executes *proc int* times.
init incr lim {proc} **for** —	executes *proc* for values from *init* by steps of *incr* until reaching *lim*.

The second group of operators is more complex, being dependent on the results of a conditional test, either outside and independent of the procedure being executed, or within it. Here you will notice a new operand type, *bool*. This represents a boolean value, either true or false. These operators are

SYNTAX	**FUNCTION**
bool {proc} **if** —	executes *proc* if *bool* is true.
bool {proc1} {proc2} **ifelse** —	executes *proc1* if *bool* is true and executes *proc2* otherwise.

and also the pair of operators

SYNTAX	**FUNCTION**
{proc} **loop** —	executes *proc* an indefinite number of times.
— **exit** —	terminates the active loop.

which are used together. This grouping of operators shows very clearly how easy and natural structured programming is in PostScript.

Structured programming is a method of developing program logic according to a specific set of rules. While this is not an appropriate place for a complete analysis of this subject, a brief discussion will help prepare you mentally to write PostScript code. One of the main rules of structured programming is that program logic should utilize only three control structures for maximum readability and logical clarity. These are the sequential control structure, the loop control structure, and the if-then-else control structure. Each of these structures is used as required to form a group of computer instructions that both conforms to strict structural requirements and performs a single logical function, which makes the code easy to read and to understand.

The sequence control structure is just a fancy way of saying that the computer executes one instruction or operation after another; this is just the ordinary sequential processing, familiar to us all. The other two control structures, loop control and if-then-else control, correspond more or less to the first two groups of operators given above. The net result is that PostScript provides the ideal set of operators to create a structured program.

We have already observed that the second group of control operators listed above depends upon testing an external object and changing control sequence based on the results of that test. PostScript provides the usual set of conditional operators to execute these tests. These operators are the following:

SYNTAX	FUNCTION
any1 any2 **eq** bool	tests whether *any1* is equal to *any2*.
any1 any2 **ne** bool	tests whether *any1* is not equal to *any2*.
num1 num2 (str1) (str2) **ge** bool	tests whether *num1* or *str1* is greater than or equal to *num2* or *str2*.
num1 num2 (str1) (str2) **gt** bool	tests whether *num1* or *str1* is greater than num2 or *str2*.
num1 num2 (str1) (str2) **le** bool	tests whether *num1* or *str1* is less than or equal to *num2* or *str2*.
num1 num2 (str1) (str2) **lt** bool	tests whether *num1* or *str1* is less than *num2* or *str2*.

PostScript also provides a series of operators for combining conditions. These are the boolean operators and consist of the following:

SYNTAX	FUNCTION
int1 int2 int	
bool1 bool2 **and** bool	logical or bitwise *and*.
int1 int2 int	
bool1 bool2 **or** bool	logical or bitwise inclusive *or*.
int1 int2 int	
bool1 bool2 **xor** bool	logical or bitwise exclusive *or*.
int int	
bool **not** bool	logical or bitwise *not*.
— **true** bool	pushes the boolean value *true* onto the stack.
— **false** bool	pushes the boolean value *false* onto the stack.

The combination of these operators allows any form of test on a PostScript object.

Procedures and Operators

The preceding section introduced you to the concept of procedures as a part of the discussion of program control and related operators. Now you can begin to make more effective use of these operators, by putting names on procedures and using those names as part of the control and flow process. To illustrate this, let's revisit some of the procedural examples that you saw before. If you don't remember any of the operators, just go back to the end of the last chapter and look them up—or you can find them in the operator summary in Appendix A.

A procedure is named and entered into the current dictionary like any other PostScript object. For example,

/average { **add** 2 **div** } **def**

defines a procedure, average, in exactly the same way that

/str (this is a string) **def**

defines the string str. All definitions are carried out in the same fashion. Procedure names can also be included in the definition of other procedures; for example, if you have defined average as shown above, then you might also define the procedure

/middlePage { 0 612 average } **def**

which would give you the average of the left and right edges of a standard page. Since the interpreter does not execute the procedure when the definition occurs, it is not necessary to have already defined average when you define middlePage. All that is required is that average be defined by the time you execute middlePage.

Notice that this procedural definition, middlePage, differs from the following definition of a named constant:

/MiddlePage 0 612 average **def**

It looks very similar, doesn't it? And it is similar, and it would (in this case) accomplish the same goal as the preceding definition. In both cases, the final result would be to leave the value of the middle of the page on the stack. The difference lies in how that result is obtained.

In the first definition, of a procedure, the calculation is carried out only at the moment the interpreter encounters the name middlePage in the program. In the second case, the calculation is carried out at the moment that the definition is encountered, and the value of that calculation is stored under the name MiddlePage. These two cases have been constructed to illustrate how these procedures work; the judgement of when to use one or the other must be made based on the requirements of each task or program. The point to note here is that, in the case of procedural definition, average does not have to be defined when the procedure is defined and the calculation of the value occurs at the moment of use. In the case of constant definition, the procedure average must be defined already, since it will be executed to compute the value to be stored, and that value, once computed, will be fixed and used whenever the named constant is invoked.

Using these techniques, we can now revisit some of the examples from the last chapter. Let's begin by defining the following procedure:

/inch { 72 **mul** } **def**

This small procedure allows you to translate inches into PostScript coordinates, which you will recall are $1/72$ of an inch in each direction. Using this procedure, the following two program segments are identical in execution:

7.5 inch

7.5 72 **mul**

However, the first is, as you would expect, much easier to understand.

Now you might define a variable, Xpos, to measure movement across the page, and a variable, Ypos, to measure movement down the page. Assume that you would like a 1-inch margin on both the left and the right edges of the page, and that you also want to start printing 1 inch from the top of the page. Then you would define

/Xpos 1 inch **def**

/Ypos 7.5 inch **def**

to begin each variable at the appropriate margin. Remember that the PostScript vertical coordinate system is positive up the page, and so a larger number represents a position higher up the page; you will subtract from the Ypos variable to measure movement down the page. Then you could write the following

/RightMargin 7 inch **def**

/outsideMargin { Xpos RightMargin **gt** } **def**

The first statement defines a position that we call RightMargin at 7 inches, and the second procedure defines a test, called outsideMargin, which checks the Xpos variable against the RightMargin position. Using these definitions we can now test whether the Xpos variable has crossed the right margin by executing the procedure outsideMargin.

Let us suppose that you have determined that movement in the vertical direction will be at 6 lines per inch. Then you could define

/lineSpace { inch 6 **div** } **def**

and

/lineDown { Ypos lineSpace **sub** } **def**

which defines the six-per-inch line spacing as lineSpace, and creates a procedure, lineDown, to subtract a lineSpace from the Ypos variable. Now you can combine these procedures to accomplish in an easily understandable way the task of moving down one line if the position across the page has crossed the right margin. This was written before as

504 Xpos **gt** { Ypos 12 **sub** } **if**

but you can now write it as

outsideMargin lineDown **if**

which is much more intelligible.

The important point here is that you have made an opaque piece of code understandable by the judicious choice of variable and procedure names. We will discuss this issue of names and procedures more thoroughly in the next section.

MANAGING MEMORY

The PostScript interpreter, like all computers, has internal memory that it uses to store programs and data for processing. In stand-alone PostScript devices, such as most laser printers, this memory is used for several main purposes. First, the PostScript interpreter itself is stored in the memory. Second, an image of the page which is to be output is stored in memory until it is time to print it. Third, the interpreter stores its internal variables and other objects, including the program that is being processed, in memory.

The memory where composite objects are stored is called *virtual memory*. This memory is the memory area which a PostScript program can access and modify. Note that the name "virtual" does not necessarily indicate that the memory is paged or provided with any special management. This can be somewhat misleading for programmers coming from other environments, where the definition of virtual memory implies that the operating system provides such management. In PostScript, you do not have to worry about memory addresses, segment size, or most other memory issues. You do, however, still have some memory management to perform if you are going to write good PostScript code. In particular, you have to ensure that you do not run out of virtual memory for your program.

As we discussed above, there are two types of objects: simple and composite. Only composite objects consume virtual memory. Simple objects are created and manipulated by the interpreter in its own memory; you don't have to be concerned about that. However, every time you create a string, array, dictionary, or other composite object, you use up some virtual memory. Since virtual memory is the only memory that you can control, from here on the word memory will refer to virtual memory, unless we specify otherwise.

To avoid using up all of the available memory, PostScript provides two memory management operators, **save** and **restore**. These are defined as follows:

SYNTAX	FUNCTION
— **save** savestate	saves the current state of PostScript virtual memory as *savestate*.
savestate **restore** —	restores PostScript virtual memory to the state represented by *savestate*.

These two operators are used together to save a picture of the virtual memory at a specific point in processing, and then to restore that state at a later point. When you **restore** the state, all composite objects in memory are returned to the state that they had at the time of the **save**. Therefore, all objects that were created and stored since the **save** are removed from virtual memory, and that memory is once again available for use. This approach has some limitations, but it does provide an efficient and effective means for a program to manage its memory resources. In the next chapter, you will see how to use these operators in your own programs.

The major drawback to this management technique is that, like the PostScript stacks, it is strictly last-in, first-out. This means that if you want to save, say, a string for later use in your program, you cannot perform a

restore until you are completely finished using that string. This may require that you use a lot of memory in the meantime. PostScript Level 2 provides additional operators that allow you to manage memory in a more explicit fashion. The two most important of these operators are the following:

SYNTAX	FUNCTION
dict key **undef** —	removes *key* and its associated value from the dictionary, *dict*.
key **undefinefont** —	removes *key*, which is a font name literal, and its associated value, which is a font dictionary, from the font directory.

There are important limitations on the effective use of these operators in Level 2 devices. If you use these operators, be sure that you are familiar with the issues discussed in Sections 3.7 and 3.9 of the *PostScript Language Reference Manual, Second Edition*.

Because of the nature of **save**, **restore** processing in PostScript Level 1, it is not realistically possible to emulate the operation of Level 2 memory management operators in a Level 1 device. For that reason, as discussed in the Introduction, we will not use these operators in any of the examples in this book.

HANDLING ERRORS

PostScript handles errors that it discovers during operation in a uniform manner which takes advantage of various PostScript language facilities. You will find that an understanding of PostScript's default error handling and reporting will aid you in reading and modifying PostScript code.

PostScript default error processing works as follows. Every PostScript error has a unique name, which is also intended to be somewhat descriptive of the nature of the error encountered: for example, **stackoverflow**, **rangecheck**, **undefined**, and so on. Possible errors for each operator are clearly identified in the *PostScript Language Reference Manual, Second Edition*. When the PostScript interpreter discovers an error during its own operation or while executing an operator, it looks up the name of the error condition in a special dictionary called *errordict*. The interpreter then executes the procedure associated with that name in errordict. In all of this, you see that the handling follows standard PostScript procedures.

Each name in *errordict* has its own associated error procedure. All of the default error procedures operate in a standard fashion. They record information regarding the error in a special dictionary, called *$error*. This special dictionary contains information about the cause of the error and about the state of the system and the interpreter at the time that the error occurred. Then the procedures stop the execution of the PostScript program and invoke the generic error-handling procedure, **handleerror**. This procedure accesses the error data stored in *$error* and prints a text message on the standard error file, which is usually identical to the standard output file.

The text message that is generated by **handleerror** conforms to a standard status message format. This means that the text is bracketed by the strings %%[and]%%, and consists of *key: value* pairs separated by semicolons. The standard format for an error message is the following:

%%[Error: errorname; OffendingCommand: operator]%%

This rather formal structure allows user application programs to extract error messages (and other status messages) from other text or data being received over the communication channel and to provide additional processing if desired. Generally, it is considered good practice to screen errors and status information from the user of an application program; hence this method of reporting errors. If you are using the interpreter in interactive mode, you will see the appropriate error message on your screen in the format shown above.

The PostScript default error processing provides better error diagnosis and messages than most computer languages, and you will generally find it sufficient for your needs as long as you are working in the interactive mode. Because this entire process uses standard PostScript facilities, however, it is possible to alter the standard error processing mechanism in various ways. The most common way is to provide printed output when an error occurs; this provides additional information when you are running in a batch mode, instead of the interactive mode that we are using here. The PinPoint utility, listed in Appendix C, is a commercial error handler which uses these techniques to help you diagnose and correct errors. Such advanced topics are generally outside the scope of this book; however, in the next chapter, we will look at some simple techniques that you can use to trap and correct errors before they are reported.

FOURTH EXERCISE: DESIGNING A POSTSCRIPT PROGRAM

To keep this exposition interesting and to help you assimilate all the material that you have been reading, let's try an additional exercise at this point. We will revisit some of the previous concepts and see how the use of procedures can both simplify and clarify them. I will leave it to you to review the third exercise and apply procedural definitions; if you will take the time, I think you will quickly see how all those repetitive blocks of two or three lines can easily be made into simple procedures.

For this section, you will undertake to program a similar but distinct page of output. It is similar in that it is set in two columns, in a text and commentary format; however, in this case it is text with marginal headings. The text represents a description of a company being analyzed; the marginal notations are subject headings.

Before you begin, however, there are several more points to be covered. You need to think more about how to analyze and then implement your page requirements in PostScript. The next section both discusses some of the considerations that you must keep in mind as you design your PostScript program and introduces you to a few useful procedures.

STATEMENT FLOW

By now, you are probably becoming more familiar with PostScript's order of notation — operands followed by an operator — and are finding it easier to read more complex PostScript statements. Because of PostScript's notational structure, complex PostScript statements are built up in concentric layers, somewhat like an onion.

The following example is a moderately complex PostScript statement, using operators you are familiar with, but not using any procedural definitions to simplify the structure of the statement. Please note that this style of programming is not recommended; it is presented here only to make a point and as an illustration of the concentric nature of typical PostScript code. For the purpose of the illustration, let us suppose that the following variables have been defined:

VARIABLE	DEFINITION
LeftMargin	left margin position (in the x-direction)
RightMargin	right margin position
StringSize	width of some string (in x-direction units)

Now suppose that we wish to position the current point in the x-direction to display this string (the one whose width is given in *StringSize*) in the center of a line. The following code will accomplish that task:

LeftMargin	%1
RightMargin LeftMargin **sub**	%2
2 div	%3
StringSize 2 **div**	%4
sub	%5
add	%6

In order to analyze this program fragment, first you need to think about how to accomplish the task at hand: namely, to determine the position, in the x-direction, where a string must begin to center it between the left and right margins. A quick analysis tells you that this point will be one-half the distance between the margins less one-half of the size of the string. That's basically the same process most people would use to center a heading on a typewritten page: space to the center of the line and backspace once for every two characters in the heading. The example above follows exactly the same process, although it may not look like it at first reading. The difference is the "onionization" of the procedure; let's analyze it by layers together.

The last thing you want to leave on the stack is the absolute x-coordinate for the display. We are assuming for the moment that movement to set the display operation will be invoked with the x-coordinate as an operand on the stack, as it would need to be for a **moveto**, for example. This x-coordinate will be the left margin plus some calculated displacement.

And so the last line, line %6, adds the result of the calculations performed in lines %2 to %5 to the variable **LeftMargin** in the first line, line %1. Here you see what I mean about the onion effect, with the last line being connected to the first. Moving inward, you see that line %2 calculates the distance between the left and right margins by subtracting the left margin from the right and leaving the result on the stack. Line %3 then divides that result by two, giving the displacement of the center of the line which now remains on the stack. Line %4 divides the length of the string, given by **StringSize**, by two to give one-half of the length and pushes that result onto the stack.

Now the stack contains three numbers: on top, one-half of the string length; next, the position of the center of the line; and finally, the left margin, still on the stack from line %1. All numbers are in x-axis units, and the top two are calculated from the left margin, as desired. Now line %5 subtracts the top two operands and returns the difference on the stack. This difference is precisely the calculated distance that we want to add to the left margin, which (not accidentally) is now the second operand on the stack. Line %6, as we discussed before, now adds the two remaining operands to provide the final, desired result. From all this, you can see how this small program consists of several layers, one inside the other.

USING PROCEDURES

We have already mentioned PostScript's affinity for structured programming, and how PostScript's control mechanisms fit naturally into the control concepts that build structured programs. At the same time, we discussed how structured programs are built of groups of instructions, or procedures, each of which performs a single logical function. In many ways, each of these procedures represents a program "fragment." When we discuss the overall considerations of program structure in the next section, you will see how these fragments are combined into pieces of a well-organized PostScript program. Because such pieces form an essential part of PostScript code, we are going to construct several fragments as a part of our exercises.

Text Manipulation

In many ways, the preceding example was a program fragment, although you may not have thought of it in that way. In fact, as your first introduction to this concept, let's rework that example into a piece of code that might be used in a real PostScript program.

Begin by making the same assumptions as previously: that the three variables, LeftMargin, RightMargin, and StringSize will be defined and set correctly independently of this procedure. For LeftMargin and RightMargin, this might be done in an initial section of the program, much as you set the named constants in the third exercise. The variable, StringSize, of course, would have to be set after you have determined the string; therefore, it would be likely to be set in the course of execution of the program, like the variables in the third exercise.

In any case, the procedural definition would look something like this:

```
/centerText

    {

            LeftMargin

            RightMargin LeftMargin sub 2 div

            StringSize 2 div

            sub add

    }

    def
```

This is the same code you saw before, only now enclosed in braces ({ }) to make it a procedure and incorporated as part of definition with the name **centerText**. How the procedure is broken up into lines is fairly arbitrary; you will read more on this issue later in the chapter.

In the same spirit, you can fashion a procedure to right-justify a string of text. In this case, suppose that you will be given a string of text on the operand stack, and the task is to create a procedure to display this string right-justified. Such a procedure will be less complex mathematically than the preceding example, but will have some additional elements in it.

The two additional elements will be, first, to determine the length of the string, and second, to display the string with the **show** operator. Such a procedure might look like this:

```
/rightJustifyText

    {

            dup

            stringwidth pop
```

```
        RightMargin exch sub

        NextLine moveto

        show

    }

    def
```

This example raises several points. The first occurs immediately with the operator **dup**, which duplicates the value on the top of the stack. This is necessary because you need the string (which we are assuming is already placed on the stack for the call to the procedure) two times, once to measure it and once to display it. The second operation is taken care of by the last line in the procedure, the **show** operator. So, at that point, you must have the string you want to display on the top of the stack. The first operation, determining the size of the string, is done by the **stringwidth** operator. Let's take a moment to look at this operator in the usual format:

SYNTAX	FUNCTION
(str1) **stringwidth** wx wy	calculates the width of the string *str1* in current units.

Note that the operator returns two distinct values, one a width in the x-direction (wx) and the other in the y-direction (wy). These are necessary because some fonts—oriental languages, like Japanese and Chinese, in particular—have width in both directions. In the case of English fonts, there is no y-direction width for a character, and hence the y-coordinate value will always be zero. The results come back with the y-value on the top of the stack, and the x-value underneath it. This is convenient since you can now discard the unnecessary y-value by using the **pop** operator.

So the first two lines of the procedure duplicate the string that you were given to start with and then determine the width of the string, leaving that calculated width on the top of the stack. Next you must subtract that width from the right margin to find out what x-coordinate value you need to have in order to display the string, ending at the right margin.

This little task is completed in the next line of the procedure. Since you want to subtract the calculated value already on the stack from the value for **RightMargin**, you need to use the operator **exch** after you place the constant **RightMargin** onto the stack to swap the top two objects and get the operands into the correct order for the **sub** operator. This leaves the correct x-coordinate for the starting point of the string on the top of the stack, with the string itself immediately underneath. For purposes of this exercise, let's assume that **NextLine** is the name of a variable that has been calculated to give the y-coordinate of the next line of text, as was done in the previous exercise. You push this variable onto the stack, which now (conveniently) is in the correct sequence to issue a **moveto**. This positions the current point at the x-coordinate that you calculated previously and at the y-coordinate, **NextLine**, ready for the **show** operator. And that's the next, and last, line of your procedure. Easy, really, once you get the hang of it.

PROGRAM EXERCISE

This exercise has many of the features of the previous exercise, but it also introduces some new material. The task is to produce a page of output about a company, Acme Widget Corporation. The required format has a centered heading of two lines with the remainder of the page set in two columns of text. The first column has topic descriptions; the second column has the text itself. Once again, the topic headings are to be aligned with the beginning of the text paragraphs; this time, however, they are to be right-justified against a 2-inch margin. Now you need to analyze how such a page might be set up.

Page Analysis and Setup

This exercise might be analyzed in several ways, all essentially correct and yet each distinct. The approach given here is only one successful approach to the problem. You will develop your own methods as you become more familiar with page-layout problems.

You must now develop a layout of the page in sufficient detail that you can program it. You can do this by working out the procedures that you will require to actually output the page. The process would proceed something like what follows.

The first output will be the heading. You will set this in Times-Bold, 16-point type on 20-point leading. There are two lines of heading, which are to be centered on the page. The left and right margins for this will be ½ inch from either edge; this gives a left margin of ½ inch and a right margin of 8 inch, based on the left edge of the paper. This portion of the layout is shown in Figure 2.2.

The paragraph titles will be in the first column, as in the second and third exercises. This means that the second column will have to be set first, as before. The first column will be right-justified on a margin 2 inches from the left margin, which will be 2.5 inches from the left edge of the paper. There will be ½ inch between the paragraph titles and the text of the paragraphs. Therefore, the body text will begin at an offset of 3 inches from the left edge of the paper. The second column will be 4.5 inches wide to the right margin. These dimensions are illustrated in Figure 2.3.

You will use Times-Roman for the body of the text and Times-Bold (the bold version of Times-Roman) for the paragraph titles; both will be set in 12-point type on 14-point leading. Space between the paragraphs within the body text will again be two lines, or 28 points.

The heading on the page will begin 1.5 inches from the top of the paper, which is 9.5 inches from the bottom edge. The text and titles will

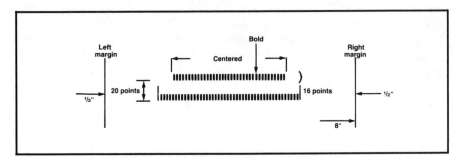

Figure 2.2: Heading layout for the fourth exercise

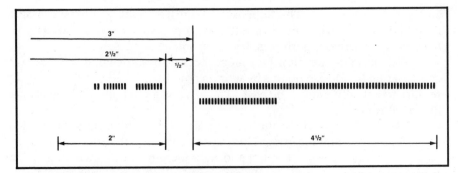

Figure 2.3: Layout of titles and body text

begin 1 inch below that, which will be 8.5 inches from the bottom. All these numbers will be incorporated into named constants for the program. This final portion of the layout is shown in Figure 2.4.

Now that you have decided on the constants, you must develop the procedures. You will set the headings in the center of their respective lines with a procedure which will display text centered in a line. Next you will display the body text. You could move a line after each display within one procedure, but then you would have to make adjustments when you get to paragraph spacing. For this reason, you want to advance the line spacing independently of the text-handling and painting procedure. Finally, you must display the paragraph headings at the correct vertical positions to match the beginning of each paragraph, and you want to right-justify each of them.

This sequence identifies the following procedures:

PROCEDURE	FUNCTION
centerText	takes a text string from the stack and centers it on the current line.
bodyText	sets a text string from the stack for the body text of the page.
rightJustifyText	sets a text string from the stack right-justified against a defined right margin.

And there are two additional procedures that will be required:

PROCEDURE	FUNCTION
advanceLine	increments the current line position by the constant for leading.
advancePara	increments the current line position by the amount of space between paragraphs.

Based on these procedures and your previous analysis, you establish the following named constants:

CONSTANT	DEFINITION
TopStart	starting point for the page titles; previously decided to be 9.5 inches from the bottom edge of the page

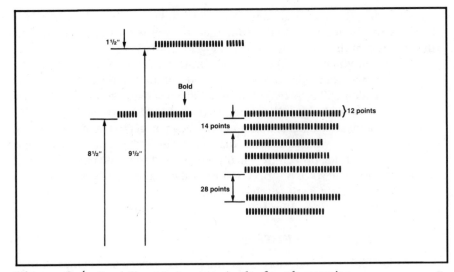

Figure 2.4: Overall page structure in the fourth exercise

CONSTANT	DEFINITION
BodyStart	starting point for the text proper and for the paragraph titles; previously determined to be 8.5 inches from the bottom edge of the page
LineSpace	space between lines, or leading; determined to be 14 points
ParaSpace	space between paragraphs; determined to be 28 points (two lines)
LeftMargin	the absolute leftmost print position; intended to be ½ inch from the left edge of the page
RightMargin	the absolute rightmost print position; intended to be 8 inches from the left edge of the page
SecondColumn	the horizontal beginning position of the body text; defined to be 3 inches from the left edge of the page

CONSTANT	DEFINITION
RightColumn	the horizontal right margin for the first column of paragraph titles; determined to be 2.5 inches from the left edge of the page
HeadFont	the font for the page titles; determined to be 16-point Times-Bold
TextFont	the font for the body text; determined to be 12-point Times-Roman
TitleFont	the font for the paragraph titles; determined to be 12-point Times-Bold

In addition, there will be several variables that will have to be defined dynamically as the program executes. The first is a vertical placekeeper, NextLine. The second are two variables, which you might name SaveCol-One and SaveColTwo, which will store the required values of the vertical position for use in positioning the paragraph headings.

You may wonder why you need to save the fonts as constants. This is simply good PostScript programming practice whenever you will be using several fonts repeatedly in a program, as you will here. There is a measurable amount of overhead in the standard sequence of operators, findfont scalefont and setfont, that you use to make a font current. You can speed up processing by only performing the findfont scalefont operations one time, saving the resulting font dictionary, and then setting it whenever you need it. This sequence is about as fast as the new selectfont operator in Level 2, which was designed precisely to speed up font handling in such cases.

Program

With this analysis and information you can now proceed to develop the required procedures and program them. In this context, we will not spend time on development of each individual routine; both of the major routines mimic what has already been covered, with minor variations. A complete analysis of each routine and line of code will be presented after you have run the exercise. Figure 2.5 gives the full text of your program.

```
/AcmeDict 25 dict def
AcmeDict begin
%--------------------------Procedures-------------------------
/inch
{
        72 mul
}
def

/advanceLine
{
        /NextLine
        NextLine LineSpace sub
        def
}
def

/advancePara
{
        /NextLine
        NextLine ParaSpace sub
        def

}
def

/centerText
{
        dup
        stringwidth pop
        2 div
        RightMargin LeftMargin sub 2 div
        exch sub
        LeftMargin add
        NextLine moveto
        show
}
def

/bodyText
{
        SecondColumn NextLine moveto
        show
}
def

/rightJustifyText
{
        dup
        stringwidth pop
        RightColumn exch sub
        NextLine moveto
        show
}
def

%--------------------------Named Constants-------------------------
/TopStart 9.5 inch def
/BodyStart 8.5 inch def

/LineSpace 14 def
/ParaSpace 28 def
```

Figure 2.5: Fourth exercise: Acme Widgets program

```
/LeftMargin .5 inch def
/RightMargin 8 inch def
/RightColumn 2.5 inch def
/SecondColumn 3 inch def

/HeadFont /Times-Bold findfont 16 scalefont def
/TextFont /Times-Roman findfont 12 scalefont def
/TitleFont /Times-Bold findfont 12 scalefont def


%-------------------------Setup page-------------------------
/PgSave save def

%-------------------------Program (Page Titles)----------------------
%Setup font for page titles
HeadFont setfont

%Move to selected position
/NextLine TopStart def

%Show titles
(ACME WIDGETS INCORPORATED) centerText

/NextLine NextLine 20 sub def
(Fiscal Year 1989) centerText

%-------------------------Program (Text)---------------------
%Set first paragraph
%       first, set the top position for both columns
/SaveColOne BodyStart def
/NextLine BodyStart def

%Set the paragraph
%       set new font for body text
TextFont setfont
%       then set the text itself
(Acme Widgets was founded in 1958 by Dippy and Daffy Acme) bodyText
advanceLine
(to produce high technology widgets for the booming aerospace) bodyText
advanceLine
(industry. Acme was quickly recognized as being the best) bodyText
advanceLine
(widget works in the country. Continued investment in new) bodyText
advanceLine
(technology and manufacturing methods has kept Acme Widgets) bodyText
advanceLine
(in the forefront of this industry. In the last year alone, Acme) bodyTe
advanceLine
(has invested over $10 million in new manufacturing tooling) bodyText
advanceLine
(and computer-aided order processing.) bodyText

%Save the current position of the second column
/SaveColTwo NextLine def

%Now set the marginal heading for the first paragraph
TitleFont setfont
/NextLine SaveColOne def
(History:) rightJustifyText
```

Figure 2.5: Fourth exercise: Acme Widgets program (continued)

```
%Continue with second paragraph
/NextLine SaveColTwo def
advancePara
/SaveColOne NextLine def

TextFont setfont
(Acme Widgets sells 72% of all widgets produced in the) bodyText
advanceLine
(United States; and it has 39% of the growing international) bodyText
advanceLine
(market.) bodyText

/SaveColTwo NextLine def

TitleFont setfont
/NextLine SaveColOne def
(Market Position:) rightJustifyText

%Continue with third paragraph
/NextLine SaveColTwo def
advancePara
/SaveColOne NextLine def

TextFont setfont
(Headquarters: Burbank, California.) bodyText
advanceLine
(Domestic sales offices in Seattle, WA; Vero Beach, FL; and) bodyText
advanceLine
(Washington, D.C.) bodyText
advanceLine
(International sales office in St. Mary Mead, Somerset, U.K.) bodyText

/SaveColTwo NextLine def

TitleFont setfont
/NextLine SaveColOne def
(Offices:) rightJustifyText
%Finally set the fourth (and last) paragraph
/NextLine SaveColTwo def
advancePara
/SaveColOne NextLine def

TextFont setfont
($223 million in gross sales for fiscal 1988;) bodyText
advanceLine
($248 million in gross sales projected for fiscal 1989.) bodyText

%Save the current position of the second column
/SaveColTwo NextLine def

%Now set the marginal heading for the last paragraph
TitleFont setfont
/NextLine SaveColOne def
(Financial Position:) rightJustifyText


%Now clean up after the page has been completed
PgSave restore
showpage

end             %AcmeDict
%all done
%quit
```

Figure 2.5: Fourth exercise: Acme Widgets program (continued)

This program is significantly longer and more complex than your previous work, but it is more like real text output. The program produces the page of output shown in Figure 2.6

There is one thing to notice about this program as you enter it. When a procedure is being defined, you do not get the PS > prompt back after a linefeed. Once you have entered the left brace ({) the interpreter waits to respond until it has received all of the input for the definition; in other words, it waits until it receives the matching right brace (}). This can be disconcerting the first time; don't worry, it's correct. Continue entering your procedure and the interpreter will reappear at the end of the definition.

Discussion and Review

The program begins by defining a small dictionary, AcmeDict, and making that the current dictionary. This places all your definitions, for procedures, constants, and variables, into one private dictionary. In this way, your page can be easily incorporated into other PostScript page descriptions and output without any problems. This also ensures that you don't have to worry about using a name for a procedure or variable that is already in use; even if you do, your definition will be in your dictionary, safely away from

---

ACME WIDGETS INCORPORATED
Fiscal Year 1986

History: Acme Widgets was founded in 1952 by Dippy and Daffy Acme
                  to produce high technology widgets for the growing aerospace
                  market. Acme was quickly recognized as being the best
                  widget works in the country. Continued investment in new
                  technology and manufacturing methods has kept Acme Widgets
                  in the forefront of this industry.

Market Position: Acme Widgets sells 72% of all widgets produced in the
                  United States; and it has 39% of the growing international
                  market.

Offices: Headquarters: Burbank, California
                  Domestic sales offices in Seattle, WA; Dallas, TX;
                  and Washington, D.C.

Financial Position: $223 million in gross sales for fiscal 1985;
                  $248 million in gross sales projected for fiscal 1986.

Figure 2.6: Output from the fourth exercise

any foreign influence and on the top of the dictionary stack, so that your definition will always be the one executed by the interpreter.

Next, the program continues with definitions of the procedures that you identified earlier. The first procedure is the little inch procedure, which will convert PostScript units into inches. Since the page layout was conceived entirely in inches, using this procedure will make your program much more readable.

The next two procedures are advanceLine and advancePara, which are essentially identical. The first moves the variable, NextLine, down by a distance which is given by the named constant LineSpace. The second procedure does the same, but uses the named constant ParaSpace. The obvious intention is that the variable NextLine will be used as part of a **moveto** to position the text output as you have seen done in the smaller examples earlier in the chapter.

The constants LineSpace and ParaSpace have to be defined and set to the values that were determined as you set up the page. These could be defined here, since they are associated with these procedures. If you do that, however, and you come back later to modify these constants, you would have to go through all the procedural definitions to find the appropriate constants. You will find that if you put all your named constants in one section of code then they will be easier to find and therefore easier to modify. So that's how it's done in this and all subsequent exercises.

Next you see the three procedures that form the heart of this exercise: centerText, bodyText, and rightJustifyText. Each of these procedures displays one type of the final output. The first procedure, centerText, will be used to display the page titles. Note that the procedure itself will display any text centered between the two variables LeftMargin and RightMargin. This procedure is essentially identical to the one you created and analyzed earlier in the chapter. The difference is that centerText takes a text string (on the stack) as an operand and displays it after having calculated the center position; in this aspect, it is identical to the procedure rightJustifyText. The rightJustifyText procedure is the third, and last, procedure defined in the program; it is identical to the procedure created and analyzed earlier in the chapter and so needs no further explanation here.

The second procedure, bodyText, is straightforward. It simply moves to a specific position and shows a string of text. Like the two other procedures, it expects the text to be placed onto the stack as an operand. Since this procedure sets the text for the body of the report, the position moved to is defined in the x-direction by the named constant SecondColumn, and in the y-direction by the calculated variable NextLine.

The structure of the program is now fairly clear. The main procedures are centerText to set the titles, bodyText to set the text for the body of the report, and rightJustifyText to set the marginal headings. The procedures advanceLine and advancePara will be used to calculate where the next line of body text will be output, depending on whether the next line continues the current paragraph or starts a new paragraph.

The next section of the program defines the named constants that are required for the program. Most of these are self-explanatory. They represent the values which were determined during the page-setup analysis. The names, of course, are arbitrary but not random or irrelevant. Choice of names is an important consideration that is discussed more fully in the next section. As in the third example, the paragraph spacing is defined independently of the line spacing, although the paragraph spacing is a multiple of the line.

The last three lines of this section define the three fonts that you will use in this program. In each case, the desired font is found and scaled, and then stored under the selected name. Once this is done, you only have to **setfont** with the desired font name to have the font you want as the current font.

The program itself is very repetitive, and you will find that this is typical of PostScript programs generally. If you have done your analysis properly, the actual production of the page or pages of output becomes simply the repetition of the procedures using the appropriate text or data as operands.

The program begins by saving the current state of the interpreter as the named variable, PgSave, in line %1. This is done to preserve the maximum amount of virtual memory as you proceed from page to page. In this case, of course, it isn't actually necessary, since you are only printing a single page. However, this is good PostScript programming technique, and you should learn to use it as a matter of course. We will discuss this requirement more in the next section of this chapter, when we look at document structure.

The program itself begins by setting the font required for the first operation, in this case, printing the page titles. Then the program initializes the variable NextLine to the position defined for the top line of the page, TopStart. Line %4 displays the first line of the titles, using the procedure centerText to center the line. Line %5 moves down one line. You can't use advanceLine here because the point size of the titles is 16 points, and the leading for the titles is 20 points, whereas advanceLine uses the LineSpace named constant as the leading. You could, of course, reset LineSpace to the desired 20 points for this portion of the program and reset it to 14 points when you get to the body of the text. If there were more than two or three lines of heading, that would be an efficient and clear way of doing the required movement; as it is, it is both easier and clearer to simply move the line directly, as line %5 does, by the desired amount—in this case, 20 points.

Line %6 finishes the titles by displaying the second line, also centered between the margins.

Line %10 sets the SaveColOne variable to the start of the first paragraph, and line %11 sets the NextLine variable to the same value to position the body output.(As in the previous examples, line numbering is not continuous; don't think anything is missing.) Then line %12 sets the font for the body of the page. The remainder of this section of the program sets the body text, using bodyText and advanceLine. Note that the vertical position at the end of each paragraph is noted and saved in a named variable, SaveColTwo. Line %15 gives an example of this. The current position, which is in the variable NextLine, is saved as the variable SaveColTwo. The ending position of each paragraph is saved for use in restoring the correct position after setting the marginal title for that paragraph.

The next three lines of the program set the marginal title or comment for the paragraph that has just been set. This section begins on line %16 by setting the font for the marginal title. Line %17 moves back to the starting line for the first paragraph of the body. Note that this is the variable SaveColOne, which was set to be equal to the constant BodyStart in line %10. That's where NextLine is set to print the first marginal title, which is done by the rightJustifyText procedure in line %18. Now you move NextLine to SaveColTwo, in line %19. This resets your current point on the page to the position at the bottom of the first paragraph. Once that's done, you simply use advancePara to move to the top of the next paragraph in line %20, and save that position for the next title in SaveColOne in line %21. The remainder of the program simply repeats these steps until the entire page is formatted.

The last lines of the program clean up the interpreter and produce the finished output. Line %30 restores all the virtual memory consumed by our page (for strings and so on) by a **restore** to the state saved in line %1 as PgSave. Then line %31 uses **showpage** to print the actual page. Finally, you end the use of AcmeDict by an **end** operator on line %32. If you are done processing, you can also now terminate the interpreter with the **quit** operator.

This program is not really difficult, yet it produces a page that is quite complex. Furthermore, you have now begun to develop a repertoire of PostScript routines that can be used in other circumstances and in other programs.

PROGRAM STRUCTURE AND STYLE

PostScript is a language that has a remarkable degree of flexibility combined with a large and powerful set of operators. But as a result of that flexibility and power, it has an equal potential to generate unsatisfactory, unworkable, and even unintelligible code. PostScript, as we observed before, has no specific structural requirements. Unlike most other computer languages, it has no reserved words and no enforced data structures. PostScript will allow any type of structure you find useful or entertaining—and it's the entertainment factor that you should worry about.

PostScript programs generally consist of a large series of procedures, or "program fragments," as we have called them. As you have read in the preceding section, procedures can be—and most likely will be—used inside the definitions of other procedures. This process is called *nesting*, and it is both a natural outgrowth of the PostScript language and a powerful tool for helping you accomplish complex page description tasks. The net result is that every PostScript program that you are likely to encounter will consist of multiple levels of nested procedures, usually culminating in a few powerful procedural definitions that accomplish large parts of the final task.

However, if this process of nesting procedures in PostScript is both natural and powerful, it also can create a chaotic program when it is carried out in an undisciplined or uncoordinated way. You can easily imagine the difficulty and frustration in trying to discover the source of an error in a procedure when you need to trace through five or six or even more layers of nested definitions. The frustration level rises rapidly if the definitions of the procedures are scattered throughout many pages of program text, and it will go into orbit if the names of the variables and procedures are short and cryptic or even completely non-descriptive. The only way to avoid most of these problems is to establish a style of programming and adhere to it tenaciously.

SELECTING NAMES

Although the examples in the preceding section are somewhat complex, and possibly difficult to follow, you can easily see that they would have been more opaque without the variable names that were used in them. Names like LeftMargin and StringSize are an important part of creating readable code because they aid you in understanding what function a program or program fragment is performing. In the example above, imagine how much more difficult it would have been to understand (or explain) if the variable names were replaced by numbers, as they well might have been. Procedure names also need to describe what the procedure does, even more than variable names need to describe what the variable contains.

This brings up another useful point, particularly for naming variables, but also to a lesser extent, procedures. Using named variables in the procedure above, rather than using the actual numbers, means that changes to the margins, for example, would not affect the procedure itself. By means of named variables, the procedure is independent of the actual margins that have been set for the page. This is a nontrival benefit, which affects both independence and maintenance as well as readability.

PostScript is an unusually good language with regard to names, because there are virtually no limits on the length of a name or on the characters used in the name. This extraordinary flexibility is a great tool if you will take advantage of it. You should make names that describe the function, not just to yourself, but also to others. If the names are too cryptic, so that only you know what they mean, you will discover that you will have forgotten your clever abbreviations and cryptic symbols when you look at the program again after a few months, or even weeks. So be warned.

There is one drawback to using long, descriptive names in your PostScript code. If you are creating a set of procedures that will be called repeatedly to create pages and pages of output (for example, if you are coding the procedures to be used by an application program, such as PageMaker or QuarkXpress), then these long names will reoccur very often as each page is generated by your application. This imposes a significant overhead when the time comes to send the output to the PostScript device. Each additional character represents one more byte of data that must be transmitted over the network, or over the connection to the PostScript device. Since the speed of printing in most PostScript devices has a direct relationship to the efficiency of transmission, in such cases names should be a short and simple as possible—although I still believe that they should be at least somewhat reminiscent of the function or variable being named. However, for our work here, this is not an issue, since these exercises are not intended for repeated use. For that reason, we will use names that fully describe the function being performed.

For the same reasons of speed and efficiency, output from applications that generate PostScript code (such as any Macintosh or Windows application) do not generate names that are of much illustrative use. The application, after all, has none of the mnemonic limitations that we, as simple humans, suffer under; and, conversely, it derives no benefit from meaningful associations. On the other hand, since the output from an application is expected to be quite long, and since the procedures will be called repeatedly for each page, there is a benefit to short names, since they reduce the amount of code that must be transmitted to the PostScript device to generate output. If you are going to do much modification of that type of output, I would strongly recommend that you use a good editor with a global search-and-replace function to modify those procedures and variables that you are working with into useful, descriptive names. This doesn't usually take long, since you will almost always be working with a small subset of the generated output.

Names are an important ingredient in creating order out of the potential chaos of any program. Names, and conventions about names—how they may be constructed, what they should look like, and so on—form an important part of program structure and style.

If you are familiar with programming at all, you have probably wrestled with the pitfalls and advantages that are associated with names in a programming environment. Basically, there are two issues relating to names that you need to think about. We've already looked at the first: how to select names so that they will be meaningful in your particular environment. The second is the use of a set of naming practices, or conventions, to ensure that you use the same or similar structure for names of the same or similar type.

Naming Conventions

Besides making individual procedure and variable names descriptive of their purpose, you will find it extremely helpful to adopt some standard conventions for names in your programs. Development and use of naming conventions is a matter of your personal style of programming; it really is an outgrowth of your experience and the requirements of the task at hand.

While no one else can define an appropriate set of conventions for you, there are two points to consider as you begin to establish your personal approach. First, PostScript is *case-sensitive*; that is, it treats uppercase and lowercase letters as distinct characters. This allows you to use capital letters to help make your names both readable and distinctive. For example, you might decide to start every variable name with a capital letter and every procedure name with a lowercase letter, with subsequent words in both names being capitalized as appropriate. Then you would write

reencodeFont   **(a procedure)**

StringSize   **(a variable)**

average	**(a procedure)**
Average	**(a variable)**
LeftMargin	**(a variable)**
testMargin	**(a procedure)**
outsideMargin?	**(a procedure)**

and so on. Use of secondary capitals in procedure names allows you to distinguish your procedures from PostScript operators. The two names *average* and *Average* also illustrate why you might want to use case as an indication of purpose or use. Using a convention like the one outlined above, you know immediately which name is a procedure and which is a variable; if you are haphazard in your capitalization, the type of name would have to be clear from the context. The last name, outsideMargin?, also illustrates the fact that you can use almost any character in PostScript names. Hence the ? character is to emphasize the test nature of the procedure.

The second point to keep in mind is the use of standard names throughout your procedures for specific variables or types of variables or procedures. There are particular variables that will reoccur throughout almost any PostScript program: a current line (vertical position), a current horizontal position, the margin settings, and so on. Similarly, there are types of variables that occur regularly: counters and strings, for example. In all such instances you will find that using a standard set of names during your programming will provide enhanced portability and readability for your procedures. For common variables, you should establish common names, even recording the names in some place where they may be readily referenced—the best situation, of course, would be to keep them in a file that could be included at the beginning of each program. Some typical examples might be

VARIABLE	DEFINITION
Xpos	the current position in the x-direction (horizontally)
Yline	the current line position or position in the y-direction (vertically)

and some of the variables we have already seen (and some obvious relatives)

LeftMargin

RightMargin

TopMargin

BottomMargin

For variable and procedure types, it is often useful to use prefixes or suffixes to indicate certain types. For example, using the prefix "test" we get

testRightMargin

testLeftMargin

testTopMargin

or using the suffix "size" we have

StringSize

ArraySize

DictSize

These are only examples. In some of the exercises you will notice that I may not follow these specific practices myself, and I'm not necessarily suggesting that you adopt them. You should be innovative and flexible and determine what works for you. Certainly you should consider carefully whatever standard names and naming conventions you do choose to adopt. As was said earlier, choice and use of conventions is a personal decision that, ideally, will grow out of your experience and the requirements of the task to be accomplished.

PROGRAM STRUCTURE

There are two types of structure that are used in a program. One type is what might be called *local structure*. This is the sort of structure that we have been discussing: naming conventions, and so on. This type also includes other issues such as spacing and indenting, use of comments, and similar issues which will be covered in the next section. The other type of structure is *global structure*. This is the overall structure of a program and it is the subject of this section.

The global structure defines the sequence of major sections of your PostScript program. It also defines what goes into each of those sections and how the sections are identified and separated from one another. The global structure of your program is completely independent of any local structure that you choose; but use of a standard global approach in your programs will influence and motivate many of the choices you must make regarding style and conventions within your program. This is particularly true when you follow the standard global structure recommended for PostScript programs.

There are compelling reasons for establishing and following some structural conventions for your PostScript programs. Some of the reasons are similar to the rationale for using naming conventions: enhanced readability, easier understanding, and improved overall clarity. Besides these common benefits, there are some additional benefits that can be gained by following a specific overall structure in the program. Unlike the naming conventions, however, recommended standards for overall program structure are published in Appendix G of the *PostScript Language Reference Manual, Second Edition*.

There are two important additional benefits that you gain from following these recommended standard conventions. First, your program will be able to be processed by automatic document management programs, such as spooling programs, which make use of these standards to identify certain portions of a PostScript program. An example of such a function would be to extract and print just certain pages of a document. Second, by following these structural recommendations, your program will have a common structural base with other PostScript programs, which can allow integration of code from other sources, and so on. Encapsulated PostScript graphics, which are discussed in Appendix B of this book, are a good example of such a use. Common structures are essential for this type of flexibility.

Desirable Qualities

Before we discuss specific recommendations for program structure and format, it will be worthwhile to establish what qualities we are attempting to create or enhance by the use of conventions. There are particular qualities which form the primary goals of structural conventions. The first and most obvious goal is one we have already mentioned: commonality. The establishment and use of common structures has several important benefits. To begin with, common structures will help you understand and analyze new programs. Most of us find it easier to find the differences between two basically similar structures than to establish common features between two very different structures. Next, common structures will help you when you want to integrate pieces from several programs into a new program. You will be able to more easily and correctly identify the specific pieces that need to be taken from each old program to do what you want in the new one. Finally, the use of a common structure within a program will aid you in maintaining and modifying the program. This occurs for many of the same reasons that you can easily take out pieces of the program: common structures allow you to isolate problems in specific sections of code and to encapsulate functions in a specific place.

The second desirable quality of any structure to be established for PostScript is page independence. This means that each section of PostScript code that produces a page of output should be independent of all other pages in the document. This goal is a little less obviously desirable than the first goal of commonality, but it is equally important. PostScript is, after all, a page-description language, and as such, its primary function is to produce pages on an output device. Most documents naturally consist of more than one page of output, and therefore most PostScript programs will be employed in generating multiple pages of output. This simple fact gives rise to several of the standard PostScript structural conventions (which will be described in detail below), all of which work to provide page independence within a PostScript program. By following these conventions, each page of output, as it is created in PostScript memory, will not depend on anything done by or output from the preceding pages. With some thought, you will see why this is desirable. Without this independence, pages could not be proofed or printed separately, and changing or maintaining individual pages would be almost impossible. Page independence also allows individual pages to be extracted from one document and inserted into another as a unit. Most of all, without it, unintended and undesired remnants from previous pages might carry forward and ruin your current page output. For these reasons, it is important that each page be independent.

The third desirable quality in program structure is ease of reading. This may seem trivial compared to the first two objectives. I can assure you, however, that working on a program that is difficult to read is like the Chinese water torture —it is insidious and excruciatingly painful. When a program is not easy to read, you must go back over procedures, definitions, and sections repeatedly to try and figure out what is being done.

Recommended Structure

Adobe Systems, the designer of PostScript, recommends following a straightforward, standard structure that will aid in achieving these admirable and desirable goals. There are two basic components in the recommended structure: *prolog* and *script*. Each of these also has subcomponents which play an important role in establishing the overall structure within a PostScript program.

However, it is important to remember that PostScript has no required program structure whatever. That is to say, the PostScript interpreter does not require any particular global information in order to correctly process PostScript statements. The only requirements (if they can be called that) are the intuitive and natural: that variables and procedures be defined before they're used, that fonts be loaded and defined before they're used, and so on; basic, obvious conditions like that.

Version 3.0 of this recommended structure is defined and described in Appendix G of the *PostScript Language Reference Manual, Second Edition*, which establishes global structural conventions to be used by any PostScript program. These conventions are primarily designed to improve handling of PostScript documents in multiuser, networked environments. They provide facilities that allow a class of programs, including print spoolers, device servers, and other postprocessors—known collectively as *document managers*—to manage printer resources efficiently and to process PostScript documents effectively in such environments.

The conventions generally allow complete cooperation between document managers at all levels, and they allow PostScript document descriptions to be created and printed to take maximum advantage of network facilities. These conventions are an external structure, neither imposed by the interpreter nor checked by it. They rely on the cooperation of the document-creation functions to implement as much, or as little, of specific conventions as are required and appropriate.

To aid in this process, Adobe Systems has also created a series of PostScript Printer Description (PPD) files, which provide printer-specific information in a standard format for use by applications and document managers. The format of a PPD file is available from Adobe Systems if you require it (see the address in Appendix C). The information contained in these files works in conjunction with the information provided by the structuring conventions to provide a mechanism for specification and use of a wide variety of device-dependent features and functions.

Published conventions such as these are particularly important in any complex environment, where there may be a number of PostScript users, perhaps connected over a network, sharing a variety of system resources such as printers or typesetters. In these circumstances, having common structures is essential if jobs are to be processed correctly and efficiently, and electronic and physical output are going to be returned to the correct destinations.

Remember that PostScript does not have any enforced global structure. This means that you, as the programmer, have a choice. You may adopt and implement all of the PostScript conventions; you may choose to work with some smaller subset of the conventions; or you may ignore or adapt the published conventions to suit your own requirements and your own environment. In many cases, you will be working in a dedicated environment, using PostScript on a microprocessor with a single PostScript output device. In this case, much of the recommended structure will be superfluous, and you might choose to work with only a minimum of overall structure to your programs.

The only thing to be cautious about in this situation is that, if your PostScript programs don't follow the standards, they may not be suitable to that more complex environment we discussed a moment ago, and they may not be able to be used with certain useful types of application programs. A simple example of such an application would be a spooler program which can reorder the printing sequence of a document. Many older laser printers stack output face up, so that the first page printed ends up face up on the bottom of the output. This creates a problem in handling long documents, since someone usually has to resequence the output. If the PostScript file that created the output is properly structured—that is, follows the standard conventions—then you can have a spooler program which will resequence the pages to print in reverse order, so that they come out of such printers in their natural order with the last page on the bottom and the first page on top. This type of application can only work when there is a well-defined structure within the PostScript document.

Another simple example is the issue of fonts and font changes within a PostScript document. PostScript supports many more fonts than are initially loaded into a typical PostScript printer. Therefore, many documents may need fonts that have to be loaded into the printer before the document can be printed. The PostScript structure allows you to specify what fonts are required by a document, or even a single page, so that a document manager can identify whether the fonts are already loaded or need to be downloaded to the printer before sending your document.

Similarly, many of the structuring conventions that are cumbersome and unnecessary in a dedicated system become essential in a more complex network environment. Generally, since it requires only a small amount of extra effort to create a PostScript program that follows the conventional structure, I strongly recommend that you follow at least the minimum structural guidelines. Upward compatibility should not be sacrificed lightly.

Structural Elements

There are two major sections required in a properly structured Post-Script program: a prolog and a script. This division is the most important one in any PostScript program; fortunately, it is also a very natural one. In fact, the fourth example, which you did earlier in this chapter, is divided into a prolog and a script.

The prolog contains procedures and named variables and constants that will be used throughout the rest of the document. The prolog will generally have been written by a programmer and will be included as the first part of every document (or script) that requires it. The prolog will usually be relatively complex, with a variety of variables and nested procedures being defined within it. The script provides setup for the document and then describes the specific elements to be produced on the output pages in terms of procedures and variables defined in the prolog, along with operand data as required.

The prolog may consist of up to three sections: the header section, an optional defaults section, and the procedures section (sometimes also called the prolog proper).

The *header section* contains two types of information. The first type of information is what might be termed creation data. This information covers who created the document, when it was created, and so on, and is primarily required in a network environment for routing and other identification purposes. The second type of information contained in the header is document information covering the resources (such as fonts, and so on) used in the document. The header section is primarily devoted to providing certain global information about the document. The most important point about the header section is that, from the viewpoint of the PostScript interpreter, it consists of comments only and does not contain any executable PostScript code.

The *defaults section* is an optional section that provides a place to specify page-level information which does not change for the entire document, and that would otherwise have to be repeated for each page. This is intended to save space in the final document and as an aid to document managers, which can use this section, if present, to simplify their work.

The *procedures section* contains the definitions and routines that will be used in the script to produce the document. This section is divided into groups of procedures, know as *procsets*, each of which can be conveniently loaded and used as a unit. Simple programs, like the exercises in this book, will generally consist of one procset; but complex programs, such as those produced by commercial applications, may contain many procsets, each of which provides a particular part of the document requirements.

The script also consists of three sections: the document setup section, the pages section, and the document trailer section.

The *document setup section* consists of procedures and definitions that are required for preparing for page output. Typically, this might include setting a page size, establishing some font settings, and so on.

The *pages section* consists of the actual document pages. These should each be functionally independent of one another, so that the pages may be extracted and printed separately, in any order. This allows document managers to perform functions like reordering pages as described earlier.

Each page in this section is expected to depend only on the prolog and any document setup information, and to be independent of all the other pages. The intention here is that it should be possible to produce any page correctly, given only the prolog, the document setup, and the description of that specific page. When the process is done well, each page description within the script will be relatively simple and probably quite repetitive, using the same procedures over and over.

The *document trailer section* contains clean-up processing and may also include certain types of document information. This is the place for document information that couldn't be easily generated in the header sections. This facility is provided for application programs that are directly generating PostScript output, and would otherwise have a problem providing the required document information in the header. For example, one of the required data items in the header is a list of fonts used in the document. This information is particularly important if the document requires nonstandard fonts which need to be downloaded to the printer prior to processing the document. If the PostScript output is being created by an application, however, it may be quite difficult to generate this information with the header, before the document itself has been created. The structural conventions therefore allow the font information to be deferred to the end of the document and put in the trailer section. You will see how this works when we discuss each of the sections and their contents in detail below.

To review, you see that a PostScript program that follows the recommended structure will consist of two major elements, each divided into three subsections. The prolog and script form the most basic divisions in any PostScript program. Within these, the various subsections provide additional information about structure so that document managers can understand and software can process PostScript output. The overall structure will always be presented within the program in the following sequence:

Prolog

    Header

    Document Defaults (optional)

    Procedures

Script

    Document Setup

    Pages

    Trailer

In addition to dividing your PostScript program into these sections, there is another practice that you should follow within the script to ensure page independence. Since each page should be independent of all other pages, each PostScript program that generates a printable document should maintain its own indicators of the current status of the PostScript document output. When the document crosses a major structural boundary, such as a page, the PostScript program should take steps to ensure that the new page is independent of all preceding pages and does not interfere with any subsequent ones.

This can most easily be accomplished by invoking the operators **save** and **restore**, which you read about and used in the fourth exercise. Since the **restore** returns to the state presented to it as an operand, it is usually easiest and best to **save** the current state at the beginning of a page as a named variable and **restore** that specific variable. If a **save** is performed at the beginning of each page, and a **restore** is performed at the end of each page to the state saved at the beginning, then each page will necessarily be independent of any other. If you have followed the recommended structure, and placed all of your procedural definitions into the prolog and all global variables in the setup, then each page will only be dependent upon the prolog, the setup, and the code between the **save** and the **restore** for that page. This practice is the fastest and most efficient method for ensuring page independence. You will remember that this is exactly what you did in the fourth exercise earlier.

Specific Format

In order to provide the necessary global information for structure, PostScript has established specific formats for the structural information to be included within the prolog and script portions of a PostScript program. Remember that there is nothing magic about these formats, nor is there anything in the PostScript interpreter that will complain if your program doesn't follow them. There may be other utility or document management programs that handle PostScript programs that require this structure and these specific formats; PostScript itself does not.

You should also understand that these specific format conventions may be subject to change. Indeed, the 3.0 on this level of the conventions shows you that there have been two earlier versions, which have been superseded by this new version. You should know that the earlier versions of the conventions are a proper subset of the version specified here; that means that any document which follows the earlier versions will process correctly under these rules. The conventions described here have been established by Adobe Systems and published, as we said earlier, in Appendix G of the *PostScript Language Reference Manual, Second Edition*. They are also available directly from Adobe in a separate document.

The important point in this sectioning process is that pieces of the PostScript program should be able to be handled and reordered, if necessary, without interpreting or executing the PostScript code itself. However, as you have already seen, the PostScript interpreter doesn't require or support any of this structure. The requirement, then, is for a method of indicating structure within a PostScript program that will be easily identifiable but transparent to the interpreter.

The conventions meet this objective by using a special form of comment to indicate sections and to provide structural information within a PostScript program. You have already been introduced to comments within a PostScript program. The standard PostScript comment begins with the character % and ends with a newline. Structural information in a PostScript program is contained in lines that begin with the characters

%% *or* %!

and end with a newline. As you can immediately see, such lines will be treated by the PostScript interpreter as comment lines and hence ignored. However, because the lines of structural information begin with this combination of special characters, they are distinguishable from ordinary comment lines by any utility or other application program that needs the information to work on a PostScript document.

The 3.0 conventions establish five categories of conventions, each relating to a distinct area, as follows:

- general conventions

- requirement conventions

- color separation conventions

- query conventions

- open structuring conventions

Each of these conventions addresses specific needs that may be present in a document-processing environment.

The *general conventions* delimit the various structural components of a PostScript document. These are the header, procedure sets, script, and trailer sections of the document, and the beginning and ending of pages within the document. They also include two additional types of information. The first is document and page setup information. This includes information relating to output routing, addressing, printer setup, and similar issues. These may be thought of as management concerns, which may affect the document as an entity or as individual pages. The second type of information is a page- or document-markup convention that establishes the beginning and ending of particular segments of the document that may require separate or special processing. This demarcation is particularly important for certain segments of the document, which may need to be removed or ignored in order to be processed successfully in specialized environments.

The *requirement conventions* are comments that are used to specify resources that are provided or required by the PostScript document. Other resource comments are used to specify device-specific requirements, such as paper size or weight, collating requirements, and so on. These features can be invoked by using specific fragments of PostScript code which are provided in the device's PPD file, thus making the actual page description more portable and useful than it otherwise might be.

Color separation conventions are used in documents that use the color extensions to the PostScript language. These perform two important functions. First, they allow document managers to direct page descriptions that require color operators to devices that support these operators. Second, they provide structural information that identify the color separation segments, define special colors, and list color use.

The *query conventions* are comments that enclose parts of a PostScript program that establish particular environmental parameters. They do this by executing certain operators, which query the selected output device to determine various characteristics or features available on the specific device and take appropriate action. A full discussion of these issues and the appropriate operators for various queries is beyond the scope of this book, but one example of such concerns would be a query to the printer regarding available fonts, for example.

Open structuring conventions are user-defined conventions. These conventions allow developers or hardware vendors to extend the standard structuring conventions to provide additional information. The only requirement for these conventions is that they conform to the guidelines given in Appendix G, section G.9 of the *PostScript Language Reference Manual, Second Edition*.

Now we are ready to discuss the exact format of the structure comments. Note that you must enter these comments exactly as shown; they are not like the regular PostScript comments, which are freeform. These comments must begin with %% and are followed by a keyword. There is no space between the %% and the keyword. As in all PostScript commands, upper- and lowercase letters are distinct, so you must enter keywords exactly as shown. In comments that require data, the keyword includes a colon (:) as the last character of the word, and again there are no spaces. There may be one or more data values whose exact interpretation depends on the keyword. The first value is separated from the colon by one space, and each subsequent value is separated from the following value by one space. A newline must appear immediately after the last value or after the keyword if there is no data. All structural comments must be no more than 255 characters long, excluding the line-termination character. This allows the comments to be read and parsed by standard application software, which may therefore use a 255 character buffer to read any comment without fearing an overflow. Comments that require more than one line can be continued on the next by starting the comment with the characters %%+ to indicate that the data on this line is a continuation of the preceding comment.

There are a large number of structural comments that are now available for PostScript documents. Many of these are specific to certain environments, or fulfill special requirements. For our look at document structure here, we will only discuss a small subset of the structuring comments. These will be the most common, and most useful of the comments; they are also the comments that you need for any conforming PostScript file.

Adobe Systems recommends that all PostScript programs begin with a comment line that starts with the characters %!. This has certain advantages in some specific environments (such as UNIX); you'll know if you are working in such an environment. In the typical micro-based environment there is no advantage to following this recommendation if you're not going to follow the other structural conventions. In a conforming program, this first line gives information regarding the structuring of the program, and is called the *version identifier*. For a conforming program, the line must look like this:

```
%!PS–Adobe–3.0
```

This identifies the PostScript program as being fully conforming to the structural conventions set out in the *PostScript Language Reference Manual, Second Edition*, Appendix G, which have been given version number 3.0. These are the same conventions as presented in this section. A program that conforms to earlier versions of the structuring conventions will begin with the same line with a different version number—either 1.0 or 2.0. A program that begins with any other line is presumed to be nonconforming.

The *general header* comments, which are the start of the prolog section, begin immediately after the version identifier. Where specific information can be postponed to the trailer section, as described earlier, the appropriate header keyword must be followed by the value (**atend**) instead of the data value or values described below. The following are general header comments, with the syntax listed first and the meaning of the comment listed below.

```
%%Title: title
```

This gives the title of the document. This can be any text string and is only terminated by a newline. The title is used for identifying documents; in some environments, this might be a file name or it might be formatted to be machine-readable.

%%Creator: name

This gives the name of the person, user or program (or maybe all of the above) who generated the PostScript document. This may be different from the person or user designated to receive the document, which may be designated by the %%For comment (see below). The name consists of any arbitrary text, terminated by a newline.

%%CreationDate: text

This gives the date and time of the creation of the document. There is no specific format for this information; all that is expected is that the text will be able to be read as a date and a time by humans. Generally, this will come from the system in whatever the standard system format may be.

%%For: userid

This is the identification of the person or user who gets the output; if this comment is absent, the output destination is presumed to be the same as the %%Creator.

%%Pages: number

This is a non-negative, decimal integer that represents the number of pages expected to be produced on the output device. If no pages will be output, the number 0 should be inserted. This comment also can be deferred to the trailer section by use of **atend**.

%%BoundingBox: llx lly urx ury

This gives the dimensions of the box that bounds all of the marks on all of the pages in the document. If the PostScript program produces more than one page, this is the largest box that bounds any page. The values are the x and y coordinates of the lower-left and upper-right corners of the page, given in the default user coordinate system; the values must be integers. This comment may be deferred to the trailer section by use of **atend**.

%%LanguageLevel: level

This indicates that the document contains operators that require the
level indicated in this comment. Currently, only 1 and 2 are defined.
This comment is required if your document uses Level 2 operators
that are not available in any Level 1 devices. Note that some Level 2
operators, such as color operators, are provided in some Level 1
devices. If you are using such operators, you should indicate that
requirement by using the %%Extensions: comment.

%%BeginDefaults

%%EndDefaults

These two comments delimit the defaults section of the prolog if that
is used in the document.

%%EndComments

This explicitly ends the header section of the PostScript program.
Because header comments must be contiguous, any line that does not
begin with the characters %X (where X is any printable character
except space, tab or newline) will end the header section
automatically.

The *general body* comments break up the executable portion of a Post-
Script program into the prolog and the individual pages of the script. If a
utility program acts on a structured PostScript program, it must respect
these markers and keep the structure intact as it operates on the program
text. In particular, it must retain the prolog at the beginning (since the pages
in the script portion depend upon it), and it must retain any trailer information at the end.

The most important general body comment is the continuation comment, as follows:

%%+ (no keywords)

This comment is used to continue any document structuring comment that
must be continued on another line to avoid exceeding the 255 character

limit on comment lines. It may also be used in cases where you want to continue a list of items, such as fonts, on individual lines, even when the comments are not greater than 255 characters.

The prolog begins with the first line after the %%EndComments statement which terminates the header section or it begins with the first line of the PostScript program that does not begin with the characters %*X* (where *X* is any printable character except space, tab, or newline). Once again, the syntax is listed first, with the explanation of the comment following.

%%BeginProlog

%%EndProlog

These two comments explicitly begin and end the prolog section of the PostScript program. The %%EndProlog is particularly important, as it has been used as a delimiter between the prolog and script portions of a document since the very first version of the structuring conventions, and many document managers look for it.

The script begins with the first line of the PostScript program following the %%EndProlog. For this reason, all documents that are divided into prolog and script must contain the %%EndProlog comment.

%%BeginSetup

%%EndSetup

These two comments delimit the setup section of the PostScript program. If present, these comments should be the first part of the script, immediately after the %%EndProlog comment and before any pages are specified.

The following comments are placed in the script code to mark page boundaries and to provide page information:

%%Page: label number

marks the beginning of an individual page within the document. The *label* and the *number* identify the page according to two methods. The *label* value is a text string which gives the page identification according to the documents internal numbering or labeling scheme. For example, this might be page ix of the Introduction, or page 2–4 (meaning the fourth page of Chapter 2, for example). The *number*, on the other hand, is a positive integer that gives the position of this page within the normal document output. This number begins at 1 and runs through n for an *n*-page document. This information is intended to be useful to utility programs; using this information, they can retrieve pages by either the internal page descriptions, that is "pages 2–4 through 2–9", or they can retrieve pages by position, that is "the last 10 pages." It also allows pages to be handled in non-sequential order; for example, if you wanted to produce pages in folio order, for book binding.

%%Trailer

This must occur only once, at the end of the pages section of the program and marks the beginning of the trailer section (if any). Any header comments that were deferred to the end of the document should be included after this comment. Any non-comment PostScript commands that follow this comment are presumed to be cleanup or otherwise not part of the page output.

%%EOF

This comment marks the end of the document; it is always the last item in the file. When a document manager encounters this comment in the file, it issues an end-of-file marker to the PostScript device. This is provided so that the interpreter does not have to understand the various end-of-file indications that occur in different network or communications setups.

The order of the header and trailer comments is not generally significant. It only becomes important if there is more than one comment with the same keyword. In that case, the data from the *first* header with the duplicated keyword is retained and used; for a trailer, the data is taken from the *last* keyword. This allows a utility program to modify the header and trailer information by simply placing the new header at the front of the PostScript program—after the version identifier, of course—and placing a new trailer at the end of the program, without having to delete any of the previous structural data. Remember, however, that the trailer data will be used only if there is a header with the same keyword and the **atend** data specification.

Besides the general conventions, the *requirement conventions* are the ones that you will use most. The requirement conventions have been changed in version 3.0. Previous versions used individual comments to mark the beginning and ending of a variety of individual types of resources, such as fonts and procsets, that might be used in a document. In version 3.0, however, all of these comments have been replaced by a single new set of comments that request and define a general category of *resources* to be used in the document. This corresponds to the new resource features in the Level 2 version of the PostScript language, which we will discuss in later chapters. These new resource comments are as follows:

%%DocumentNeededResources: resourcetype resourcename . . .

Lists the resources required by the document by name. The resource type may be any one of the following keywords: *file*, *font*, *form*, *pattern*, *procset*, or *encoding*. Of these, fonts and procsets are the most commonly required resources. The name of the resource must be identical to the name that can be used to retrieve that resource; for example, for a font, the name must be identical to the PostScript font name. For a procset, this is the procedure sets name, followed by a version number and a revision. The version number may have a decimal point and values after that, such as 1.2; the revision must be an integer.

%%DocumentSuppliedResources: resourcetype resourcename . . .

Lists the resources supplied in the document file itself. This list is mutually exclusive of the resources listed in the %%DocumentNeededResources comment. Every resource in this list should be in the document file, surrounded by %%BeginResource and %%EndResource comments.

%%BeginResource: resourcetype resourcename maxvm minvm

%%EndResource

These two comments explicitly begin and end all resources that are included in the document. The variables *maxvm* and *minvm* are optional integer numbers that indicate the maximum and minimum amount of virtual memory required by this resource. If present, these values may be used by a document manager to help control memory resources in the output device. An alternative to using these values is to include the special %%VMusage comment after the %%BeginResource comment.

%%IncludeResource: resourcetype resourcename

Tells the document manager to include the named resource at this point in the document. The resource type and name specified must match an entry in the %%DocumentNeededResources comment. Even if the document only uses standard fonts as resources, it should use this method to indicate that to a document manager; not all PostScript devices have the standard fonts available.

The remaining types of conventions, color separation conventions, query conventions, and open structuring conventions are more specialized and therefore are not discussed here. If you want to know more about these, you can look them up in the *PostScript Language Reference Manual, Second Edition*, as mentioned earlier.

Structuring Example

You can certainly be forgiven if, at this point, you still don't really have a clear picture of how these comments would look in an actual program. To illustrate these in a concrete manner, let's add a standard set of comments to the program that you produced in the fourth exercise, earlier. The result looks like Figure 2.7.

As you can see, the program starts with a series of header comments. The first line is the required %!PS–Adobe–3.0. This is followed by standard comments, described individually above, which tell you (and any document manager software) who created this document, when it was created, and so on. The %%BoundingBox: values for this example were derived by simple inspection of the actual page; you can easily calculate these values if you want. Remember that the box simply has to enclose all the marks on the page; that means that you can use values that are larger than the actual minimum box. If you have any problems calculating this box, you can always use a standard page size; for example, the maximum bounding box for an 8.5 by 11 inch page would be 0 0 612 792.

```
%!PS-Adobe-3.0
%%Creator: Cheshire Group
%%CreationDate: 1:25:21 PM  12/3/91
%%Title: Figure 2.7
%%For: Understanding PostScript (3rd Edition)
%%BoundingBox: 80 340 525 695
%%Pages: (atend)
%%DocumentNeededResources: font Times-Roman
%%+ font Times-Bold
%%EndComments
%%BeginProlog
%%BeginResource: procset Acme 1.0 0
/AcmeDict 25 dict def
AcmeDict begin
%---------------------------Procedures-------------------------
/inch
{
        72 mul
}
def

/advanceLine
{
        /NextLine
        NextLine LineSpace sub
        def
}
def

/advancePara
{
        /NextLine
        NextLine ParaSpace sub
        def

}
def

/centerText
{
        dup
        stringwidth pop
        2 div
        RightMargin LeftMargin sub 2 div
        exch sub
        LeftMargin add
        NextLine moveto
        show
}
def

/bodyText
{
        SecondColumn NextLine moveto
        show
}
def

/rightJustifyText
{
        dup
        stringwidth pop
        RightColumn exch sub
        NextLine moveto
        show
```

Figure 2.7: Acme Widgets program with structuring comments

```
}
def
end            %AcmeDict
%%EndResource
%%EndProlog

%%BeginSetup
%%IncludeResource: font Times-Roman
%%IncludeResource: font Times-Bold

%-------------------------Named Constants-------------------------

AcmeDict begin

/TopStart 9.5 inch def
/BodyStart 8.5 inch def

/LineSpace 14 def
/ParaSpace 28 def

/LeftMargin .5 inch def
/RightMargin 8 inch def
/RightColumn 2.5 inch def
/SecondColumn 3 inch def

/HeadFont /Times-Bold findfont 16 scalefont def
/TextFont /Times-Roman findfont 12 scalefont def
/TitleFont /Times-Bold findfont 12 scalefont def

%%EndSetup

%%Page: 1 1
%--------------------------Setup page--------------------------
/PgSave save def

%--------------------------Program (Page Titles)----------------------
% Set up font for page titles
HeadFont setfont

% Move to selected position
/NextLine TopStart def

% Show titles
(ACME WIDGETS INCORPORATED) centerText

/NextLine NextLine 20 sub def
(Fiscal Year 1989) centerText

%--------------------------Program (Text)----------------------

% Set first paragraph
%        first, set the top position for both columns
/SaveColOne BodyStart def
/NextLine BodyStart def

% Set the paragraph
%        set new font for body text
TextFont setfont
%        then set the text itself
(Acme Widgets was founded in 1958 by Dippy and Daffy Acme) bodyText
advanceLine
...
...
...
```

Figure 2.7: Acme Widgets program with structuring comments (continued)

```
% Now set the marginal heading for the last paragraph
TitleFont setfont
/NextLine SaveColOne def
(Financial Position:) rightJustifyText


% Now clean up after the page has been completed
PgSave restore
showpage

%%Trailer
end          %AcmeDict
%%Pages: 1
%%EOF
```

Figure 2.7: Acme Widgets program with structuring comments
(continued)

The %%Pages comment shows you an example of information which is deferred to the trailer section of the document. The %%DocumentNeeded Reesources comment lists the two fonts that you have used in the document and shows you an example of using the continuation comment as well. It is quite common to list each required resource on a separate line like this, and Adobe recommends that at least each individual type of resource should be on a separate line. The %%EndComments terminates the header section.

For this document, there is no defaults section since there is only one page in the document. Remember that defaults are optional and are intended to simplify document structure, which is not required here.

The procedures section begins with the standard %%BeginProlog comment. The beginning of the set of procedures for this document is indicated by the %%BeginResource: comment. The type of resource is a procset, and we have given it the name "Acme" with a version number of 1.0 and no revision. If there is no revision number, it is good practice to insert a 0, as you have done here. The procset ends with the required %%EndResource comment.

You should note here that there are two small, but significant, changes in the program code in this version to comply with the requirements of the structuring conventions. These are the **end** operator at the end of the procset, matched by a **AcmeDict begin** at the start of the document setup. You didn't require these in the first version of the program, because the dictionary was created, filled with procedures and variables, and then used, all at once. Here, however, two additional things have happened. First, the structuring conventions require that procsets (or any other resource for that matter) should be able to be load separately from the document file. This allows document managers to remove a procset that is used in several documents and download it separately into the output device to save time and processing. This can't be done if the dictionary that you create isn't removed from the dictionary stack at the end of its creation. Second, you have added the two %%IncludeResource: comments between the end of the procset and the beginning of the setup. Now, for our purposes, these two fonts are already loaded into memory, so no actual font needs to be included. However, if one were included, it would be inserted here. It would be bad programming, and possibly cause an error, if you left a private dictionary on the dictionary stack while you were defining a common resource like a font. Therefore, this version of the exercise removes the dictionary at the end of its creation and then reinstates it at the beginning of the page setup, as you see here.

The document setup begins with the %%BeginSetup comment, immediately followed by the two %%IncludeResource: comments for the two fonts that you require. Then you place **AcmeDict** onto the dictionary stack and define the global parameters as before. Note that the two required fonts must be included and defined before you can successfully execute the lines that setup the fonts for the heading, text, and titles. The setup section then ends with a %%EndSetup comment.

The single page of output begins with the %%Page: comment. In this case, both the literal page number and the page sequence number are 1.

At the end of the page, and the program, there is the %%Trailer comment. This is followed by the cleanup processing; in this case, simply an **end** operator to remove the private **AcmeDict** from the dictionary stack. Then comes the %%Pages: comment that you deferred at the beginning in the header. The file finishes with the %%EOF comment, which is, as it must be, the last line in the file.

PROGRAM STYLE

Everybody who writes programs has a programming style, just as anyone who writes a paragraph has a prose style; style is just your personal way of organizing your thoughts and expressing yourself in a language. It's easy enough to understand what "style" means in regard to natural language, but what does it mean when applied to writing programs, particularly PostScript?

As we briefly discussed earlier in the chapter, there are two components to programming style. These may be thought of as global structure and local structure. The global structure concerns where you put procedural definitions, how you name variables and constants and where you define them, and how you structure program flow. The local structure covers decisions regarding indentation, line breaks, and use of comments.

The preceding sections of this chapter have explained in some detail how you might approach global structure for a PostScript program. Some of this structure is contained in the recommended (but not required) structural format using the comments previously described. Some of the global structure is inherent in the nature of the PostScript language itself, such as how you create and use procedures. Overall, at this point, you should have a clear understanding of these issues.

Local Structure

Global structure has been the main focus and concern of this chapter up to now, primarily because global structure has a much greater impact on the overall usefulness of a program than local structure. However, you will generally discover that good global structure is supported by good local structure, and vice versa. So there are some points to make regarding local structure in your PostScript code.

There are basically three decisions involved in local structure: where to break lines, how to indent code, and how to use comments. With the exception of the few rules about breaking lines in comments and so on, PostScript does not provide much guidance on issues of local structure. Essentially, in this area, as in the area of names and naming conventions, you are free to do whatever you decide based on your best judgement and experience. While it is your personal choice and style that will decide what local conventions you use, I would offer you some advice and suggestions.

The first advice is in regard to indentation and line breaks. These should be used as tools to clarify the overall structure of your program, and there are three rules to follow for best results. First, use line breaks at every logical operation and try to keep one operator to a line; where you decide not to do this (for example, when setting fonts), at least keep one logical thought to one line. Second, use indentation to create an outline format for your procedures. This is particularly important and useful when you are doing logical tests. Finally, be consistent in your use of these tools. Don't put multiple operators together one time and put them all on separate lines on another. If you look back at the previous exercises, you will see how I have chosen to structure procedures and variables.

Consistency is particularly important in PostScript. Of course, consistency within a program is essential; but, with PostScript, you will find that you develop a library of common routines to accomplish certain functions. You will come to rely on these routines and to include them in many of your programs. As you do so, you will discover that such routines need to follow a common format for maintainability and utility in a wide variety of programs.

The use of comments is also a personal decision. Many program instruction books recommend using many comments for clarity and explanation. Personally, I find them less useful than good notes or other documentation, and I generally don't trust them—too often, someone has changed the code and not the comment. Nevertheless, they are useful and have a place in your local conventions. I would recommend that you use them in at least three places. First, as full lines to break the prolog and script into useful sections. This would be in addition to the structural comments, of course. Second, use them at the beginning of procedures to describe what the procedure does, what it expects on the stack, and what (if anything) it returns to the stack. It is probably useful to establish some standard format for this information, particularly for your library routines. I will give an example of such a format with the next exercise. And, finally, use comments to annotate any portion of the program that is especially opaque, complex, or otherwise out of the ordinary. One common example of this is the use of a comment with the **end** operator to indicate what dictionary is being removed from the dictionary stack. This helps you identify the range of statements where you are using a specific dictionary.

OPERATOR REVIEW

This section presents the same information given earlier in the chapter for a variety of operators. It is repeated here for your review and convenience.

Dictionary Operators

SYNTAX	FUNCTION
int **dict** dict	creates a dictionary *dict* with the initial capacity for *int* value pairs. In Level 1 devices, this is also the maximum number of pairs that can be contained in the dictionary.
dict **begin** —	pushes *dict* onto the dictionary stack and makes it the current dictionary.
— **end** —	pops the current dictionary from the dictionary stack.
key value **def** —	associates *key* and *value* in the current dictionary.

Control Operators

SYNTAX	FUNCTION
{proc} **exec** —	executes *proc*.
int {proc} **repeat** —	executes *proc int* times.
init incr lim {proc} **for** —	executes *proc* for values from *init* by steps of *incr* until reaching *lim*.
bool {proc} **if** —	executes *proc* if *bool* is true.
bool {proc1} {proc} **ifelse** —	executes *proc1* if *bool* is true and executes *proc2* otherwise.
{proc} **loop** —	executes *proc* an indefinite number of times.
— **exit** —	terminates the active loop.

Relational Operators

SYNTAX	FUNCTION
any1 any2 **eq** bool	tests whether *any1* is equal to *any2*.
any1 any2 **ne** bool	tests whether *any1* is not equal to *any2*.
num1 num2 (str1) (str2) **ge** bool	tests whether *num1* or *str1* is greater than or equal to *num2* or *str2*.
num1 num2 (str1) (str2) **gt** bool	tests whether *num1* or *str1* is greater than *num2* or *str2*.
num1 num2 (str1) (str2) **le** bool	tests whether *num1* or *str1* is less than or equal to *num2* or *str2*.
num1 num2 (str1) (str2) **lt** bool	tests whether *num1* or *str1* is less than *num2* or *str2*.

Logical Operators

SYNTAX	FUNCTION
int1 int2 int bool1 bool2 **and** bool	logical or bitwise *and*.
int1 int2 int bool1 bool2 **or** bool	logical or bitwise inclusive *or*.
int1 int2 int bool1 bool2 **xor** bool	logical or bitwise exclusive *or*.

SYNTAX	FUNCTION
int int	
bool **not** bool	logical or bitwise *not*.
— **true** bool	pushes the boolean value *true* onto stack.
— **false** bool	pushes the boolean value *false* onto stack.

Memory Management Operators

SYNTAX	FUNCTION
— **save** savestate	saves the current state of PostScript virtual memory as *savestate*.
savestate **restore** —	restores PostScript virtual memory to the state represented by *savestate*.
dict key **undef** —	removes *key* and its associated value from the dictionary *dict*.
key **undefinefont** —	removes *key*, which is a font name literal, and its associated value, which is a font dictionary, from the font directory.

3

Introducing Fonts and Graphics

T HIS CHAPTER INTRODUCES A variety of PostScript graphics concepts and operators. It also provides a formal introduction to and discussion of PostScript fonts, which you have been using informally so far.

The chapter begins with a section on basic PostScript graphics concepts. Most of this section is an expanded discussion of PostScript graphics. The section leads into these topics by examining the nature of PostScript graphic images. This nature is precisely defined by and primarily a function of PostScript's target output devices, which are examined in detail.

The exploration of page layout revives issues that were discussed in Chapter 1 in a less formal and detailed manner. After this review, you are introduced to simple PostScript graphics constructions. There are several examples using straight-line segments to illustrate both the old concepts and new operational issues. The examples proceed from straight-line segments to the creation of closed figures made from straight lines. Then the figures are filled with shades of gray. The examples proceed naturally, each building on the previous work so you can easily follow the structure.

The examples also illustrate how to create procedures that generate standard shapes and how such procedures can best be structured to be useful on a variety of pages and in a range of formats. These issues of flexibility and independence, which are tightly connected, will remain with us throughout the chapter.

The next section is concerned with fonts and PostScript font machinery and also recapitulates some of the earlier material about text and text output. The section starts with some observations and definitions regarding fonts generally and proceeds to the specifics of PostScript fonts. This is an important topic. The section does not require any operators other that the ones you are already familiar with; however, the actual function of each of the operators is discussed in detail, whereas before you were only given minimal information for practical application.

Because PostScript treats fonts and text as graphics objects, you need to have some insight into the PostScript font machinery to establish real control over the text output. The ultimate objective is to understand the process and be able to manipulate text and graphics output comfortably on a PostScript page.

The third section of the chapter continues the previous discussion of the use of graphics. It adds curve-lined segments to straight lines and produces a series of examples similar to the examples developed around straight lines. This work leads into an examination of the PostScript coordinate structure and PostScript methods for transforming an ideal page—which is what you are working in—into a concrete page of output on a specific device. This PostScript facility, which is inherent in the PostScript design objective of device independence, can also be used advantageously by the PostScript programmer to adjust the page. The three most common adjustments are translation, rotation, and scaling of coordinates. Each of these is discussed in detail, with examples.

But coordinate adjustment is only part of the story. The section continues by returning to the issues of procedure construction that were raised earlier in the chapter. Now you have all the concepts and tools to make independent and flexible graphics procedures. This portion of the chapter shows you, by discussion and example, how to do that.

The chapter ends with a fifth exercise that uses all the preceding work and integrates the techniques that you have been reading about and practicing. In this exercise you will create a simple, stylized logo for an imaginary company. The logo is reasonably complex and yet simple to create with the tools you have been learning. This example also leads into later chapters, which uses the logo as a graphics element in a simple document.

GRAPHICS CONCEPTS AND BASICS

PostScript was designed from its inception as a language with powerful graphics capabilities. The PostScript language has many features in common with other computer languages, since it addresses the same or similar tasks and must overcome the same problems as they do. But PostScript goes far beyond traditional computer language tasks to provide the ability to handle and output graphics images of all types. In many ways, all the other features of PostScript are centered on and support this unique capacity to describe graphics objects.

You have already been introduced to the PostScript graphics concept of ''painting onto a page''; that is, rendering an image or other graphic onto an output device. This is a natural and intuitive way to think about graphics; and this conceptual model of graphic output is satisfactory because, to a great extent, it approximates what graphic artists actually do as they work. However, the computer and its associated output devices do not work in that way; they require their instructions in mathematical forms.

I make this point simply to explain the necessary intrusion of certain mathematical concepts into portions of this chapter. By their design, Post-Script graphics operators insulate the user from most mathematical considerations. There is, however, an irreducible minimum of mathematical information that is involved in particular graphics objects. Take a circle as a good, simple example. When a graphic artist wishes to put a specific circle on a specific page, he or she need only pick the place and draw the circle. To create a circle on a laser printer, however, requires two mathematical data: a radius (or diameter) and a center. This is what I mean by the "irreducible minimum" of mathematics that will intrude upon us as we proceed through the chapter.

To continue with the circle as an example, PostScript does not have a simple operator that produces a circle. Instead, PostScript has operators that produce arcs, arbitrary portions of a circle. These operators can then be used, with the proper operands, to create a new procedure that will generate a circle. In fact, you will create and use such a procedure in the last exercise in this chapter. By combining PostScript graphics operators into such procedures, you will be able to generate a wide array of graphics objects for your use. This chapter will show you the basics of the creation and use of such procedures.

GRAPHIC IMAGES

Human beings have a strong visual orientation. Our languages are full of visual imagery. In English, we say "I see" when we mean that we understand something, and the saying "a picture is worth a thousand words" has become a cliché. It is this visual orientation that inspires the need to render images into a permanent and concrete form, through pictures or other graphics.

A variety of means is available to create images. The most ancient, surely, is to apply paint or some other opaque medium to a prepared surface. By this method we get paintings and drawings of all types: oil, watercolor, acrylic, enamel, and so forth; and by extension we have collage and similar assemblies. Another method of capturing or creating images is through photography, by using light to create chemical changes on special media, which can then be translated into images. This happens because the images are captured by millions of tiny dots on the photographic surface. All methods of rendering images involve one or another of these techniques, or a combination of both.

Printing, if you think about it in these terms, is painting with ink. With text, each character on a printed page is a continuous line of ink, just like a line in a drawing. When it comes to reproducing pictures or graphic images that don't involve lines, however, modern printing technology, on high-speed presses, becomes more like the photographic process. An image is broken down into a set of dots, which are then grouped together to render the image onto paper. This process of grouping dots to re-create an image is called *screening*, and it plays an important role in PostScript image handling.

Raster Output Devices

The PostScript language is designed to work with a general class of output devices, known as *raster output devices*. You may be surprised to learn that the television is the original and prototypical raster output device; in fact, that's where the term "raster" comes from. Raster devices are characterized by having a number of dots that are activated in some manner to make up an image. On a television screen, these dots are composed of phosphorescent material activated by a beam of electrons, but the dots may be created by any mechanism. Essentially, the image is created by using dots and a screening process, just like the printing process described above. Unlike printing, however, raster output devices render text characters as a series of dots; there is no such thing as a continuous line on these devices.

Each dot on a raster output device represents one picture element, or *pixel*. Although these elements are also conventionally called "dots," this is a generic term and doesn't necessarily represent the actual pixel shape. Pixels may be round, square, oval, or rectangular—whatever shape is most appropriate and convenient for the specific output device manufacturer. Generally, pixels, like binary numbers, are either off or on, zero or one. You can immediately understand how well this concept fits into a digital-processing framework.

Some devices have pixels that can be varied in intensity by various methods. This translates into more than binary values for each dot. Even in devices with a single intensity, pixels may be grouped together by the screening process to create the effect of varying intensity.

As so often in life, there are advantages and disadvantages to this process of composing in dots. The advantage is that this mechanism produces both text and graphics without distinction. Each character or image is simply a set of pixels to be set appropriately. The disadvantage is that there is not a continuous boundary for a character or other graphic, so that, at the finest and smallest level, all objects look ragged and uneven.

Resolution

Naturally, the intention is to produce text or graphics that appear continuous to the eye, although ultimately they are composed of dots, or pixels, in a given area. The number of pixels per unit area is called the *device resolution*.

Because resolution is measured by area, it has both horizontal and vertical components. Many devices have identical resolution in both directions; such devices generally provide resolution measurements as *dots per inch* (dpi). Where the resolution is different in the horizontal and vertical directions, each resolution must be expressed separately, such as 240 by 300 dpi.

Obviously, the greater the device resolution, the better it can fool the eye into seeing a continuous line instead of a string of dots. But even on devices of high resolution, there is still the issue of how to define the boundary of an image. This process is particularly critical for text characters because quick recognition of the distinctive shapes of characters has a major impact on speed and ease of reading. This issue of adjustment of pixels at image boundaries is called *tuning*, and although it is important, it is also extremely device dependant. This is just one reason to choose an intermediary language like PostScript, which provides both flexibility and control without requiring concern about specific device characteristics.

Device Classification

It should be clear from this discussion that all typewriters and similar devices are not raster output devices. This includes old-style "letter quality" printers, which are essentially based on typewriter technology. Such devices rely on preformed letters and shapes, and ink onto paper transfer to produce their results. They have no screen facilities and so cannot successfully represent generalized images.

Dot-matrix printers, even though they are impact printers, are raster output devices, with resolutions typically between 100 and 200 dpi. Most page printers—laser printers, ink-jet printers, and so on—have resolutions between 300 and 600 dpi. Typesetting machines, using photographic techniques to create pixels, achieve resolutions between 1000 and 2800 dpi; some very high-resolution systems go even higher.

Obviously, higher resolution devices have more information per unit of area and so impose significantly greater demands on system resources, such as computational power. All of this is reflected in higher costs for using such devices.

Displays on computer terminals are also raster output devices. These generally have the lowest resolution of the raster output devices, ranging between 50 and 100 dpi. At such low resolutions, tuning becomes most important and poor tuning is most noticeable. For this reason, text characters and graphics figures may appear ragged on the terminal, although they will appear smooth enough on a higher resolution device, such as a laser printer.

POSTSCRIPT GRAPHICS CONCEPTS

At this point you are familiar with PostScript page structure and the PostScript page coordinate system, both from your previous reading and from the exercises. Let's quickly review these key concepts now to set the stage for further discussion.

PostScript operates on an ideal page, called a current page. Positions on the page are given by x and y coordinates that work like mathematical coordinate systems. The origin point (0,0) is in the bottom-left corner of the page; movement in the x-coordinate is horizontal with positive movement toward the right of the page, while positive movement in the vertical, or y-coordinate, direction is up the page. The default coordinate units are $1/72$ inch.

Line Concepts

PostScript creates images on the page by tracing a current path, which can then be "painted" to become visible. There are several methods of painting the current path. The end of the current path is the current point. So far, you have not actually dealt with the current path; you have only moved the current point around on the page to govern the location for text output. Working with a specific current path wasn't necessary because the **show** operator, which is used for text output, handles those issues automatically. Now that you are starting to produce graphics, however, you need additional information, along with more operators, to deal with the current path.

The current path can be composed of both straight- and curved-line segments, and it can also have multiple, discontinuous segments. The path may close or cross itself, creating enclosed areas, or figures, on the page. Remember that the current path itself is not visible; it is only made visible on the page by painting operators, which have various properties that will be explained later. Finally, after all the desired areas have been painted onto the page, the page must be output on the device by specific commands.

Operator Review

You have already used several of the most basic PostScript operators that relate to the current page. The **moveto** operator sets the current page at the current point. The **show** operator also sets the current point to the position following the last character of the output string. Finally, you have used both the **showpage** and the **copypage** operators to create output on the printer.

Simple Lines

Not all output is text, however, and if text was all you wanted to output you could find many ways other than PostScript to produce it. You will begin to develop your PostScript graphics vocabulary in this section by learning to draw simple, straight lines. All of the examples in this chapter will assume that you are already in the interactive mode, at the PS > prompt, and ready to proceed.

For the first example, you will create two lines, 2 inches long. Each will begin at a point 3 inches from the left edge of the paper and 6 inches from the bottom edge. This can be done with the code in Figure 3.1. It produces the page of output in Figure 3.2.

```
%Begin simple line example
/inch                                        %1
        {     72 mul  }
    def
3 inch 6 inch moveto                         %2
5 inch 6 inch lineto                         %3
stroke                                       %4
newpath                                      %5
.1 inch setlinewidth                         %6
3 inch 6 inch moveto                         %7
3 inch 8 inch lineto                         %8
stroke                                       %9
showpage                                     %10
%all done
```

Figure 3.1: A simple line example

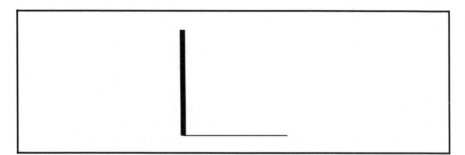

Figure 3.2: First example output: a vertical and a horizontal line

From here on, for simple examples like this, I won't show you the entire page, but just the relevant figure output. By now you understand the PostScript coordinate system and can reasonably picture the location of these figures on the page.

This short program introduces several new operators. The inch procedure, on line %1, is already an old friend; you will see it again and again in these examples. Line %2 moves to the position designated as the beginning of the lines, 3 inches from the left side and 6 inches from the bottom of the page. The next line contains the first new operator, **lineto**. This operator takes x and y coordinates as its operands and draws the current line from the current point to the designated point. The designated point then becomes the current point. The effect is like a putting your pencil down on a specific point and moving it up to a designated spot on the page. The **lineto** operator doesn't actually make a mark on the current page; remember, that is done by the **stroke** operator in line %4.

That completes the first line, which is 2 inches horizontally. You know it is because the coordinates of the end of the line, given to **lineto** in line %3, are 2 inches further in the x-direction than the current point, which was set in line %2; and the coordinates are the same in the y-direction. The next line will be 2 inches vertically, because the coordinates will be 2 inches greater in the y-direction and the same in the x-direction.

Line %5 presents another new operator, **newpath**. This operator does just what you would expect: it clears the current path. Note that it doesn't erase the line you have already painted onto the page; it only eliminates any segments of the current path that have not been painted.

This is followed by another new operator, **setlinewidth**. This operator sets the width of the current line to the given number. Here, you have defined a line 0.1-inches wide. The default width of a line is 1 unit, or $1/72$ inch, which is what the first line was. Then lines %7 through %9 repeat the actions of lines %2 to %4 and create another line; however, this time it's a thicker, vertical line instead of a horizontal one.

Finally, line %10 outputs the entire page with the **showpage** in the usual fashion. This is a simple procedure, and yet it illustrates several important PostScript graphics commands.

The next example is a variation on the theme. Let's mark two X's on the page, along the same line, 5 inches from the bottom of the page. The first X will be on the left side of the page, 3 inches from the left edge; the second will be on the right, 6 inches from the left edge. Each X will be 1 inch high and 1 inch wide.

Before you begin coding, briefly review Figure 3.3 with me. This figure lays out the coordinates for the first X in inches. Note the coordinates of the ends of the crossed lines that form the X. As you can see, we need to draw two lines to make the figure, one from the lower-left (3,5) to the upper-right (4,6), and the second, from the lower-right (4,5) to the upper-left (3,6). Of course, which end of the line you choose to start from is arbitrary; either line could just as well be drawn in the opposite direction. I will leave it to you to work out the coordinates of the second X.

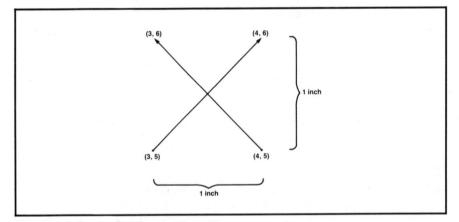

Figure 3.3: Layout for the first X

The second example is shown in Figure 3.4. Note two points about the coding before you begin. First, if you are continuing from the previous example without exiting from PostScript, you don't need to define the inch procedure again; but it won't hurt anything if you do. Second, if you have just started the PostScript interpreter, the **newpath** command is not strictly necessary since nothing is in the current path; but again, it can't hurt anything, and it is a good habit to get into. As you would expect, the code produces two *X*'s on a line, as in Figure 3.5.

There are no new operators in this short program, and nothing should come as a surprise. We have already discussed lines %1 and %2; whether you need them depends on whether you are starting PostScript fresh or are continuing from previous work. In either case, you are familiar with these operators. We have already discussed the endpoint coordinates of the first *X*; in lines %3 and %4 you see how the first line of the *X* is constructed. Then you move your electronic ''pencil'' to the opposite corner of the *X* and make the second line. Finally, you ink in the two lines with the **stroke**

```
%Begin second example
newpath                          %1
/inch                            %2
       { 72 mul }
       def
%Do first X at (3, 5)
3 inch 5 inch moveto             %3
4 inch 6 inch lineto             %4
4 inch 5 inch moveto             %5
3 inch 6 inch lineto             %6
stroke                           %7
%Do second X at (6, 5)
6 inch 5 inch moveto             %8
7 inch 6 inch lineto             %9
7 inch 5 inch moveto             %10
6 inch 6 inch lineto             %11
stroke                           %12
%Now to show the output
showpage                         %13
quit                             %14
```

Figure 3.4: Second example: two *X*'s on a line

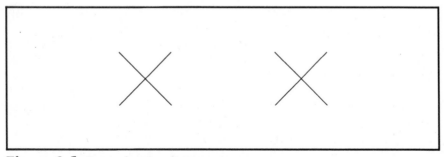

Figure 3.5: Second example output

command in line %7. The second *X* is constructed in an identical fashion, but starting, as defined, at the point (6,5). Then the entire page is printed, and you're done.

To finish this section on simple lines, let's review the operators that have been introduced here and put them in our conventional format.

SYNTAX	FUNCTION
num1 num2 **lineto** —	adds a straight-line segment to the current path. The line segment extends from the current point to the *num1* x-coordinate and the *num2* y-coordinate. The new current point is (*num1, num2*).
num **setlinewidth** —	sets the current line width to *num*. This controls the thickness of the lines painted by subsequent **stroke** operators.
— **stroke** —	paints a line following the current path and using the current color.
— **newpath** —	initializes the current path to be empty and causes the current point to be undefined.

Closed Figures

Now that you can draw straight lines, let's use those lines to make some figures. Closed figures are just a collection of lines, (straight or otherwise), that finish at the point where they began. Figures of this type are certainly some of the most typical graphic elements, and PostScript has several operators to help you construct and display them.

The first two examples of this section will draw squares at various points on the page; and all dimensions, as before, will be in inches. These two examples will have similar features, but will be positioned at different places on the page so that you can do them in one session with the interpreter, if you want to.

In the first example of the set, you will draw a 1-inch square with its bottom-left corner at the point (3,5); that is, 3 inches from the left edge of the page and 5 inches from the bottom edge. Then you will move to the point (6,5) and draw a box that is tilted to the left, so that the bottom of the box is a line from (6,5) to the point (7,6), like the first line of the *X* in the last example. The layout of these two squares is shown in Figure 3.6.

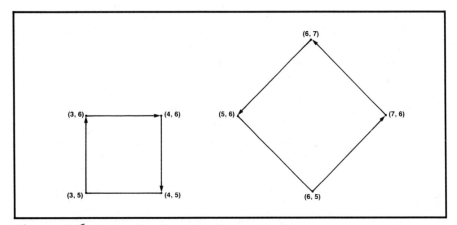

Figure 3.6: Layout for the square box example

The essence of any closed figure is that the original line returns to its starting point. PostScript provides a special operator to close a figure, the **closepath** operator. There is a particular reason to use this operator to finish a figure, which is not entirely obvious. As you saw in the earlier examples, PostScript lines have an actual width, like the stroke of a brush or of a calligraphic pen. Since a line begins and ends precisely at the line to the starting point using most PostScript operators, you will have a small space at the end of the line where it joins the original line-that is not filled in. This is illustrated is Figure 3.7.

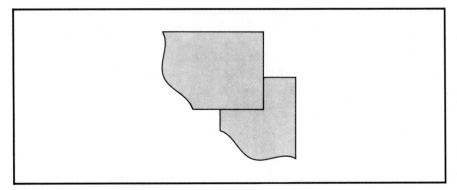

Figure 3.7: Line join

This problem can be avoided by using the **closepath** operator. If you use **lineto** or any other PostScript operator to finish the figure and close the path, the interpreter doesn't register that this last junction of lines is anything special; when you use **closepath**, it will finish the figure and fill in the resulting join for you automatically. The program for these first two figures is shown in Figure 3.8. It produces the output in Figure 3.9.

This example is really straightforward and only has one new operator, **closepath**, which has already been discussed. Each box is begun by moving to the desired location. Then each side of the square is put in by drawing a line to the next corner of the box, as in Figure 3.6. The **closepath** operator

```
%Begin square box example
/inch                                              %1
      { 72 mul }
      def
newpath                                            %2
%Do first square
3 inch  5 inch  moveto                             %3
3 inch  6 inch  lineto                             %4
4 inch  6 inch  lineto                             %5
4 inch  5 inch  lineto                             %6
closepath                                          %7
stroke                                             %8
%Do second square
6 inch  5 inch  moveto                             %9
7 inch  6 inch  lineto                             %10
6 inch  7 inch  lineto                             %11
5 inch  6 inch  lineto                             %12
closepath                                          %13
stroke                                             %14
%Now see what was done
copypage                                           %15
```

Figure 3.8: Square box example

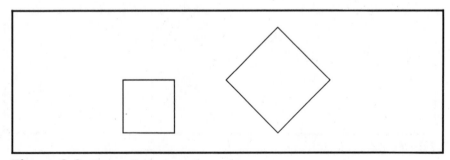

Figure 3.9: Square box example output

returns the line to the starting point from the last corner, finishing the four sides. Finally, the **stroke** operator inks the fours sides of the box. The only possible surprise here may be the use of the **copypage** for the output; I did that so both this example and the next example will show on the next page. If you want, you can use **showpage** instead and leave these boxes off the next page of output.

The next example produces two boxes identical to the first two, but it uses some new operators to create them *relative* to a starting point—in this case, the first coordinate, the lower-left corner of the first box. These two new operators are **rmoveto** and **rlineto**. These are identical to the two matching operators, **moveto** and **lineto**, with which you are already acquainted, except that the operands these new operators use are relative to the current point rather than absolute page coordinates. Let's use the first square as an example.

This square is 1 inch on each side. Using **lineto**, you must calculate the coordinates of each corner of the square to use as operands. Thus you start at (3,5), make a line up to (3,6), go across to (4,6) and down to (4,5), and then close the path at the starting point. Using **rlineto** instead, you can code this starting at (3,5)—just as before—but then move 1 inch on the y-axis and 0 units on the x-axis, relative to the current point. This takes you to the next corner, just as before, and from there you proceed 1 inch in the x-direction and 0 units in the y-direction to the next corner, and so on. All of this is shown in Figure 3.10.

In the first example, after you finished the first square, you moved the current point to the starting point of the next box, (6,5). Now you can move

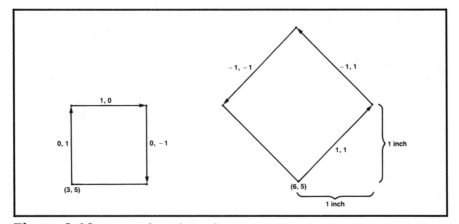

Figure 3.10: Layout for relative boxes

the current point relative to the corner of the first box to start the second box. This distance, as shown in Figure 3.10, is 3 inches in the x-direction and 0 units in the y-direction. These new commands are valuable precisely because they do not require that you know where on the page you began; they simply allow you to create movement and lines relative to where you are at this moment on the page. When we construct graphics procedures, you will see how useful this facility is.

The program for our new boxes is given in Figure 3.11. Note that the set of boxes now begins at the point (3,2) rather than (3,5). This allows you to print both sets of boxes on one page, if you used **copypage** before, and compare them. You may find this instructive. The program produces output indistinguishable from that produced by the first example, as shown in Figure 3.9.

The output from this program was designed to be identical to that from the previous example. When you look at the two programs (see Figure 3.8), you will immediately notice that they are almost identical as well, except that the equivalent relative commands have been substituted for the prior operators and there is only one **stroke** operator. The only absolute coordinates in the program are in line %3, which is the first **moveto**. This must have an absolute coordinate. The previous **newpath** command has cleared the current path, and consequently, no current point is defined. Therefore, there is nothing to move relative to, and the use of any relative operator (or any operator that requires a current point to work from, such as **lineto**) would give you an error.

```
%Begin second square box example
/inch                                              %1
       { 72 mul }
     def
newpath                                            %2
%Do first square
3 inch  2 inch  moveto                             %3
0  1 inch  rlineto                                 %4
1 inch  0  rlineto                                 %5
0  -1 inch  rlineto                                %6
closepath                                          %7
%Do second square
3 inch   0 inch  rmoveto                           %8
1 inch   1 inch  rlineto                           %9
-1 inch  1 inch  rlineto                           %10
-1 inch  -1 inch  rlineto                          %11
closepath                                          %12
stroke                                             %13
%Now see what was done
showpage                                           %14
```

Figure 3.11: Relative boxes example

You also notice that, in this example, you drew both boxes before you issued the painting command, **stroke**. The previous example could have been done in the same way, using one painting command, if you wanted to. However, in this example, it is essential to paint the figures only once because **stroke** erases the current path as it works, having the same effect as a **newpath**. If you painted the first box at the same point in the program as in the preceding exercise, before moving on to the second box, you would get an error in this program, because the **rmoveto** command would have no current point to move from. Therefore, you only stroke the path once, at the end of the procedure.

It is important to note that this program will work at any point on the page, once you have changed the coordinates in line %3. Thus, if you set line %3 to point (3,5), as in the first example, none of the remaining code would have to be altered to produce the two boxes at exactly the same points. In contrast, if you tried to reuse the code from the previous example, you would have to change every coordinate, which means almost every line. You can see how you can use these relative commands to great advantage in creating procedures. You will put this knowledge to use in the next section as you continue to develop graphics.

Before you leave this section, let's recap in the standard format the operators that have been introduced here.

num1 num2 **rmoveto** —

(relative moveto) starts a new segment of the current path in the same manner as **moveto**. However, the new current point is defined from the current point (x,y) to $x + num1$ as an x-coordinate and $y + num2$ as a y-coordinate. The new current point is (x + $num1$, y + $num2$).

num1 num2 **rlineto** —

(relative lineto) adds a straight-line segment to the current path in the same manner as **lineto**. However, the line segment extends from the current point (x,y) to $x + num1$ as an x-coordinate and $y + num2$ as a y-coordinate. The new current point is $(x + num1, y + num2)$.

— **closepath** —

closes the segment of the current path by appending a straight line from the current point to the segment's starting point (generally the point specified in the most recent **moveto** or **rmoveto**).

Shading

Not all figures are simply line drawings. You might want to fill in the figure with a color or pattern. PostScript has a wide variety of operators that will help you accomplish such tasks. As an introduction to these operators, let's begin with the simplest and most obvious operation: filling a figure with black.

By this time, you are probably getting tired of drawing boxes; this exercise will draw two triangles instead and color them black. The dimensions and other data for these triangles are given in Figure 3.12.

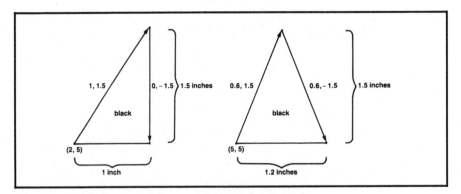

Figure 3.12: Layout for the two-triangle example

This example will also introduce procedures to create these figures. As you see from the figure, these are two triangles: one is a right triangle and the other is an isosceles triangle. You will define two procedures, one for each triangle, which will need to be positioned with the current point at the left corner of the triangle and with the base (or bottom dimension) and the height of the triangle on the stack. Let's call these two procedures right-Triangle and isoTriangle.

Remember to take the operands off the stack in the reverse order than you put them on when you called the procedure. In this case, you will call the procedure like this:

height base **rightTriangle**

Then you will take *base* off the stack first, since it will be on top, and take *height* off next. Since these procedures are your creations, and not Post-Script operators, the order of operands is completely arbitrary. For the example, I have chosen to put *height* on the stack followed by *base*.

With that preliminary out of the way, let's go on to the example on Figure 3.13, which produces the output in Figure 3.14.

There are several instructive points to this example. The example is set up into the prolog-and-script format that you read about in the last chapter. The previous examples in this chapter haven't contained any procedures other than **inch**; now that you are beginning to code procedures, you

```
%Begin triangle procedure example
%------------------------Procedures----------------------
/inch                                                   %1
      { 72 mul }
      def
%define graphic procedure for right triangle
/rightTriangle                                          %2
%called as: height base rightTriangle                   %2.1
      {     /Base exch def                              %2.2
            /Hgt exch def                               %2.3
            Base Hgt rlineto                            %2.4
            0 Hgt neg rlineto                           %2.5
            closepath }                                 %2.6
      def                                               %2.7
%define graphic procedure for isosceles triangle
/isoTriangle                                            %3
%called as: height base isoTriangle                     %3.1
      {     /Base exch def                              %3.2
            /Hgt exch def                               %3.3
            /HalfBase Base 2 div def                    %3.4
            HalfBase Hgt rlineto                        %3.5
            HalfBase Hgt neg rlineto                    %3.6
            closepath }                                 %3.7
      def                                               %3.8
%------------------------Program-------------------------
newpath                                                 %4
2 inch 5 inch moveto                                    %5
1.5 inch 1 inch rightTriangle                           %6
fill                                                    %7
5 inch 5 inch moveto                                    %8
1.5 inch 1.2 inch isoTriangle                           %9
fill                                                    %10
showpage                                                %11
%all done
```

Figure 3.13: Triangle procedure example

Figure 3.14: Triangle procedure output

should follow the standard format. You remember that, in the standard for-mat discussed in the last chapter, a PostScript program will consist of four sections: a header, a prolog, a script, and a trailer. We are still not including the header and trailer sections because to do so would make these short pro-cedural examples too formal and bulky—and it wouldn't add to the clarity or readability of the examples. When you begin to code complete exercises in the next chapter, we will use the full structuring conventions.

The prolog contains three procedures: inch, rightTriangle, and isoTriangle. The basic requirements of the two-triangle procedure were discussed before you started the coding, but there are several points you should note about the actual code of each procedure. Let's take them in order.

The rightTriangle procedure begins by defining two variables: Base and Hgt. These two variables represent the base and height, respectively, that are on the stack when the procedure is called. The comment line at %2.1 shows what operands are expected on the stack and in what order. In this case, the base is on the top of the stack (and was the last of the operands, remember). To define Base, you push the name literal /Base onto the stack, and then you exchange the literal and the desired number and execute the **def** operator. The exchange is necessary because **def** requires the value to be defined on top of the stack and the name literal to be associated with that value next. You will see this technique used often in PostScript procedures.

Base and Hgt are each defined in the same manner, removing the value from the stack as they are defined. Once the variables are safely stored, you can begin to draw the lines. Line %2.4 draws the first line from the current point to the point defined by base, height. Now you want to move straight down to the corner of the triangle to form the right angle. To do this, however, you must move in a negative direction on the y-axis. The natural thought would be sim-ply to put a minus sign in front of Hgt, but that won't work. Hgt is a name in the dictionary that represents a number; it is not a number itself. It becomes a num-ber again as soon as it is retrieved from the dictionary; therefore, you must retrieve it (by using its name), store it on the stack, and then negate the number on the stack by means of the **neg** operator. That's what was done in line %2.5. Then **closepath** finishes the figure.

The isosceles triangle is constructed in much the same way. The only difference is that, in this case, you need to calculate the displacement for the top of the triangle, since the second side does not equal the height and the third side does not equal the base as in the right triangle. This calculation is performed in line %3.4, which divides the base value in half. Since the two sides of an isosceles triangle are equal, the top point must have an x-displacement that is one-half the base. This value is calculated as the variable Halfbase in line %3.4, and it is used as the x-displacement in the remainder of the procedure, which is straightforward.

Now that the procedures are finished, the prolog is complete and the script portion of the program can begin. As you were promised, the script is relatively short and repetitive. Line %4 clears any path debris, and line %5 moves to the bottom-left corner of the first triangle. The **rightTriangle** procedure is then called with operands of the height of 1.5 inches and a base of 1 inch.

The resulting figure is not stroked, however. This time, you use the **fill** operator to fill the figure completely with black. If you had wanted another line figure, you could have used **stroke** instead; nothing in the procedure constrains you. This is a positive feature of the PostScript concept of creating a current path and then filling it using whatever painting operator you wish.

Next you move the current point to the left corner of the second triangle and repeat the process, using the isoTriangle procedure and the height and base of 1.5 inches and 1.2 inches, respectively. After filling in the triangle, the resulting page is printed.

There is no **quit** operator at the end of the above example because you may want to continue these short exercises. For this reason, we will not repeat the inch, rightTriangle, or isoTriangle procedure. Let us assume that you are continuing directly on to the next example. (If you don't, just reenter those procedures from the previous example.)

This example will define a squareBox procedure, to complement the previous triangle procedures. This box will be used in conjunction with the triangles to illustrate the use of shades of gray in filling a figure—all the way up to white. It will also demonstrate what happens when one figure overlays another.

Let us begin by drawing two square boxes and an overlapping isosceles triangle, as laid out in Figure 3.15. You will notice several things about this figure. First, it gives all the essential dimensions for the program. Second, it assumes that you will define the squareBox procedure to take a size parameter as an operand from the stack. The figure shows the starting point of each of the figures; (2,5) for the first box, (2.5, 5) for the triangle, and (4,5) for the second box. Both boxes have 1-inch sides, and the triangle is 2 inches along the base and 2 inches high. Each of the figures is filled with gray; dark gray for the first box, medium gray for the triangle, and light gray for the last box. The figures will be produced in order, left to right: box, triangle, and box.

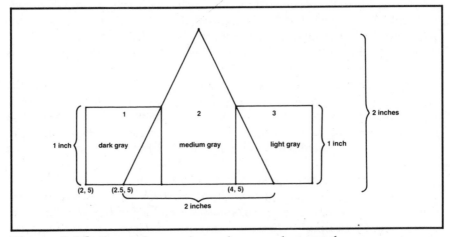

Figure 3.15: Layout for overlap and gray-scale example

You will adjust the gray value that fills in each figure by means of a new operator, **setgray**. This operator takes an operand between 0 and 1, with 0 being *black* and 1 being *white*. Any number outside the range 0 to 1 is an error. For this example, you will use 0.25, 0.5, and 0.75 to set the gray level for each figure.

The use of 0 for black and 1 for white may seem confusing. The analogy is to light rather than to ink on a page. With light, 0 represents no light, or black, and 1 represents full light, or white. Thinking of 0 and 1 as light may help you remember the two values.

The example code is given in Figure 3.16. It generates the output in Figure 3.17. You will notice that each of the figures completely overlays the preceding one, even though the preceding figure is darker. This would remain true no matter what colors were used. The effect is that of opaque paint or of a solid piece of paper. There is no mixing or bleeding of colors in the electronic world, nor are the colors transparent.

```
%Begin overlap and gray scale example
%-----------------------Additional Procedure---------------
/squareBox
      (      /Dim exch def
             0 Dim rlineto
             Dim 0 rlineto
             0 Dim neg rlineto
             closepath )
      def
%----------------------Program----------------------------
newpath
%Do first box
2 inch 5 inch moveto
1 inch squareBox
.25 setgray
fill
%Do triangle
2.5 inch 5 inch moveto
2 inch 2 inch isoTriangle
.5 setgray
fill
%Do last box
4 inch 5 inch moveto
1 inch squareBox
.75 setgray
fill
%Now show the results
showpage
```

Figure 3.16: Examples of overlapping figures and gray scale

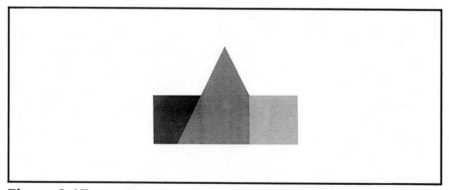

Figure 3.17: Overlap and gray-scale output

This effect can be handy, and we will end this section with one last example to illustrate this point graphically. In this example, you will generate a square box and fill it with black. Then you will generate a right triangle at the same origin and color it white. The dimensions, coordinates, and design of the output are given in Figure 3.18. I will assume again that you are continuing from the preceding exercise, and will not include the procedures. With that caution, the program is shown in Figure 3.19. It provides the interesting output shown in Figure 3.20.

This output should reinforce the previous discussion; you see how the white triangle has overlaid the black square to give the effect of a single, reversed black triangle. This overlay process can be used to good effect, as you will see in an exercise later in this chapter.

We will end this section with a recap in the standard format of the two new operators.

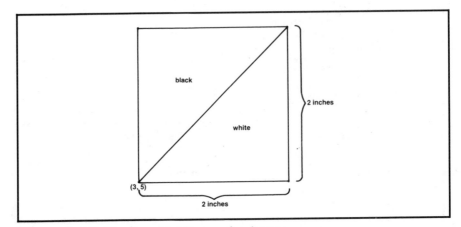

Figure 3.18: Black-and-white overlap layout

```
%Do box and triangle
newpath
%First do box in black
3 inch 5 inch moveto
2 inch squareBox
0 setgray
fill
%Then do triangle at same origin in white
3 inch 5 inch moveto
2 inch 2 inch rightTriangle
1 setgray
fill
showpage
```

Figure 3.19: Black-and-white overlap example

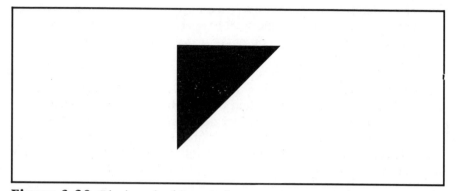

Figure 3.20: Black-and-white overlap output

SYNTAX	FUNCTION
num **setgray** —	sets the current color to a shade of gray corresponding to *num*. *num* must be between 0, corresponding with black, and 1, corresponding with white, with intermediate values corresponding to intermediate shades of gray.
— **fill** —	paints the area enclosed by the current path with the current color; clears the path.

FONTS

You have already been informally introduced to fonts in the exercises and examples in Chapters 1 and 2. Up to this point, you have been given font commands for the exercises without much explanation, since you were concentrating on character placement, string handling, and similar basic operations. You also needed some basic graphics concepts and operations before beginning serious work with PostScript fonts. Now you are ready to proceed to a broader discussion of fonts, their management, and their use in PostScript.

This approach has meant that we have skipped over, but not ignored, PostScript font operations. You probably feel comfortable with the font operators you have worked with so far, and you may have an intuitive feeling for how they operate. PostScript font operators offer a natural approach to font access and use, and you have probably not found this informal approach either difficult or disconcerting.

However, you will want to make more extensive use of fonts as the exercises become more complex, and you will need to understand more about the choices and operations that are available when working with PostScript fonts. In this section, you will begin to explore these issues. This does not require introducing any new PostScript operators. Instead, it requires a fuller discussion of fonts generally and a more detailed and systematic look at PostScript font operations specifically.

FONT DEFINITION

A *font* is defined as a set of type—meaning a complete collection of characters and punctuation—in one style and size. Perhaps a font can be most easily understood if you think of it as being like the type-ball in an IBM Selectric typewriter, which gives a specific form and size to each letter or character that you type. For example, most people are familiar with the Courier type style, which is a standard office typewriter font. Just as a typewriter can't type without a type-ball or element, the PostScript interpreter can't create letter images without an active font.

This section and the next discuss general font issues. Many of these topics apply to all fonts in any environment; some apply only to raster output devices; none, however, are limited to PostScript alone. Later we will discuss font issues that specifically relate to PostScript fonts and font operators.

Type as a Graphic Element

Before we examine all the technical aspects of fonts, let's discuss type as a graphic object. The form of letters is one of the most ancient of graphic elements. As soon as humans began to write, they began to think about and modify the shapes that they used to convey language. Indeed, many languages, ranging from ancient Egyptian to modern Chinese, use stylized pictures to represent words and concepts. The design of modern print typefaces grew out of the formal writing of medieval Europe, when printers tried to imitate calligraphy. Each letter in a good typeface is a small work of art; each is an object of intricate graphic design.

Aesthetics and utility are merged in perfect harmony in the best type designs. The beauty of a typeface is directly related to how well it performs its utilitarian functions of clarity, emphasis, and legibility. Each style of type is designed to enhance these qualities in various settings. Each style fulfills these functions in a way that is complementary to specific page environments or design requirements.

Fonts for Raster Output

Typefaces were originally designed for printing applications, and as we observed earlier, type in such applications consists of solid and continuous lines of ink. The task, then, is to translate these beautiful and essential objects from continuous lines into dots for display on a raster output device. This task is neither easy nor trivial, particularly for devices with low or medium resolution.

The essential problem is to carry over all the fine nuances of the typeface design into the series of dots that form an image on the raster output device. The process of converting the outline of the character on a font into pixels is a special case of the process known as *scan conversion*. In many cases, fonts are further enhanced when human judgement is applied to adjusting the pixels to create the most harmonious and attractive characters at a given font size. This process is known as *font tuning*. Obviously, the rendering of a typeface by conversion to pixels is going to be noticeable at very small type-sizes, where the features of individual letters may be only a few pixels. In this case, the characters may appear ragged or uneven; in extreme cases of small type on low-resolution devices, certain characters may become indistinguishable.

USING FONTS

Fonts are changed within a document for many reasons. Sometimes it may be only for fun, to show off the variety of fonts available with a laser printer. Usually, however, there is a more serious reason. In some cases—for example, in insurance policies—there is a legal requirement regarding the text. Sometimes font changes are necessary to make a point stand out or to differentiate certain portions of the text, such as instructions from data on a form or headings from body text. In any case, the requirements for fonts generally fall into one or another or a combination of three categories.

First, fonts are used for legibility. This is probably the most obvious, but also the most overlooked requirement. The object of printing anything is to have it read with a minimum of strain and a maximum of ease. Many fonts were designed specifically for clarity and readability, particularly where space is limited. The use of a crisp, clear font helps pack the maximum amount of information into a small space while retaining reading ease. Thus, readability is the first thing to think about when evaluating fonts.

Fonts are also used to emphasize a point or to make a statement. Sometimes this objective clashes with the issue of legibility, as in some of the fonts that imitate handwritten script of Gothic lettering. Generally, however, emphasis is provided by the use of either bold or italic fonts, or by increasing the size of the font used, or sometimes both. This use is especially important to divide one type of information from another on a page; for example, instructions on a form are often printed in italic type to make them stand out from the information requested.

Finally, fonts are used to enhance the quality of the finished output. A typeset page certainly has more impact, and possibly more credibility, than one that is typewritten. Typeset-quality fonts provide immediate letter recognition to the eye. This clarity of shape is an essential element of a fine font.

Overall, the selection of a correct font for a given task is an important part of creating an acceptable page. The font or fonts selected will help you make a clear, readable document. You can use them to emphasize specific items or to distinguish certain portions of the page from others, and they will provide you with output that can be immediately and easily understood by you and your readers.

Font Families and Font Names

There are a variety of ways to group fonts. The simplest and most obvious is by design, or *typeface*. Most typefaces have names, which represent the complete range of fonts with a common design but in different sizes and styles. Such a set of fonts is called a *font family*. Remember that a font, properly speaking, is only one size in a particular style of typeface design. You may have noticed that I have been using the term ''font'' for what we have now defined as a font family; for convenience, I will continue to use ''font'' in this way whenever there will be no confusion.

These font families can be classified into three categories by distinct design elements. The first category comprises the *serif* fonts. Serif fonts have smaller lines that finish off the major strokes of each letter, similar to the effect of a chisel on stone or of a calligraphic pen on paper. The Times font family, which you have been using for text output so far, is a serif font family. The second category is called *sans-serif*. As you might guess, these fonts are distinguished by the absence of the serif lines. The Helvetica font family is a sans-serif font family. Generally, serif fonts look more traditional, while sans-serif fonts have a more modern appearance. Finally, some fonts don't fall easily into either of these two groups; one such font is Courier, which, as we discussed before, is primarily used for typewritten output. Fonts such as Courier are *typewriter* fonts.

Font Sizes

Fonts vary in size within a family as well as in design between families. Every character in a font has a height and a width. The width of a character within a font is called the *pitch*. All characters in a typewriter font have a single width. Such fonts are called *fixed pitch* or *monospaced* fonts. Characters in most fonts, however, have different widths depending on the shape of the individual character; these are called *variable pitch* or *proportional* fonts. Thus, in a typewriter font like Courier, the letter *i* takes up as much space as the letter *w*, just as it would on your typewriter, while in a proportional font like Helvetica, the *w* will be much wider than the *i*.

To say that the width of characters in a font is proportional is not to say that there is a fixed mathematical relationship between them. Typefaces are designed so that all their characters will fit together aesthetically, and proportions that seem to be mathematically correct may look ungainly when the letters are put together on the page. Arriving at "optically correct" proportions is a long process of trial and error, and one of the advantages of using traditional typefaces is that you have the benefit of many people's experience.

Font height is generally given in points, just like the spacing on the page. The most usual size for reading type is 10-point. Smaller point sizes indicate smaller type, with 4 to 6 points being about the smallest type that most of us can read. You remember that there are 72 points on an inch, so that 36-point type, for example, is $\frac{1}{2}$-inch from the top of the ascender of any character on that font to the bottom of the descender (for example, from the top of the letter *k* to the bottom of the *p*, with capital letters and *x*-height letters appearing smaller). Type size is often varied for much the same reasons that type styles are varied: to achieve an effect or to mark off special sections of text, and so forth, as required.

Font Access

All fonts must be made available to the interpreter before they can be used by PostScript operators. To begin with, every PostScript output device has some fonts that come with it, or are *built-in*. At a minimum, all PostScript-equipped devices have the Times family, the Helvetica family, and the Courier family. Some PostScript devices have more than these three families, but all have at least these three. All the fonts that you will use in this book are from this minimum set of built-in fonts.

Apart from the fonts that always reside in your printer, there are two methods of making fonts available. One method is by sending a copy of the font from your IBM-PC or Mac to the printer to be stored in the printer . This process is called *downloading*. The other method is to create a new font using PostScript code; it will be covered, along with some other complex font procedures, in Chapter 4.

Each copy of a font requires memory within the printer controller, and each make and model of printer can hold a different number of fonts in its memory. Sometimes there is a trade-off between the number and size of the fonts and the size and complexity of the pages that can be handled by the printer. We will examine some techniques to deal with such trade-offs in Chapter 6, which covers advanced text handling.

Font Sources and Ownership

If you are not familiar with the world of printing and typesetting, it may surprise you to find out that not all fonts are public property: the designs are licensed to companies that want to incorporate the fonts into various devices. Adobe Systems, the developer of PostScript, has licensed a wide variety of classic fonts for use with PostScript; for example, Times-Roman and Helvetica are licensed fonts.

POSTSCRIPT FONTS

PostScript treats text characters as general graphic objects subject to appropriate operators just like any other graphic; a box or a triangle is conceptually no different to the interpreter than a *g* or an *R*, and vice versa. Because PostScript makes no distinction between text and other graphics, it has no problem combining text and graphics on a page. In a real sense, all pages are graphic images to the PostScript interpreter. You could actually draw every character of a font on a page using PostScript operators, but that would be tedious and difficult. Instead, PostScript provides a variety of high-level operators to handle text conveniently and efficiently.

PostScript describes fonts though the use of a *font dictionary*. Each font dictionary is referenced by a PostScript name literal and provides information and procedures for building all the characters in that font. You have already seen the PostScript font mechanism at work in the exercises. The name of a PostScript font is used as a key into a special dictionary that returns the associated value, which is a font dictionary. This font dictionary is then used by the PostScript interpreter to define the process for rendering characters on a string onto the current page. The interpreter uses each character as an index to select the correct definition process.

There are two important points to remember here. First, PostScript actually does draw each character, using appropriate graphics operations; and second, the PostScript interpreter creates characters through the use of a font dictionary that contains all the information required to produce a given font, including the appropriate procedures for rendering each character.

Types of Fonts

Most PostScript fonts contain characters that are defined as outlines in the font dictionary and are then processed by the interpreter and filled in to make the character. By using this process to create characters, PostScript can render all sizes of text with a minimum of distortion and can perform many other graphics operations on the characters or using the characters. Both Times and Helvetica are defined as outline fonts.

A few PostScript fonts contain characters that are defined as lines to be stroked rather than outlines to be filled. Courier is such a font.

It is also possible to create PostScript fonts directly, as images that are rendered by the interpreter as a series of pixels. Such fonts are called *bit-mapped* fonts. PostScript has no built-in fonts of this type, but it is possible for a PostScript user to create and work with these fonts. We will discuss all these issues—graphics operations with fonts, changing fonts, and creation of new fonts—in Chapter 4.

Because the characters in PostScript fonts can be stroked or filled as required, they can also be modified by means of the **setgray** operator to show on the page in the usual range of black to white, depending on the **setgray** operand. This provides an easy and effective way to show white lettering against a dark or patterned background, for example.

Font Metrics

Earlier we discussed how all characters have height and width. In PostScript fonts, each character's width is given as an (x,y) displacement. This pair of numbers makes up the value that represents the distance from the beginning of the present character to the point where the next character can begin; essentially these are the coordinates for a relative move command. Most Indo-European alphabets have a positive x-component and a zero y-component for this value; other alphabets may differ, having negative x-components or non-zero y-components. The values returned by the **stringwidth** operator are the sum of these (x,y) coordinates for all the characters on the string under evaluation.

Characters in PostScript fonts also have height. A font specifies the shape of the characters on one standard height. This size is defined as the minimum vertical separation necessary to ensure that two successive lines of text do not interfere with one another; that is, that the top of an *f* in one line doesn't run over the bottom of a *g* on the line above it. All PostScript fonts are set up so that this height is 1 unit. In the default coordinate system that you have been using, that would be 1-point high.

Such type would be too small to read, and it also would be difficult to convert into dots. In order to get the type size you want on the output page, you must expand the type to the correct size in both the *x* and *y* dimensions. This process is called *scaling* the font.

Font Manipulation

Now you have covered all the basic considerations in dealing with PostScript fonts. In order to use PostScript font, the following steps are required.

1. The font name must be looked up to retrieve the font dictionary.

2. The characters in the font must be scaled to the correct size for output.

3. The scaled font must be identified to the interpreter as the font to be used for text output.

Each of these tasks has its own operator, and each operator performs its job in such a way as to leave the information for the next task's operator on the stack. In this way, the operators can be invoked naturally in the sequence above.

This is what you've been doing in the earlier exercises. The first operator, **findfont**, identifies the font dictionary by its special name, taking a name literal as an operand, looks it up in the special dictionary, and returns the associated font dictionary onto the stack. If you give it a name it doesn't find, it will return an error; on the Apple LaserWriter, it issues the error message and uses a default font dictionary(Courier). The **scalefont** operator performs the second task. This operator requires two operands: a number that represents the scaling factor and a font dictionary that is to be scaled. You provide the scale number, and the font dictionary is usually on the stack already as a result of a previous **findfont**. The operator returns a properly scaled font dictionary to the stack, where it is used as an operand by the next operator on the series, **setfont**. This operator, as its name suggests, makes a font dictionary on the stack into the *current font*. This is the name for the dictionary that the interpreter uses for all subsequent text output.

At this point, we have returned to our original definition of a font as a set of type in one style and one size. Now you know both how to go about setting up and using a PostScript font and how PostScript itself treats and works with fonts.

Let's recap these font operators in our standard format.

SYNTAX	FUNCTION
name **findfont** font	obtains a font dictionary specified by *name* and puts it onto the operand stack
font scale **scalefont** newfont	applies *scale* to *font* to create *newfont*, whose characters are enlarged in both the *x* and *y* directions by the given scaling factor when they are printed
font **setfont** —	establishes *font* as the font dictionary to be the current font for all subsequent character operators

COMPLEX GRAPHICS

So far in this chapter you have read about and worked with straight lines and characters from fonts as graphic objects. You have built a variety of shapes and figures, both stroked and filled, and you should be familiar and comfortable with basic PostScript operations.

With this background, you are now ready to extend your graphics vocabulary in two directions. First you will work with arcs, circular shapes, and figures composed of both curved- and straight-line segments. Second, you will become acquainted with PostScript measurement and coordinates in more detail.

This will prepare you for a final summary of PostScript graphics, which will explain the conceptual and practical framework of all PostScript graphics procedures. You will learn how to formulate, define, and use Post-Script procedures that are independent of page structure and that will not affect or be affected by other graphics operations.

CURVES

Most interesting shapes and figures are not composed of straight lines alone. Curved lines are generally an important part of dynamic and visually attractive designs. Operations to create and use curved-line segments are therefore essential in any comprehensive set of tools for rendering graphic objects.

By their nature, curved lines present more problems in a computer environment. By now you are used to PostScript's ability to describe any point on a page as a pair of numbers (x, y) that give measurements from a specific point on the page. These coordinates are called *rectangular* coordinates, because the two dimensions, measured by x and y, are at right angles to one another. Straight lines are natural on rectangular coordinates, which you have been using to move around the PostScript page. Curved lines, however, require more work to define and more information to use; unfortunately, they also require additional mathematics. We will begin with the easiest form of curved lines: circular arcs.

Circular Arcs

Even in rectangular coordinates, the mathematics necessary to describe a circle precisely are relatively simple. You needed two pieces of information, or *parameters*, to place a square box on the page, although you may not have thought of it this way. In order to use the **squareBox** procedure, you needed to set the current point to the position for the bottom-left corner of the box and you needed to give a width for the box. The circle also requires two parameters in order to be positioned on the page. These two parameters are the location of the center of the circle, and the radius of the circle which are equivalent to the corner of the box and width the box, respectively.

Circular arcs are just portions of a circle. To define a circular arc requires two additional parameters: the points that form the beginning and the end of the arc. While there are various ways to specify the endpoints of an arc, PostScript uses a simple and straightforward method, specifying the two angles that measure the beginning and ending radii of the arc, taken counterclockwise from the horizontal axis. This measurement process is illustrated in Figure 3.21.

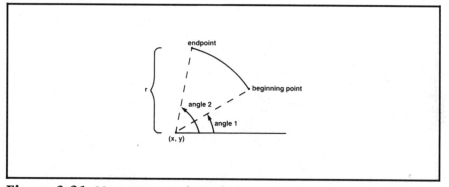

Figure 3.21: Measurement of circular arcs

In this figure, the center of the circle is at point (x, y) and the radius is r. The arc of the circle to be drawn begins at *angle1* and runs counterclockwise to end at *angle2*. These five values (two for the center point and one each for the radius and two angles) are the operands that are required for the PostScript **arc** operator.

The **arc** operator takes these five values and creates a circular line segment that begins at the point specified by *angle1* and ends at that given by *angle2*. This endpoint becomes the new current point. The **arc** operator may perform one additional step. If the current point is undefined when you call **arc**, it just draws the circular segment as described above. If, however, the current point is defined, **arc** draws a straight-line segment from the current point to the beginning point of the arc and then constructs the arc.

Let's try an example to help you practice these operations using **arc**. Like the early examples with straight lines, this won't be visually exciting, but it will illustrate the possibilities.

This example will produce a page with three arcs, one above the other and each demonstrating the use of the operator. The three figures and their relevant dimensions are shown in Figure 3.22. The solid lines on each figure will be stroked onto the output page; the dotted lines and the angular

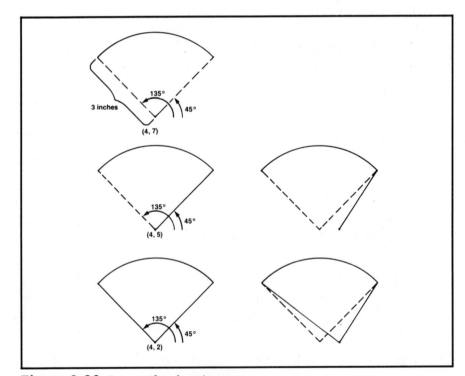

Figure 3.22: Layout for drawing arcs

measurements are inserted for reference. The example program looks like Fig ure 3.23, and the output page shown in Figure 3.24.

The program consists essentially of three **arc** operators. The first **arc**, you notice, begins right after a **newpath**, which means that the current point is undefined. The **arc** operator is invoked in line %3 with the operands that were defined before: center at (4,7), radius of 3 inches, and beginning and ending angles of 45° and 135°, respectively. This segment is then stroked. Since **stroke** performs an implicit **newpath**, there is once again no current point. Therefore, the program performs a **moveto** to the point (5,5), making it the current point. In line %6, **arc** is called again with the same operands except that the center is shifted to the point (4,5). This generates a straight line from the current point (5,5) to the beginning of the arc and then generates an arc identical to the preceding one. This path is stroked. Finally, in lines %8 and %9, the same sequence is repeated with the points (5,2) and (4,2); but the result is closed by **closepath** in line %10 before being stroked.

PostScript has a matching operator, **arcn**, which performs the same functions as **arc** and requires the same operands, except that **arcn** draws the arc clockwise. That means that, if you wanted to reproduce the first arc presented in the program using **arcn**, you would code the operator as

    4 inch 7 inch 3 inch 135 45 arcn

If you reversed the angles back to 45 135,

    4 inch 7 inch 3 inch 45 135 arcn

```
%Begin arc examples
/inch
      { 72 mul }                              %1
      def
newpath                                       %2
4 inch   7 inch   3 inch   45 135 arc         %3
stroke                                        %4
5 inch   5 inch   moveto                      %5
4 inch   5 inch   3 inch   45 135 arc         %6
stroke                                        %7
5 inch   2 inch   moveto                      %8
4 inch   2 inch   3 inch   45 135 arc         %9
closepath                                     %10
stroke
showpage
```

Figure 3.23: Example of multiple arcs

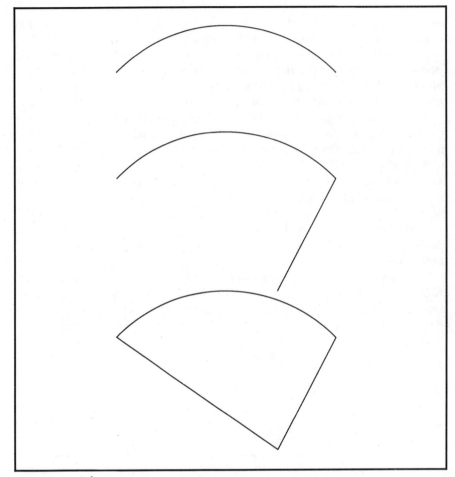

Figure 3.24: Multiple arc output

you would get an arc like one in Figure 3.25, which forms an arc from the part of the circle not painted by the first arc by moving clockwise from 45° to 135°.

Closed Curves

Now let us proceed to closed figures that combine circular arcs and straight lines. You will see that all the techniques you applied to straight-sided figures can be used with circular ones as well.

As you saw in the last example, adding straight-line segments to a circular arc is easy. Therefore, as a change of pace, the next example will draw and shade a circle. This example will draw a circle and fill it with a dark (0.25) shade of gray. Then it will move down the page and draw a square of the same dimensions and shading as the circle and place a circle, colored white, within it. The program is shown in Figure 3.26. This produces the expected output, shown in Figure 3.27.

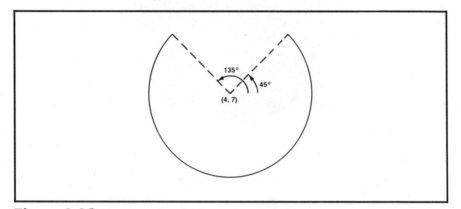

Figure 3.25: Reverse circular arc using **arcn**

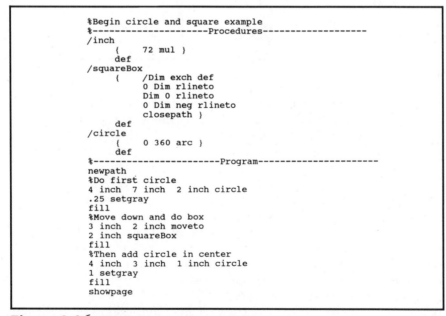

```
%Begin circle and square example
%--------------------Procedures-------------------
/inch
      (      72 mul )
      def
/squareBox
      (      /Dim exch def
             0 Dim rlineto
             Dim 0 rlineto
             0 Dim neg rlineto
             closepath )
      def
/circle
      (      0 360 arc )
      def
%--------------------Program--------------------
newpath
%Do first circle
4 inch  7 inch  2 inch circle
.25 setgray
fill
%Move down and do box
3 inch  2 inch moveto
2 inch squareBox
fill
%Then add circle in center
4 inch  3 inch  1 inch circle
1 setgray
fill
showpage
```

Figure 3.26: Circle and square example

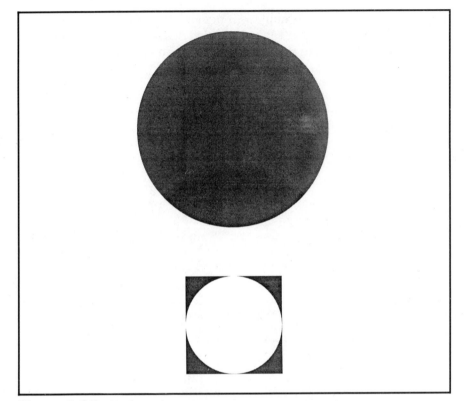

Figure 3.27: Circle and square output

This example is clear by itself, and we won't spend much time on explanations. The **inch** and **squareBox** procedures are familiar to you; the new procedure, **circle**, is just the **arc** operator, moving 0° to 360° to complete the circle. The **circle** procedure requires the other three operands to be on the stack when it executes.

The only other point that may give you pause is how to establish the coordinates for the center of the circle that is overlaid onto the square. In this case, the dimensions are shown in Figure 3.28.

The next example is a little more interesting, and it introduces you to a new operator, **arcto**. This operator draws arcs by connecting two lines, rather than using a center and a radius. In this example you will use **arcto** to draw a square with rounded corners; it looks a bit like a television screen, so we'll call the procedure **screenBox**. The example uses the procedure twice, once to draw the box and stroke it and then again to draw the box inside a square. The square is filled with gray (0.25) and the screen is filled with light gray (0.8).

Before we begin the example, let's look at the operator **arcto**, which forms the heart of the program. In order to follow this discussion, look at Figure 3.29. This operator, like **arc** and **arcn**, adds the arc of a circle to the current path, possibly including a straight line. In this case, however, the arc drawn is defined by the radius r and two tangent lines. The tangent lines are from the current point—(x_0, y_0) in the diagram—to the point (x_1, y_1) and from (x_1, y_1) to the point (x_2, y_2). Unlike the previous arc operators, **arcto** requires a current point to start from.

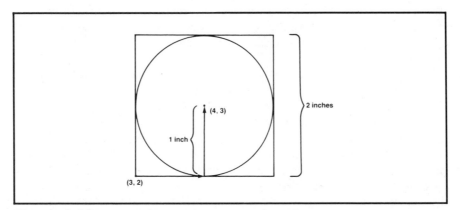

Figure 3.28: Layout for overlapping circle and square

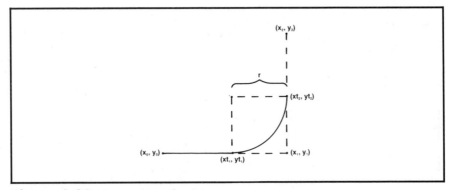

Figure 3.29: Operation of **arcto**

The center of the arc is located at the intersection of the two lines that are perpendicular to the tangent lines at the distance r. (If you remember geometry, you will remember that there is only one such point.) The center lies inside the inner angle formed by the two lines. The arc begins at the first tangent point, (xt_1, yt_1) on the first line from (x_0, y_0) to (x_1, y_1), and ends at the second tangent point, (xt_2, yt_2) on the line from (x_1, y_1) to (x_2, y_2). Before constructing the arc, **arcto** adds a straight-line segment from the current point (x_0, y_0) to the first tangent point (xt_1, yt_1), unless the two are the same point. At the completion of the operation, the point (xt_2, yt_2) becomes the current point.

Finally, the **arcto** operator, unlike other line-drawing operators, returns the coordinates of the two tangent points on the stack: xt_1, yt_1, xt_2, yt_2. I don't know what use this operation has; every program of example that I know of using **arcto** throws away this information by executing four **pop** operators to clean up the stack after the operation. The complication is annoying, but hardly onerous.

Let's design the **screenBox** procedure to see how **arcto** works in a concrete example. Suppose that you want to create a procedure that will work like **squareBox** but produce a square with rounded corners. This means that the current point will be positioned at the lower-left corner of the box when the procedure is invoked, and the desired size of the box should be on the stack. For this exercise, assume that the radius of the corners (the one additional piece of information that you will need) is fixed at 0.25 inches; in the next section you will see how to scale the corners to the size of the box.

Now look at Figure 3.30. If the current point is (x, y), then the four corners of a square with the width d will be the points (x, y), $(x + d, y)$, $(x + d, y + d)$, and

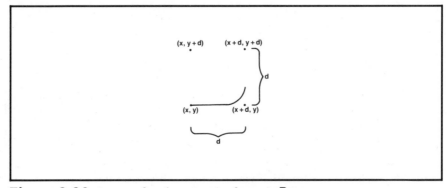

Figure 3.30: Layout for the corner of screenBox

($x, y + d$). Because you want rounded corners tangent to the lines connecting these points, they represent the operands required for the **arcto** operator.

Since you want all the corners rounded, you must save the current point and then move some distance down the first side before you start the **arcto** commands. If you didn't do this, the first **arcto** would draw a straight line beginning at the current point, which is also a corner of the box; and a small portion of the line would stick out when the corner was rounded on the finished surface. The result would have a bottom-left corner that looks like Figure 3.31.

Here is the design of the screenBox procedure:

- Save the width value (d) off the stack.

- Save the current point values.

- Move some distance in the x-direction to start the lines.

- Perform four **arcto**s using the following pairs of points:

1. ($x + d, y$), ($x + d, y + d$)
2. ($x + d, y + d$), ($x, y + d$)
3. ($x, y + d$), (x, y)
4. (x, y), ($x + d, y$)

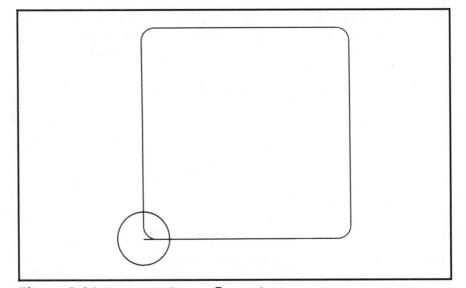

Figure 3.31: Example of screenBox without **move**

- Finish by closing the figure to ensure that the end of the last **arcto** meets the starting point.

Having outlined what the procedure should look like, you can now design the page. In this case, you have two figures to create: a simple, stroked screenBox and a filled screenBox inside a squareBox. The first of these is easily set up; you simply decide where to position the bottom-left corner of the screen, move there, and call the procedure with an appropriate width argument. In this case, the corner is placed at (3,7) and the width is set as 2 inches.

For the second figure, you can position the squareBox in the same way you did the preceding screenBox, but you will need to calculate where to position the screenBox that you want to place within it. Consider the layout in Figure 3.32, which gives all the necessary dimensions to execute the program. Note that, in choosing (3,3) as the bottom corner for the square, you will have 2 inches between the bottom of the preceding figure—at (3,7)—and the top of this box at (3,5). In addition, notice that you can center the screen inside the square by leaving 0.25 inches on each side, which makes the point (3.25,3.25) the starting point for the screen and makes the width 1.5 inches.

Having discussed **arcto**, the design of screenBox, and the precise layout of the figures, let's put all this to use. The program is given in Figure 3.33. It produces the output in Figure 3.34.

This program begins with a prolog that contains three procedures. The first and second procedures, at lines %1 and %2, are already familiar. The screenBox procedure begins at line %3. You have already analyzed the

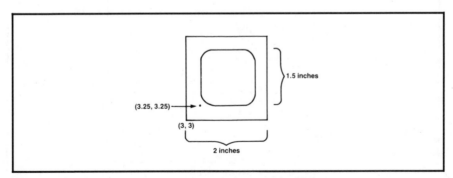

Figure 3.32: Layout for overlapping screen and box

```
%Begin rounded corner example
%--------------------Procedures-------------------
/inch                                               %1
    {    72 mul }
    def
/squareBox                                          %2
    {    /Dim exch def
         0 Dim rlineto
         Dim 0 rlineto
         0 Dim neg rlineto
         closepath }
    def
/screenBox                                          %3
    %expect stack: size                             %3.1
    {    /Dim exch def                              %3.2
         currentpoint                               %3.3
         /Ypos exch def                             %3.4
/Xpos exch def                          %3.5
         .5 inch 0 rmoveto                          %3.6
    %first side                                     %3.7
         Xpos Dim add Ypos                          %3.8
         Xpos Dim add Ypos Dim add                  %3.9
         .25 inch arcto                             %3.10
         4 {pop} repeat                             %3.11
    %second side                                    %3.12
         Xpos Dim add  Ypos Dim add
         Xpos Ypos Dim add
         .25 inch arcto
         4 {pop} repeat
    %third side                                     %3.13
         Xpos Ypos Dim add
         Xpos Ypos
         .25 inch arcto
         4 {pop} repeat
    %last side and corner                           %3.14
         Xpos Ypos
         Xpos Dim add  Ypos
         .25 inch arcto
         4 {pop} repeat
    %and close up the figure
         closepath }                                %3.15
    def
%------------------------Program------------------------
newpath                                             %4
3 inch  7 inch moveto                               %5
2 inch screenBox                                    %6
stroke                                              %7
3 inch  3 inch moveto                               %8
2 inch squareBox                                    %9
.25 setgray                                         %10
fill                                                %11
3.25 inch  3.25 inch moveto                         %12
1.5 inch screenBox                                  %13
.8 setgray                                          %14
fill                                                %15
showpage                                            %16
```

Figure 3.33: Example of screen and box

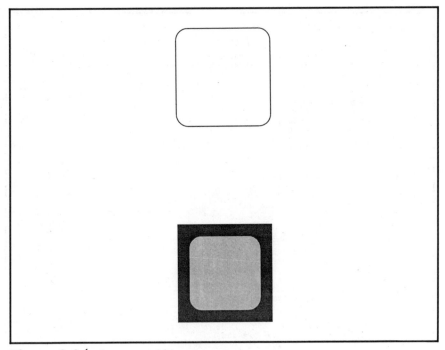

Figure 3.34: Screen and box output

requirements for this procedure above; the only points to be discussed here are how to implement the design requirements.

Line %3.2 takes the width operand off the stack and saves it as the variable Dim. This is exactly like squareBox. Line %3.3 introduces a new operator, **currentpoint**, which does what you might expect and pushes the x and y values of the current point onto the stack. Remember from the design of screenBox that you need to save the current point to calculate the points for the four **arcto** operators. This takes place in lines %3.4 and %3.5, where the current values of x and y are stored as Xpos and Ypos. Next you have to move away from the corner, as described in the design. This is done in line %3.6 by an **rmoveto**, moving 0.5 inches along the x-axis. You could move any distance greater than 0.25 inches, but you must move at least the radius of the arc (in this case 0.25 inches) to be sure that you won't have a bit of line sticking out. If you look back at Figure 3.32, you will see how that works.

Line %3.7 begins the first side of the screen. Line %3.8 calculates the first point $(x + d, y)$ using Xpos, Dim, and Ypos. Line %3.9 calculates the second point for the first side, $(x + d, y + d)$. Then line %3.10 sets the radius of the arc at 0.25 inches and calls **arcto**. Finally, line 3.11 executes **pop** four times to throw away the extraneous coordinates that **arcto** leaves on the stack.

The remaining three sides of the figure are done in the same manner, each pair of points being calculated according to the setup design. The resulting figure is finished in line %3.15 by a **closepath** to fill in the small segment of line that would otherwise remain between the end of the fourth **arcto** and the point where the figure started.

The script portion is, as always, simple and easy to follow; all the hard work has been done in the prolog. Line %4 clears any path debris so that you start with an empty page. Lines %5 and %6 create the first figure, an outlined screen, with the dimensions laid out earlier. Lines %8 to %11 create the desired square and fill it with 0.25 gray. Line %12 moves the desired distance into the square to set up for the screen. Lines %13 to %15 create the screen figure and fill it with a light (0.8) gray. Finally on line %16 the entire page is output.

This example shows more complex procedures than the earlier ones. With the screenBox procedure, you are getting near to what you want graphics procedures to look like. However, before you can go on to completely independent graphics, there are two issues that still must be covered: measurement and its relation to coordinates, and PostScript graphics machinery. These are the subjects of the next two sections.

Before proceeding to those topics, however, here are the three new operators for drawing circular arcs.

x y r ang1 ang2 **arc** —

Adds a counterclockwise arc of a circle to the current path, possibly preceded by a straight-line segment. The arc has radius r and the point (x, y) as a center. ang1 is the angle of a line from (x, y) with length r to the beginning of the arc, and *ang2* is the angle of a vector from (x, y) with length r to the end of the arc. If the current point is defined, the **arc** operator will construct a line from the current point to the beginning of the arc.

x y r ang1 ang2 **arcn** —

Performs the same function as **arc**, except in a clockwise direction.

x1 y1 x2 y2 r **arcto** xt1 yt1 xt2 yt2

Creates a circular arc of radius *r*, tangent to the two lines defined from the current point to *(x1,y1)* and from *(x1,y1)* to *(x2,y2)*. Returns the values of the coordinates of the two tangent points *(xt1,yt1)* and *(xt2,yt2)*. The **arcto** operator also adds a straight-line segment to the current point, if the current point is not the same as the starting point of the arc.

MEASUREMENT AND COORDINATES

PostScript provides a number of facilities to control and adjust coordinates. These operators make PostScript coordinate systems both flexible and independent. The flexibility allows, for example, coordinates to be different parts of the same page; and PostScript coordinates, which are independent of the device, can also become largely independent of the nominal page coordinates. This flexibility and independence come about because PostScript maintains a coordinate system, the user space, which is separate from the coordinates used by the specific output device, called the device space.

You will remember that we defined and discussed the default user space in Chapter 1. This is the coordinate system that you have been working in for all of the procedures and programs until now. This is the entire set of coordinate parameters—(0,0) origin at the bottom-left corner of the page and the *x* and *y* dimensions of 1/72 inch—that you are familiar with. This system is satisfactory for most of your PostScript coding, and you will continue to use it to the end of the book. It is not, however, the necessary or only coordinate system for PostScript. It is simply the *default* system: what you get when you start a fresh page.

Device Space

Let me emphasize again that this coordinate framework (the user space) bears no intrinsic relationship to the physical output device (the device space). As discussed earlier, raster output devices vary greatly in their individual ability to resolve images. At current technological levels, for example, a typical laser printer has a resolution of 300 dpi both vertically and horizontally. Moreover, each output device has an individual addressing system to identify points on the output page. The specific addressing mechanism for the device is what forms the basis for the device space.

Individual devices use a wide range of methods to address points on their output area. Devices vary in a number of ways: paper path, resolution, scanning direction, and so on. Each of these variables may influence the coordinate system native to the device. Some devices, such as terminals, even have differing resolutions in the vertical and horizontal directions. All of these limitations must be avoided to obtain device independence. For those circumstances in which it is essential to know specific information about the output device, PostScript provides operators that can access this information.

User Space

We have defined the user space as the coordinate system that programs use to specify points on the current page. We also have discussed a default set of values that allow a program to work on the page. These default values offer both simplicity and convenience, and thus represent an excellent starting point. They are, nevertheless, completely arbitrary and can be changed at will. Both unit size and orientation are not constrained in any way. Specifically, they are not tied to the resolution or coordinate system of the output device; generally, they are not fixed to any particular page structure.

This admittedly arbitrary set of default coordinates does provide the PostScript program with a consistent place to start page construction. As the process of page composition continues, the PostScript program may need to modify the user space to accommodate specific requirements. This is done by means of coordinate transformation operators, powerful operators that provide much procedural flexibility. At this point, keep in mind that the coordinates in the user space are not rigid, like a sheet of graph paper. Instead, the coordinates are on a kind of rubberized sheet that can be shrunk, expanded, or twisted as necessary.

Thus, there are two key points to remember about coordinates in user space:

- They are independent of the output device.

- They can be transformed into any orientation on the current page.

Transformation of Coordinates

This ability to transform coordinates in user space into any form that you want is a direct outgrowth of the need to transform user coordinates into device coordinates. This process is performed by the *current transformation matrix* (CTM). A transformation matrix is a mathematical device that changes one set of (x,y) coordinates into another set in a uniform way. You don't have to be concerned here with how this works; you should just understand that it is happening.

Since the PostScript interpreter needs to make this transformation from user space to device space in any case, it turns out that adding an additional transformation, or even several transformations, is easy. This means that you can map an infinite variety of changes onto the default user space.

PostScript provides operators that will perform the most common transformations in a natural way. There are three coordinate changes that are most often needed and used, and each of these transformations has a special PostScript operator. They are the following:

OPERATOR	FUNCTION
— translate —	moves the user-space origin (0,0) to a new position with respect to the current page, while leaving the orientation of the axes and the unit length along each axis unchanged.
— rotate —	turns the user-space axes about the current origin by a particular angle, leaving the origin and the unit length along each axis unchanged.
— scale —	modifies the unit lengths independently along the current x and y axes, leaving the origin and the orientation of the axes unchanged.

These powerful modifications can be performed individually or in sequence to provide a wide variety of effects on the coordinate system. Let's look at some of the previous examples, using these operators to demonstrate what they can do and how they might be used in a program environment.

Translation

Translation is simply moving the coordinates around on the page. An example might look like Figure 3.35. In this case, the coordinates are translated to (7,5). After the translation, the same code that produced the square at (2,1) would produce a square at (2,1) in the new coordinates, which would be (9,6) in the old coordinates. Both the old and new coordinates and the two boxes are shown in Figure 3.35.

This translation process wouldn't be of much use for drawing boxes. After all, the squareBox procedure works from the current point, which can be set by a simple **moveto**. A translation would take as much coding and work as a move, perhaps more. Nevertheless, while this observation is correct for the square, let's consider the effect of using a translation with screenBox. You remember that you had to save the current point during this procedure, and you used the x and y values in a number of calculations to create the screen. Look at how the use of translation simplifies this procedure is Figure 3.36.

Note that all the labor and confusion of getting and saving the current point and adding up the various corners is now gone. This screen starts at

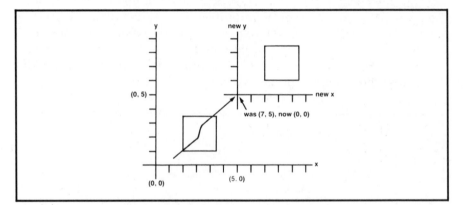

Figure 3.35: Example of translation

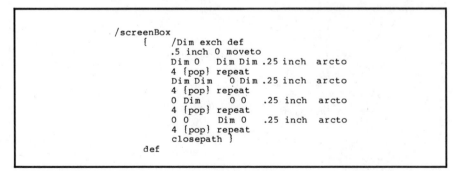

Figure 3.36: Revised screenBox procedure

the point (0,0) and therefore has corners at the points—for **arcto** purposes—of (0,0), (d,0), (d,d), and (0,d). Note also that the **rmoveto** is now changed to a straight **moveto**, since you begin the procedure at (0,0). Of course, this series of instructions will only execute correctly if the bottom-left corner of the screen is point (0,0); otherwise, it will produce strange results or fail entirely.

Translation will take care of that problem, however. Look at the example in Figure 3.37, which produces the page of output shown in Figure 3.38. There are two points to note about this example. The first one is the use of the **translate** operator. As you see, this operator takes two operands: the *x* and *y* coordinates of the point on the current page where you want the new origin. In this example, the screen has been moved around the page without any concern for the location of the current point. For the screen-Box procedure, the current point is always the origin (0,0). The second point to note is that the **translate** procedures are cumulative; that is, each one is a movement relative to the current origin, not the original origin, as would be the case with **moveto**. Once you understand the operation of the **translate**, the rest of the program is easy for you to read.

```
%Begin translation example
%-------------------------Procedures----------------------
/inch
        {       72 mul }
        def
/screenBox
        {       /Dim exch def
                .5 inch 0 moveto
                Dim 0    Dim Dim .25 inch   arcto
                4 {pop} repeat
                Dim Dim   0 Dim .25 inch   arcto
                4 {pop} repeat
                0 Dim      0 0    .25 inch   arcto
                4 {pop} repeat
                0 0        Dim 0   .25 inch   arcto
                4 {pop} repeat
                closepath }
        def
%-------------------------Program----------------------
newpath
.25 setgray
1 inch  1 inch translate
1.5 inch screenBox
fill
2 inch  2 inch translate
1.5 inch screenBox
fill
2 inch  2 inch translate
1.5 inch screenBox
stroke
showpage
```

Figure 3.37: Example of translated figures

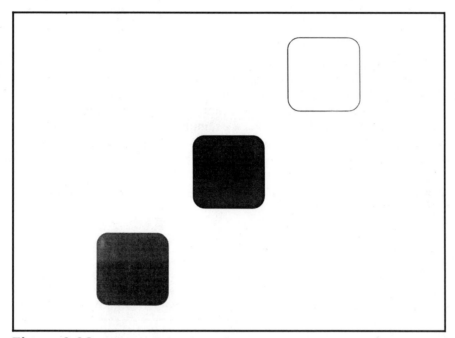

Figure 3.38: Output of translated figures

The point that may raise a question is the first translation of (0,0) to (1,1). This was necessary because point (0,0) in the device space on the LaserWriter is not within the imageable area of the printer; that is, a spot at (0,0), while it's correct, won't print. The *imageable area* of a device is the actual area that is visible for reproduction. The imageable area of a default, letter-size page on the Apple Laser Writer is 7.68 by 10.16 inches, centered on an 8.5 by 11.0-inch sheet; that is, there are left and right margins of 0.41 inches and top and bottom margins of 0.42 inches. Anything you attempt to print outside these boundaries will not be printed on this device, although the coordinates are valid and may produce output on another PostScript device.

Rotation

Rotation is much like translation, except that it turns the coordinates around the current origin rather than moving them laterally. This is illustrated in Figure 3.39. Rotation can be used independently or combined with other operators like translation. Consider the example in Figure 3.40. This produces the output in Figure 3.41. This program example was given to you without the usual preliminaries; if you are unclear about how anything in the example works, go back for a moment and reread it.

You will notice that this example has been treated, like some of the previous examples, as a continuation of other work. It assumes that the procedures, which are quite familiar to you, have already been defined; there are no changes in the procedures for this example.

As with most recent examples, the example begins with a **newpath** in line % 1 to give the current path a fresh start. Line % 2 translates the origin to

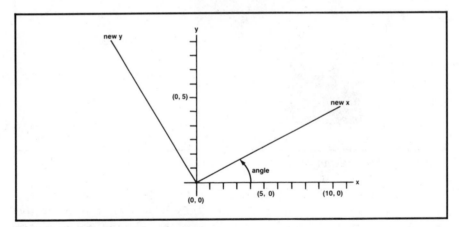

Figure 3.39: Example of rotation

```
%Begin rotation example
newpath                              %1
1 inch  1 inch translate             %2
30 rotate                            %3
1.5 inch screenBox                   %4
stroke                               %5
4 inch  2 inch translate             %6
1.5 inch screenBox                   %7
stroke                               %8
2 inch  2 inch moveto                %9
15 rotate                            %10
2 inch squareBox                     %11
stroke                               %12
showpage                             %13
```

Figure 3.40: Example of rotated figures

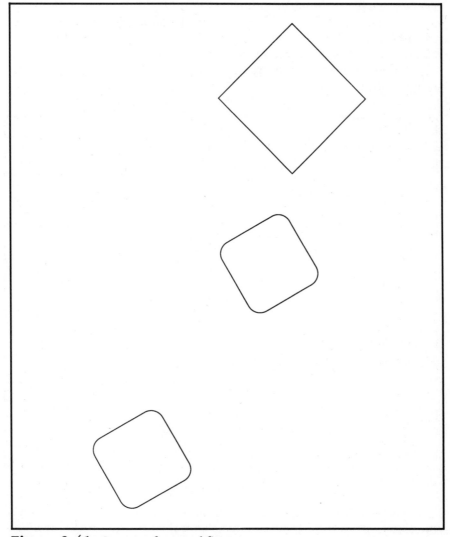

Figure 3.41: Output of rotated figures

(1,1) in current coordinates, while line %3 rotates the coordinates 30°
counterclockwise. Then lines %4 and %5 create the screen figure and
stroke it. Line %6 moves the coordinates again, this time to point (4,2) in
current coordinates. Remember that this movement is cumulative and relative to the current (not the original) coordinates; as a result, the new origin

has been moved to a point at an angle to the original coordinate system. You may have noticed that the second screen figure is not where you would have thought it would be. It is further away on the y-axis than on the x-axis, although the translate moved further on the x- than on the y-axis. This happens because the coordinates are tilted. Figure 3.42 gives you a graphic picture of what has happened.

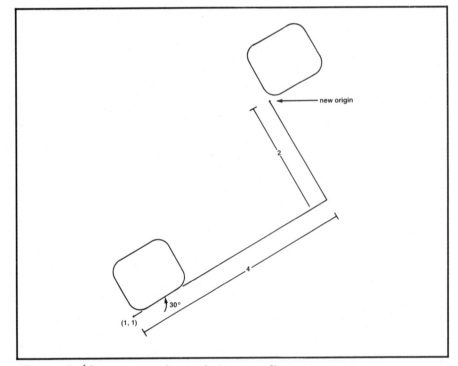

Figure 3.42: Diagram of cumulative coordinate movement

Lines %7 and %8 stroke another screen figure. Then line %9 moves the current point to (2,2) in the current coordinates. The axes are rotated a further 15°, making a tilt of 45° in all. The program draws and strokes a 2-inch square in lines %11 and %12, and the page output in line %13 finishes the example.

This program illustrates again the cumulative effect on the coordinate transformation operators. It also demonstrates that these operators can be used together, as in lines %2 and %3, for example, or they can be used separately, as in line %11.

Scaling

The last transformation operator that you are going to work with here is the **scale** operator. This operator changes the size of the x and y dimensions of the user space; that is, by means of the **scale** operator, you could make 1 inch (in our default coordinates) into ½ or 2 or 12 (or whatever) inches. More important, you could eliminate the inch procedure entirely.

Look at the example in Figure 3.43. This program produces the output shown in Figure 3.44. This program is interesting for what it *doesn't* have; namely, it doesn't have any references to inch except in the **scale** operator. These references have been retained for convenience and clarity; but they too could have been eliminated be replacing 1 inch with 72, and so on, using the actual scale in the default coordinates. If you had done that, there would be no reference, and hence no need, for inch at all.

```
%Begin scaling example
newpath                             %1
1 inch  1 inch scale                %2
2 2 moveto                          %3
2 squareBox                         %4
fill                                %5
4 6 moveto                          %6
.5  2 scale                         %7
2 squareBox                         %8
.25 setgray                         %9
fill                                %10
showpage                            %11
```

Figure 3.43: Example of scaled figures

Because you have scaled all the axes to units of 1 inch, all the coordinate values are automatically inches. So lines %3 and %4, for example, produce the same results as the following lines of code within the default coordinate system:

3 inch 5 inch moveto

2 inch squareBox

At line %7, the coordinates are scaled to ½ inch by 2 inches, and then the same size square coded on line %4 is drawn again on line %8. Remember that you have already scaled the coordinates to 1 inch and that all transformations are cumulative; hence, you need the simple numeric values to

Figure 3.44: Output of scaled figures

rescale the coordinates. Normally, you would have had to include the inch procedure after the numbers to rescale the coordinates.

The sides of the figure are the same size in the procedure, but as you can see, they are not the same size on the output. The result isn't even a square anymore, it's a rectangle. This results from the rescaling of the axes in a non-uniform manner. In particular, the x-axis has been shortened to ½-inch, while the y-axis has been lengthened to 2 inches. The net transformation is that one unit along the x-axis is one quarter the size of a unit along the y-axis, the ratio of ½ to 2; therefore, what was previously a 2-unit square becomes a 1-unit by 4-unit rectangle. These two figures provide an excellent example of the **scale** operator in action.

To end this section properly, let us list these three new operators in the standard notation.

SYNTAX	FUNCTION
tx ty **translate** —	moves the origin of the user space to (tx,ty) in the previous coordinate system.
angle **rotate** —	rotates the user space around the origin by *angle* degrees.
sx sy **scale** —	scales the user space by the factor *sx* in the x-dimension and by the factor *sy* in the y-dimension.

GRAPHICS PROCEDURES

You have now been introduced to a number of "current" settings. You know how to manipulate the current path, set text or draw figures from the current point, and fill in figures or stroke lines in the current color. In the previous section, you learned how to transform the current PostScript coordinate structure into virtually any shape you want. As you have seen, these transformations are cumulative and can be combined. This creates a powerful tool that can generate multiple shapes out of a simple graphic object, but it also raises some questions and problems.

The very power and persistence of these operators causes some concern. How can you be sure that the page structure is what you wanted, or thought it would be, when you designed a procedure? You have already been using operators like **newpath** to ensure that you don't get unexpected results. And in the original screenBox procedure, you saw how you needed to access the value of the current point for the procedure to function correctly. As these current-state variables increase—and there will be more in this book—we need to develop a method of controlling these values in a unified manner. Luckily, the PostScript interpreter faces a similar problem and provides a solution.

Graphics State

There are a number of other implicit arguments that are necessary for the painting operators to function properly. These consist of objects such as current color, current line width, current font, and so forth. All of these parameters, which together are necessary for the correct operation of the painting operators, are contained in a PostScript data structure called the *graphics state*. This structure defines the context, or background, for each of the painting operators. Most of the time, as you work on a page, you will want the same context for your graphics operations; therefore, setting these once as a global structure makes writing PostScript easier and more straightforward than if you had to specify these arguments for each operation.

The graphics state is not itself a single PostScript object, nor can it be directly accessed or modified. It is, rather, a collection of objects that form the control parameters, and these can be both read and altered by various graphics operators. In this way the current context can be changed as necessary to produce the output you want.

The graphics state is a data structure and is maintained by PostScript in a separate graphics stack. PostScript provides a **gsave** operator to push the current graphics state (or context) onto the graphics stack and a **grestore** operator to pop the topmost state on the stack and make it the current graphics state. This provides a valuable and necessary mechanism for controlling the current context for graphics operations.

In Level 2, you also can save and restore a specific graphic state without using the **gsave**, **grestore** or the graphics state stack. This allows you to set various graphics state parameters directly and save that state by using the new **gstate** and **currentgstate** operators. The **gstate** operator places an empty *gstate* object onto the operand stack, and then **currentgstate** converts that object into the current graphics state as a *gstate* object on the operand stack. Once there, you can save it as you would any other PostScript object. Once you have saved the *gstate*, you can restore that state at any time by using the **setgstate** operator, which takes the desired *gstate* as an operand. This type of manipulation is generally not required when creating pages on a output device, where the standard **gsave**, **grestore** mechanism is quite adequate. However, when working on a display, or in some unusual situations, this facility can be extremely important.

Before leaving this topic, let's look at these operators in our standard format.

SYNTAX	FUNCTION
— **gsave** —	saves a copy of the current graphics state on the graphics state stack.

SYNTAX	FUNCTION
— **grestore** —	resets the graphics state by restoring the state on the top of the graphics state stack.
— **gstate** gstate	makes a new, empty gstate object and saves it on the operand stack.
gstate **currentgstate** gstate	enters the current graphics state parameters into the *gstate* operand and returns state.
gstate **setgstate** —	sets the graphics state to the values contained in the *gstate* operand.

Developing Independent Procedures

So the graphics state is the place where these current values, including the current transformation matrix, are stored. You can control the status of the graphics state, to some extent, by explicitly saving and restoring it. This is not just one more thing to worry about; on the contrary, this is the means of your liberation—or at least of the liberation of your PostScript procedures.

In the previous section, you saw several examples of how procedures were partially freed from specific page position and coordinate measures. These same techniques, coupled with **gsave** and **grestore**, can create procedures that are entirely free from the page structure in their design. The procedures can be constructed, as it were, in their own coordinate system and then placed onto the page when and where you want them, in the shape and size that you decide; they need not disturb the remainder of the page in any way. Such independence is important when you want to develop a library of procedures that you can use repeatedly in different documents and with varied page designs. The best demonstration of this is to take some of the previous examples and rework them into independent procedures of the type just described.

Graphics Examples

In this section we will rewrite one of the procedures used in a previous example in a completely independent format. The object will be to illustrate how to create procedures that can be moved anywhere on the page and used at any size you wish. This requires a change, not only within the procedure itself, but also in how you invoke it within a program, or script. As you designed each procedure, you had to establish a context for its operation, and you had to determine what operands would be required for its execution. These context and operand requirements have not changed; but your ability, via transformation operators, to shape and modify the environment has changed. The net result is that each procedure must be rethought and reworked, and each program using the procedure will require the same type of effort.

Let's use the screenBox procedure as our illustration. This procedure was already partially modified for independence in the previous section. I say "partially" because it still contains references to the inch procedure in two important places. That means it still assumes that the default coordinate units are in effect—that one unit on the axes is $1/72$ inch. You will remember from our earlier discussion that the arc of the curved corner should be proportioned to the length of a side; if you were to use the previous procedure to make a screen figure with a very short side, for example 0.5 inches, the round arc would take up almost all of the side. Conversely, if the figure had a large side, say 8 inches, the rounding at the corners would hardly be noticeable. Similarly, you had to move some distance along the base of the figure to avoid having an extraneous line segment, and that distance was also proportional to the radius of the arc at the corners.

Now all these considerations and limitations can be removed and all the dimensions scaled to the figure itself, without any outside references. Look at the revised procedure in Figure 3.45.

See how much simpler the procedure has become. This new screenBox is designed to be called after two things have taken place. First, the coordinate system has to be translated to the point on the page where you want to position the bottom-left corner of the screen figure. This is the same technique that was used in the previous example; you saw how it worked there. Second, this new procedure requires the coordinates to have been scaled to the correct size to create the figure you want. In the default coordinate system, this procedure would create a box 1 unit ($1/72$ inch) on a side— hardly big enough to see. However, by means of scaling you can draw the box any size you require. You can even make it a rectangle rather than a square.

Let's see a concrete example of independent procedures in use. First, you will put a 1-inch square screen at the point (3,8)—all dimensions here are in inches, as always. Then you will put a rectangular screen, 1-inch wide

```
/screenBox
      (     .5 0  moveto
            1 0   1 1 .25 arcto
            4 (pop) repeat
            1 1   0 1 .25 arcto
            4 (pop) repeat
            0 1   0 0 .25 arcto
            4 (pop) repeat
            0 0   1 0 .25 arcto
            4 (pop) repeat
            closepath )
      def
```

Figure 3.45: Coordinate-independent screenBox

by 2-inches high, at point (5,8). Finally you will both outline (stroke) and fill a 2-inch-high square screen at (3,3). The example is given in Figure 3.46, which produces the page shown in Figure 3.47. This example illustrates how you can create programs and procedures that work together. Let's review it, line by line. The prolog consists of the two procedures, inch and screenBox. The screenbox procedure is as presented above; inch is included to make coordinate movement easier and more intelligible.

The script, or program section, begins with **newpath** for the usual reasons. Then, on line %1, appears the first of several sets of **gsave**, **grestore** pairs. Remember that all coordinate transformations are cumulative, and so you need to keep track of them. The best and easiest way to do this is to preserve the original, default graphics state, make the needed transformations, and then restore the original state saved earlier. In this way, each transformation begins from the same basic condition, and each change will have the anticipated result.

The first **gsave**, on line %1, is matched by a **grestore** at the end of the first screen figure, on line %1.6. Line %1.1 moves the origin to the desired location at (3,8). Line %1.2 scales the x- and y-axes uniformly to 1-inch units. Then lines %1.3 to %1.5 create the figure and fill it with dark (0.25) gray.

The next **gsave, grestore** pair is in lines %2 through %2.6. This time, the x- and y-axes are scaled non-uniformly, so that 1 unit on the x-axis is 2 inches, while 1 unit on the y-axis is 1 inch. Note here that the corners of the figure are "rounded" on the same proportions as the axes are scaled; hence the corners are no longer really round, but rather elliptical. Also notice that the box is black, since you don't set the gray value. This occurs without regard to the **setgray** that you executed within the preceding segment, because the gray value set there was reset by the **grestore** at %1.6 to the default value (black).

```
%Begin procedure independence example
%-----------------------Prologue---------------------
/inch
      {      72 mul }
      def
/screenBox
      {     .5 0 moveto
            1 0   1 1 .25 arcto
            4 {pop} repeat
            1 1   0 1 .25 arcto
            4 {pop} repeat
            0 1   0 0 .25 arcto
            4 {pop} repeat
            0 0   1 0 .25 arcto
            4 {pop} repeat
            closepath }
      def
%-----------------------Script----------------------
newpath
gsave                                           %1
      3 inch  8 inch translate                  %1.1
      1 inch  1 inch scale                       %1.2
      screenBox                                  %1.3
      .25 setgray                                %1.4
      fill                                       %1.5
grestore                                         %1.6
gsave                                            %2
      5 inch  8 inch translate                  %2.1
      2 inch  1 inch scale                       %2.2
      screenBox                                  %2.3
      fill                                       %2.5
grestore                                         %2.6
gsave                                            %3
      3 inch  3 inch translate                  %3.1
      2 inch  2 inch scale                       %3.2
      screenBox                                  %3.3
      gsave                                      %3.4
            .5 setgray                           %3.4.1
            fill                                 %3.4.2
      grestore                                   %3.4.3
      1  2 inch div  setlinewidth                %3.5
      stroke                                     %3.6
grestore                                         %3.7
showpage
```

Figure 3.46: Example of independent procedures in use

The last set of **gsave, grestore** is in the lines %3 to %3.7. See how the save and restore functions are paired on the portion of the example. Remember that the graphics state is maintained by the interpreter on a separate, but otherwise usual, PostScript stack mechanism, just like the operation stack or the dictionary stack. Each **grestore** puts back the state saved by the last **gsave**. Here you have one **gsave, grestore** pair within another. Note that the use of indentation here provides a visual clue to the effect and relationships of the paired operators.

Figure 3.47: Output of independent procedures

Now that you know what is being done, you may ask why is there a
gsave on line %3.4? To answer that, you must consider the effect of the
stroke and **fill** operators. Both of these require a current path to work on,
and both erase the current path after they have executed. Since you want to
both stroke and fill the last screen figure, you need to preserve the current
path while also using it for each operator in turn. Also, you want the line
stroked to be black, while the interior of the figure should be lighter. For
these reasons, you want to save the graphics state, including the current
color and the current path, after you have created the figure but before you
fill it with gray. This allows you to restore everything with the **grestore** in
line %3.4.3.

You are probably wondering why line %3.5 exists. Line %3.5 restores the
line width to the default unit coordinate, one point. It does this by taking
the reciprocal of the current scaling factor, 2 inches, and making that the current line width. This is necessary because the **stroke** operator would paint a
line 2 inches wide otherwise. You will remember that **stroke**, by default,

always paints a line 1-unit wide in the current coordinate units. Actually, in the earlier discussion, no mention was made of coordinate units; we just said the line was 1 unit and left it at that, or adjusted it to multiple units. However, the line is 1 unit in the current coordinates; if you have scaled those coordinates, the line will take on the size of the scale factor. In this case, the scale factor has been set to 2 inches on line %3.2. If you just issued a **stroke**, without any adjustment, you would get a line 2-inches wide all around the figure—which is now what you want. Note that the adjustment of the line width does not affect subsequent operations like the **stroke** on line %3.6, which is what you want.

Now that you've seen how all these concepts fit together in a small example, let's put them into a larger context. The next section will show you how to combine these techniques to create a larger figure.

FIFTH EXERCISE: DRAWING A LOGO GRAPHIC

This exercise will build on and make concrete the set of concepts that you have been reading about, thinking about, and working with throughout the chapter. Although the examples have illustrated the concepts presented and many of them have built on preceding work, this exercise is intended to integrate much of this material and allow you to see many of these ideas in a practical setting.

This exercise builds a logo for an imaginary sporting goods company, which will be called Mountain Sports, Ltd. The logo consists of a simple, stylized figure of three mountains, one behind the other two, with the sun overhead. The mountains are represented by triangles shaded in gray and the sun, by an uncolored circle. All the elements of this design are easily constructed with the tools you have at this point. Figure 3.48 shows the layout and dimensions of the logo design.

You will notice some differences between this figure and previous figures that you have worked with. First, the dimensions are given in units, not inches. The dimensions here are all relative dimensions: they represent the sizing and placement of the various elements in space and in relation to one another. For this exercise, the actual output will be scaled with 1/2 inch being 1 unit on the figure. Since the figure has an overall width of 17 units, or 8.5 inches at

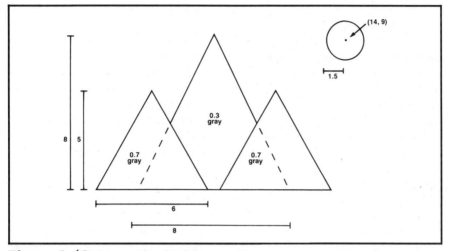

Figure 3.48: Layout for the logo graphic

the scaled dimensions, you will display the figure along the length of the paper. This orientation of the paper—printing along the length in- stead of the width—is called *landscape* orientation. The normal print direction, printing across the page, is called *portrait*.

You are, by now, quite able to analyze such layouts for yourself and to work out the necessary operations to create the figure presented. Let me just suggest that there is room here for four procedures. Two of them will draw the two figure elements, one for the hill and one for the sun. Following the principle of clarity for procedure names, these will be called hill and sun in the exercise.

The third procedure will be halfinch, which is the desired measure and scaling factor. The fourth procedure in the exercise is called landscape, and it reorients the coordinates for the landscape mode of printing. This proce- dure is only invoked once during the program, and so you may wonder why it should be a procedure at all. There are two reasons. First, when you are working in the interactive mode, you may want to play with the figures you've created—to try out various positions, for example, or various shad- ings. You may have an error on your code or in your typing and have to redo the page several times to correct it. In any case, making such transforma- tions in a procedural form ensures that they are the same for each exercise or variation. The second reason is one that we have touched on before: you will probably want to develop a library of PostScript routines for use in your environment. A procedure such as this is an excellent candidate for inclusion in that library.

Let me encourage you to take a few moments to work out your own approach for this figure and to write down a few notes on how you might code the program itself. Remember that any approach that produces the desired output is correct. The program that follows is just one way to get the output; there are certainly others. In any case, it will prove valuable for you to try some coding on your own and then check it against the program provided in Figure 3.49. This program produces the expected output, shown in Figure 3.50.

Let's review this exercise in detail. The exercise begins with two general procedures. The first, halfinch, is a variant of the inch procedure that you are familiar with. It simply multiplies by 36 instead of 72. The second procedure is the landscape procedure that we discussed above. This procedure does three things. First, it scales the coordinates to $1/2$-inch, using the halfinch procedure. Then it translates the coordinates to the bottom-right corner of the page, in preparation for changing to landscape orientation. This may surprise you; you have to visualize the coordinates on the page, and when you do, you will see that the bottom-left corner of the page in landscape mode is the same as the bottom-right corner in portrait mode. After the translation, the coordinates are rotated 90° to set up the landscape orientation. Note that the bottom-left corner of the page is still the origin.

The next two procedures in the prolog are specific to the task at hand: hill and sun. The sun procedure is simply a circle procedure, assuming that the center of the circle is at the origin and that the radius of the circle is on the stack. The hill procedure is similar to the procedure you used earlier to construct an isosceles triangle, except that the corner of the triangle is assumed to be at the origin and there is no **closepath** to finish the bottom side (since you might want to use the figure stroked rather than filled and you may not want a baseline). You don't need to be concerned about using **fill** under such circumstances since the **fill** operator will perform an implicit **closepath** before it fills in the figure. Note that the procedure must start with a **moveto** to the origin, so that the **lineto** (or **rlineto**, for that matter) will have a place to start.

Lines %1 to %3 of the script set up the coordinates on the page by means of landscape and then correct the current line width to a 1-point size to compensate for the scaling, as you did in the last example, and move the initial origin inside the imageable area of the page. Lines %4 to %9 form the first figure. This is the background hill, which must be constructed first so that the hills in the foreground will overlay this image. Position, size, and coloring are as specified in the layout. The **grestore** in line %9 resets all the coordinates to what

```
%!PS-Adobe-3.0
%%Title: Logo Exercise
%%Creator: David Holzgang
%%CreationDate: 4:01:50 PM  12/30/91
%%For: Understanding PostScript Programming (3rd Edition)
%%BoundingBox: 85 70 470 635
%%Orientation: Landscape
%%Pages: 1
%%EndComments
%%BeginProlog
%%BeginResource: procset Logo 1.0 0
/LogoDict 10 dict def
LogoDict begin
%---------------------------Prologue--------------------------
/halfInch
%create a procedure to convert user units to use halfinches
     {
     36 mul
     }
def
/landscape
%create a procedure to print in landscape (sideways) format
     {
     1 halfInch 1 halfInch scale
     17 0 translate
     90 rotate
     }
def
/sun
     {
     /Radius exch def
     0 0 Radius 0 360 arc
     }
def
/hill
     {
     /Base exch def
     /Hgt exch def
     /HalfBase
     Base 2 div def
     0 0 moveto
     HalfBase Hgt lineto
     Base 0 lineto
     }
def
end         %LogoDict
%%EndResource
%%EndProlog

%---------------------------Script--------------------------
------
%%BeginSetup
LogoDict begin
 %set up unit measures
landscape                                               %1
1 1 halfInch div setlinewidth                           %2
2 4 translate                                           %3

%%EndSetup

%%Page: i 1
%---------------------------Setup page------------------------
/PgSave save def
```

Figure 3.49: Example of the logo graphic

```
%begin logo
%do background mountain
gsave                                                    %4
        3 0 translate                                    %5
        8 8 hill                                         %6
        .3 setgray                                       %7
        fill                                             %8
grestore                                                 %9
%do left and right hills
gsave                                                    %10
        %left hill
        5 6 hill                                         %11
        .7 setgray                                       %12
        fill                                             %13
        %right hill
        7 0 translate                                    %14
        5 6 hill                                         %15
        fill                                             %16
grestore                                                 %17
%do sun
gsave                                                    %18
        14 9 translate                                   %19
        1.5 sun                                          %20
        stroke                                           %21
grestore                                                 %22
%logo finished

% Clean up after the page has been completed
PgSave restore
showpage                                                 %23

%%Trailer
end        %LogoDict
%%EOF
```

Figure 3.49: Example of the logo graphic (continued)

was in effect at line %4, when the **gsave** was done. In particular, the origin returns to the point (2,4) in the user coordinates; that is, to a position 1 inch from the left edge of the paper and 2 inches from the bottom edge when the paper is held sideways. You can see here the power of the save and restore combination.

The second set of **gsave** and **grestore** runs from line %10 to line %17. This set builds the left and right hills, which will overlap the background hill in the correct way. Again, the layout specifies all the required dimensions and the coloring. The final set of **gsave** and **grestore** in lines %18 to %22 creates the sun over the mountains. The only point to note here is the earlier setting of the line width, which is essential to ensure that the **stroke** operator in line %21 will work as you expect. The page is then output.

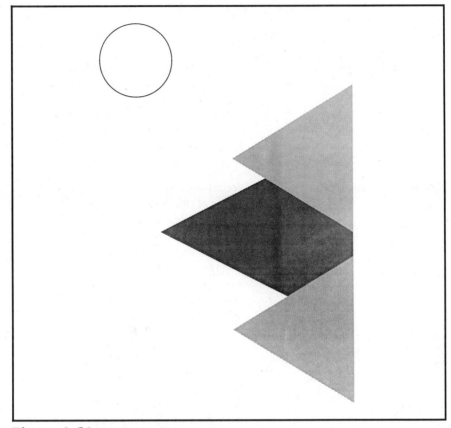

Figure 3.50: Logo graphic output

You also see that this exercise conforms to the structuring conventions laid out previously. In this regard, it is a good example of how to code and implement these conventions.

OPERATOR REVIEW

This section recapitulates all the operators from this chapter. As before, there is nothing new here; this section is a review and reference.

Drawing Operators

SYNTAX	FUNCTION
num1 num2 **lineto** —	adds a straight-line segment to the current path. The line segment extends from the current point to the *num1* x-coordinate and the *num2* y-coordinate. The new current point is (*num1, num2*).
num1 num2 **rmoveto** —	(relative moveto) starts a new segment of the current path in the same manner as **moveto**. However, the new current point is defined from the current point (x,y) to $x + num1$ as an x-coordinate and $y + num2$ as a y-coordinate. The new current point is $(x + num1, y + num2)$.
num1 num2 **rlineto** —	(relative lineto) adds a straight-line segment to the current path in the same manner as **lineto**. However, the line segment extends from the current point (x,y) to $x + num1$ as an x-coordinate and $y + num2$ as a y-coordinate. The new current point is $(x + num1, y + num2)$.
x y r ang1 ang2 **arc** —	adds a counterclockwise arc of a circle to the current path, possibly preceded by a straight-line segment. The arc has radius r and the point (x,y) as a center. *ang1* is the angle of a line from (x,y) with length r to the beginning of the arc, and *ang2* is the angle of a vector from (x,y) with length r to the

SYNTAX	FUNCTION
	end of the arc. If the current point is defined, the **arc** operator will construct a line from the current point to the beginning of the arc.
x y r ang1 ang2 **arcn** —	performs the same function as **arc**, except in a clockwise direction.
x1 y1 x2 y2 r **arcto** xt1 yt1 xt2 yt2	creates a circular arc of radius *r*, tangent to the two lines defined from the current point to *(x1,y1)* and from *(x1,y1)* to *(x2,y2)*. Returns the values of the coordinates of the two tangent points *(xt1,yt1)* and *(xt2,yt2)*. The **arcto** operator also adds a straight-line segment to the current point, if the current point is not the same as the starting point of the arc.

Graphics Operators

SYNTAX	FUNCTION
— **stroke** —	paints a line following the current path and using the current color.
— **fill** —	paints the area enclosed by the current path with the current color; clears the path.
— **newpath** —	initializes the current path to be empty and causes the current point to be undefined.

SYNTAX	FUNCTION
— **closepath** —	closes the segment of the current path by appending a straight line from the current point to the segment's starting point (generally the point specified in the most recent **moveto** or **rmoveto**).

SYNTAX	FUNCTION
num **setlinewidth** —	sets the current line width to *num*. This controls the thickness of the lines painted by subsequent **stroke** operators.
num **setgray** —	sets the current color to a shade of gray corresponding to *num*. *num* must be between 0, corresponding with black, and 1, corresponding with white, with intermediate values corresponding to intermediate shades of gray.
— **gsave** —	saves a copy of the current graphics state on the graphics state stack.
— **grestore** —	resets the graphics state by restoring the state on the top of the graphics state stack.
— **gstate** gstate	makes a new, empty *gstate* object and saves it on the operand stack.
gstate **currentgstate** gstate	enters the current graphics state parameters into the *gstate* operand and returns that state.
gstate **setgstate** —	sets the graphics state to the values contained in the *gstate* operand.

Font Operators

SYNTAX	FUNCTION
name **findfont** font	obtains a font dictionary specified by *name* and puts it onto the operand stack.
font scale **scalefont** newfont	applies *scale* to *font* to create *newfont*, whose characters are enlarged in both the *x* and *y* directions by the given scaling factor when they are printed.
font **setfont** —	establishes *font* as the font dictionary to be the current font for all subsequent character operations.

Coordinate Transformation Operators

SYNTAX	FUNCTION
tx ty **translate** —	moves the origin of the user space to (tx,ty) in the previous coordinate system.
angle **rotate** —	rotates the user space around the origin by *angle* degrees.
sx sy **scale** —	scales the user space by the factor *sx* in the x-dimension and by the factor *sy* in the y-dimension.

4

Creating and Modifying Fonts

T HIS CHAPTER PROVIDES MORE
information on how fonts work in PostScript and on how you can control
and affect the font machinery. It includes information on how to modify
fonts and on how to add additional fonts to your PostScript output device,
either by downloading more fonts or by creating new ones.

The chapter starts out with a discussion of the PostScript font mechanics that is quite detailed. The detail is necessary if you are going to adjust
the fonts in the kinds of ways that we are going to discuss, but the detail is
also useful to aid you in making efficient use of PostScript fonts. The first
topic covered is the font dictionary. This is the place where PostScript stores
all the information related to a given font. The second topic is how the interpreter uses the dictionary to create characters and how those characters are
treated when you place them on an output page.

With this information as a guide, you proceed to the first task: modification of a PostScript font. The first exercise is to access some of the accented
characters that are available in most PostScript fonts. This is a particularly interesting exercise: it introduces you to some real, effective code such as you might
find in an actual application prolog. The exercise is complex, so each step is
examined in some detail; the final result is your complete understanding of an
important PostScript technique. Then you proceed to modification of a font to
create characters that are outlines, rather than solid shapes. This is quite a bit
easier, as you will discover, but it is still an interesting and valuable way to modify characters.

The next section deals with two related but different topics. The first is
the topic of global modification of fonts. Up to this point in the chapter, all
the modifications have been done character by character; now you modify
all the characters in the font at once. The most common, and the most useful
global change that you make to fonts is to the size of the characters. This is
the related second topic of this section, font measurement, or metrics. This
section of the chapter shows you how to make size changes in two different
ways, then you use the techniques you have read about in an example,
where you create and display both condensed and expanded versions of a
PostScript font.

The last major section in the chapter is a short discussion about adding
fonts to your PostScript device. The two ways of adding fonts to PostScript
are downloading additional fonts and creating new fonts. The major focus
in this section is on understanding the process and the options available,
rather than on actually performing the task. This is done because the task is
inherently complex and because the actual process depends to some extent

upon your environment. It is important to understand the process, however, so that you can make informed choices about font sources and font use. There is a careful discussion of things you should be aware of in using additional fonts in your PostScript document.

The chapter ends with an operator review similar to the ones in Chapters 2 and 3. Like them, this final section is intended as both a review and a reference; it provides in one place and in one standard format all the PostScript operators that have been introduced or reviewed in this chapter.

FONT MECHANICS

Until now, you have been using PostScript fonts that are supplied with every PostScript device. Moreover, you have been using these fonts in the most natural way; that is, by setting text in the font and then displaying that text on a page. All of the work that you have done so far with fonts has been oriented toward this type of text output. This is the most typical use of fonts generally, whether in PostScript or in any other reproduction technology. There have been enough challenges in producing typeset-quality documents without adding complexity by altering the type itself.

You have mastered the basic font operations and should be quite comfortable with positioning and displaying text on an output page. This enables you to move beyond simple text and use PostScript fonts in a more creative way.

PostScript is a powerful language, oriented toward producing graphic units (pages) on raster-output devices. It is also, as we have discussed earlier, a language with a natural affinity for graphics. In particular, PostScript treats characters in fonts as graphic objects. This concept allows you to make interesting and useful modifications to PostScript fonts, and, indeed, even to create your own fonts.

Your first response to that thought may be to wonder why you would ever want to modify or create a font. After all, the fonts are already provided, and they work quite well. There are two reasons. First, PostScript fonts actually contain more characters than can be accessed from the keyboard. There are 256 available characters in a PostScript font, while there are less than 100 keys on your keyboard. Obviously, the keyboard contains the most often used characters: the alphabet, both uppercase and lowercase, numbers, and common punctuation. But there are additional characters, less frequently used in English, that are still included in the standard Post-Script fonts. These additional characters include the tilde, the symbols for the British pound and the Japanese yen, the cents sign, the upside-down exclamation point and question mark (used as punctuation in Spanish), and many others. All the additional characters that are included in the standard PostScript fonts are clearly set forth in Appendix E, "Standard Character Sets and Encoding Vectors," of the *PostScript Language Reference Manual, Second Edition.*

These additional characters are referenced by using the *ddd*, notation which we mentioned when we discussed strings in Chapter 3. Let's expand on that notation. The form *ddd* is used within a string to indicate to the PostScript interpreter that you wish to reference the character indicated by the octal value, *ddd*. If you look in Appendix E of the *PostScript Language Reference Manual, Second Edition,* you will see that each character has an octal code assigned to it. When you want to include a character in your string that isn't on the keyboard, you can look up the octal code in this table and use that code, in the form *ddd,* to reference the character. For example, the tilde (˜) is shown as code 176; that means that you would code \\176 to insert a tilde into a string. An entire string including such a code would look like this:

(This string has a tilde, \\176, included in it)

When you perform a **show** on that string, the tilde character would appear between the commas. Since every character has a code, you could use all octal numbers to create a string, but that would be a waste of time for characters that exist on the keyboard. I only mention it so that you understand that this isn't an exclusive arrangement; every character can be referenced by number if you choose, and there isn't any difference for the interpreter between "a" and "\\141."

You may think this an embarrassment of riches; but PostScript doesn't stop there. When you use the techniques presented in this chapter, you will have an additional 56 characters available to you for special work. These special characters make up all accented characters that are used in various languages. PostScript creates them on your command.

This is different from the process of referring to characters not on the keyboard that we outlined above. In that case you really don't have to do anything special to the font to access the characters; in this case, you must modify the font to get PostScript to make the characters that you want. You are going to learn these techniques for font modification in this chapter.

You might want to modify fonts for a second reason. Fonts have their own measurements, called *metrics,* included within them. You can access and change these metrics in several ways to produce new fonts with interesting and valuable properties. Techniques for doing this are also part of the chapter.

You can also create your own fonts; however, PostScript fonts supplied by Adobe and other font vendors generally will satisfy even the most demanding graphic artist. The available fonts are of high quality and there is an extensive selection, with more fonts being added almost every month. Font vendors now include both purveyors of strictly electronic fonts, such as Adobe, BitStream, and others, and traditional font vendors, such as Linotype, Agfa-Compugraphic, and so on. More important to my mind, if a bit more subtle, the fonts have been tuned and formed to present a satisfactory graphic image on a wide range of output devices. Many of these font vendors either own or have licensed high-quality fonts with long histories and excellent reputations. This aspect of quality is not easily acquired nor is it something to trifle with.

Creation of even decent fonts, therefore, is not an easy or a quick job. The task is complex and it requires a good understanding of PostScript font machinery. In addition, there is the essential but indescribable requirement for aesthetic quality. Nevertheless, it is sometimes necessary for a particular application, or even an unusual document, to require a created font. Actual creation of a new font is beyond the scope of this book, but we will go through font concepts and machinery in sufficient detail so that you will be well-equipped to undertake such a task if you wish.

The important point here is to understand the workings of PostScript fonts in some detail. This understanding is the key factor that you will acquire in the chapter. Effective and efficient use of PostScript fonts requires that you have a good, working knowledge of font structure and font mechanics. Even if you never modify a font—much less create a new one— you will find this knowledge invaluable in creating PostScript documents. Whether you are programming PostScript directly or using an application program, you will be able to understand good font handling practices and distinguish them from those that are poorly conceived and poorly executed. You will apply these techniques here; you will understand why you are applying them; and you will be able to distinguish them in other PostScript programs as well.

·OPERATIONS REVIEW

Before you start working on the new material, there are two types of PostScript operations that we should review here: font operations and dictionary operations. The font operations are clearly important, but you may wonder why dictionary operations should be included. The answer is that PostScript fonts are implemented by means of dictionaries. In all aspects of using fonts, you will be constantly working with dictionary objects. The fonts themselves are dictionaries; and, as you will see, they contain subsidiary dictionaries as well.

Font Operations

PostScript provides a simple method for accessing and using fonts. This is the method that you have been working with during the previous examples and exercises. The first task is to identify the font to be used. This is done by putting its name onto the stack and invoking the **findfont** operator. Next the font must be set to the correct point size that you want to use. This is done by the **scalefont** operator which requires the desired size on the stack as a numeric operand. Finally, the font must be identified to the PostScript interpreter as the current font, that is, as the font to be used for all subsequent text operations. After the font is made the current font, operators such as the **show** operator can be invoked to use that font to display strings onto the output device.

This simple sequence normally looks like this in the code that you have been using:

/Helvetica **findfont** 12 **scalefont setfont**

If you remember the first time you did this sequence, however, you remember that these are each three separate and independent, but related, operators. Each one has a place and a purpose, and they sometimes must be separated to do certain tasks. In fact, the entire PostScript font machinery is quite complex, and this sequence of operations is deceptively simple. Details of this process will be presented below; for now, you just need to refresh your memory concerning each of the three distinct operations.

Level 2 devices allow you to combine these three processes into a single operation by using the new **selectfont** operator. To perform the same function as shown above, you would use

/Helvetica 12 **selectfont**

Dictionary Operations

Dictionaries are an essential component of PostScript generally, and are the major implementation mechanism for fonts in particular. Most of the dictionary work that you have done up to now has involved defining and retrieving objects from the default *userdict*, or from small procedure dictionaries. But since PostScript fonts are themselves dictionaries, you now have to refresh your memory about general dictionary operations and learn some new operators that will help you access and use the font dictionaries.

This refresher isn't intended to be a full recapitulation of things you already know; instead, it is meant to be more like a series of one-liners to help you to recall certain aspects of dictionary operations. If any of this isn't clear, or doesn't come back to you, don't hesitate to review the topic in Chapter 2 and then return here when you're ready. You're under no compulsion to forge ahead before you feel comfortable. The new material, of course, will be fully covered and presented in the usual way.

To review, a dictionary is a PostScript object that contains key, value pairs. The key is used to access the value from the dictionary. There are at least two standard dictionaries that are always present: the *systemdict* and the *userdict*; in Level 2 devices, there is a third, *globaldict*. PostScript works with a dictionary stack, and you may have more dictionaries than just these two or three. The topmost dictionary is called the current dictionary. The normal search method for dictionaries is for the interpreter to take a key, usually a name, and search downward through the dictionary stack until it finds a match to the key. The interpreter then retrieves the value associated with the key and returns it to the stack or executes it as appropriate.

Values are associated with keys, and entered into the current dictionary, by means of the **def** operator. No special operator is required to retrieve a value from the dictionary. When the interpreter receives a name, it looks up that name in the dictionary stack. Operators are no different from any other PostScript name in this respect; the main difference is that operators are defined in the *systemdict*.

As we said before, fonts themselves are PostScript dictionaries and can be handled and accessed with the appropriate dictionary operators. Each font dictionary also contains additional internal dictionaries, which make up a set in a hierarchical order. All this will become clearer when you begin to work with the font dictionaries. The list of all available fonts is maintained in a master dictionary, called the **FontDirectory**. Each font has its own dictionary, and is referred to by its name, like Helvetica, or Times-Roman, which is the key for that font in the **FontDirectory**.

The font handlers actually take care of most of the manipulation of the font dictionaries for you, but, for investigative and de-bugging purposes, you need to remember how to begin using a new dictionary—in other words, how to add it to the dictionary stack—and how to stop using it. These two operations require the two operators that you originally met in Chapter 2, presented here again as follows:

SYNTAX	FUNCTION
dict **begin** —	pushes *dict* onto the dictionary stack and makes it the current dictionary.
— **end** —	pops the current dictionary off the dictionary stack and makes the dictionary that was immediately below it the current dictionary.

As mentioned earlier, the default dictionaries (*systemdict* and *userdict* in Level 1, and additionally *globaldict* in Level 2) are permanently installed on the dictionary stack. Any attempt to pop them by using an **end** operator, for example, without having issued a **begin**, will cause an error.

Resources

In PostScript Level 2, fonts are one example—probably the most common example—of a more general category of *named resources.* One new feature of Level 2 is its use of named resources for many types of features. Generally, a *resource* is a collection of PostScript objects that control certain features in the language. By their nature, the size and number of resources is arbitrary.

The perfect example of a PostScript resource is a font. Fonts, as you already know, are dictionaries which are referenced by name, and which provide the necessary definitions and procedures for drawing all the characters in the font. All currently available fonts are named in a special directory dictionary, called the **FontDirectory**, as described earlier. (You will learn more about this directory and about fonts in the next section.) However, many different fonts might be used for printing a document; too many to keep in the printer's memory at once. The problem, then, is how to access the fonts required by a document that are not already available in printer memory.

Fundamentally, there are only two mechanisms to solve this problem. One is to ensure that any font required by the document is included with the document itself. This means including all the necessary PostScript code, both to create the font and to draw all its characters, within the prolog of your document. This guarantees that the font is there when required, but also has some obvious drawbacks. For example, it requires that the font be included with each document, which increases the size of the document and the time required to transmit the document to the printer.

The second mechanism is to preload the font into the device. There are several methods of preloading fonts. One alternative is to store the font information internally in the printer in read-only memory (ROM). This is the approach that is used for such commonly used fonts as Helvetica and Times, which you have used in these exercises. An alternative strategy is to have the interpreter load the font from some external device, such as an attached hard disk drive, when the font is needed by the document. Finally, if certain fonts are commonly used in a document, you can manually download them to the printer's memory. Fonts loaded in this fashion are said to be ''permanently'' loaded since they do not disappear at the end of a job like most composite objects in memory. However, the font will not stay in memory when the printer is reset or turned off; once that happens, the font needs to be downloaded again.

This problem with fonts can also be generalized to cover a wide variety of other resources that might be needed in a document: forms, patterns, procedure sets, halftones, images, and other common objects. Level 2 provides a common approach for handling all these named resources. There are two essential ingredients in this process. First, the objects must be able to be accessed by name. Second, they must be collected into a central dictionary that registers the currently available names. Besides supporting a wide variety of standard resources, Level 2 allows you to define and use your own resource categories in the same way as you would use standard resources.

FONT DICTIONARY

Every PostScript font dictionary follows a set format. This means that specific keys must be present in the dictionary, and other keys may be present. The values associated with each of these keys may vary, but the type of object associated with a specific key is invariable. This makes perfect sense, because the PostScript font machinery cannot work without some specific information.

Other than the set format, there is nothing special about a font dictionary. It is created and manipulated by all the same operators that work on regular dictionaries. The only special handling comes when you want to identify a specific dictionary as a font dictionary. That is done by using the **definefont** operator, which checks the new dictionary for the correct format, and then enrolls the name that you give the dictionary into the master font directory, **FontDirectory**. The **definefont** operator also adds a special fontID object with the name **FID** to the new directory. All of these required and optional keys are listed below.

In Level 2, fonts are a special case of named resources. A font dictionary is an instance of a **Font** resource. Resources can be loaded into either local or global memory. In a Level 2 device, you may also use the new **defineresource** operator to define a font instead of **definefont**, which is simply a special case of **defineresource** in Level 2.

Font Types

There are three types of font dictionaries defined in the PostScript language. Each type is distinguished by the value of the **FontType** entry in the font dictionary. The types of PostScript fonts are as follows:

- A **FontType** entry of 0 indicates a composite font. A *composite font* is a hierarchical collection of other fonts, called *base fonts*. Composite fonts exist in all Level 2 devices and in some Level 1 devices.

- A **FontType** entry of 1 indicates a base font that contains character descriptions that are defined in a special encoded format. These descriptions are stored in the **CharStrings** dictionary, which is described below. This format is faster to interpret and more compact than standard PostScript. The format is defined and explained in the *Adobe Type 1 Font Format* manual.

- A **FontType** entry of 3 indicates a base font that contains character descriptions that are defined in ordinary PostScript procedures. These procedures are controlled by **BuildGlyph** or **BuildChar** procedures as described below.

Naturally, the first question everyone asks when they see the **FontType** list is "What happened to Type 2?" According to Adobe, Type 2 was part of the initial design of PostScript but was ultimately absorbed into the other two types of fonts before the PostScript language was finalized and released to the public. Sort of a fossil footprint in the language.

Font Entries

Depending on the type of font, there are a variety of entries that may exist in a font dictionary. This section describes these entries in four groups: entries that exist in all fonts; entries that exist in all base fonts; entries that exist only in Type 1 fonts; and entries that exist only in Type 3 fonts.

There are seven entries which occur in all types of font directories; six of them are supplied by you (or whoever creates the font), and the seventh is created by the **definefont** operation. Of these, two of the supplied entries are required and the rest are optional. These keys and their associated meanings are listed here:

KEY	TYPE	DEFINITION
FontMatrix (required)	array	Converts character coordinates into user coordinates. The characters are built in their own coordinate system (called the *character coordinate system*) that is independent of the user coordinate system; the size of each character is one unit high in the user coordinates to begin with.
FontType (required)	integer	Indicates by a number where the information for character descriptions is to be found and how it is represented. Type 0 indicates a composite font; types 1 and 3 indicate base fonts.
FontName (optional)	name	Contains the font's PostScript name. This is for information only; it is not used by the font machinery. Usually this name will be the same as the name passed to the **findfont** or **selectfont** operator, but that isn't required.

KEY	TYPE	DEFINITION
FontInfo (optional)	dictionary	Contains optional information about the font. This information is entirely for the benefit of PostScript programs that use the font; the PostScript font machinery ignores this information. Table 4.1 shows what is contained in this dictionary.
LanguageLevel (optional)	integer	Indicates the minimum level of the PostScript language that is required for the font to image correctly. Fonts that specifically use Level 2 features should set **Language-Level** to 2 to indicate that. This should only be set when the font contains Level 2 features as a part of the character definitions. If the font will print correctly on a Level 1 device, even if it contains other Level 2 information or entries, it should use a **LanguageLevel** of 1. If this entry is not present, the language level is assumed to be 1.
WMode (optional)	integer	indicates whether vertical or horizontal metrics will be used when painting the characters in a font. A **WMode** of 0 (the default) means that horizontal writing will be used; a **WMode** of 1 indicates that vertical writing will be used. This is required because, in some writing systems—notably Japanese and Chinese—the same characters may be aligned either vertically or horizontally. This option is only meaningful when composite fonts are supported by the output device.

KEY	TYPE	DEFINITION
FID (created)	fontID	Serves internal purposes in the font machinery; this entry is automatically created by the **definefont** or **defineresource** operator.

Table 4.1: Contents of the Optional FindInfo Dictionary

KEY	TYPE	DEFINITION
Notice	string	the trademark or copyright notice (if applicable).
FullName*	string	the full text name of the font.
FamilyName	string	the name of the "font family" to which this font belongs.
Weight	string	the weight of the font, for example: Bold, Italic, Light, or Ultra.
version*	string	the font's version number.
ItalicAngle	number	the angle in degrees counterclockwise from 90° of the dominant vertical strokes of the font.
isFixedPitch	boolean	a value that, if *true*, indicates that the font is a fixed-pitch (monospaced) font.
Underline Position	number	the distance in character coordinate units from the baseline of the characters to the underline.
Underline Thickness	number	the stroke width in character coordinate units for the underline.

* Used primarily for documentation, these names are not organized in any systematic way and have no effect on the font keys used with **findfont** *and* **definefont**.

All base fonts (fonts that do not have a **FontType** of 0) have certain entries. These are as follows:

KEY	TYPE	DEFINITION
FontBBox (required)	array	An array of four numbers in the character coordinate system giving lower-left x, lower-left y, upper-right x and upper-right y for the box that encloses all characters in the font, called the *font bounding box.* That is a box that is just large enough to enclose all marks made by any character in the font, if all the characters were printed one on top of the other at the same point.
Encoding (required)	array	An array of 256 names that maps the character codes (the numeric values) to a set of character names. This process and what is included in this array is more fully described in the section on font encoding below.
UniqueID (optional)	integer	An integer that identifies this font; it must be unique to the font. Every different font, no matter how small the difference may be, should have a different value of **UniqueID**. This entry is not required; but if it is present, it will be used by the font cache mechanism to help the cache run more efficiently.
XUID (optional)	array	An array of integers that uniquely identifies this font or any variant of it. This is only used in Level 2 devices.

In addition to these basic entries, there are a number of additional entries which are present in PostScript built-in fonts or in any Type 1 font. These contain the following additional keys with associated values:

KEY	TYPE	DEFINITION
PaintType (required)	integer	A code that indicates how the characters in the font are to be painted. The valid codes are as follows:

0   characters are filled

2   characters are outlined

Type 1 fonts are normally created with a **PaintType** of 0. If you want to change this value, you should check that it is 0; the only reasonable change is from 0 to 2 (filled to outlined). Previously, types of 1 and 3 were also documented; these are no longer supported and were never appropriate for general use. However, the Courier Type 1 font, in most devices, has a **PaintType** of 3. You should never change Courier (or any font that does not have a type of 0 or 2) to any other value for **PaintType**.

CharStrings (required)	dictionary	Associates character names (from**Encoding**) with shape descriptions in a special encoded format.
Private (required)	dictionary	Contains internal information about the font. See the *Adobe Type 1 Font Format* manual for additional information.
StrokeWidth (optional)	number	Gives the stroke width in character coordinate units for outline fonts. This field is not initially present in filled fonts, and must be created when making an outline font from a filled font.
Metrics (optional)	dictionary	Contains width and side-bearing information for any character in the font in writing mode 0. This entry is not normally present in built-in fonts; if it is present, it will override the widths and side bearings encoded in the character description of whatever characters are included here.
Metrics2 (optional)	dictionary	Contains metric information for any character in the font in writing mode 1. This entry is only used in devices with composite fonts.
CDevProc (optional)	procedure	Changes the font metrics by applying the calculations in the procedure. This is only available in devices with composite fonts.

A Type 3 font has the basic entries given above, and another two additional entries which may be present. These contain the following additional keys with associated values:

KEY	TYPE	DEFINITION
BuildGlyph	procedure	Draws the characters in the font. When a character is requested from a Type 3 font, the interpreter calls the font's **BuildGlyph** procedure with the font dictionary and the character name on the operand stack. **BuildGlyph** must remove these two operands and draw the requested character. **BuildGlyph** is only supported in Level 2 devices; Level 1 devices use the **BuildChar** procedure described next.
BuildChar	procedure	Draws the characters in the font. When a character is requested from a Type 3 font, the interpreter calls the font's **BuildChar** procedure with the font dictionary and the numeric character code on the operand stack. In Level 1 devices, the interpreter always calls **BuildChar**; this makes it a required entry in Level 1 devices. In Level 2 devices, the interpreter first calls **BuildGlyph**; if there is no **BuildGlyph** procedure, the interpreter then calls **BuildChar**. Either **BuildGlyph** or **BuildChar** must be present in a Type 3 font.

A Type 3 font may have both **BuildGlyph** and **BuildChar** procedures. This allows new fonts to be used by both Level 1 and Level 2 interpreters with maximum efficiency. In either case, the Build procedure is responsible for all parts of creating and handling the characters in a font. Typically this will include selecting the correct character drawing procedure, drawing and painting the character, and setting the correct metrics for the character. If the font is designed to be cached, the Build procedure must use the necessary PostScript operators to ensure that caching takes place. We will discuss font caching later in this chapter.

Note that, although a Type 3 font may have entries such as those described above in a Type 1 font, there is no automatic mechanism for using them. For example, a Type 3 font may have a **PaintType** entry, but changing it will not necessarily change the font from filled to outlined. The Build procedure in the font would have to check the **PaintType** and change the painting from filled to outlined for this to work; the font machinery will not do it automatically.

That completes the list of keys in a font dictionary and the types of objects associated with each key.

Uses for the Font Information

Most of this information has little or nothing to do with the average PostScript programmer; it is useful to know, some of it is interesting, but generally it doesn't affect how you handle the PostScript fonts. Some of the entries must be modified to create certain effects or when you change characteristics of the font. Most of the time, such manipulation is dangerous and potentially disastrous.

There are two components which do lend themselves to modifications, however. These are the font **Encoding** and the **FontMatrix**. Both of these components provide you with powerful change mechanisms that can be used advantageously. We will discuss these changes in the rest of this chapter.

In addition, you might want to change the font **PaintType**. This is one way to derive outlined fonts, although we will discuss and work with an alternative method for showing strings in outline format later in this chapter. The general process of font modification is discussed in detail in the corresponding section of this chapter, and some examples of common modifications are given. After you have completed the examples in that section, you should be able to make other changes, such as from filled to outlined, without difficulty.

Mechanism of Normal Operation

The normal operation of PostScript base fonts uses the information in the font dictionary to create the images of the characters that are to be painted onto the output device. Let's consider exactly how this operates in detail. As you remember, Level 2 does the same steps, but can use a single operator for the complete process.

You begin the process by putting a name literal, which represents a font name, onto the operand stack and invoking the **findfont** operator. That typically looks like this:

/Helvetica **findfont**

This operator takes the name literal off the operand stack and looks it up in the **FontDirectory**. If it doesn't find the name, it attempts to find the font on any external file system, if one is present. If there is no external file system, or if the font is not found there, it will usually substitute a default font (typically Courier) or return an error, as we discussed in an earlier chapter. If it does find the name, it returns the associated value to the operand stack. This value is a pointer to the named font dictionary.

It may surprise you to know you get a pointer back, and not the object itself. Remember that a dictionary is a composite object, and that values of composite objects are shared, not duplicated, as we discussed in Chapter 2. This sharing is done by using pointers to the objects, instead of moving around the objects themselves. Therefore what you get back on the operand stack is a pointer. If you display the stack by using the **pstack** or = = operators, you will see something like this:

PS>/Helvetica findfont

PS>pstack

– dictionary –

PS>

This is what you expect, and shows you what type of object the pointer on the stack points to.

Next you would issue the command to set the point size for the font, like this:

12 **scalefont**

This operator, **scalefont**, takes the value on the operand stack and uses it to scale **FontMatrix** from one unit to the number of units given. The result is stored into a new **FontMatrix**, and the pointer to the modified font is returned to the stack. Now you issue the **setfont** operator. This takes the pointer off the operand stack and stores it into the graphics state as the current font. Once that has been done, the modified font can be retrieved from the graphic state by execution of the **currentfont** operator. Remember that all of this has been done using pointers, not the actual objects themselves. Using pointers is quicker and more efficient than manipulating entire dictionaries.

How to Access and Read Font Information

You can't retrieve the font information listed above simply by executing the name of the desired object and then looking on the stack, as you might with a typical object. The information is unavailable because the font dictionary is not on the dictionary stack, where the interpreter is looking for the information. To retrieve the information, you must move the desired font dictionary to the dictionary stack and make it the current dictionary.

The explanation that follows depends more heavily on the interactive mode than any of the previous examples; consequently, we will stop at several points between prompts for explanations. Before going on each time, let the interpreter come back to the PS> prompt. Also, note that we are not discussing how to access the font as a font; we are talking about accessing the font information in the font dictionary as listed above, which is a different matter. You already know how to access the font in a normal way; what you want to learn is to be able to examine items in the font dictionary, for example, the **FontName**.

Let's look at the built-in Helvetica font first. This is a good example of how you can access PostScript font information. You would start like this:

```
PS> /Helvetica findfont

PS> pstack

- dictionary -
```

These lines tell you that you have retrieved the Helvetica font dictionary, and that the pointer (for our purposes, the dictionary) is on the operand stack. Normally you would continue with **scalefont** and **setfont**, but not this time. Instead you continue as follows:

```
PS> begin
```

This line takes the dictionary off the stack, puts it onto the dictionary stack, and makes it the current dictionary. That's what we previously said would be necessary for you to retrieve information from the font dictionary as though it were a regular dictionary. Let's make sure that the dictionary is there, like this:

PS> FontName

PS> =

/Helvetica

This process assures you that the Helvetica font dictionary is now on the dictionary stack, since you can retrieve information from it by giving the interpreter the name, or key, and getting the associated value back on the operand stack.

You will notice that you used the = operator, instead of the **pstack** operator that was used above. The **pstack** operator shows you the entire stack without disturbing or altering the stack in any way; the = , on the other hand, shows you only the topmost item on the stack, and it pops that item. In the first instance, you saw the dictionary on the stack and left it there, since you wanted to use it; whereas in this case, you popped the name literal since there was no reason to leave it on the stack.

Going down another level is just the same technique applied again. For example, suppose you now want to access the **FontInfo** dictionary. You would do it like this:

PS> FontInfo

PS> pstack

– dictionary –

PS> begin

PS> Notice

PS> =

(Helvetica is a registered trademark of Allied Corporation)

PS> end

Here you have used the **end** operator to pop the **FontInfo** dictionary off the dictionary stack when you were through with it. Remember that you can't access the **FontInfo** dictionary until you have performed the earlier step of getting a font dictionary and putting it onto the dictionary stack. If you try to access **FontInfo** before that, you will get an error; the **FontInfo** dictionary is included within the font dictionary, just like the other font information.

FONT ENCODING

The preceding section discussed and reviewed the operations required to select a font and put it into use. Now you are going to explore, in the same detail, the operations that actually place a character onto a page using a font. This is an important issue for working with and modifying fonts. In the process of actually painting characters on the page, called *font encoding,* you can have a marked effect on the efficiency of PostScript programs. This is also the first process that we will modify (just slightly) to create a revision to an existing font.

The Encoding Process

We will use the **show** operator as the example since this is the operator that you have worked with so far, but the same process applies to all the character rendering operators. In the ordinary course of work in PostScript, **show** is called with a string as an operand. Let's use abcd as the example; then you would write

    (abcd) show

to paint the string onto the output page. This assumes, of course, that the **currentfont** is set to what you want it to be. For the rest of this section, we will assume that a current font has already been provided, and we will look at the standard operation when the current font is a Type 1 font.

The **show** operator is going to work on each character in the string in an identical fashion, so we will only look at the process for one character. The **show** operator takes the first character and uses the character code, which is the numeric value of the character as given in Appendix E of the *PostScript Language Reference Manual, Second Edition,* as a key into the **Encoding** array. This array matches the value of the character with a name. You notice that this is kind of the reverse of the normal dictionary process, where a key is a name and returns a numeric value; in this case the index, or key, is the numeric value and the associated element is the name literal. Names of simple alphabetic characters in the **Encoding** array are just the single letters themselves, but other characters have names that are complete words, such as "plus," "comma," and "cent." The names of all the characters are given in Appendix E, section E.5, "Standard Roman Character Set," of the *PostScript Language Reference Manual, Second Edition,* along with the octal codes for the characters. Notice particularly that the numbers also have word names, like "one," "three," and so on.

You will also notice that there are two sets of octal numbers next to the character names. These represent the codes for the two built-in encoding vectors that are present in most PostScript devices: Standard and International Standards Organization (ISO) encoding. The standard encoding is the default encoding that is normally used by PostScript fonts; it is stored in *systemdict* as **StandardEncoding**. The ISO has also defined a standard encoding for use in text output; this encoding is somewhat different from the standard PostScript encoding. In particular, ISO encoding includes more accented characters as standard and fewer ligatures and other characters. The ISO standard encoding is stored in *systemdict* as **ISOLatin1Encoding**. By using the techniques that you will learn in this chapter, you may use either one of these encoding vectors, or you may modify one of them to make a special version for your own use.

The character name extracted from the chosen encoding vector is then used as a key into the **CharStrings** dictionary for the current font. **CharStrings** tells the interpreter how to construct the given character. This is done by normal PostScript graphic operations, just as you might draw a character using PostScript procedures. When the character is fully formed at the correct size, it is imaged onto the page at the current point. Then the current point is moved by the appropriate distance for positioning the next character.

The formed character is also stored into the *font cache.* The font cache is an area that is set aside to help speed the process of rendering characters. Once a character has been used in a page, it will stay in the font cache for a period of time. This means that the next occurrence of that same character doesn't have to go through the entire process outlined above; instead, the interpreter uses the image of the character that has been already created and stored in the font cache. This makes the process of printing the character on the order of a thousand times faster than executing the entire procedure again.

If the font is a Type 3 font, the process is quite similar. The character is still looked up in the **Encoding** array. In a Level 2 device, the font dictionary and the character name are then passed to **BuildGlyph**, if it's present.

Otherwise, the font dictionary and the character code are passed to **Build-Char**. In Level 1 devices, as you learned above, **BuildChar** is always used. The procedure that draws the character must use special PostScript operators within the character definition to include the character in the font cache. If it does, the character is included in the font cache as described above; otherwise, the character is drawn individually every time.

That gives you a detailed look at the complete process of handling fonts and rendering characters in fonts. You now can see that there are several points where you might make changes to font operations to create certain useful effects. The simplest of these changes is the subject of the first example in the next section.

Font Imaging Methods

There are three ways to image or draw a font, corresponding to the three types of graphic images that PostScript can represent. These are

- outlined fonts

- stroked fonts

- bit-mapped fonts

Outlined fonts may be rendered onto the page either as outlines, or, more commonly, as filled shapes. In either case, they behave like a box or a circle on a page. Stroked fonts, on the other hand, are made up of lines rather than shapes: they resemble the straight lines you produced in earlier examples. Just as you could not fill a line, so you cannot fill a stroked font. You can use a technique we will mention in the next section to change a stroked font into a fillable shape. Both of these types of fonts use PostScript operations to render the fonts onto a page. Generally, all Type 1 fonts are outline fonts.

The third type of font, bit-mapped, is somewhat different. We are not going to discuss bit-mapped fonts in detail, but I want to mention them for the sake of completing the list and because you will probably hear them mentioned as you read about computers and graphics. Bit-mapped fonts are direct pictures, as it were, of a letter. Similar to the pictures of Christmas trees produced in computer departments by printing zeros and ones on a page, they are a series of dots (the bits) which are turned on to make up a letter. Generally, such fonts do not provide the best typeset quality to your output. These fonts require a lot of coding and design, and further discussions or examples of bit-mapped fonts are beyond the scope of this book.

Advantages of PostScript Fonts

Characters in PostScript fonts are generally created by the equivalent of the path construction and painting operations. This is entirely consistent with the design of PostScript and the notion of type as a graphic object. This approach provides several benefits for the user which may not be obvious at first glance.

First, this approach to creating characters preserves the quality of the fonts. In very fine (and expensive!) typesetting, each letter of each font is hand-crafted to give the look and feel that the type designer had in mind. This may mean, for example, that the stroke-widths or relative sizes of letters within the same font group but at different point sizes are subtly different. While PostScript can't go quite that far, it comes closer to this careful craftsmanship than any alternative I am aware of. In particular, since Post-Script effectively draws each character at the correct point size, it preserves the relative size and weight relationships down to the finest resolution available to it. In addition, since PostScript is an interactive language, smaller sizes of a font may be ''tuned'' to provide the best quality image at the desired size. Many electronic fonts, on the other hand, are simply reductions or enlargements of a fixed size of characters; this means that the font becomes coarse and unappealing at sizes quite different than the design size. This doesn't happen with PostScript fonts.

In addition, this process of drawing the characters also forms an important part of the device independence that PostScript provides. Because Post-Script is independent of device-specific qualities such as resolution, it must have a way to represent characters that will be able to place the characters in the same relative positions on different devices and yet allow the maximum resolution that the device is capable of producing. After all, you wouldn't be very interested in using, and paying for, a high-resolution device if it did not provide output of a higher quality.

MODIFYING FONTS

Now that you have covered the operation of PostScript fonts in detail, it's time to use this deeper knowledge to help you make some changes to the available fonts. This section of the chapter will show you how to modify fonts and characters within fonts to provide some effects that you may not be able to get in any other way.

Remember that the font machinery is complex, for all its ease of use, and that you have to be careful when you work with the fonts. Arbitrary or unplanned changes are likely to result in poor-quality output at best, and a disaster at worst. Be sure to read the exercises carefully before you begin, and follow the explanations so that you know what is intended. With that small caution, you will find that modification of characters and fonts is both useful and fun.

CHARACTER MODIFICATION

The first type of modifications that you will work with are modifications of individual characters. These are both the easiest modifications to make, and the most common. You will find this work very interesting, because it allows you additional freedom to use characters as graphic objects.

All modifications to a font ultimately come down to modification of characters. What character modification means here is modification to specific individual characters within a font, rather than global modifications to a font that change all the characters uniformly. Such global modifications will be covered in the next section. The first character modifications that you will do are those that change the font encoding to allow you to access characters that are otherwise unavailable to your program.

Reencoding Fonts

The use of the **Encoding** array to output a character onto the page may have seemed rather indirect. So it is, but it offers substantial benefits. One of these benefits is the ability to render characters that are not in the standard encoding; another is that standard characters may be rearranged into an alternative encoding scheme if necessary. In this example, you will modify the standard encoding to add some additional characters. The additional characters that are available are those that have a dash next to the character name in the "Std" column in section E.5, "Standard Roman Character Set," of the *PostScript Language Reference Manual, Second Edition*.

You will note that all of the characters that we will add to the standard character set are already present in the ISO encoding. If you wished, you could simply substitute the ISO encoding for the standard encoding. However, that wouldn't teach you how to modify an Encoding vector, which is what you want to learn here. Therefore, you will use the standard encoding and change that to add the desired characters. After all, there are some characters that you might want to use, for example the trademark symbol, that are not encoded in either character set.

You now have enough information to follow where these characters come from. These are characters that have names and procedures in the **CharStrings** dictionary for the built-in fonts, but that do not have names in the **Encoding** array **StandardEncoding**. What you have to do is make entries for those characters that you want to use in a new **Encoding** array with the names of the characters at the positions that you choose. Let's work an example.

This example is a portion of a menu for a fancy dinner, which presents some interesting combinations of food and wine. You want to produce a menu with correctly accented letters where required. After reviewing the food and wine, you make a list of the additional letters, with accents, that you will need for the wording on the menu. Now you look in Appendix E of the *PostScript Language Reference Manual, Second Edition* to determine the correct name for each of these letters. The complete list of letters that you will use, along with their correct names, is shown in Figure 4.1.

Executing these names in **CharStrings** will cause the interpreter to build the accented characters. The task now is to include these character names into an encoding vector so you can use them in your menu.

First of all, you have to decide what character codes you want to use to make these letters. Theoretically, you might choose any character between the codes of 0 and 255; however, that really isn't practical. Your document is already using ordinary text and punctuation, so you don't want to substitute any of these special characters for the regular ones. The special characters aren't on the keyboard, but we have already discussed how you can use the octal codes to call out characters that are not on the keyboard. So now you need to determine what octal codes you want to use for these characters.

One choice would be to use the positions that these characters have in the ISO encoding. This would overlay some existing characters in the standard encoding, but they are not ones that you want to use in this document. If you were creating general output for an application, this would be a good solution, since it would maintain compatibility between the two encoding schemes for accented letters. Here, however, you are simply creating a one-time encoding for this menu project, so you can adapt a simpler approach.

Character	Name
â	acircumflex
à	agrave
è	egrave
é	eacute
û	ucircumflex
ü	udieresis
ó	oacute

Figure 4.1: Accented letters for menu example

You have identified seven accented characters that you want to use on the menu. Look at the section E.6, ''StandardEncoding Encoding Vector'' in Appendix E of the *PostScript Language Reference Manual, Second Edition*. This section gives the standard encoding vector for normal fonts, which is the vector you will be working with. You see that some spaces are shaded in gray on the table to mark empty spaces in the encoding vector. The block of lower numbers, from \000 to \037, are positions where there is a potential conflict with the normal control characters that your computer might send. However, the remaining blocks indicate codes that are entirely unused. You can see that there is a continuous block of unused codes from \330 to \336; these are the codes you will use for your accented letters. Note, however, that if you wanted to use other positions, even ones that are currently used, you could do that.

Before you get to the example, there is one more point to discuss: the choice of font for the menu and the method of changing the encoding vector for that font. In this example, you will use 10-point Times-Roman font for all the type. You certainly don't want to modify the encoding vector for Times-Roman permanently. Therefore, the correct way to produce a small modification of the encoding vector is to duplicate the font before you modify it.

Here are the steps that you need to take in the program to produce the menu output:

1. Duplicate the Times-Roman font.

2. Reset the encoding vector to include the new codes and the associated character names.

3. Set the menu text using the appropriate octal codes for the accented characters.

The program necessary to perform this example is given in Figure 4.2. It produces the results pictured in Figure 4.3.

This is not an easy program to follow, so we will go through each portion of it in detail. First of all, the program begins by defining the two variables, **Ps** and **Lead**. These two will be used in the program to determine the point size for the output and the line leading. They have been made variables to provide an easy method for changing and adjusting the output.

Next, in line %3, the program defines an array, **Menuvec**, which has the revised encoding in it. Specifically, this array consists of pairs of entries: an octal number specifying the code, and the name of a character from the list in Figure 4.1. This array introduces you to the use of square brackets ([ ]) as delimiters for arrays, as was mentioned in Chapter 2. The use of brackets is precisely like the use of braces ({ }) for procedures. The array itself consists of lines %4 to %10. Each line contains a pair of objects: a number and a name literal. The number is an octal number, denoted by the prefix 8#, followed by the three digits of the character position. In this case, the positions are those chosen earlier, 330 to 336. The name is the name for the character that you want to image when you invoke that character code; the names are taken from Figure 4.1. These names must correspond to the keys in the font's **CharStrings**.

Two simple, short procedures follow. The first, **ss**, shows a given string at the point specified by the variables, **Xpos** and **Line**, and moves down the page by the size of the **Lead** variable. The second procedure, **nextblock**, moves the vertical place variable, **Line**, down the page by a fixed distance, 40 units. These procedures will be used to display the text on the page at appropriate locations.

Line %14 begins the portion of the program that is most interesting: the part that reencodes the font. The section begins by defining a working dictionary, so that nothing that you define here will be contingent on or affect the permanent dictionaries. The new operator, **dict**, takes an integer

```
%---------------------------Variables---------------------------          %1
/Ps 12 def            %set point size                                     %1
/Lead 14 def          %set leading                                        %2

%-----------------------Modified Encoding Vector---------------          %3
/Menuvec [                                                                 %3
   8#330 /acircumflex                                                      %4
   8#331 /agrave                                                           %5
   8#332 /egrave                                                           %6
   8#333 /eacute                                                           %7
   8#334 /ucircumflex                                                      %8
   8#335 /udieresis                                                        %9
   8#336 /oacute                                                          %10
  ] def                                                                   %11


%-------------------------Procedures---------------------------
/inch
{
     72 mul
}
def

/ss                                                                       %12
{
     Xpos Yline moveto show
     /Yline Yline Lead sub def
}
def

/nextblock                                                                %13
{
     /Yline Yline 40 sub def
}
def

%-------------------------Re Encode Font----------------------
/ReEncodeDict 12 dict def                                                 %14
/ReEncodeDict begin                                                       %15
     /BasefontDict /Times-Roman findfont def                             %16
     /NewfontDict BasefontDict maxlength dict def                        %17
     BasefontDict                                                        %18
     {
         exch dup /FID ne                                                %19
         {
             dup /Encoding eq                                            %20
             {
                 exch dup length array copy                              %21
                 NewfontDict 3 1 roll put                                %22
             }
             {
                 exch NewfontDict 3 1 roll put                           %23
             }
             ifelse                                                      %24
                                                                         %25
         }
         {
             pop pop                                                     %26
         }
         ifelse                                                          %27
     }
     forall                                                              %28

     NewfontDict /FontName /Times-Roman-Menu put                        %29
```

Figure 4.2: Menu example

```
        Menuvec aload                                        %30
        length 2 idiv                                        %31
        {
              NewfontDict /Encoding get 3 1 roll put         %32
        }
        repeat                                               %33
        /Times-Roman-Menu NewfontDict definefont pop         %34
end                                                          %35

%-----------------------Program (Wines)--------------------
%Setup re-encoded font as current font
/Times-Roman-Menu findfont Ps scalefont setfont             %36
%Position and show wines
/Xpos 5.5 inch def                                           %37
/Yline 8 inch def                                            %38

(Louis Roederer Cristal 1979 ) ss                           %39
(        Brut ) ss

nextblock                                                    %40
(Ch\330teau Clerc Milon 1970) ss                            %41
(Ch\330teau La Gaffli\332re 1970) ss                        %42

nextblock                                                    %43
(Ch\330teau Cheval Blanc 1970) ss
(Ch\330teau Haut-Brion 1970) ss
( ) ss

nextblock
(Ch\330teau Les Forts de Latour 1970) ss
(           (en magnum) ) ss

nextblock

%-----------------------Program (Food)---------------------
%Position and show courses
/Xpos 1 inch def
/Yline 8.5 inch def

(Oxtail Rillettes) ss
(  with Catalan-style Tomato Bread) ss

nextblock
(6-Lily Risotto) ss
(  with Black Sesame Seeds) ss

nextblock
(Saffron-flavored Rago\334t of Chicken,) ss
(  Chicken-of-the-Forest Mushrooms,) ss
(  and Parsnips) ss

nextblock
(Roast Triangle Tip of Beef with Bordeaux Basil Butter,) ss
(  Pencil-thin Asparagus,) ss
(  and Stuffed Baby White Eggplant) ss

nextblock

%Move toward center of the page
/Xpos 250 def

(Assorted Cheeses \331 la Red Smith) ss
```

Figure 4.2: Menu example (continued)

```
nextblock
(Marc de Gew\335rztraminer (Gilbert Miclo),) ss
(Marc Mascar\336, and other alcohols) ss

nextblock
(Caf\333 Demi-decaf\333in\333) ss

showpage
```

Figure 4.2: Menu example (continued)

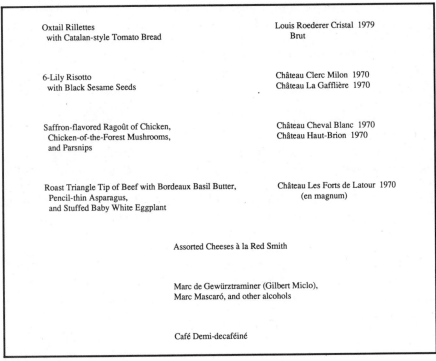

Figure 4.3: Menu example output

operand and creates an empty dictionary big enough to hold the number of entries equal to the integer value of the operand, and returns the new dictionary to the stack.

Line %15 issues a **begin** to push the new dictionary, ReEncodeDict, onto the dictionary stack, and to make it the current dictionary. Line %16 defines the variable BasefontDict to contain a copy of the Times-Roman font dictionary, which was retrieved by the **findfont** operator. You will use this dictionary everywhere in the following code. Line %17 uses another new operator, **maxlength**, to determine the maximum size of BasefontDict. This number is used as an operand by another **dict**, and the resulting dictionary—which is still empty—is defined as NewfontDict. This is the dictionary that will become your new font. Notice that NewfontDict is exactly the same size as the original font dictionary.

Lines %18 through %28 fill in the new font dictionary with entries from the original font dictionary, represented by BasefontDict. The **forall** operator on line %28 executes the procedure defined in lines %19 through %27 for every element in the BasefontDict dictionary.

Fundamentally, this procedure copies each element of BasefontDict into the new NewfontDict. This is done by a rather clever use of two new operators, **put** and **roll**. To begin with, you want to insert key, value pairs into a dictionary that is not on the dictionary stack. You can do this by the use of the **put** operator. This operator takes three operands: a dictionary, a key, and a value. The value must be on the top of the stack, followed by the key, followed by the dictionary. Remember this order, as it is critical to what you have to do next. You will retrieve each entry from the BasefontDict, and the key for each entry will be put onto the stack by the **forall** operator, followed by the value—except somehow you need to get the NewfontDict dictionary onto the stack below the key. You can do this trick with the **roll** operator. Let's look at the stack after **forall** has done its work; for this example, we'll use the **FontName** entry, but remember that **forall** is going to get each and every entry in the dictionary. The stack at this point is shown in Figure 4.4.

Now you push the dictionary, NewfontDict, that you want to work with onto the stack, which now looks like Figure 4.5. Note the small numbers to the

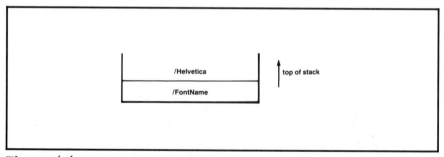

Figure 4.4: Stack entries after **forall**

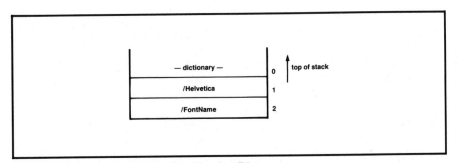

Figure 4.5: Stack entries after NewfontDict

right; these are not part of the stack, but they are essential for understanding how **roll** works.

Now you invoke the **roll** operator, which takes two more operands, 3 and 1. These two numbers tell **roll** that you want to affect the top three operands on the stack, and you want to move them all up one position. That means that the key, in this case the name literal /FontName, at position 2 will roll up to position 1; and the value, at position 1, will roll up to position 0. Of course, that action can't be continued because the dictionary, at position 0, has no position above it to go to. So **roll** does what you might have suspected from its name, and puts the top element, the dictionary, marked 0 in Figure 4.5, after the lowest element that you moved, the key /FontName, marked 2. This rolls all the operands into the new positions shown in Figure 4.6, which is what you need for the **put**. Now, when you execute the **put**, you will get an entry into the dictionary NewfontDict that matches the original entry from BasefontDict.

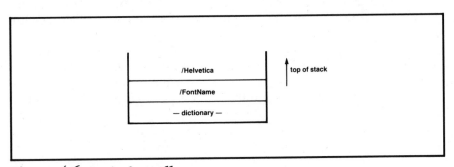

Figure 4.6: Stack after **roll**

You want exactly the same entries, but with two exceptions. (Naturally, nothing could be that simple.) These two exceptions are handled by a pair of **ifelse** conditions within the larger procedure.

The first exception is the original **FID** entry. You may remember, from our previous discussion, that this entry will be created by the **definefont** operator; therefore you can't copy it onto the new font. This exclusion is handled by the first **ifelse**, which has the conditional test on line %19 matching the **ifelse** on line %27. Let's analyze this process.

First of all, you have to identify the **FID** entry. You can do that by testing for the key, the name /FID, except you know that the key went onto the stack first, followed by the value. Therefore, you must reverse the order on the stack by using an **exch** before you can do the test. So that's what you do first on line %19. Then you need to test for the name literal /FID. When you perform the test, using the **ne** operator, it will consume the two objects on the stack used for the test, and return a boolean value **true** or **false**. Because you will use up the key by doing the test, you first must use a **dup** operator to get an extra copy. Then you push the name literal, /FID, onto the stack and make the comparison. If the comparison is **true**, the **ifelse** operator executes the first procedure, from lines %20 to %25, if it is **false**, it executes the second procedure, given on line %26. Since the test is whether the entry is not equal to /FID, it will execute line %26 if the key is /FID and lines %20 to %25 for all other keys. That works fine, since line %26 consists of two **pop** operators, which simply throw away the /FID entry from the original dictionary. Notice that this leaves one unused entry in the new dictionary, since the new dictionary was created to hold the same number of entries as the old one. This space will be used by **definefont** for the new **FID**.

Lines %20 to %25 form the second **ifelse** test. In this case, you are looking for the **Encoding** array. You may want to know why you can't copy the original **Encoding** array and then modify it. For the answer, recall the discussion of composite objects in Chapter 2. An array is a composite object, and when you duplicate a composite object, you share the values between both copies. That means that, if you were to simply **put** the old encoding array into the new font dictionary, the two arrays would be sharing the same values. Thus, when you modify the encoding array, you would affect the old array as well as the new one, and you don't want to do that. Instead, you want a new version of **Encoding** with the same values.

PostScript provides one operator, **copy**, that will copy values from one composite object to another. You will use the **copy** operator to generate the new encoding array to go into NewfontDict.

First of all, you have to test for the **Encoding** entry. This is just like the one for the **FID**, except that you don't have to swap the top two operands on the stack first, because you already did that for the previous test. You will duplicate the key on the top of the stack and test whether it is equal to the name literal /Encoding. If it is not equal, then the **ifelse** on line %24 executes the second procedure, on line %23. This procedure is basically the routine that we analyzed earlier, using the **put** and **roll** operators. However, it has to be preceded by another **exch** operator. This is necessary because you took the key and the value from the original dictionary and reversed them to perform the **ifelse** tests on lines %19 and %20. Now you have to put these back the way they came from BasefontDict originally.

If the test is true, and the entry is the encoding array, the **ifelse** executes the procedure on lines %21 and %22. This procedure starts out by swapping the operands on the stack again, for the same reasons the procedure on line %23 had to—namely, to put the key and value back in the order that they were in originally. This also, not coincidentally, places the actual encoding array on the top of the stack for further work.

The last part of the procedure is also familiar, since it consists of the same sequence of **put** and **roll**. The new part is on line %21, where you have to provide a new copy of the encoding array. You begin this task by duplicating the array on the stack and then using the **length** operator to determine how many entries it has. The **length** takes the array and returns an integer value, the size of the array, to the top of the stack. This value is the operand for the **array** operator, which generates an empty array of the given size. So the operand stack now contains the following items, from the top down: an empty array that is exactly equal in size to the original encoding array, the original encoding array, and the /Encoding name literal. Now you can apply the **copy** operator, which moves the values from the original array to the empty array, one by one, and returns the new, filled array to the top of the stack. This leaves the new array, followed by the name literal on the stack. You perform the same exercise to enroll this object into the new font dictionary.

You have created a new font dictionary, NewfontDict, which has an independent copy of the original encoding vector and does not yet have a **FID** entry, but has room for one. Having enough room is essential, because when you eventually issue the **definefont** command in line %34, there must be a place to enter the new **FID** entry in the font dictionary. In line %29, you change the **FontName** entry in the new font to the new name that you want to use—in this case, /Times-Roman-Menu.

Now you must modify the encoding vector to add the entries for the additional characters that you want to use. This is done in lines %30 to

%33. This piece of code is also tricky, but it is similar to the preceding task, in lines %18 to %28. First you put Menuvec on the stack. Menuvec has seven pairs of entries that must be added to the encoding vector inside the new font dictionary; your first task is to unravel Menuvec into its component parts so they can be placed into the new encoding array in the correct locations. This can be done by the **aload** operator, which takes an array on the operand stack and converts it into all its parts. It places all the parts onto the stack in order, with the last element on the top. Finally, **aload** pushes a copy of the original array onto the stack. Applying this operator to Menuvec, results in the stack looking like Figure 4.7.

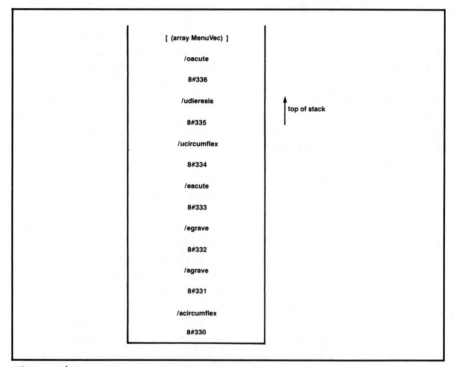

Figure 4.7: Stack after **aload** of Menuvec

Now you have to insert these values into the encoding array in NewfontDict. This task is done by the **repeat** operator in line %33, which needs to execute the procedure on line %32 once for each pair of entries in the new vector. The number of times to execute the procedure is calculated on line %31. First, the **length** operator is used to determine how many entries there are in the array, which was on the top of the stack after the **aload** as shown in Figure 4.7, and is now replaced by the results of the **length**. This number is twice the correct number, since the entries come in pairs. Therefore you divide the number by two (well, almost). The **repeat** operator requires an integer number on the operand stack; the **div** operator returns a real number in all cases, even if the actual numbers used in the division are integers. The answer here is to use a variant of divide, **idiv**, that solves this problem. This operator returns only an integer result; any remainder is discarded. Using this, the integer 7 is pushed onto the stack as a result of the operations at line %31.

Now look at the procedure in line %32. This uses the familiar **roll** and **put** sequence to insert the entries in Menuvec into the new encoding vector. The process is the same as the earlier sequence that you used, but here you are working on an array instead of a dictionary. Actually, **put** will work on three types of objects: arrays, strings, and dictionaries. All of these objects can be indexed and thus used with the **put** operator. This use of **put** is discussed more fully in the "Operator Review" section at the end of the chapter.

The procedure retrieves the new encoding vector from the new font dictionary, NewfontDict, by executing the **get** operator. This operator takes two operands: first, a string, an array, or—in this case—a dictionary; next, an index (for a string or array) or a key (for a dictionary). Here you give it the dictionary NewfontDict, and the key, the name literal /Encoding, and it returns the value associated with the key in the dictionary, the encoding array itself, on the operand stack.

This is what is required for the insertion of the new encoding values. Now you **roll** an index and a value from Menuvec into position, and the **put** operator adds the key,value pair to the /Encoding array. When the **repeat** is finished, the new values have been transferred from Menuvec to the new **Encoding** entry in NewfontDict.

You may wonder why you don't have to issue a **put** to match the **get** and restore the encoding array to the font dictionary. Again, this is a situation created by the shared values of composite objects. As we observed earlier, an array is a composite object, and therefore two duplicate arrays share values. In this case, the array on the stack that you are working with is a duplicate of the actual array in the font dictionary, and the two copies share values. So, when you change the values in the copy on the stack, you are simultaneously changing the values for the copy in the font dictionary.

Now you have constructed a well-formed font dictionary in NewfontDict and are ready to put it to use. It is enrolled in FontDirectory by the

definefont operator in line %34, using the name /Times-Roman-Menu that you inserted into the dictionary before. That definition does not automatically affect the name that you use here; it's up to you to keep the two names the same. Finally, the whole set of definitions and all is cleaned up by popping the temporary dictionary, ReEncodeDict, from the dictionary stack.

The rest of the program follows the usual form, and is quite straightforward. The new font is used, like any other font, in a **findfont** operation in line %36. Since the font has all the normal characters, you can use it for all the text on the page.

The text for the menu is printed in two columns, wine on the right and matching food courses on the left. The two procedures, **ss** and **nextblock**, position the text as you want it on the page. The only further point for comment is the use of the special characters. As we discussed before, these are not characters that appear on the keyboard. Therefore they have to be placed into the display strings by use of the *ddd* convention. You see a typical example in line %42, where the characters acircumflex and egrave are printed by using their octal codes, \\330 and \\332, in the output string.

There is one more point to make regarding these additional entries in the encoding vector. You remember that these are characters that exist in the PostScript font but are not encoded into the standard encoding. If you look at the list of the standard encoding for a PostScript font, you will see, besides all the alphabet and the punctuation, a series of individual accent marks. These marks, together with the appropriate letters, make up the additional accented letters that you called for when you reencoded the font. These accented character are called *composite characters* because they are made up of two other characters. For example, the acircumflex that you used above in the exercise (\\330) is actually built up out of the a (\\141) and the circumflex accent in the font (\\303). In Level 1 devices, both characters that make up the composite character must be available in the new encoding for the encoding of the composite character to work properly. Although this is not essential in Level 2 devices, it is still good practice to keep both items in the font when you reencode it.

This completes your exercise in reencoding a font. You can see here how flexible and powerful PostScript font machinery is, and how you can work with it to take maximum advantage of its features.

You have been introduced to a number of new operators in this exercise. All of these operators are included in the Operator Review section at the end of the chapter, where they are presented in the standard format that we have been using throughout the book. I encourage you to look them up and review them there to see their full range of capabilities.

Outline Letters and Fonts

There are other methods for manipulating the PostScript font characters. One of the most useful, after being able to reencode the font, is to be able to use the fonts as either filled or outlined figures. In this portion of the chapter, you will learn how to change certain PostScript fonts into outline letters rather than filled ones.

This technique is only useful with fonts that are generally filled, rather than stroked. You remember the **PaintType** indicator from the font dictionary, which specifies whether a font is outline or not. If the font is not outline, it is still possible to derive a kind of outline representation for it, but that representation is not at all what you might expect, is harder to deal with, and is not a subject that we will cover here. Of the standard PostScript fonts, only the Courier font family is not outlined; both the Times-Roman and the Helvetica families and the Symbol font are outlined or filled.

This approach to the creation of outline letters can be used, with some alterations, on any string that will be displayed onto the output page. As an example, let's create a headline for the menu you just printed. This won't be very involved; just the words DINNER MENU will be included in capitals across the top of the page. You will center the text 1 inch from the top of the page in 36 point Times-Italic, and make the headline outlined type, rather than filled.

This program is easy enough (in contrast to the previous exercise) that it can just be listed here, without any additional preliminary setup work. The actual program is listed in Figure 4.8. This short program produces a simple line of output, shown in Figure 4.9.

If you wanted, you could combine this program with the preceding one to produce the complete menu; however, this is very similar to exercises you did earlier in the book, and is not necessary to repeat here.

The program shown in Figure 4.8 has only one new feature: the display of the text string (DINNER MENU) in outline rather than filled form. This changes two things in what you were previously doing. The first change is in the procedure **centerText**. In the version of this procedure that you were using before, the procedure finished with a **show** operator. This operator is now removed, so you can change the string for outline display.

The second change is use of the new **charpath** operator. This is the operator that changes the string to outline form and adds the outlines to the current path. It requires two operands: the first is the string to be changed, and the second is a boolean value that directs the operation. The boolean value **false** tells

```
%------------------------Prologue ------------------------
/inch
{
      72 mul
}
def

/centerText
{
      /Right exch def
      /Left exch def
      dup
      stringwidth pop
      2 div
      Right Left sub 2 div
      exch sub
      Left add
      Line moveto
}
def

%-----------------------Script-----------------------------
/Times-Italic findfont 36 scalefont setfont
/Line 10 inch def
(DINNER MENU) 1 inch 7.5 inch centerText
false charpath
stroke

showpage
```

Figure 4.8: Menu headline example

Figure 4.9: Main headline output

charpath that you want to get a path that is suitable for stroking; the value **true** would indicate that you want a path suitable for filling or clipping. (Clipping is an effect that we will discuss in detail in Chapter 7). This distinction only really becomes important in dealing with fonts that are not outline, like Courier—that is, fonts with a **PaintType** that is not 0 or 2. For most of the fonts, which are outline fonts and have a **PaintType** of 0 or 2, there is no difference in the resulting path, whether the boolean operand is **true** or **false**.

However, you will always get the expected result if you use **false** when you are going to use **stroke**, and use **true** otherwise. If you inadvertently use **charpath** with **true** and the Courier font, for example, you are likely to get unexpected and probably unsatisfactory results.

In this case, you have correctly chosen the Times-Italic font, which is an outlined font; and so the **charpath** operator returns an outlined image of each character that is added to the current path. When **charpath** is done, you invoke the **stroke** operator to outline the letters. This **stroke** works the same way as it would for a box or any other figure that you might create. In particular, the line width used is the current line width in the graphic state; in this case, it is the 1-point default line. Since the font is scaled to 36 points, this is just fine; but if you were using a smaller point size, you might want to adjust the line width accordingly to avoid having the line overpower or even entirely fill some portions of a letter.

The program is now easy to follow. First you define the two procedures that you will require: inch and centerText. These are familiar by now; the center-Text procedure has the one change already discussed. Then you define the font you want to use, Times-Italic in this case, and you scale the font to 36 points and set it as the current font. Next you set the **Line** variable for the line you want the text to show on.

The actual text string is then pushed onto the stack, and the centerText procedure is invoked to center the string between the 1-inch and 7.5-inch margins. This procedure leaves the text string unaffected on the stack, where it is available as an operand for **charpath**. After the **charpath**, the resulting figures are stroked and finally the entire page is printed.

Although this process works fine for short strings such as the one here, it will not work on an arbitrarily long string. Character outlines are quite complex, and there is a maximum number of line segments that you can add to the current path before exceeding device limits. On a high-resolution image-setter, even the short string that you used here might well cause an error.

There is an easy technique that will eliminate this problem: only draw and stroke a single character from the string at one time. Since each character is added to the path and then stroked, the path never contains too many line segments as long as a single character is processed at a time. Although this technique is somewhat more complex than the example shown here, it follows the same principle, using **charpath** for the conversion. The major difficulties lie in selecting a single character at a time from the string. In Chapter 6, you will learn how to handle strings in this way and you will be able to build a procedure to outline any arbitrary string.

It is also possible to change the **PaintType** code in the font dictionary to create an outline font. To make an outline font, you need to change the **Paint-Type** from 0 to 2, and create and set the **StrokeWidth** entry in the font dictionary. Doing this makes a global change to the font mechanism, rather than changing individual characters as you have been doing. The process for changing from filled to outline characters uses the same mechanisms and techniques that you used earlier to change the encoding for the font, coupled with some of the techniques for global font modifications described in the next section. After you have worked through that section, you will be able to do this as an exercise, if you want to do it.

FONT METRICS

You have now worked through, in some detail, the process of modifying individual characters. This section will discuss modification of the font dictionary in ways that change all the characters in the font at the same time, in the same way.

The most common global change made to a font is to change its size. Actually, you have done this operation every time you have used a font, by using the **scalefont** operator. In this section, you will learn how to adjust the size of the font in a more general way. The measurement of size in a font and the coordinates used by the font are distinct from those used in user space; these characteristics are called *font metrics.*

Actually, the changes to a font work in a way that is analogous to changes in the coordinate system in general. The main difference is you can change the font coordinates without making any changes to the page coordinates as a whole. This is what **scalefont** does; it works on the font coordinates in exactly the same way that the **scale** operator works on the entire page.

How Fonts Are Measured

Before you can change the font measurements, you need to know how the characters within fonts are measured. Figure 4.10 shows two typical characters, a *g* and an *h,* positioned one after the other. The figure also shows some of the important measurements that affect characters and character placement.

Let's discuss these measurements in detail. First of all, all the measurements for characters are done in a separate *character coordinate system.* This coordinate system is distinct from the coordinates in the user space,

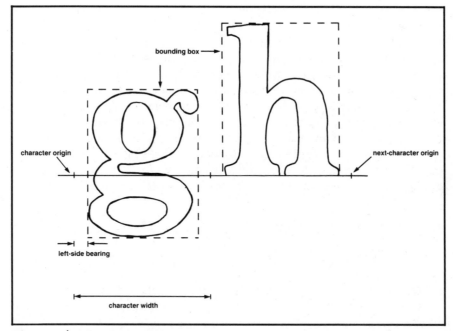

Figure 4.10: Character metrics

and can use any scale that you want. For built-in fonts, the characters are usually scaled in a coordinate system of 1000 units. This works in the same way as the graphics procedures that you defined before; each character has its own *character origin* (0,0) that is separate from any page reference. You used a similar approach to create, locate, and output the logo graphic in the last chapter.

This character origin is also called the *reference point,* and is the point that **show** (and other text painting operators) will position on the current point of the user space when the character is painted onto the page. The reference point is the connection between character coordinates and user coordinates.

The *width* of the character is the distance between the origin of one character and the origin of the next character when they are printed consecutively on the page. In other words, the *next character origin* shown in Figure 4.10 is the character origin plus the width; and this is the point that **show** will return to you as the current point if this is the last character in the string. As you noticed in the exercises where you used the **stringwidth** operator, character width is a vector in the character coordinate system; it has both x- and y-coordinate values. For our purposes, the y-coordinate value will always be zero, but you should know that it exists.

The character is enclosed in a *bounding box*. This bounding box represents the smallest rectangle that will completely enclose all the marks that make up the character. You will remember the **FontBBox** entry in the font dictionary; that is the largest bounding box of all the characters in the font.

Finally, there is the *left-side bearing* of a character. This is the distance from the character origin to the left edge of the character's bounding box. This distance, like all the measurements for characters, is in character coordinate units. Note also that it may be negative; that is, instead of starting on the right of the character's origin, the character may start on the left. This occurs, for example, in alphabets where the characters read from right to left.

Modification of Font Metrics

We have already discussed the most ordinary change that you might make to a font's size: namely, scaling it to the correct point size by using the **scalefont** operator. This is fast and convenient, but it doesn't have the flexibility that **scale** has, since you can only scale a font uniformly in both x- and y-coordinate units using **scalefont**.

The **scalefont** operator works by changing the **FontMatrix** array in the font dictionary. This array gives the transformation required to change the character coordinates into user coordinates. Since characters in the built-in fonts are typically sized in 1000 units, the typical **FontMatrix** divides all the character coordinates by 1000, by multiplying them by .001. The **FontMatrix** array contains six numeric entries that represent mathematical coefficients for the transformation, which sounds more formidable than it is. Let's examine the typical **FontMatrix** array, which looks like this:

[.001 0 0 .001 0 0]

The first element of the array is the multiplier for the x-coordinate. As you see, and as expected, it is .001 to change from the 1000-unit character coordinate system into 1 unit in the user coordinate system. Similarly, the fourth element of the array is the multiplier for the y-coordinates. The remainder of the six entries affect the font coordinates in other ways that we won't discuss here.

When you execute a **scalefont** operation, what you would see in the font dictionary is a revised matrix that would look like the following, if you scaled the font to 12 points:

[.012 0 0 .012 0 0]

As you see, you have simply multiplied the x- and y-coordinates by the scale factor of 12.

This example suggests how you can scale fonts in unequal proportions; you simply change the x- and y-coordinate multipliers in the **FontMatrix** by different amounts. This can't be done by **scalefont**, but PostScript has thoughtfully provided another, more general, operator that will allow you to do it. This operator is called **makefont** and works like this:

font matrix **makefont** newfont

applies *matrix* to *font*, and produces *newfont*, whose characters are transformed by the values in *matrix* when they are printed. The operator first creates a copy of *font*, then replaces the **FontMatrix** in the copy with the result of combining the original **FontMatrix** and *matrix*. The resulting *newfont* is returned to the stack.

The **makefont** operator is used in the same place and in the same way as the **scalefont** operator, which isn't surprising, since **scalefont** is simply a special case of the more general **makefont**. In addition, the matrix that you use for the operation must have all six elements, not just two. However, the matrix looks just like the **FontMatrix** that we discussed earlier, so the first element is the x-scaling factor and the fourth element is the y-scaling factor.

You can make expanded and condensed fonts, using the **makefont** operator. The short example that follows will show an arbitrary string in both expanded and condensed Helvetica. The program to do this is given in Figure 4.11. It produces the output shown in Figure 4.12.

The program itself is simple. You start by defining two of our old friends: inch and centerText. This is the original centerText with a **show** at the end. Next you define three fonts: one condensed, one expanded, and one the normal Helvetica. These definitions all follow the same pattern. First you push the name for the scaled font onto the stack. Then you use **findfont** to get the basic font and put it onto the stack. Then you issue either **makefont** or **scalefont** with an appropriate operand. Finally, you store the scaled font under a new name.

```
%----------------------Prologue-------------------------
/inch
    (        72 mul       ) def

/centerText
{
    /Right exch def
    /Left exch def
    dup
    stringwidth pop
    2 div
    Right Left sub 2 div
    exch sub
    Left add
    Line moveto
    show
}
def

%----------------------Script---------------------------
%first define the new condensed font
/HCondensed
    /Helvetica findfont
    [ 10 0 0 12 0 0 ] makefont
def

%then define the new expanded font
/HExpanded
    /Helvetica findfont
    [ 15 0 0 12 0 0 ] makefont
def

%finally define normal Helvetica for comparison
/HNormal
    /Helvetica findfont
    12 scalefont
def

%now make test strings
/StrCond
    (This is a test of Helvetica condensed font - units 10 on 12)
def
/StrExp
    (This is a test of Helvetica expanded font - units 15 on 12)
def
/Str
    (This is a test of Helvetica normal font - 12-point)
def

%now use each font
%first the normal 12 point
HNormal setfont
1 inch 9 inch moveto
Str show
/Line 6 inch def
Str  0  8.5 inch centerText

%next condensed 10 on 12
HCondensed setfont
1 inch 8 inch moveto
StrCond show
/Line 5 inch def
StrCond  0  8.5 inch centerText
```

Figure 4.11: Example of condensed and expanded fonts

```
%next expanded 15 on 12
HExpanded setfont
1 inch 7 inch moveto
StrExp show
/Line 4 inch def
StrExp  0  8.5 inch centerText

showpage
```

Figure 4.11: Example of condensed and expanded fonts (continued)

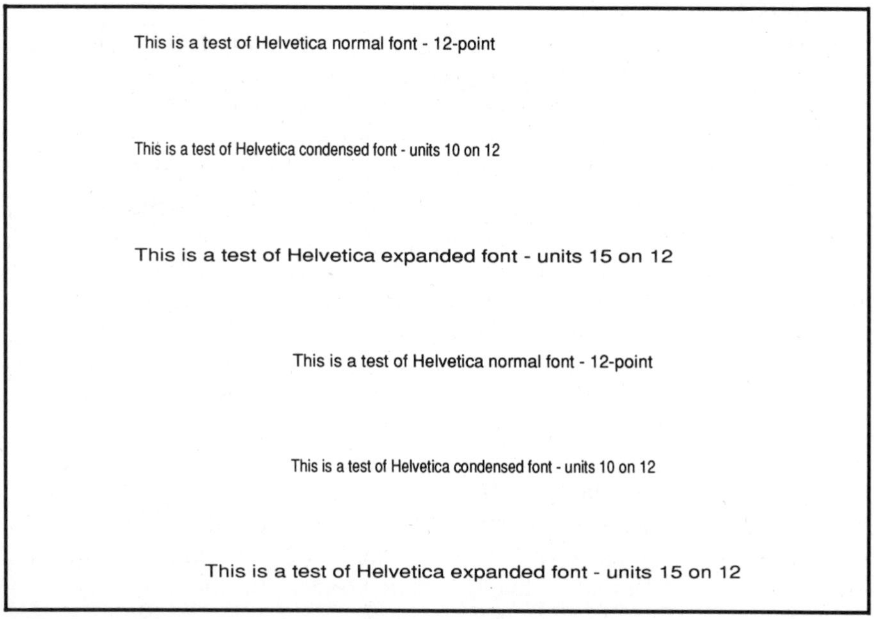

This is a test of Helvetica normal font - 12-point

This is a test of Helvetica condensed font - units 10 on 12

This is a test of Helvetica expanded font - units 15 on 12

This is a test of Helvetica normal font - 12-point

This is a test of Helvetica condensed font - units 10 on 12

This is a test of Helvetica expanded font - units 15 on 12

Figure 4.12: Output using condensed and expanded fonts

In the case of the condensed font, this is a scaling of the font by 10 units in the x-direction and 12 units in the y-direction. Because point size is a measurement of the font in the y-direction, this is a 12 point font. Since the x-scale is 10 points instead of 12, this will result in a condensed font; that is, the characters will be narrower in the x-direction than in the y-direction. In the case of the expanded font, the reverse is true. Here the scaling is 15 units in the x-direction, but 12 units in the y-direction. You still have a 12-point font, but it is expanded by about 25 percent. Finally, you define a normal version of Helvetica, scaled to 12 points for comparison.

You will create three separate strings to test each of the fonts. The first portion of each string is the same to help you see the differences and similarities in the letters; the last portion of each string is unique to identify the different strings. Then comes the substance of the program. First you use the normal font, showing the normal string left-justified on a line 9 inches from the bottom of the page; then again, using centerText, you center it on a line 6 inches from the bottom. The centering is done between the edges of the paper, 0 and 8.5 inches respectively. Next you do the same thing for the condensed font, moving each line an inch below the previous normal text. Finally you show the expanded text in the same way, one inch below the condensed font.

This is an interesting and instructive little program. It is the first time that you have defined fonts in this way and saved them for use in a multifont document. You will see more of this, and a discussion of the most efficient ways of handling fonts, in the next section.

There is one point to make about the condensed font that you have been using in this example. Typographers distinguish between condensed fonts and narrow fonts. In this terminology, *condensed fonts* are fonts that have been designed to have tighter spacing than the normal font, whereas *narrow fonts* are mathematically compressed versions of the normal font. A condensed font, therefore, will have a **FontMatrix** that shows no scaling effect, that is

[.001 0 0 .001 0 0]

while the narrow font will show different numbers as the x- and y-coordinate multipliers. By that definition, the font that you have created and used above is a narrow font, and not a condensed font. This font closely approximates the Helvetica Narrow font that is built into many PostScript printers.

MULTIFONT DOCUMENTS

Text representation is one of the most time-consuming and resource-intensive activities that is normally performed in creating page descriptions, yet it is also one of the most common. PostScript has an efficient and well-designed mechanism for handling text, as you have read above. Nevertheless, you can do specific things to aid the interpreter in working on your pages, and you should avoid other things so that you don't slow the output down to a crawl. One area of special concern is pages that contain multiple fonts. A number of issues that are particularly important in dealing with multi-font pages are discussed in the following sections.

Efficient Font Changes

The execution of the **findfont** and **scalefont** or **makefont** operators requires significant resources. You need to design your work to use these operators efficiently. The best way to do this is to avoid making procedures that use these operations; instead, execute the operators once and save the resulting font dictionary for use later. You may have noticed that this was the technique that you used in the last example; that was not accidental. In the case of the example, the overhead would have been the same whether you had done the font changes in-line, made procedures to do them, or used the saved font dictionaries as you did. Because each font on the page was used only once, each operation had to be executed once. But in many multi-font pages it is not possible to predict, as you did in the example, where condensed text, for example, will be positioned on the final page. In those cases, you might have to set the same font multiple times on the same page. As a result, the overhead of finding and scaling a font becomes quite significant. If you use the technique in the example, you will minimize that overhead.

Streamlining Font Handling

There are some additional points to be sensitive to in handling Post-Script fonts. Using many different fonts on a page is a potential problem. Setting aside aesthetic considerations, the number of fonts that will fit into PostScript memory at one time is limited. Note that this is not a limitation of the PostScript language, but a limitation of how the language is realized in a specific device. Each device has a specific amount of room for fonts to be stored and used internally. Some devices also store fonts externally, in cartridges or on disk; and some fonts, like the built-in fonts that you have been using in the examples and exercises, are stored permanently in the device to increase speed of handling. All such efficiencies are device-dependent, however, and should not be relied upon for most PostScript pages.

To insure that you have reasonably quick font handling, you want to use a minimum of font changes on a page. This is not intended to inhibit you from changing fonts; just be aware that every font change—and a change in point size is a font change for our purposes—has a cost in terms of performance and page output.

Font Cache Concerns

Because font character conversion is resource-intensive, PostScript uses the font cache as a means of speeding up text processing. You saw earlier in the chapter how the process works to insert characters that you are putting onto the page into the font cache for reuse. This is one of the important considerations in designing efficient PostScript code.

Here again, minimizing the number of font changes is an important issue. Every character that differs from a preceding one in either size or style causes the interpreter to convert it from the font; whereas every character that is reused can be, and is, taken directly out of the font cache, rather than reconverted. As I said earlier, the process of retrieving a character from the cache is almost a thousand times faster than the process of conversion. Whatever you can do to minimize changes that will cause the interpreter to have to do additional conversion will improve your performance measurably.

When a font has an **UniqueID** value in the font dictionary, the interpreter uses that value to identify cached characters. This allows the interpreter to reuse cached characters from one job to the next, which can make multiple jobs which use the same font run faster and more efficiently. In addition, on devices with an attached, external hard disk, some of the font cache is stored on the disk. This allows the interpreter to keep many more characters than can be stored in the internal cache and is another improvement in efficiency.

ADDING FONTS

You are well versed in the PostScript font machinery, and you have worked on various types of modifications that can be made to PostScript fonts. In all of this, you have been working with the built-in set of PostScript fonts. In this final section of the chapter, you will see how to add more fonts to your PostScript device.

There are two ways to add more fonts to PostScript. You can download additional fonts from your computer or make your own new fonts. We will examine both of these methods in this section.

FONT DOWNLOADING

Probably the best way to get additional fonts into your PostScript device is to download fonts from your computer to the device. *Downloading* is the process of sending the font information, essentially the font dictionary and all its subsidiary information, to the PostScript printer and installing it so the printer can use it. This section of the chapter discusses downloading fonts in general terms, and describes some of the considerations you need to keep in mind as you work with downloaded fonts. Specific directions on how to install, initialize, and download fonts for your system are contained in the package when you purchase downloadable fonts.

Downloadable Fonts

There are several sources for PostScript-compatible fonts. The bibliography in Appendix D lists a book that contains an extensive compilation of fonts that are available. In this section of the book, however, we will only discuss those PostScript fonts that are Type 1 fonts. Such fonts are available from Adobe Systems and from other vendors. These are probably the most common additional fonts that you may come across, and the process of downloading fonts is well defined for these fonts, making them the best choice for an example.

Fonts that are to be downloaded to the PostScript output device must be installed on the host computer before they are available for downloading. Besides the installation of the font (or fonts) onto some accessible place (usually a hard disk), you must install the associated screen fonts and font-metric files. The screen fonts contain characters that accurately imitate the style and size of the printer fonts. You install them so that your application programs can show you what your finished output will look like. Screen fonts are not essential, particularly if you use a utility such as Adobe Type Manager, which can derive screen fonts directly from the PostScript font outlines. But screen fonts will speed up text display on your computer and may be important for some applications.

The font metric files have the file extension .AFM (for Adobe Font Metrics), and they provide an application program that uses them with information on the size and spacing for each character in the font. This is important for the application to know when it is doing justification and kerning, for example. Only some applications make use of AFM files, however, and if yours does not, you may not want to include these files in your installation. Check the font documentation for details.

These are one-time tasks that you have to carry out to make the new fonts work on your system. They are not difficult, but they do take some time. Of course, the instructions that are shipped with each additional font package are the final word on the correct procedures to follow for initialization and installation. This discussion is intended to give you a short overview of what has to be done to make these additional fonts work on your printer.

Types of Downloading

Now that the new fonts are correctly installed, how can you make use of them in your documents? The basic concept should be clear. You must send the font information, essentially the font dictionary and all the supporting information that you learned about above, to the PostScript printer and have the interpreter enter the new font into the **FontDirectory**. Once that is done, you may use the font like any built-in font.

If you have a hard disk attached to your printer, you have an alternative. You may send the font to the hard drive and store it there. The **findfont** operator, as you read earlier, will look on the hard disk to see if a font is there when it doesn't find it in memory. If the font is there, **findfont** will load it into memory and enroll it in the **FontDirectory**.

Adobe provides a program, called the *Font Downloader,* to do this downloading task. It will process the font information from your disk, send it to the PostScript output device, and make the font available to the interpreter.

There are two methods of downloading fonts for a PostScript document. These methods do not differ in the process that is used; in both cases, the font download process is as outlined above. Instead, the two methods differ in when the download is performed, and how much you, as the user, have to be involved. The two methods are manual downloading and automatic downloading.

Some PostScript applications will automatically download the fonts that you request when you create a document. They check to see if the fonts are already on the printer; if they are not, they automatically look up the font information on the disk and download the required fonts. In particular, the standard printing services on the Macintosh (the LaserWriter driver and its associated

LaserPrep file) provide automatic downloading for all Macintosh applications that use standard printing.

If your system does not provide this service, or if you want to avoid using it, you may download the required fonts manually. There are some important performance considerations in the automatic downloading process that we will examine in the next section of the chapter. (You may have the reason to avoid automatic downloading.) Manual downloading means that the user controls the downloading process by sending the chosen fonts to the printer to be stored for subsequent use.

Concerns and Cautions

There is one major concern that you must have when you are downloading fonts. This has to do with the space available in PostScript memory to hold fonts. Earlier in the chapter, we briefly discussed the limitations on the number of fonts that can be held in any specific PostScript device. This limit specifically applies to downloaded fonts. Each font consumes memory resources and, inevitably, there is only a limited amount of memory in any device. Before you download a font, you should check the amount of memory available for the font before. This operation is automatically performed by the Font Downloader supplied by Adobe. The test is critical because, if you exceed memory, the printer will reset itself, just as if you turned it off and then on again. You will lose whatever is currently in the memory: procedures, fonts, and your document, if you are in the middle of processing.

You should also be cautious in your use of fonts, particularly when your system or application provides automatic downloading. You may find that the system downloads the required fonts and then erases them after completing the individual document that used them. This happens because of the memory limitations that we examined above; the process avoids leaving excess data in memory. That's a good attitude, but if you're printing a series of documents that use a downloaded font, you will find that your documents print more slowly because the required font is being downloaded each time. Downloading is quite a lengthy process; a lot of information is included in the font dictionaries. If you add this overhead to every document that you print, you will suffer some measurable degradation in performance. You can imagine the results if you have two or more fonts in your document that need to be downloaded.

You can avoid this problem by using manual downloading. In this case, you will control the downloading process, generally downloading once for your series of documents. Then, when the application is ready to print, it "sees" that the fonts are already present in the printer and doesn't issue a download on its own.

FONT CREATION

In addition to adding fonts that are supplied by others, such as the Adobe fonts, you can also create fonts of your own. The entire font creation process requires much work, and design and layout skills (not to mention PostScript procedures) that are beyond the scope of this book. However, we will look into the types of fonts that you might want to create and give you an overview of the process you would have to follow to create a new font.

Types of Fonts

The fonts that you have been using, and all fonts that are supplied by Adobe, are drawn using PostScript operations as we have discussed. We also mentioned bit-mapped fonts. These fonts are not drawn, but are a collection of dots that closely approximate a character in all aspects: point size, typeface, rotation, and so on. Generally, bit-mapped fonts are significantly lower quality than drawn fonts.

You are most likely to encounter bit-mapped fonts when running applications that have fonts on the screen that are not (for one reason or another) available in PostScript format for use on the printer. Results in this case are, of course, dependent upon the application and the hardware being used; but at least in the case of the Apple Macintosh, you will be given bit-mapped versions of fonts if the correct fonts are not either already available on the printer or available to be downloaded to the printer. If this happens to you, consult your hardware documentation for corrective action; if you are using Adobe downloadable fonts, consult the *Adobe Type Library User's Manual* for further information.

You can also use a combination of re-encoding and drawing to associate alternative shapes with various codes. You might use this technique to create bullets or small open circles to be used as part of an outline in your text. You could associate any arbitrary figure in place of a code. For example, you could take the logo graphic that we created in Chapter 3 and associate it with an arbitrary code or even replace a letter code, say *L* (for

Logo) and have the graphic print out when you entered the code or the letter. Needless to say, I don't recommend replacing letters (or any keyboard character) in such a way; it might be quite confusing unless you had a specific purpose in mind. The point here is that you can, if you wish, associate arbitrary graphic procedures with any character code, as well as the usual letter shapes. After all, the letters and other characters in a font are just graphic shapes themselves.

How to Create Fonts

Font creation in PostScript is very similar to modifying the encoding vector, which you did earlier in the chapter as an exercise. In fact, it uses all the same techniques and adds a few. Let's briefly look at the process of font creation.

To begin with, a user-defined font must follow all the rules laid down by PostScript for fonts. In particular, all the required entries for the font dictionary must be in place and be correct. This can be done using the same procedures that you used in the example of reencoding a font. The **FontType** must be set to 3, to indicate that this is a user-defined font. In addition, the font dictionary must contain a procedure named **BuildChar** or **BuildGlyph**. This procedure is used to create characters in the new font.

The process works like this. When a PostScript program invokes an operator that displays a character, for example **show**, the interpreter looks first to see if the character is in the font cache. If it is, the image in the cache is used; but if it isn't (and no character of the new font will be at first), the interpreter pushes the current font dictionary onto the operand stack, followed by the character code (an integer number between 0 and 255), and then executes the font's **BuildChar** procedure. Type 2 devices will push the current font dictionary followed by the character name (like the name in the **Encoding** vector) onto the operand stack and then execute the **BuildGlyph** procedure if that is present. If **BuildGlyph** is not present, then the character name is changed to the character code, and **BuildChar** is executed.

In either case, this procedure must use the supplied information to construct the requested character. This will involve determining what character has been requested, usually by using the character code as an index into the **Encoding** array and determining the character name, or else by using the name directly. The name provides the key for retrieving a procedure which is executed to create the character: it supplies character metric information, constructs the character, and paints it.

The **BuildChar** or **BuildGlyph** procedure works within a **gsave**, **grestore** pair, so that changes to the graphics state do not affect any other operations. It can assume that the coordinate system has been properly set to reflect both the font matrix defined in the current font and the current user coordinates. It should then use ordinary PostScript operators to construct the desired character and paint it.

Once the Build procedure is done, the interpreter takes the completed character and transfers it both onto the output device and into the font cache. The character is included into the font cache only if that was requested within the Build procedure by use of the appropriate operator.

This is all that we will present here regarding creation of new fonts in PostScript. If you want more information, there is a full discussion of the appropriate methods and procedures, including a full discussion of the requirements for **BuildChar** and even a short example, in the *PostScript Language Reference Manual, Second Edition.*

OPERATOR REVIEW

This section presents all the new operators that were introduced to in this chapter in the standard format. Please do look at each of these operators; in some cases, you will find that they are quite powerful and have additional capabilities that were not discussed in the text. Also, several of the operators are listed below in more than one section; most notably **get**, **put**, and **copy**. Each of these performs somewhat different functions, depending on the nature of the operands that you give it; for that reason, I have chosen to list the operators several times, under each type of operand that you might be using. Please note that it is the change in operand that determines how the operator's results change; there is no change in the operator itself.

DICTIONARY OPERATIONS

SYNTAX	FUNCTION
int **dict** dict	creates an empty dictionary with an initial capacity of *int* entries and places the created

SYNTAX	FUNCTION
	dictionary onto the operand stack. *int* must be a non-negative integer. For Level 1 devices, *int* is also the maximum capacity of the dictionary.
dict **begin** —	pushes *dict* onto the dictionary stack and makes it the current dictionary.
— **end** —	pops the current dictionary off the dictionary stack and makes the dictionary that was immediately below the current dictionary.
dict **length** int	returns *int* as the current number of key-value pairs in *dict*. (See also **maxlength**.)
dict **maxlength** int	returns *int* as the maximum number of key-value pairs that *dict* can hold using the current amount of memory allocated to it. For Level 2 devices, this can increase as long as additional memory is available; for Level 1 devices, this is the absolute maximum number of entries, as defined by the **dict** operator that created *dict*.
dict key **get** any	looks up the *key* in *dict* and returns the associated value. If *key* is not defined in *dict*, executes the error procedure **undefined**.
dict key value **put** —	uses *key* and *value* and stores them as a key value pair into *dict*. If *key* is already present in *dict*, its associated value is replaced by the new *value*; if it is not present, **put** creates a new entry.
dict1 dict2 **copy** dict2	copies all elements of *dict1* into *dict2*. The **length** of *dict2* must be 0; that is, *dict2* must be empty when the **copy** takes places; **copy** returns the revised *dict2* onto the stack. *dict2* must have a **maxlength** that is at least as great as the **length** of *dict1*.

ARRAY OPERATIONS

SYNTAX	FUNCTION
int **array** array	creates *array* that initially contains *int* null objects as entries. *int* must be a non- negative integer less than the device-dependent maximum array length.
string index array index **get** any	looks up the *index* in *array* or *string* and returns the element identified by *index* (counting from zero). The *index* must be between 0 and $n-1$, where n is the number of elements in *array* or *string*.
string index value array index value **put** —	stores *value* into *array* or *string* at the position identified by *index* (counting from zero). *index* must be in the range 0 to $n-1$, where n is the number of elements in *array* or *string*.
string array **length** int	returns *int* as the number of elements that make up the value of *array* or *string*.
string1 string2 substring2 array1 array2 **copy** subarray2	copies all elements of *array1* or *string1* into *array2* or *string2*. The types of the two operands must be the same, that is array or string. The length of the second operand must be at least the

SYNTAX	FUNCTION
	length of the first; **copy** returns the changed elements of the second operand onto the stack as *subarray2* or *substring2*. If the second operand is longer than the first; the remaining values are unaffected by the **copy**.
array **aload** $A_o...A_n$array	successively pushes all *n* elements of *array* onto the operand stack, where *n* is the number of elements in *array*, and finally pushes *array* itself.

FONT OPERATIONS

SYNTAX	FUNCTION
key font **definefont** font	registers *font* as a font dictionary associated with *key*, which is usually a name literal. **definefont** also creates an additional entry in the dictionary, whose key is **FID** and whose value is an object of type fontID; *font* must be large enough to add this entry.
font matrix **makefont** newfont	applies *matrix* to *font*, and produces *newfont* whose characters are transformed by the values in *matrix* when they are printed. The operator first creates a copy of *font*, then replaces the **FontMatrix** in the copy with the result of combining the original **FontMatrix** and *matrix*. The resulting *newfont* is returned to the stack.

SYNTAX

string bool **charpath** —

FUNCTION

makes character path outlines for the characters in *string* as if it were shown at the current point using **show**. These outlines are added to the current path, and form shapes suitable for general filling, stroking or clipping. If *bool* is *true*, the resulting path is suitable for filling or clipping; if *bool* is *false*, the result is suitable for stroking. This distinction only affects stroked fonts (**PaintType** 1); when the current font is an outline font (**PaintType** 0 or 2), the results will be identical. (Nevertheless, as discussed in the text, I recommend that you use *false* for results that you want to **stroke**, and *true* otherwise.)

OTHER OPERATIONS

SYNTAX

$any_1 \ldots any_n$ int **copy**
$any_1 \ldots any_n$ $any_1 .. any_n$

FUNCTION

when the top element on the operand stack is a non-negative integer *int*, **copy** pops *int* and then duplicates the top *int* elements of the operand stack.

$any_n \ldots any_0$ int **index**
$any_n \ldots any_0$ any_{int}

index pops *int* and then duplicates the item on the stack which, is *int* items from the top of the operand stack. The items on the stack are indexed with 0 as the top item on the stack. The operand *int* must be a non-negative integer between *0* and *n*, and there must be at least *int − 1* elements on the stack.

SYNTAX	FUNCTION
$any_{n-1} \ldots any_0$ n int **roll** $any_{(j-1)mod\ n} \ldots any_0$ $any_{n-1} \ldots any_{j\ mod\ n}$	performs a circular shift of the contents of the operand stack. The top n objects on the stack are shifted by amount *int*. A positive value of *int* indicates movement up the stack, that is, toward the top of the stack; a negative value indicates movement down the stack. The operand n must be a non-negative integer, and there must be at least n elements on the stack below the top two operands. The operand j must be an integer.
int1 int2 **idiv** result	divides *int1* by *int2* and returns the integer portion of the quotient as *result*; any remainder is discarded. Both operands must be integers, and the result is an integer.

5

Building a
Basic Document

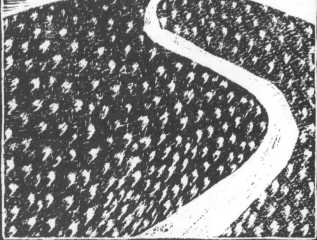

THIS CHAPTER HAS TWO PRIMARY purposes. First, it gives you an overview of the features that have been improved or added to the PostScript language in Level 2, and it discusses how you can use those features in a way that allows your code to run on both Level 1 and Level 2 devices. Second, it integrates the techniques and procedures that you have been learning by means of a long and detailed exercise. The purpose of this exercise is to produce a basic document that combines text and graphics on one page. Also, in the course of that exercise, it illustrates, in a concrete way, how you can take advantage of Level 2 features in your PostScript code while still remaining compatible with Level 1 devices.

POSTSCRIPT LEVEL 2

The Level 2 version of the PostScript language contains some new features and consolidates some advances that had previously been incorporated into PostScript in various devices. PostScript is not, and never was expected to be, a static language. Since its inception the PostScript language has grown and changed both to adapt to new devices and environments, and to take advantage of new technologies as they became available. Thus, the Display PostScript language extensions, for example, provide facilities for a programmer to display graphic images on a screen, or other display device, rather than on a printed page. After some five years of this progress, Adobe Systems, the creators of the PostScript language, decided to wrap all of these enhancements and extensions, along with some new features, into a single, upgraded language version. This new version is called PostScript Level 2. The amazing thing about the PostScript language is not that it has changed, but how little was required to adapt it to new opportunities and requirements as they became available.

LEVEL 2 FEATURES

The additional features in PostScript Level 2 that were not present in the first definition of the PostScript language can be divided in two groups: features that were implemented in some devices during the development of Level 1, and features that are new in Level 2. Let's look at these two groups.

Consolidated Features

Consolidated features include those that are available in some, but not all, Level 1 devices. One of the purposes of Level 2 is to consolidate all these features into a single version, so that PostScript programmers do not need to test explicitly for each possible feature. At present, some of these features are widespread; some of them are fairly common (being present in a specific class of output device, for example); and some of them are fairly rare. These features are packed array processing, color operations, composite fonts, and the new features that are in the Display PostScript environment.

It seems that PostScript programmers have been running out of memory in their output devices almost since the first LaserWriter hit the market. Since PostScript arrays, in the form of procedure definitions, are one of the most common composite objects, one method of saving memory is to pack arrays so that they use less space. *Packed arrays* function the same way that standard arrays do, except that packed arrays are always read-only. By using the special **setpacking** operator, procedures can be created in packed format to conserve memory. This feature is available in most current Level 1 devices.

Red, green and blue (RGB) and hue, saturation, and light (HSL) color operators have always been present in all PostScript output devices. This allowed PostScript programs to define colors which were then transformed into gray values for display. However, with the advent of standard color output devices and the use of PostScript to describe complex color pages, the RGB model become too cumbersome for regular use. To correspond to the standard methods of color printing, the cyan, magenta, yellow and black (CMYK) color operators were introduced into PostScript. CMYK operators are already present in most Level 1 color output devices; but they are generally not available in black-and-white devices. However, advanced device-independent color space features and operators are new in Level 2.

The standard PostScript font mechanism used in most Level 1 devices was designed to access up to 256 characters per font. However, some languages, particularly those which use writing systems based on Chinese characters, require significantly more characters for standard text output. *Composite font operators* implement a hierarchical array of font definitions that allow virtually unlimited character definitions. These operators are available in Level 1 devices that support Japanese and Chinese characters, and are now available in all Level 2 devices.

Computer systems, such as the NeXT system, which use Display Post-Script for output, have a number of features which have now been incorporated into Level 2. Some of them support binary token encoding instead of the standard ASCII encoding, user paths and other specialized operators for faster performance of standard graphics tasks, and so on. However, because of the nature and requirements of display output as opposed to standard printed output, there are (and I suspect there always will be) some features of Display PostScript which are unique to that environment.

New Features

Besides consolidating existing extensions to the PostScript language, Level 2 adds some new features as well. Some of these are completely new, while some are extensions or consolidations of existing features to make them more accessible and more consistent across the wide array of devices that now support the PostScript language. These features cover various aspects of managing the output device, optimization features, and communication improvements.

PostScript is, by design, independent of the target output device. However, by the same token, printing on any given device has always required access to specific device features or other software components. PostScript Level 2 has consolidated many of these requirements into a standard format and uses a standard approach for handling them. I have grouped all these here as various aspects of managing the finished document on your output device.

One new feature of Level 2 is its use of named resources for many types of features. As discussed in Chapter 4, a font is a perfect example and paradigm of a named resources. Fonts, as you already know, are dictionaries which are referenced by name, and which provide the necessary definitions and procedures for drawing all the characters in the font. Furthermore, all currently available fonts are named in a special directory dictionary, the **FontDirectory**.

Besides fonts, forms and patterns are two of the most common resources that you will work with. We will discuss both of these briefly here so that you can see a little about how these important resources work. Then, in the exercise in this chapter, you will use forms in a resource environment. This will help you get a clearer picture of how resources are used and what they mean for PostScript programmers.

Forms are generally standard documents that are used in business to collect and organize information. As such, a form may contain arbitrary graphics, just like any other document. The thing that makes a form unusual as a document is that it is likely to be output repeatedly with slightly different information each time it is printed. Because so much of a form is the same from one printing to the next, it is convenient and much more efficient to not have to repeat the PostScript code that draws the basic form, but to only repeat the new information to be used on the form. For example, the exercise in this chapter is an order form. The ideal is to send the form definition only once, and then send only the variable information, such as ordered items, name and address, and so on, repeatedly. Since the form definition is quite large, this speeds up processing and can save on transmission time and storage. In Level 2, it is also possible to save the actual form image, so that repeated impressions do not require as much repeated work by the interpreter to draw the form.

As you saw in Chapter 3, the PostScript interpreter paints an area using the current color, which is generally a shade of gray, or a color on color output devices. However, it is often the case that you want to fill an area, not with a solid color, but with a repeating figure, called a *pattern*. Level 2 allows you to define any arbitrary graphic which can then be used by the interpreter as a pattern to paint or fill a given path.

There are two issues to consider when you are making patterns. First, you must create the *pattern cell,* which is the actual figure to be repeated over the given area. Second, you must define the *tiling,* which defines how the pattern cell is repeated.

One of the major improvements in Level 2 devices is the new memory management techniques that are now available. These new techniques supplement, but do not replace, the older **save, restore** mechanism, which you have already met in the exercises. These techniques provide several new features, the most important of which is the distinction, new in Level 2, between *local* and *global* virtual memory. In Level 1 devices, all objects are contained in the same pool of virtual memory. If you perform a **save** and then later do a **restore**, all the objects that you created in the time between these two operations are lost, and the memory that they required is recovered. Generally, this is exactly what you want, and allows you to return to the same state that you left earlier. In Level 2, local virtual memory behaves in this same fashion.

Sometimes, however, this process is not exactly what you want. For example, suppose that you are creating a series of pages for your document, some of which use a special font. You want to define the font just before you use it, to save memory. However, if you encapsulate each page in a **save, restore** pair, then the font definition must be repeated for each page or it will be lost. The only alternative is to define the font at the start of the document and keep it in memory for the entire run, even though it is only required for a certain group of pages. Neither of these options is quite satisfactory. The same problem arises, with even more force, when you have a font that you wish to use in several documents.

Level 2 provides a special global memory allocation where you can place resources, such as procedure sets and fonts, which you don't want to remove when you do a **restore**. Generally, the idea is to place all objects whose lifetime is directly related to the document into local memory, and to place objects whose lifetime is independent of the document into global memory.

Level 2 also provides an automatic, internal mechanism to reclaim previously used memory. This feature is known by the rather colorful name *garbage collection*. As you remember, whenever you create a composite object, such as a string for display, you consume memory in the interpreter. However, even after the string is no longer available in memory, the memory that it used is not reclaimed in a Level 1 device. In Level 2, however, this memory can be reclaimed and returned to use by the garbage collector.

Consider this example. Suppose that you create a simple string,

(Hello World!)

and then display it with a **show** operator. Once the **show** is complete, the string is no longer on the operand stack; and it was never defined in the current dictionary. For all practical purposes, the string can never be used again. However, it did exist and it used some memory for storage. In a Level 1 device, the only way to recover that memory and reuse it is with a **save** at some point before the string existed followed by a **restore** sometime after you use it. Otherwise, the memory used by the string is taken up until your document or job is completed. In Level 2, however, the garbage collector can recognize that the memory, previously used by the string, is now available. It then returns the memory to use and allows you to continue adding more information without losing memory.

The presence or absence of the garbage collection feature should not directly affect your programming style. The **save** and **restore** operators are still available, and they are the most efficient method for directly recovering memory when you have allocated objects in your program. In the same way, where you need to create temporary objects, such as strings or arrays, to hold data, you should create one object and reuse it. The garbage collection feature is designed to handle cases, such as the one outlined above, where a string or other object is created and directly consumed by some operator. It does this very efficiently and allows you to be less concerned with specific memory management.

Besides providing garbage collection, Level 2 allows you to remove objects directly from memory by using certain operators. In Level 1, the only way to remove an object was to use **save** and **restore**. Although effective, this removed all objects defined after the **save** and could not be used to remove only one object. In Level 2, you can use the **undef** operator, which works just like the reverse of **def**, to remove a single object from memory. Level 2 also has other operators to remove certain special types of objects; for example, the operator **undefinefont** is used to remove a font from memory.

In Level 1 devices, the graphics state stack is a simple, push-down, pop-up stack that is used to store and restore the graphics state with the operators **gsave** and **grestore**. You have already been introduced to this in the exercises that you have done so far. In Level 2, however, you can create a given graphics state as a *gstate* and save it with a name. This gives you additional flexibility in setting and restoring a graphics state. Generally, you will find that the **gsave** and **grestore** mechanism is sufficient for your needs when you are creating document output. However, if you are working on a screen display, for example, then you may needed to use named graphic states.

In addition to packed arrays, mentioned earlier, Level 2 also provides a new feature that allows you to speed up drawing procedures for many types of objects. These are called *user paths,* and they allow you to specify any drawing path, usually one to be used repeatedly, in a compact format that allows the object represented by the path to be drawn very efficiently.

A user path is a collection of operators that create and mark a path. The only things that can be placed in a user-path definition are path construction operators, like **moveto**, **lineto**, and so on, and the required coordinate operands, which must be literal numbers. The user path offers several advantages over standard path construction. First of all, because of its strict limitations, it is much simpler and quicker to interpret and draw than standard operations. Also, it allows you to cache the resulting object and reuse it.

Level 2 consolidates and, to some extent, simplifies the problems of managing a specific output device. The basic PostScript language is independent of any specific device characteristics. However, when you actually go to output a page, there are certain device features which you may want to use. For example, if your printer has a manual feed, you may want to use that to feed the paper rather than use the standard paper tray. Such features depend on the exact type of device that is actually being used.

On Level 1 devices, operators used to control device-specific output are stored in a special dictionary known as **statusdict**. Applications can get the information about what features are available on a device in two ways. First, the information is available as a PostScript language supplement for the device. This information can then be coded into the application. The user is then asked to select one of the known printers for output and the application adjusts the features and output to conform to the chosen printer. Second, the information is available in a PostScript Printer Description (PPD) file for the device. In this case, the information can be parsed from the file by an application which then uses the PostScript code given in the file to access the desired features.

Neither of these solutions is entirely satisfactory. The first one limits the user to those printers which were known to the application developer; if the user has a device that isn't listed, he or she must try to map it to some listed device. The second approach is better, since it is not intrinsically limited to existing devices, but it requires a significant amount of additional code in the application to support reading and parsing the PPD file. Also, PPD file formats do change (albeit not often), so there is still an issue of updating these files.

Level 2 takes a somewhat different approach to the problem of setting up and controlling the output device. Applications can still parse and use PPD files to access features, and this is the most secure method for doing so, since it will work on any PostScript device. However, Level 2 devices have a new **setpage-device** operator, that provides a standard framework for setting initial conditions for the output and for controlling the various features that are specific to the device. One of the most important feature of **setpagedevice** is that it provides default actions when an application asks for some feature that is not present on that device.

Level 2 offers some new operators to simplify and speed up common tasks. These are all things that can also be done in Level 1, but they require several steps to accomplish. Since they are quite common in many environments, Level 2 offers additional support for these requirements. Level 2 provides new, optimized operators for these three areas: adjusting lines for uniformity on output, creating and using rectangular paths, and setting a font.

The first of these areas is automatic support for stroke adjustment. You read about possible problems when drawing multiple lines and how to adjust the line stroke to compensate for this in Chapter 3. By using the new **setstrokeadjust** operator, you provide automatic adjustment to force all lines to be a uniform width on your output device.

Rectangular paths are used repeatedly for many purposes. Therefore the second area of optimization is in handling rectangular paths. Level 2 provides a set of operators that will draw a rectangular path and stroke or fill the path, or clip to the path. This allows an application to specify rectangles directly in a natural way, and provides some speed enhancements over using a PostScript procedure to draw them.

Since text is probably the most common graphic on a page, and since using text inherently requires setting a font, Level 2 also offers a streamlined font access mechanism by means of the **selectfont** operator. As you read earlier, this combines the actions of **findfont**, **scalefont**, and **setfont** into a single operator, with corresponding savings in overhead.

Typically, one of the major complaints about printing is that it is not fast enough. Because PostScript is an interpreted language, this can be especially noticeable in PostScript devices, as files must be sent to a printer and then interpreted before they can print. Speeding up the transmission time for a file, therefore, is an important component in speeding up the printing process overall. This becomes especially noticeable as faster, RISC-based (reduced instruction set) processors are used in printers. Such printers can interpret the output page much more quickly than their older siblings, but if the transmission time remains the same, the overall improvement in printing may not be very significant.

Level 2 provides some major enhancements that allow an application to speed up the transmission of a file to the PostScript device. These fall into two categories. First, a Level 2 interpreter can compress data in a file in several ways. As a result, Level 2 interpreters can accept and send data directly in several compressed or improved formats, thus saving transmission time and improving processing speed. Second, a Level 2 or Display PostScript interpreter can use binary tokens for transmission when the connection between the computer and the printer supports binary data. This speeds up transmission and can also speed processing in some modes.

LEVEL 1 AND LEVEL 2 COMPATIBILITY

There are a variety of issues that you should examine when you are considering whether or how to incorporate Level 2 features into your Post-Script code. Depending on the decision, once you have examined these issues, you may still need to look at how you are going to provide that support. This section looks at the specific questions that you should ask yourself. It also suggests some ways of incorporating Level 2 code into your own procedures. As you will see, there is one method that you can use which gains you at least some Level 2 functionality at a small cost and which allows you to run the same code on Level 1 and Level 2 devices. We will discuss this method, and then you will use it as you create the document that makes up the sixth exercise, which forms the bulk of this chapter.

Compatibility Strategies

As you have seen, PostScript Level 2 provides a variety of features that are well worth having and exploiting in your PostScript code. In this section of the chapter, we will look at how you can determine the language level of your specific output device.

Once you know the language level of the PostScript output device, you can tailor your code to use the operators and functions that are available for the given level. If necessary, as we discussed earlier, you can emulate many Level 2 features on a Level 1 device. Since this may add significant overhead in both processing and transmission, you can choose to use emulations whenever you know that the output will be sent to a Level 1 device, or when you are not sure what the final output device will be. On the other hand, if you know that your device supports Level 2, you can use Level 2 features directly without any additional overhead for emulation.

Clearly, the next question is how to determine what type of device you have for output. If your code only runs in an environment with a single printer, or only runs in one environment where you can control the output device, this becomes a trivial problem: you know exactly what device you have set for output. However, if you are running in a more complex environment, or if you are creating code to be run in many different environments, this is an important issue.

Fundamentally, there are four methods for determining what type of output device you have, and whether that device supports PostScript Level 2. These are to

- query the device directly,

- query a printer description (PPD) file,

- ask the user, or

- make your code self-configuring by testing for the required features when it begins operation.

Let's briefly examine each of these alternatives.

The first alternative is to query the device and determine whether it is a Level 2 device or not. You can do this by sending a special query job to the device, receiving it, and analyzing the return. To determine the language level supported by the device, you would send the following code.

```
%!PS–Adobe–3.0 Query

%%Title: Query to determine if this is a Level 2 printer

%%?BeginPrinterQuery

/languagelevel where

        {pop languagelevel}

        {1}

        ifelse

= flush

%%?EndPrinterQuery: 1
```

Let's look at this job and the associated code for a moment.

The job overall follows the 3.0 Structuring Conventions for a device query. The first line is familiar to you from the discussion of structuring conventions in Chapter 2. However, notice the addition of the **Query** keyword, which identifies this as a job whose special purpose is to query the device for information. Note that all queries should be sent to the device as a separate job. They should never be included with a document description, since you need the information returned from the query to set up the document output correctly. The **Query** keyword allows document management software to handle such queries correctly and not mix them with standard jobs. The %%Title entry is entirely optional, and is used here simply to remind you what this query does.

The actual query is surrounded by a pair of comments

```
%%?BeginPrinterQuery

%%?EndPrinterQuery: default
```

that delimit the actual query code itself. There are several types of query, and using these comments allows you to include more than one query type in a single job. The comments themselves are very similar to the structural comments that you saw before in Chapter 2. The major difference is that these comments have an additional ? after the requisite % % to indicate that these are query comments and do not affect document structure. The %%EndPrinter-Query comment also has an optional *default* response field. This indicates the response that a spooler or document manager should return if the query cannot be completed for some reason. In our query, the default response is naturally 1.

The actual code that you use works by using the new, Level 2 operator **languagelevel**. This operator returns an integer that tells you what level of the language is supported by this device. The only catch in this approach is that Level 1 devices don't have this operator. The code above, therefore, first tests to see if the key **/languagelevel** is present in any dictionary. If it isn't, then this is automatically a Level 1 device, so the value *1* is placed on the stack. If it is, then the dictionary returned by **where** is removed from the stack and the operator is executed. This returns the integer value of the language level on the stack. So now you have an integer on the stack that represents the language level, whether the operator **languagelevel** is present or not. This value is returned to the querying application by the use of **==** **flush**, which sends the value back immediately. And that's what you want. Now you can simply have your application test the returned value to determine whether you are running on a Level 2 device or not.

The only drawback to this method is that, very often, the target output device is not connected to your application by a two-way connection where you can retrieve the value returned by your query. Also, sending a query to the device uses time and network resources that you may want to save. As an alternative, you can query the PostScript Printer Description (PPD) file for the target printer. This file contains a lot of important device information in a format that can be easily parsed by an application program. You can get a complete description of this file format and its contents from the Adobe Systems Developer Support Group.

To determine the language level of the printer from the PPD file, you should parse the file for the keyword ***LanguageLevel:** and test the following integer value, which will be the language level of the device. Conceptually, this is exactly the same as sending a query to the device, except that the device does not have to be attached or available.

Another strategy for determining the device language support is to simply ask the user. In this approach, the idea would be to display a query, such as a dialog box, and ask the user to set the language level that he or she wishes to use for output. In this case, of course, no further action is required, provided that the user is familiar with the actual device that will be used for output.

Obviously, these approaches are not mutually exclusive; you can combine them in various ways. For example, you might use a PPD file if it is available, and fall back on either the query or the dialog with the user if it is not available. In any case, you should always have a default plan if none of these produces satisfactory results.

There is one additional issue that you should consider when you are making this type of test. If you are creating output as a PostScript file, or if you are creating output for a spooler, then you should always assume that the output device only supports Level 1. The only exception would be in the case where you have used user input, such as a dialog, to set the language level for your code. In that case, of course, you should trust the user and stick to his or her decision. For the other cases, however, you cannot simply stay with the device response, since the output may be redirected to some device other than the one that you expected. In that case, although your query or the PPD file indicates that Level 2 support is available, the final output device may not actually be compatible with Level 2 operations and features. In these cases, therefore, you should always prepare your code as if it were going to run on a Level 1 device.

Compatibility Issues

As you have already seen in the exercises so far, one of the great strengths of PostScript is that it is a programming language. This allows you to define new procedures to create any desired graphics or to undertake other tasks that can be done inside your PostScript interpreter. Therefore, one natural approach to compatibility is to attempt to emulate the new Level 2 operators by creating PostScript procedures that provide the same functionality. This strategy is fundamentally sound, and it is one that we will explore in this section.

The added features in Level 2 can be divided into three groups:

- features that cannot be emulated in Level 1 devices;

- features that can be emulated in Level 1 devices, but only at a significant cost in either programming or device overhead; and

- features that can easily be emulated in Level 1 devices.

Items in the first category are new features, such as advanced memory management, that depend on enhancements in the Postscript interpreter itself. For obvious reasons, these operators and their associated actions cannot be emulated by existing PostScript code.

Items in the second and third categories can be emulated in existing Level 1 devices. The issues are how difficult these features are to emulate, how much overhead they require, and how much you need them in order to create your document.

There are three types of support that you, as a programmer, can provide in your PostScript code. First, you can provide basic support for all Level 1 features and functions. This may sound a bit strange, but it is an important point. Your first task, as a PostScript programmer, is to use the Level 1 features in a correct and efficient manner. This book, and others referenced in Appendix D, will help you do that.

After providing solid Level 1 support, you can go further and organize your code to take advantage of Level 2 features where appropriate and available, without requiring a Level 2 device. This is, I think, the best compromise for most of us. This allows your code to execute at its optimum level in all devices, but still allows you to run on the large number of Level 1 devices that are installed in the user community.

Finally, you may either need or want to write PostScript code that requires a Level 2 device for proper output. This strategy is best suited to circumstances where you can control the device that produces your output. The simplest example of this would be if you are developing code for a single device, and you know that the device supports Level 2. Another example would be if you are writing code for your company and you know that at least one Level 2 device is available; in that case, you may choose to use only that device for output. This would be particularly appropriate if your application truly requires some of the special Level 2 features.

Portable PostScript

A commercial application developer, however, would be better off creating code that is compatible with both Level 1 and Level 2 devices. We might call this "writing portable PostScript," or code that will run on both Level 1 and Level 2 device while taking advantage of the improvements in Level 2 when they are available. This process is not so difficult as you might think, and a little effort can pay big dividends. The exercise in this chapter will show you how to use this strategy in your own code.

The major drawback to writing portable PostScript is that it requires additional code and time in the PostScript device to test for and emulate Level 2 features. However, the overhead is generally small, and the potential benefits are substantial. First of all, using this technique ensures that your code will run on the currently installed base of Level 1 devices and still take advantage of the higher performance features of Level 2 devices when those are available. This will help you to avoid changing your PostScript programs for each new device, and therefore enhances the natural portability of the

PostScript language, which is, after all, one of the main reasons to use Post-Script for output description in the first place.

There is also a second, and somewhat more subtle, reason to use this approach. The PostScript language did not evolve in an ivory-tower, academic environment. On the contrary, PostScript has been improved in direct response to the requests and requirements of a multitude of users who have embraced it as a solution to the manifold problems of creating and storing documents. As a result, shaping your code toward the Level 2 features also helps you get the best possible structure for your PostScript code. The resulting programs will be easier to maintain, more stable, and more flexible than they might be without this discipline, even when you are only using a Level 1 device for output.

The query example above gives you some idea of how you can solve the problem of producing code that will run equally well on both Level 1 and Level 2 devices. The basic approach is to test in your procset for Level 2 features and then set up your code accordingly, using emulation if the required features are not present.

There are two methods of testing for Level 2 features. The first is the one shown earlier, where you test for the language level itself. This can be done early in your procset and then used later when you need to determine whether to emulate or invoke Level 2 features. The following code gives you one way to do this.

```
%%BeginResource: procset MyProc 1.0 0

/MyProcDict 20 dict def

MyProcDict begin

/languagelevel where

        {pop languagelevel}

        {1}

ifelse

2 ge

/L2 exch def

    . . .
```

This code sets a boolean variable, L2, which is true if the language level is 2 or greater and is false otherwise. Once this is set, you can simply use it directly when you are creating procedures to determine whether you want to create an emulation or use Level 2 features directly.

This is generally the correct approach when you need several of the Level 2 features. However, if you only need some of the Level 2 enhancements, it is both more correct and safer to simply test for the required features directly. For example, if you only require color operators for your document, you should simply test for one of the CMYK color operators and use that test to determine whether the extended color operators are present, rather than testing for **languagelevel**. This ensures that your code will run whenever the required operators are present, even if the device is not a full Level 2 machine.

For the exercise here, you will use the first method, as shown earlier, to test for the language level and then set up emulation or direct use of the required operators. However, you should keep in mind that, when you simply need one specific set of operators, then you should test just for the functionality you require, and not for anything more.

SIXTH EXERCISE: CREATING A BASIC DOCUMENT

In this exercise, you will design and create a basic document, one that might be used in real-life circumstances. This document is a single-page form, an order, and will be designed to work with the output from a typical application program—not, in this case, any real application but instead a generic application output such as you might get from a database or spreadsheet. This exercise addresses a common concern that occurs in many situations: how to create and fill out a form. Such tasks are typical in everyday business operations, and sometimes in personal life as well, and this exercise is a useful illustration of ordinary complexity in handling page output.

Forms are particularly illuminating not only because they are a regular part of ordinary life, but also because they are conceived and used as complete pages. In this respect, they differ from text output or most computer-generated reports, for example, where the page structure is a way to organize a continuous stream of output into a readable unit. Since PostScript is a page-description language, in this exercise you will see how the PostScript page concepts fit naturally into the design and use of forms.

Forms also have some special requirements when they are being generated and printed; in particular, because a form will generally be printed repeatedly with only small changes, efficiency and speed are important issues when using forms. Level 2 provides new and more powerful tools for handling forms for these reasons. This allows you, in this exercise, to design a program that combines Level 1 and Level 2 features for forms handling.

This exercise can also be accomplished with the tools that you have developed so far. You may be surprised, but think of all the points you have covered. You have worked with text as captions, as labels, and as individual lines making up small paragraphs. You have worked with graphic figures of various shapes and sizes; and you finished the last chapter by designing and printing a simple logo as a graphic unit. These tools are ready to be combined and used in the task of creating and filling in a simple form.

EXERCISE STRUCTURE

Before you can proceed to any other problems in designing and creating this exercise, you must consider the overall structure of the task at hand; that is, how to create an order form and fill it with data produced by an application program. A number of points must be resolved before you can complete this job successfully. This section of the chapter presents a simple but elegant approach to structuring this or any similar task.

The page in this exercise needs to be structured to accommodate both the fixed-form information and the variable data provided by the application. Both the fixed and the variable parts of the page have their own requirements and impose constraints on the page design, and yet each must fit into the other. The solution is to consider the design of each part of the page separately.

Actually, the exercise is designed as two separate pages. The pages are complementary, so that the final output is created by overlaying one page with the other. You might think of each page as transparent, with the fixed data, the form, on one sheet and the data to be filled in on another. The two sheets are complementary in the sense that the fill-in sheet is constructed so that the location of the data matches the places on the form that require data. The technique is to place one image onto the output device, lay the other image over the first without erasing or disturbing anything, and then output both as one unit.

We will use this method to create the output in this exercise. Each page will be designed individually, with all the required procedures and variables placed in the prolog. Then each page will be created (but not printed out) individually by the final script, so that each page is essentially independent of anything except the prologue. The end of the program will print the finished document, which will consist of both pages, superimposed, like a double exposure in film.

You can see how much depends on the design of the form and the fill-in sheet. Yet this is no different from, and no more laborious than, the considerations that must be made when designing a form initially and when designing output from an application to match the preprinted form. Since the natural sequence would be to design a form and then set up the application output to match, we will follow that sequence here.

Form

The first page to consider is the form itself. You may think of this as just an ordinary blank form. In this case, however, you will only print a test version of the blank form; once the form is correctly programmed, it will be printed with the associated data page as described above.

The first consideration is what information is required on the form for it to perform its function. In this case, the form is an order form for an imaginary company, Mountain Sports, Ltd. The basic information on any order is a list of items purchased and a total for the entire list. Therefore, the body of the form will consist of lines for the ordered items with a total at the bottom.

As a step toward designing this form, you may consider the information requirements as a series of blocks; for now, you may treat these blocks as units for positioning and analysis. The first block has already been identified as the list of items purchased. This block will occupy the center of the page, taking up most of the space; its size will depend on the other blocks of information that need to be fitted around it.

The second block will contain the total of the items above and any additional information related to that total, such as shipping or handling charges, sales tax, and so on. There might also be a trailer block to finish the page; this would be optional, variable information—for example, a company motto or a variable sales message a line or two long. In this exercise, for the sake of simplicity and clarity, a trailer block will not be included; but you should keep the possibility in mind for use if you need it. That completes the information at the foot of the page.

Above the major data block there will also be two blocks of information: a header block and a logo block. The header block will contain variable information such as the name and address of the customer, the date of the order, and perhaps other pertinent data such as terms, delivery date, and so on. The logo block will consist of the graphic logo plus the name and address of the company. Presumably these elements would have been designed as a unit and would be used as such; but each element (the graphic and the pieces of the name and address) could be handled separately for specific effects. In this exercise, the logo will be treated as a unit, with some alternative treatments discussed at the end of the chapter.

The entire set of blocks will come together on the page in something like the block diagram in Figure 5.1.

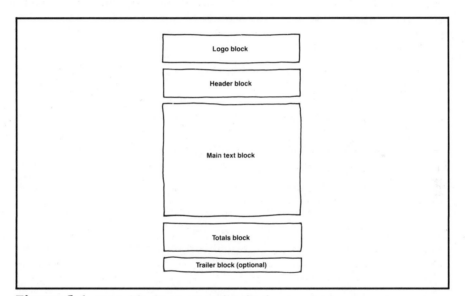

Figure 5.1: Basic block structure for the form output

The order of the blocks is natural and derives directly from the analysis of the information in each block. You began with the body block in the center of the page; the totals block, by its nature, must follow directly below the main data block, and any optional trailer block would come below the totals. On the top, the logo would naturally come first, with the heading data immediately preceding the main body.

Before you can define a final layout for this form, you must perform several more steps, as follows:

1. Identify specific information (data elements) to be included in each box.

2. Decide on the size and placement of data elements in each box.

3. Determine the overall size of each box.

4. Position and scale each box onto the final form layout.

Although you are still working with a blank form, you can see that the nature of the data that will fill in the form is becoming important, and you can't effectively finish the design of the blank form without considering the data to be on it.

Fill-In

The data that will fill in the order form might be generated by any application. This application needs to perform the following tasks:

- provide an entry method for those data elements that must be entered;

- calculate specific data elements;

- display information and titles on the screen for editing and review;

- output data element on a consistent format for integration onto the final form output.

Now you need to decide what data elements belong in each block. In a real systems analysis, you would need to identify what data was required for processing the order and what data was required on the order to tie back into the inventory and order-processing methods in use at the store. For the exercise, data elements used in each section will represent an arbitrary, but fairly typical, selection of data that may be required on a standard order.

As before, let's start with the main or body block. In this case, a line of body data will consist of the following data elements:

1. Item number

2. Item description

3. Quantity ordered

4. Quantity delivered

5. Unit price

6. Extended price

Of these six data elements, the first five will have to be entered into the application, while the sixth, extended price, can be calculated as quantity delivered multiplied by unit price.

This leads to a consideration of the second block of data, which contains the totals. In this section there will be four data elements, as follows:

1. Item total

2. Sales tax

3. Shipping and handling charges

4. Order total

The shipping and handling charge might be entered or derived from a database. Each of the remaining elements can be calculated. The first element, item total, is the sum of the extended prices of the lines above. The sales tax is a percentage of the item total; in the California county where I live, this would be 7.5 percent. Finally, the order total is the sum of the three preceding fields. This completes the bottom of the spreadsheet.

Data in the header block is more complex and generally has a wider variation in required elements than data in the body or totals sections. For simplicity of design and ease of programming, the data elements selected for this exercise will be kept to a minimum set of commonly used elements. These will be the following:

1. Name and address

2. Order number

3. Date

The name and address data is presented as a block of four lines of text that will be transferred as a unit to the form. The order number might be generated or entered. The date is commonly available from most computer systems, and in this case is provided as a text string for display only. If the application is taking the date from the system, this might require changing the format or type of the system data.

You have finished identifying the required data elements in each box. Now you need to determine the size—the length and width—and the placement of these data elements within each box.

Remember that the form and the fill-in sheet are complementary; they are designed so that the application data will fall into the proper spaces on the form. In this process, it is easiest to design "backwards" so to speak, at least partially working out the size and placement of the data elements and then designing the form around them. This approach is effective because the data is the essential information being presented; the form is just a method of organizing the data.

The approach is also effective because the length and width measurements for the data are easier to determine. The form might be constructed in a variety of formats using different typefaces; however, the data has some constraints on presentation that will help you determine the length and width of the elements. In this exercise, and in most cases of form construction and fill-in like this, you want to make the data appear to be typed. This differentiates the data from the form and corresponds to the most common presentation of data on forms. Because Courier is a common typewriter font and is available in PostScript, data output for the application will be in Courier. Most typewriter fonts are monospaced fonts, typically 10 or 12 characters per inch. PostScript Courier is also monospaced, and you can select a point size to give the desired character spacing—in this case, you select a 10-point font to give a spacing of 12 characters per inch.

Line spacing is also fairly rigid for this type of output, usually 6 or 8 lines per inch. Both 6 and 8 divide into 72 (which is the number of PostScript units per inch), giving 12-and 9-point spacing respectively. Nine-point spacing will not work with the 10-point type that you have chosen; however, 12-point spacing will work well. This provides 10-point type on 12-point leading, which you already recognize from our previous discussions as acceptable spacing for normal purposes.

You may be wondering why 10-point type will give you 12 characters per inch. If the type is 10 points, doesn't that imply that there will be about 7 characters per inch? Or if you want 12 characters per inch and an inch is 72 points, shouldn't you use 6-point type? The calculations ($72/10 = 7$ and $12 \times 6 = 72$) are certainly correct; the confusion stems from the concept of point size. From our previous discussion of point size and font metrics, you may remember that point size was the size necessary to ensure that two lines of type don't overlap one another, and that the width (for proportional fonts) varied according to the character. Here you are using a monospaced font, so the width is the same for each character; but the point size still fulfills the same function of providing clearance between the lines. As you may recall, the vertical measurement to ensure adequate spacing must include both ascenders and descenders. These are the parts of the letters that extend above and below the line of type, like the top of the letter *b* of the bottom of the letter *y*. If you look at Figure 5.2, you will see how these are measured.

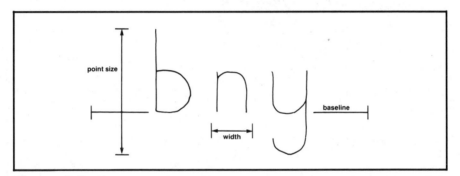

Figure 5.2: Character measurements

Because point size is a vertical measurement, the width of the character is always less than the point size; in effect, a box that fits around every character in a font would always be taller than it would be wide. Therefore, about seven lines of 10-point type will fit in a vertical inch, but the characters (in a monospaced font) will come out 12 to an inch. Of course, in a proportional font, the width of each character, and hence the number of characters per inch, will be variable.

Using these measures of 12 characters per inch and 6 lines per inch, you can work out the space required for the data in each of the lines. In this section you will work with the data elements only, as you might do for printing onto blank paper. The form measurements and layout will come later in the chapter, after you have worked out the data layout.

To begin with, the physical page is 8½ inches wide. You have to allow for margins on all sides, both for printing and aesthetic reasons, and allow room for the form to be printed. In this case, suppose that you establish 1-inch margins on both sides of the page. This leaves a maximum of 6½ inches for each line of data. The logo block at the top of the page is part of the form, and you will want it to print as close as possible to the top of the page. At the bottom, however, you should leave a margin of about 1 inch so that the data doesn't appear to run off the page.

The maximum line width is primarily a concern in the main block, which contains the list of purchased items. At 12 characters per inch, there will be a maximum of 78 characters across a $6\frac{1}{2}$-inch line, including all spaces and punctuation. Using the previous list of data elements, you might allocate the spacing as follows:

DATA ELEMENT	NUMBER OF CHARACTERS	TYPE
item number	8	alphanumeric characters
	5	spaces
item description	25	alphanumeric characters
	3	spaces
quantity ordered	5	four digits and sign (– 9999)
	3	spaces
quantity shipped	5	four digits and sign (– 9999)
	3	spaces
unit price	6	three digits, decimal, and two digits (999.99)
	3	spaces
	2	spaces
extended price	10	– 99,999.99
	—	
	78	characters

Notice that you must provide room for a sign in several of the fields and for appropriate punctuation in the currency fields. The signs will be required for processing credits and returned items. You will also notice that the spaces between unit price and extended price have been divided into two parts: 3 spaces and 2 spaces. The 2-space section is provided to allow room for aligning the totals (which will be larger than any individual price) under the extended price column.

The totals block contains four short data elements, which will be aligned under the extended price column from the main text block. Nothing in the totals block is going to approach the maximum line width, and spacing can be allocated as follows:

DATA ELEMENT	NUMBER OF CHARACTERS	TYPE
item total	11	– 999,999.99
sales tax	9	– 9,999.99
shipping and handling	10	– 99,999.99
order total	11	– 999,999.99

Similarly, nothing in the header block will be maximum width, either. The name and address data will consist of four lines, one below the other, while the order number and date are relatively short numeric items. Space might be allocated as follows:

DATA ELEMENT	NUMBER OF CHARACTERS	TYPE
name and address (4 lines)	30	alphanumeric characters
order number	6	digits (999999)
date	9	*DD–MMM–YY*

You have now completed width allocation for all the data elements that have been identified. But you still must determine how many lines each block will require, which can best be done after discussing how you are going to merge the form and the data into one document.

Integration

You have already worked out the method for producing a completed form by overlapping the blank form and the data onto a single output sheet.

The data will be placed over the form, and both will be printed out together. The form clearly has to be designed and built like any other PostScript page, using the techniques that you have practiced in earlier chapters. You might, however, think that the application output could be printed onto the form without further processing, using whatever printing method the application provides.

In a Level 2 device you might do this by storing the form in the printer and then reusing it. However, in a Level 1 device, this becomes more difficult and potentially wastes memory. Of course, this would require that your application produce the correct PostScript output, with the required calls for your form. In any case, that is not the approach that you will use here; instead, you will construct both the form and the data as a single output unit, even though the two parts are conceptually distinct.

Even if you cannot modify your application to produce the required output directly, it is not difficult to adapt standard output to the PostScript environment. The problem is to insert the necessary PostScript procedures into the application output so that the data will go onto the page with the structure required to match the form. You can do this easily by following these steps:

1. Print the application output to a disk file.

2. Edit the disk file to add PostScript procedures.

3. Send the revised file to the printer.

Later in the chapter, you will read about other methods of working with application output, but the method presented here is easy to understand and to work with.

As you have already discovered, PostScript structure is best used by creating powerful procedures to handle large segments of the desired page. You can use such procedures to process large pieces of the application output, treating output elements as strings and positioning an entire group on the page as required for the result you want. Knowing this, you can see that only modest editing would be necessary to prepare the application output for printing.

We have completed the initial analysis that was necessary before you could begin detailed layout and programming. Let's review what you have accomplished so far. You have structured the output page, both form and data, into major output blocks. You have also identified and positioned data elements for each block. The size of each data element and the horizontal spacing of elements within a line in the main text block—which is the largest portion of the form and contains the most data—have all been established. Finally, the minimum line spacing will be six lines per inch; however, the overall vertical spacing remains to be finalized because it depends on the detailed structure of the form itself.

FORM

You are ready to begin the detailed layout and design of the form. Because both parts of the final output must fit together exactly to work properly, this section frequently refers to the location of data elements on the other part of the output; and the same thing will happen in reverse when you design the data output in the next section. This natural back-and-forth should not be a surprise and would be equally necessary if you were designing a form to be printed and used on a typewriter or on a computer printer. In all cases, the form and the associated data make up a single output unit and ultimately must be considered and designed as such.

Layout

Let's consider how to structure and lay out the form. You know that the minimum desirable spacing between lines is 6 lines per inch, or 12 points per line. This information provides a basis for starting the final layout. In addition, several design elements are important to consider.

In laying out any page, there are a number of issues regarding form design and data placement that need to be resolved on aesthetic grounds or that may involve arbitrary choices. Such decisions are usually arrived at by a process of trial and error, making each judgement based on how the output looks (this is why WYSIWYG, or "What You See Is What You Get", is so important in page-composition software). To avoid making this exercise tedious and repetitive, I have completed this trial-and-error process and the layout shown in Figure 5.3 is the result.

As before, this layout contains design elements, such as the box around the purchased items and the totals, and the marks around the name and address, that are purely arbitrary; the same applies to some of the spacing decisions that are incorporated into the layout. Nevertheless, all these elements are taken from actual forms and are commonly used.

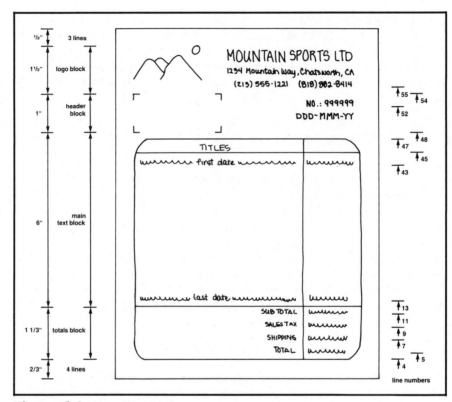

Figure 5.3: Form layout

All vertical dimensions are given in inches or lines, or both, using the previously established basis of 6 lines per inch for the output. One of the first things you notice about this design is that the main text and totals have both been enclosed in a box, similar to the figure produced by the **screenBox** procedure that you worked on in the previous chapters.

Let's analyze this layout, working form the bottom up and starting with this box. Working from the bottom of each of the elements and blocks makes sense. This position represents the baseline for the text and defines a precise y-coordinate to be used for positioning both text and graphic elements. In keeping with standard PostScript measurements, all the lines are numbered from the bottom of the page. This means that there are 66 lines on the page (11 inches at 6 lines per inch) with line 66 being the top of the page. With this housekeeping out of the way, let's review the form layout in detail.

The bottom of the data box is at line 4, leaving a $^2/_3$-inch margin at the bottom of the page. The data elements within the totals block are double-spaced and located as follows:

DATA ELEMENT	LOCATION
item total	line 11
sales tax	line 9
shipping and handling	line 7
order total	line 5

This portion of the data box represents the totals block that was discussed earlier. The box is designed to enclose both the main text block and the totals block; but before you can determine the position for the top of the box, you need to position the top two blocks on the form. The base of the topmost block, the logo block, is at line 55. This leaves 12 lines, or 2 inches, to the top of the physical page. The detail of the logo has not been designed yet, but you can esti-mate, based on the work in the last chapter, that you will require 1 $^1/_2$ inches for the logo, leaving a $^1/_2$ inch as a top margin. Since the top of the logo is jagged and not uniform across the page, this top margin is not precise, but the estimate gives you a rough box to work with that is 1 $^1/_2$ inches high and 7 $^1/_2$ inches wide—a convenient ratio of 1:5.

The base of the header block is at line 48. You will note that the name and address information, which is 4 lines of data, is enclosed in an area set off by a series of graphic elements that look like corner tabs. This element is common in many forms and is designed (so I'm told) to help align the name and address space for window envelopes. In any case, the data elements in the header block are positioned as follows:

DATA ELEMENT	LOCATION
name and address (4 lines)	lines 52 to 49
order number	line 52
date	line 50

The top two "corners" are located on line 54, while the bottom two are on line 48. The word "Order" and the title "No.:" are also on line 52, before the position for the order number.

Now that these two blocks are positioned, the remaining area is available for the main text block. The data box, which encloses both the main text and the totals, will have its top line on line 47. You will need titles for the data within the box, so set aside the top two lines of the box for title information and start the first data line two lines below that, on line 43. The last data item that will fit into the main text block should also be double-spaced from the totals. That places it two lines higher than the item total; therefore, it would be located at line 13.

You have now established the overall vertical spacing of the form as follows:

DATA ELEMENT	LOCATION
logo block	top at line 63
	baseline 55
header block	top at line 54
	baseline 48
main text block	top at line 47
	baseline 13
totals block	top at line 11
	baseline 4

In addition, the main text block and the totals block have been combined by means of a box that surrounds all the data elements from both blocks, combining them into a single graphic unit.

Main Text and Totals

Now you need to set up and program each of the blocks in detail. You can begin with the box that encloses both the data items and the totals. Remember that you are not concerned with the positioning of the data or the totals themselves, but are creating the places on the form where those items will appear after they are output by the application. The top of the box will look like Figure 5.4.

This figure shows you the detail of the top of the box, along with the title information and the first line of the item list. The outer edge of the box will consist of a 2-point line, double the usual line width. A horizontal line of 1 point will be used to separate the title information from the data, and vertical lines of 1 point will be used to separate data elements down the page into columns. The positioning of these lines is shown in Figure 5.5, along with the x-coordinate required to position each of them.

These coordinates were calculated using the character spacing for the data that will be below them; you remember that the data will be spaced 12 characters to the inch, which means that each character is 6 points wide.

The titles themselves will be in 10-point Helvetica and based 6 points (a half line) above the horizontal line that divides the title area from the data. This will approximately center the titles in the boxed area formed by this line and the top of the large data box, allowing 8 points above and 6 points below the title text. As discussed earlier, there is a double space down to the first line of data, on line 43. The data, the list of items purchased, will be entered from the spreadsheet, and that spacing will be discussed when we design the application output in the next section. In any case, the last data item that can be printed will

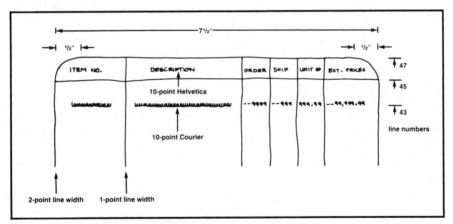

Figure 5.4: Titles and first-line layout

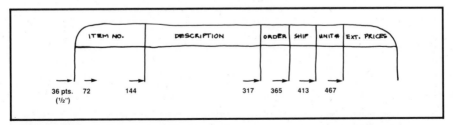

Figure 5.5: Column positioning

be on line 13. The setup information for the bottom of the box, which is the bottom of the form, is presented in Figure 5.6.

This figure starts at the last data item and continues to the end of the form. This portion of the form contains totals information from the spreadsheet, which is placed next to appropriate labels, double-spaced in lines 11 to 5. The last data line is set off from the totals by a 1-point line positioned 6 points (half a line) below line 13; this will be line 12.5. The bottom of the box that encloses the data and totals is on line 4; as before, the line that forms the entire box is 2 points wide. The vertical line that divides the extended prices on the data portion of the form is brought down through the totals section to divide the numeric values from the labels; there is room enough for the larger totals fields because you allowed an extra two spaces on the extended-price column just for this purpose. The rest of the vertical lines end at the horizontal line that divides the data section from the totals.

The labels for the totals are in 10-point Helvetica-Bold and are right-justified at a position 4 points to the left of the vertical line.

You are ready to develop the procedures that are required to produce the main data block and the totals block. You will develop these procedures together because you have enclosed these two blocks with the data box, effectively making them into one graphic unit. There isn't much overlap between this portion of the form and the other blocks, so you may as well make the procedures specific. When you have produced the final version of the program, it should follow the conventions discussed earlier; for now, you can break the program into prologue and script sections that can be integrated into a completely structured PostScript program later.

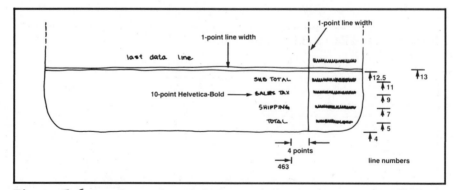

Figure 5.6: Last line and totals layout

The major procedures for this part are as follows:

SYNTAX	FUNCTION
screenBox	produces the box that encloses the data and totals sections. This procedure differs from the earlier version in that it requires two operands for height and width (because this box is not a square).
dataTitles	produces the title information at the top of the data box, including both the titles and the horizontal line underneath them.
footTitles	produces the titles for the totals and the horizontal line above them; also produces the vertical line that separates the titles from the data.
verticalLines	produces the vertical lines that divide the columns of data. The lines extend from the top of the data box to the horizontal line that divides the last line from the totals area.

Each of these procedures will use additional procedures. In real Post-Script programming, you might begin to write the program using these procedures at this point. Let's look at Figure 5.7 to see what the program (that is, the script) portion might look like.

```
    %------------------------Main Text Script---------------------
    %Setup for test
    /Pg save def

    %------------------------Main Text Block---------------------
    gsave
            .5 inch 4 line translate
            2 setlinewidth
            7.5 inch 43 line screenBox
    grestore
    verticalLines
    dataTitles
    footTitles

    %Print for test
    Pg restore
    copypage
```

Figure 5.7: First draft of the form script

The program flow follows what has been discussed previously. You will notice that, first, the entire script section is enclosed in a **save, restore** pairing of operands on lines %1 and %10. This is good PostScript practice, as you learned when these operators were introduced. Second, you will notice that the screenBox procedure now strokes the box. Because of this, you need to set the line width at line %4 before creating the figure in line %5. Also notice that the entire procedure is enclosed in a **gsave, grestore** pair on lines %2 and %6 in order to avoid mis-setting the other elements elsewhere on the page.

This program also identifies two more procedures that you will want to write: inch and line. You can see that the measurements on the page are given both in inches and lines; whichever is easiest and most natural has been used. The net result is that most y-coordinates are in lines, while the x-coordinates are either in inches or just in the native x-values. For this reason it is easier to use two procedures to help position items, instead of trying to convert one into the other.

Now you are ready to write the procedures. The figures that follow give each of the procedures identified so far, along with a short discussion. Figure 5.8 gives you the revised screenBox, based on the familiar screenBox procedure as you finally developed it in Chapter 3.

There are three differences that you will see between this version of screenBox and the earlier one. The **stroke** is now included in the procedure; another difference is that there are now two dimensions required to

```
    %----------------------Form Prolog ------------------
/screenBox
(
        newpath
    /DimY exch def
    /DimX exch def
    .5 inch 0 moveto
    DimX 0   DimX DimY .25 inch arcto
    4 (pop) repeat
    DimX DimY  0 DimY .25 inch arcto
    4 (pop) repeat
    0 DimY       0 0      .25 inch arcto
    4 (pop) repeat
    0 0       DimX 0      .25 inch arcto
    4 (pop) repeat
    closepath
    stroke
)
def
```

Figure 5.8: Revised screenBox procedure

develop the box, rather than one, which leads to the definition of two variables. If you don't remember the **arcto** operator, you should review it in the opperator summary at the end of Chapter 3.

Finally, the two variables are defined using a **store** operator instead of **def**. The **store** operator works very much like **def**, except that it searches the dictionary stack for the given key before it defines it. If the key exists already in any dictionary on the stack, the previous value is replaced by the new one in that dictionary, even if it isn't the current dictionary. If the key does not exist, **store** works just like **def** and creates a new entry in the current dictionary. This technique is used here for compatibility with Level 2 processing; we will discuss it later when you read about emulation of the **execform** operator. The choice of the starting point (0.5 inch) and the size of the radius (0.25 inch) are arbitrary; you may adjust them to any values you find satisfactory.

Now you can move on to the next procedure, verticalLines, in Figure 5.9. This procedure moves to the top of each of the columns identified in Figure 5.5 and rules a line from the top of the box, at line 47, to the bottom of the data area, at line 12.5. It doesn't stop at line 13, which is the last data line, because there is a horizontal line 6 points (a half line) below the data and it would look best to run the vertical lines into the horizontal one.

```
/verticalLines
{
        newpath
        144  47 line moveto
        144  12.5 line lineto
        317  47 line moveto
        317  12.5 line lineto
        365  47 line moveto
        365  12.5 line lineto
        413  47 line moveto
        413  12.5 line lineto
        467  47 line moveto
        467  12.5 line lineto
        stroke
}
def
```

Figure 5.9: The verticalLines procedure

The next procedure is dataTitles, in Figure 5.10. This procedure is also straightforward; but it creates a need for an additional procedure to support it. The dataTitles procedure starts by moving to the point identified for the horizontal line dividing the data from the titles and draws that line. Then it moves to the position for the title text, which is 6 points, or a half line, above the horizontal line at line 45.5.

You will also notice that, instead of setting the font directly in this procedure, you simply reference a variable F1 which must be set to the correct font and size. In this case, as you determined earlier, that will be 10-point Helvetica. This approach is compatible with both Level 1 and Level 2 devices and is generally the fastest and most efficient way to switch between fonts in your PostScript code. You will use this approach throughout this exercise.

At this point, you realize that you must decide where to display the title headings. You have already established the location of the vertical lines that divide the data elements into columns; an obvious solution is to center the titles between the columns. This is performed by the new procedure, centerText, which takes three operands; the string to be displayed, and the left and right positions between which the string is to be centered. The procedure will need to set the current point for the **show**, and a natural way to do this would be to use the current line as the vertical position. Therefore you insert a **moveto** before setting the titles to establish the y-coordinate position.

This centerText is similar to the previous procedure for centering text that you developed in Chapter 1, with some minor variations. That procedure centered a text string between predefined margins; this one centers it between arbitrary x-coordinates. We will discuss the variations in this procedure later when you examine these auxiliary procedures.

```
/dataTitles
{
        newpath
        .5 inch 45 line moveto
        7.5 inch 0 rlineto
        stroke
        .5 inch 45.5 line moveto
        F1 setfont
        0 45.5 line moveto
    (ITEM NO.) 72 144 centerText
    (DESCRIPTION      ) 144 317 centerText
    (ORDER) 318 365 centerText
    (SHIP) 366 413 centerText
    (UNIT $) 414 467 centerText
    (EXT. PRICE) 468 540 centerText
}
def
```

Figure 5.10: The dataTitles procedure

The positions chosen for the centering are derived from the column positions shown in Figure 5.5. The first column begins at position 72, or 1 inch from the edge of the paper. No vertical line is ruled here as it would be redundant; the line at the edge of the box is sufficient to create a column for the data. The second and subsequent columns are used as positioned, except that the starting position for the centering has been moved right 1 point to allow for the width of the line that creates the column.

The final procedure that was identified initially is footTitles, shown in Figure 5.11. This procedure also requires a newly identified helper, rightJustifyText, which takes a string, followed by y- and x-coordinate positions and displays the string at the y-coordinate, right-justified against the x-coordinate. It uses a new font which is given the font code of F2.

```
/footTitles
{
        newpath
    .5 inch 12.5 line moveto
    7.5 inch 0 rlineto
    stroke
    467 12.5 line moveto
    467 4 line lineto
    stroke
    F2 setfont
    (SUBTOTAL) 11 line 463 rightJustifyText
    (SALES TAX) 9 line 463 rightJustifyText
    (SHIPPING)  7 line 463 rightJustifyText
    (TOTAL).    5 line 463 rightJustifyText
}
def
```

Figure 5.11: The footTitles procedure

The basic procedure begins by creating the necessary horizontal and vertical lines that were previously identified. Then the titles of the totals are each positioned and right-justified. The process is identical for each title: the rightJustifyText procedure is invoked to set the desired string at the correct locations.

Now that these major procedures are defined, you need to turn your attention to the supporting ones in Figure 5.12. Each of these procedures resembles the procedures used previously for these same functions; there are, however, some minor variations that make these procedures a bit more flexible than the ones you have seen before.

```
        /inch
        {
                72 mul
        }
        def
        /line
        {
                12 mul
        }
        def

        /centerText
        %procedure to center a string between arbitrary margins
        %called as:  string left right  centerText  --
        {
                2 index
                stringwidth pop
                2 div
                3 1 roll
                1 index sub
                2 div
                3 -1 roll
                sub
                add
                currentpoint exch pop
                moveto
                show
        }
        def

        /rightJustifyText
        %procedure to center a string between arbitrary margins
        %called as:  string y x  rightJustifyText  --
        {
                2 index
                stringwidth pop
                sub
                exch moveto
                show
        }
        def
```

Figure 5.12: Auxiliary procedures for the form

Let's look first at the new centerText procedure. This takes three operands: a string for display, and the two x-coordinates for the right and left margins for centering the string. The procedure, as mentioned earlier, assumes that current point is already set to the correct y-coordinate for the display. Unlike the previous version of centerText, this version does not define the operands as variables; instead, it uses them directly from the operand stack. This is more efficient than saving and recalling them, and it saves memory and dictionary space. However, it does require some additional stack manipulation. The procedure begins by retrieving the string and placing a copy of it onto the top of the stack using the **index** operator. (The **index** operator is given in the standard format in the operator review at the end of Chapter 4.) The string is the third item on the stack; since stack entries are numbered from 0, the string is index number 2. Once the string is on top of the stack, the routine determines the **stringwidth** and divides that by two, just as before. Now you must move the adjusted **stringwidth** down underneath the left and right margins, using the **roll** operator that you met in Chapter 4. This places the **stringwidth** as the third item on the stack, with the right and left coordinates above it. Now you move a copy of the right coordinate to the top of the stack, subtract that from the left, and divide by two. Now the string width is returned to the top of the stack with a reverse **roll**, and is subtracted from the result of the previous calculation. This gives you the starting offset for the string display which you now add to the original right margin setting to give the correct x-coordinate for the string. The next line determines the current point by using the **current-point** operator and throws away the present x value while saving the y-coordinate on the top of the stack. You now have the current y-coordinate on the top of the stack and the desired x-coordinate beneath it; so you **moveto** that point. The only item remaining on the stack is the original string, which you now display with a **show** operator. In this way you avoid any internal definitions within the procedure by using the operands directly from the operand stack. If you have any questions about the basic operation of this procedure, reread the appropriate sections of Chapter 2.

The rightJustifyText procedure is very similar. Again, it uses the same algorithm as the earlier version, but takes its operands directly from the stack instead of defining internal variables and reusing them. It retrieves the string using the same technique that you saw in centerText and calculates the string width. Then it subtracts the width from the x-coordinate value to get the correct starting point. Next it exchanges the x- and y-coordinate values on the stack and then performs a **moveto** and **show** to output the string.

The entire data box can now be produced by running the procedures and the script as previously identified. The program so far looks like Figure 5.13. All this is familiar territory for you. This program produces the page of output in Figure 5.14—not our full form yet, but a good start.

You will notice that a **copypage** appears at the end of this program segment. It was placed there so that you can proceed directly to the next portion of the form without rerunning the program to get both elements together. This saves a bit of time and effort; as you can see, the actual program is compact and would be easy to rerun if you needed to do so.

You will notice that you are reusing procedures that were developed earlier in the book, either in the same or in a slightly modified form. This is characteristic of PostScript and illustrates what has been said before about developing a library of PostScript procedures to work from. With such a

```
%-------------------------Main Text Block--------------------

%-------------------------Main Text  Prolog------------------

%-------------------------Support Procedures-----------------
/inch
{
        72 mul
}
def
/line
{
        12 mul
}
def

/centerText
{
        2 index
        stringwidth pop
        2 div
        3 1 roll
        1 index sub
        2 div
        3 -1 roll
        sub
        add
        currentpoint exch pop
        moveto
        show
}
def

/rightJustifyText
{
        2 index
        stringwidth pop
        sub
        exch moveto
        show
}
def

%-------------------------Fonts & Variables------------------
/F1
        /Helvetica findfont 10 scalefont
def
/F2
        /Helvetica-Bold findfont 10 scalefont
def

/DimX 0 def
/DimY 0 def

%-------------------------Main Text Procedures---------------
/screenBox
{
        newpath
  /DimY exch def
  /DimX exch def
  .5 inch 0 moveto
  DimX 0  DimX DimY .25 inch arcto
  4 {pop} repeat
  DimX DimY  0 DimY .25 inch arcto
  4 {pop} repeat
```

Figure 5.13: Program for the data block

```
        0 DimY      0 0     .25 inch arcto
        4 (pop) repeat
        0 0       DimX 0    .25 inch arcto
        4 (pop) repeat
        closepath
        stroke
)
def

/verticalLines
(
        newpath
        144 47 line moveto
        144 12.5 line lineto
        317 47 line moveto
        317 12.5 line lineto
        365 47 line moveto
        365 12.5 line lineto
        413 47 line moveto
        413 12.5 line lineto
        467 47 line moveto
        467 12.5 line lineto
        stroke
)
def

 /dataTitles
(
        newpath
        .5 inch 45 line moveto
        7.5 inch 0 rlineto
        stroke
        .5 inch 45.5 line moveto
        F1 setfont
        0 45.5 line moveto
    (ITEM NO.) 72 144 centerText
    (DESCRIPTION      ) 144 317 centerText
    (ORDER) 318 365 centerText
    (SHIP) 366 413 centerText
    (UNIT $) 414 467 centerText
    (EXT. PRICE) 468 540 centerText
)
def

/footTitles
(
        newpath
    .5 inch 12.5 line moveto
    7.5 inch 0 rlineto
    stroke
    467 12.5 line moveto
    467 4 line lineto
    stroke
    F2 setfont
    (SUBTOTAL) 11 line 463 rightJustifyText
    (SALES TAX) 9 line 463 rightJustifyText
    (SHIPPING)  7 line 463 rightJustifyText
    (TOTAL)     5 line 463 rightJustifyText
)
def


%-------------------------Main Text Script---------------------
%Setup for test
/Pg save def
```

Figure 5.13: Program for the data block (continued)

```
%-------------------------Main Text Block----------------------
gsave
        .5 inch 4 line translate
        2 setlinewidth
        7.5 inch 43 line screenBox
grestore
verticalLines
dataTitles
footTitles

%Print for test
Pg restore
copypage
```

Figure 5.13: Program for the data block (continued)

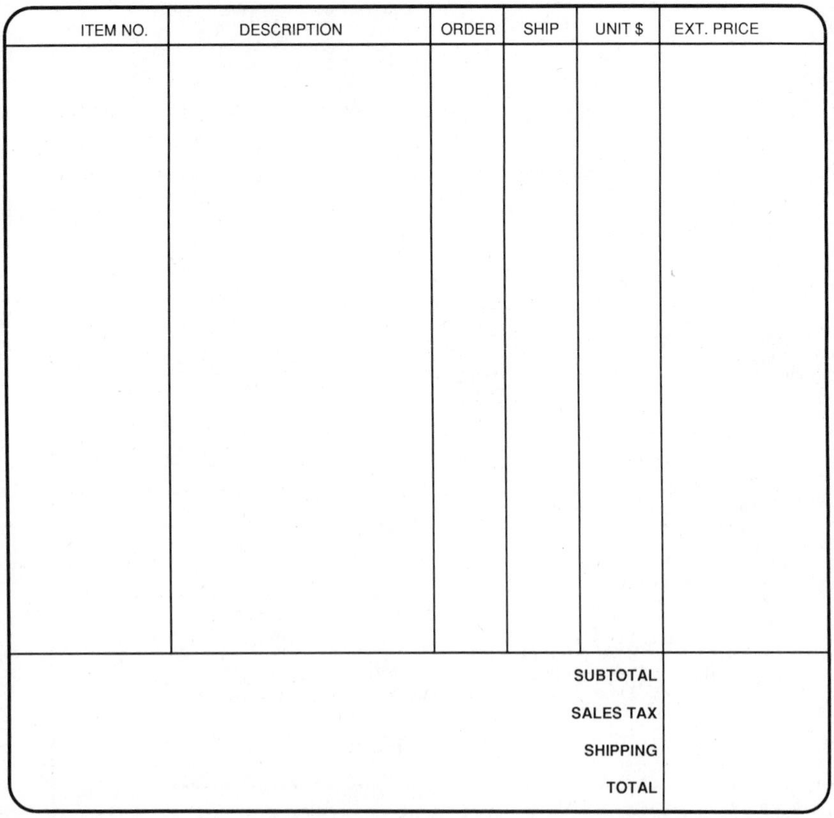

Figure 5.14: Main text block and totals block

library of tested procedures, you will find that you can produce a variety of relatively complex pages in a short time. We will discuss this in more detail later in the chapter.

Header

Now you can move on to set up and program the header block in detail. In this case, the setup is fairly easy because you have already done most of the required work.

There are three data elements in this block: name and address, order number, and date. Of these, only the order number has any impact on the setup of the header block within the form. You have already allocated space inside the small graphic "corners" for the name and address, and the date will be on a line by itself. Only the label for the order number needs to be positioned and integrated with the data output. The easiest way to do this is to set an arbitrary margin on the right side of the page that leaves enough room for the order number and then right-justify the label against that margin. If you wanted to be fancier, you could use the string for the order number to calculate the position for the label; but for this exercise, using a margin will suffice.

This procedure produces a setup for the title information within the header block, as shown in Figure 5.15. This figure shows you both of the labels necessary in the header block and their respective positions and sizing. The ORDER label will be centered between the page margins of 0.5 inch and 8 inches and set in 15-point Helvetica-Bold at line 52, as established on the original form design. The NO.: label, for the order number, is set in 12-point Helvetica-Bold and also is located at line 52. In this case, the label is right-justified against an arbitrary 7-inch margin, which leaves 1 inch for the number itself.

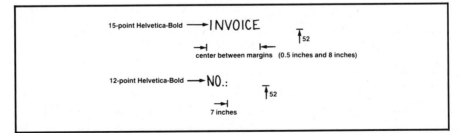

Figure 5.15: Header title information

The setup for the ''corners'' is equally easy and is shown in Figure 5.16. The box bounded by these ''corners'' is 6 lines, or 1 inch, high and must fit 25 characters across. As discussed earlier, there will be 12 characters to the inch, so allowing for spacing and position adjustment, you can make this box 2.5 inches, or 30 characters, wide. The ''corners'' themselves are 12 points in each direction, and the baseline of the entire figure is at line 48.

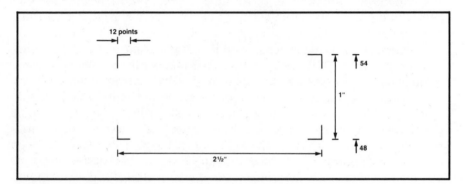

Figure 5.16: Name and address box in header

In this case, you can see that the following two procedures will make up the header block:

SYNTAX	FUNCTION
headTitles	produces the title information for the header.
cornerBox	produces the box made out of the small ''corner'' graphic elements.

Following the same methods used before, you can work out what a simple script using such procedures might look like:

```
%---------------------Header Block------------------

headTitles

gsave

        .5 inch 48 line translate

        2.5 inch 1 inch cornerBox

grestore
```

This section of the program looks, unsurprisingly, much like the preceding section for the data block. Once again, the graphic portion of the figure, which is produced by the cornerBox procedure, is enclosed in a **gsave**, **grestore** pair so that the changes made within the procedure don't affect anything else in the program. In particular, the effect of the **translate** that you use to move the origin to the bottom-left corner of the box is confined to the procedure itself. The titles stand by themselves, since they are positioned by lines relative to the original coordinate system and don't require any special movement to work correctly.

This only leaves you the task of working out these procedures. Taking both together, you have the code in Figure 5.17. You will notice that the headTitles procedure makes use of the previously developed supporting

```
/headTitles
{
        %first set invoice title
        F3 setfont
        0 52 line moveto
        (ORDER) .5 inch  8 inch  centerText
        %now set number title
        F4 setfont
        (NO. :) 52 line 7 inch rightJustifyText
}
def

/cornerBox
{
        newpath
        /DimY exch def
        /DimX exch def
        %bottom left corner
                0     0    moveto
                0     12   rlineto
                0     0    moveto
                12    0    rlineto
        %bottom right corner
                DimX 0    moveto
                0     12   rlineto
                DimX 0    moveto
                -12   0    rlineto
        %top left corner
                0 DimY   moveto
                0 -12    rlineto
                0 DimY   moveto
                12    0    rlineto
        %top right corner
            DimX DimY moveto
                0 -12    rlineto
            DimX DimY moveto
            -12    0    rlineto
        stroke
}
def
```

Figure 5.17: Header block procedures

procedures, centerText and rightJustifyText. This illustrates how you need to think about procedure structure as you're working through a PostScript program; often you will find that there are common supporting procedures that you can use throughout the program. When you find such procedures in several programs, they become strong candidates for inclusion in your library of PostScript routines.

The cornerBox procedure is long, but simple. It is easy to see how this procedure operates. It begins at the bottom-left corner, which is the origin for the figure, and produces two 12-point line segments, joined at the vertex; one segment to the right in the x-direction and one down the page in the y-direction. The **rmoveto** before the two **rlineto**s is a simple convenience, since it allows you to move to the corner and then to the beginning of the line. You might think to start each part of the line from the common vertex; but you will recall that this will not produce a correct corner, since the lines will not be joined. Therefore you move to one end of the lines and create both of them as two, joined segments. This is done for each of the box corners. Notice that you again use **store** rather than **def** to set the dimensions for the procedure.

After creating the bottom-left corner, you move over to the bottom-right corner with an explicit **moveto** command and create the next corner. Here the lines extend down the page in the y-direction as before, but go back across the page in the x-direction; hence, the negative sign is required on the **rmoveto** for the line in the x-coordinate as well as on the line for the y-coordinate. The rest of the corners function in exactly the same way; only the negative signs change to indicate the proper direction for each relative motion.

The final result is a program that is a combination of the previous elements and looks like Figure 5.18. This program produces the output in Figure 5.19.

There are a couple of points to note here. First, this portion of the program assumes that you are continuing your work from the preceding segment; therefore, the necessary support procedures should be already defined. If they were not, you would get an error as you tried to execute the procedures that depend on them. This assumption is made to save space here; if you need to redo the procedures, go back to the preceding section and copy them again.

The second point is that the preceding section, like this portion of the form, ends with a **copypage**. If you have continued from the previous exercise, you will see both elements of the form on your output, because the **copypage** will have left the output generated by the earlier segment still on

```
%------------------------Header Block----------------------

%------------------------Header  Prolog-------------------

%------------------------Fonts & Variables----------------
/F3
        /Helvetica-Bold findfont 15 scalefont
def
/F4
        /Helvetica-Bold findfont 12 scalefont
def

/DimX 0 def
/DimY 0 def

%------------------------Header Procedures----------------
/headTitles
{
        %first set invoice title
        F3 setfont
        0 52 line moveto
        (ORDER) .5 inch  8 inch  centerText
        %now set number title
        F4 setfont
        (NO. :) 52 line 7 inch rightJustifyText
}
def

/cornerBox
{
        newpath
        /DimY exch def
        /DimX exch def
        %bottom left corner
                0    0   moveto
                0   12   rmoveto
                0  -12   rlineto
                12   0   rlineto
        %bottom right corner
                DimX 0   moveto
                0   12   rmoveto
                0  -12   rlineto
                -12  0   rlineto
        %top left corner
                0 DimY   moveto
                0  -12   rmoveto
                0   12   rlineto
                12   0   rlineto
        %top right corner
            DimX DimY moveto
                0  -12   rmoveto
                0   12   rlineto
            -12    0   rlineto
        stroke
}
def

%------------------------Header Script--------------------
%Setup for test
/Pg save def
```

Figure 5.18: Header block program

```
%-------------------------Header Block-------------------------
headTitles
gsave
        .5 inch 48 line translate
        1 setlinewidth
        2.5 inch 1 inch cornerBox
grestore

%Print for test
Pg restore
copypage
```

Figure 5.18: Header block program (continued)

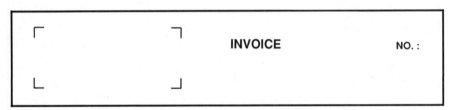

Figure 5.19: Header block output

the page. Figure 5.19 shows only the output generated by the current program segment; therefore, don't think it's an error if the output from the previous segment is also present.

Logo

The logo block is the one block that remains to be set up and programmed. This block will use the graphic element that you developed at the end of Chapter 3 as a logo graphic and will integrate the name of the company and its address information to make a complete logo for the firm.

The setup of the logo block has to begin with the consideration of the graphic element, which needs to be sized and positioned before you can do anything with the text elements. When you built the graphic in the previous chapter, you created an element that was 17 units wide by 11 units high, and produced the output graphic using ½ inch as a unit. Now you must fit the graphic into a defined space; the space that you left at the top of the form for the logo block. Here is where the power and elegance of the PostScript language become evident. The graphic is not a particular size; it is 11 by 17 *units*. Since you want the height to be about 1½ inches, you need to divide 1½ inches by 11 to get the appropriate scaling factor. In this case, a cursory examination shows you that 1½ inches is an inconvenient measure for this division, so you quickly that into 108 points; dividing 108 points by 11 gives 9.8 points per unit. For ease of calculation, you may round that number down to 9.5 points; you don't want to round up, since that would push the graphic out of the block that you have designed and into the top of the page.

Using that factor, and doing some arithmetic, you can figure out that the horizontal dimension of the graphic will be approximately 2¼ inches (17 × 9.5 / 72). Now you can leave an open rectangle of those dimensions on the detail setup for the logo and proceed to lay out the text elements as shown in Figure 5.20.

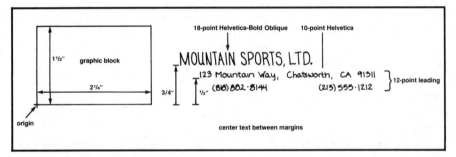

Figure 5.20: Logo block layout

All measurements on this figure start from the bottom-left corner of the box that will contain the graphic element; in other words, unlike the previous blocks, the logo block is self-contained. Note that either approach is possible; for the logo, making all references within the graphic to a single, internal origin allows you to reuse the logo in other documents. The entire logo, graphic and text form a complete aesthetic and practical unit, which can be moved or adjusted as required without reference to any other element on a page. This allows the block to be reused in a variety of contexts, if required.

The name of the company, Mountain Sports, Ltd., is set uppercase in 18-point Helvetica-BoldOblique type. As the name implies, this type is both bold and slanted and serves to emphasize the name in the logo. The name is based on a line that is 0.75 inches above the logo baseline, which will be about halfway up the graphic. The name and address lines are all centered between the margins. The address lines begin 0.5 inches from the logo baseline, making them 18 points (a quarter-inch) below the name. This means that they are set the same distance from the name text as the name is high.

Since the address lines are set in 10-point type, this is a good distance, and it sets them off enough from the name to be easily legible. The two address lines are set in 10-point Helvetica with 12-point leading.

This analysis suggests two procedures, one for the graphic and one for the text. These can be defined as follows:

SYNTAX	FUNCTION
logoTitles	sets the company name and address text for the logo.
logoGraphic	produces the graphic element for the logo.

However, the entire logo is measured and located as a unit. In this case it is useful to create a third procedure to connect one logo procedure to the other; the best method will be to define a new procedure, logo, that will contain both logoTitles and logoGraphic. Although you could simply invoke each of these individual procedures directly from the main body of the program, making a new procedure allows you to reuse this graphic element as a unit in other contexts—the same reasoning that lead you to make the logo a self-contained unit in the first place.

This procedure simplifies the body of the program, which now need only contain the following lines to generate the logo block:

```
%-------------------------Logo Block----------------------------

gsave

        .5 inch 55 line translate

        logo

grestore
```

Let's look at the procedures individually. You can begin with the titles, shown in Figure 5.21, because they will be the most straightforward. As before, the auxiliary procedures for centering and right-justifying text strings are required. With those available, the rest of the procedure is easy. Note that the measurements are, as discussed earlier, all based on the logo origin and not the page origin as in the previous procedures for the header and data text.

```
/logoTitles
{
        F5 setfont
        0 .75 inch moveto
        (MOUNTAIN SPORTS, LTD.)
        0 8 inch centerText
        F1 setfont
        0 .5 inch moveto
        (123 Mountain Way,   Chatsworth, CA   91311)
        0 8 inch centerText
        0 .5 inch 12 sub moveto
        ((818) 882-8144                    (213) 555-1212)
        0 8 inch centerText
}
def
```

Figure 5.21: The logoTitles procedure

The procedure for the graphic element is an adaptation of the fifth exercise in Chapter 3, making it into a procedure instead of a program. It looks like Figure 5.22. This uses the same supporting procedures that were required in the earlier exercise: sun and hill. These procedures are shown in Figure 5.23.

There are a few changes to these procedures which you should notice. They now use some of the techniques that you learned earlier to avoid defining operand data from the stack; instead, they use the data directly. The sun procedure requires the radius of the circle as an operand. This must be passed to the **arc** operator as the third operand. To do this, you simply **roll** the operand into the correct position after placing the two operands that **arc** requires before the radius onto the stack. The hill procedure requires two operands: a base and a height. The base is also divided by two for use in drawing the first part of the hill. Here, you duplicate the base value on the stack, divide it by two, and then **roll** the operands to create the desired order. After the **roll** the half-base is underneath the height. Then you perform a **lineto** to draw the first line segment of the hill. You follow that by placing a 0 onto the stack above the remaining base value. Another **lineto** makes the second line segment for the hill, and a **closepath** finishes off back at the origin. This approach is more efficient than defining internal variables for these procedures.

This only leaves the logo procedure to be defined, as follows:

```
/logo

{

        logoTitles
```

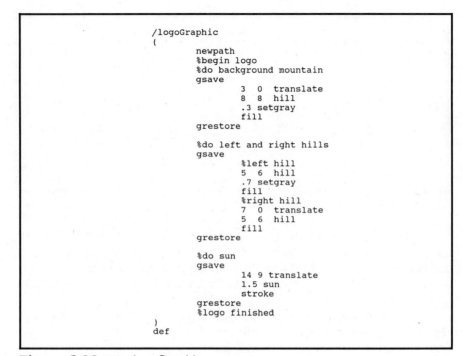

```
/logoGraphic
{
        newpath
        %begin logo
        %do background mountain
        gsave
                3   0   translate
                8   8   hill
                .3 setgray
                fill
        grestore

        %do left and right hills
        gsave
                %left hill
                5   6   hill
                .7 setgray
                fill
                %right hill
                7   0   translate
                5   6   hill
                fill
        grestore

        %do sun
        gsave
                14 9 translate
                1.5 sun
                stroke
        grestore
        %logo finished
}
def
```

Figure 5.22: The logoGraphics procedure

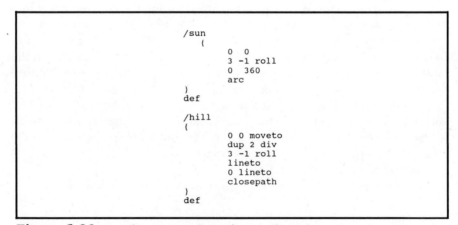

```
/sun
    {
            0   0
            3 -1 roll
            0   360
            arc
    }
def

/hill
    {
            0 0 moveto
            dup 2 div
            3 -1 roll
            lineto
            0 lineto
            closepath
    }
def
```

Figure 5.23: Auxiliary procedures for logoGraphic

```
       9.5 9.5 scale

       1 9.5 div setlinewidth

       logoGraphic

   }

   def
```

This procedure does just what is required and no more. It calls the procedure logoTitles, then it scales the coordinates for the graphic, resets the line width to 1 point, and calls logoGraphic. All saving and restoring of the graphic state and any required translation of the coordinates is left for the main line program. In fact, both of those actions are required to invoke logo for this form, as you saw earlier.

To finish the final block, before you proceed to the completed form program, the short program for the logo itself is shown in Figure 5.24. This procedure, by itself, produces the output in Figure 5.25. You will notice that the program doesn't use **copypage** this time. If you have been working continuously, now you will see the entire form on your output; in either case, you need to clear the page for the final form output, which comes in the next section.

Entire Form as a Unit

Even though you have built each of the blocks individually, some work is still necessary to make all the blocks into a single form and to adapt this form so that it will work on both Level 1 and Level 2 printers. To do this, you should establish the full PostScript structure around your program; until now, the structure has been minimal.

In order to adapt the form for use in Level 2 devices, you need to learn some things about form handling in Level 2. Forms in a Level 2 device are produced by using the **execform** operator. This operator takes a *form dictionary* as an operand, and produces the form defined in that dictionary. A *form* is a self-contained description of any arbitrary graphic unit, possibly including text, graphics, or bit-mapped data, which will be produced multiple times, either on one page or multiple pages.

The form dictionary is a type of resource, and, like a font dictionary or other resource, it requires certain entries so that **execform** can create the

```
%-------------------------Logo Block------------------------

%-------------------------Logo Prolog-----------------------

%------------------------Support Procedures-----------------

/sun
{
        0  0
        3 -1 roll
        0   360
        arc
}
def

/hill
{
        0 0 moveto
        dup 2 div
        3 -1 roll
        lineto
        0 lineto
        closepath
}
def

%------------------------Logo Procedures--------------------

/logoGraphic
{
        newpath
        %begin logo
        %do background mountain
        gsave
                3   0   translate
                8   8   hill
                .3 setgray
                fill
        grestore

        %do left and right hills
        gsave
                %left hill
                5   6   hill
                .7 setgray
                fill
                %right hill
                7   0   translate
                5   6   hill
                fill
        grestore

        %do sun
        gsave
                14 9 translate
                1.5 sun
                stroke
        grestore
        %logo finished
    }
    def
```

Figure 5.24: Logo block program

```
/logoTitles
{
        F5 setfont
        0 .75 inch moveto
        (MOUNTAIN SPORTS, LTD.)
        0 8 inch centerText
        F1 setfont
        0 .5 inch moveto
        (123 Mountain Way,   Chatsworth, CA  91311)
        0 8 inch centerText
        0 .5 inch 12 sub moveto
        ((818) 882-8144                 (213) 555-1212)
        0 8 inch centerText
}
def

/logo
{
        logoTitles
        gsave
                9.5 9.5 scale
                1 9.5 div setlinewidth
                logoGraphic
        grestore
}
def

%-------------------------Logo Script------------------------
%Setup for test
/Pg save def

%-------------------------Logo Block-------------------------

gsave
        .5 inch 55 line translate
        logo
grestore

%Print for test
Pg restore
showpage

%----------------------------Required Entries-----------------------
/FormType 1 def
/BBox [ 0 0 612 792 ] def
/Matrix matrix def
/PaintProc
{
        begin    %OrderForm dictionary
        1 setlinewidth
        0 setgray
        %produce logo block
        gsave
                .5 inch 55 line translate
                logo
        grestore
        %produce header block
        gsave
                headTitles
                .5 inch 48 line translate
                2.5 inch 1 inch cornerBox
        grestore
        %produce main text & totals block
```

Figure 5.24: Logo block program (continued)

```
        gsave
            .5 inch 4 line translate
            2 setlinewidth
            7.5 inch 43 line screenBox
        grestore
        verticalLines
        dataTitles
        footTitles
        %form page finished
        end             %OrderForm dictionary
    }
    def
```

Figure 5.24: Logo block program (continued)

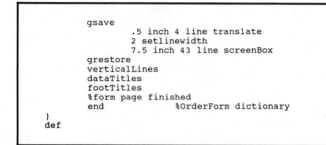
MOUNTAIN SPORTS, LTD.
123 Mountain Way, Chatsworth, CA 91311
(818) 882-8144   (213) 555-1212

Figure 5.25: Logo block output

desired form. The required entries in a form dictionary are as follows:

KEY	TYPE	DEFINITION
FormType	integer	must be 1.
Matrix	matrix	a transformation matrix that can be combined with the CTM (current transformation matrix) to map from the form coordinates to user coordinates. The combination of this entry with the CTM establishes the *form coordinate system.*
BBox	array	an array of four numbers representing the lower-left *x,* lower-left *y,* upper-right *x* and upper-right *y* in the form's coordinate system for the box that encloses all marks made by the form.

KEY	TYPE	DEFINITION
		This is used in caching the form and for clipping the form image; any marks made outside this box will not print.
PaintProc	procedure	a procedure that draws and paints the form.

The form dictionary can contain other information, including procedures and constants that are used by the **PaintProc** to create the form. The form is defined in its own coordinate system, which is created by combining the form's **Matrix** entry. Both the **BBox** coordinates and the **PaintProc** use the form coordinate system. The form is created by executing the new operator, **execform** with the form dictionary as an operand. The **execform** operator sets up the form coordinates, clips the form to the dimensions set by the **BBox** entry, pushes the form dictionary on the operand stack, and executes the **PaintProc** within a **gsave**, **grestore** pair to draw the form.

The **PaintProc** must be self-contained to execute correctly; that is, it must follow certain restrictions. It must not use **showpage**, **copypage**, or any device setup operators; generally, it cannot use any of the operations that are unsuitable for use in an EPS file (see Appendix B for a complete discussion of these restrictions). It must remove the form dictionary from the operand stack and leave all other dictionaries unchanged. It should depend only on information defined in the form dictionary and it must produce the same result every time it is called. In particular, it cannot define any variables or allocate any object that will consume virtual memory.

Form Dictionary

Figure 5.26 shows you how you might define the required entries for this form dictionary. Let's review each of these entries in turn. The **Form-Type** is set to 1, as required. The **Matrix** entry is set to the default identity matrix, which is generated by the **matrix** operator. Since the form here is a full page and uses the default coordinate system, it is not necessary to have any coordinate transformations for this form. The **BBox** entry gives the dimensions of the form as 0 0 612 792. Since there is no change in coordinates for the form, this means that the form's bounding box is the default user origin for the lower-left corner, and 8½ by 11 inches (612 by 792 points) for the upper-right corner. This takes in the complete form as previously laid out. Notice that the form actually falls slightly inside these margins; it is not essential that the bounding box be as small as possible. What is essential is that the bounding box be large enough so that no part of the form is outside the box.

```
%---------------------------Required Entries-------------------------
/FormType 1 def
/BBox [ 0 0 612 792 ] def
/Matrix matrix def
/PaintProc
{
        begin   %OrderForm dictionary
        1 setlinewidth
        0 setgray
        %produce logo block
        gsave
                .5 inch 55 line translate
                logo
        grestore
        %produce header block
        gsave
                headTitles
                .5 inch 48 line translate
                2.5 inch 1 inch cornerBox
        grestore
        %produce main text & totals block
        gsave
                .5 inch 4 line translate
                2 setlinewidth
                7.5 inch 43 line screenBox
        grestore
        verticalLines
        dataTitles
        footTitles
        %form page finished
        end             %OrderForm dictionary
}
def
```

Figure 5.26: The form dictionary for the order form

    Finally, you must define the **PaintProc** for this form. Actually, this isn't hard at this point. As shown in Figure 5.26, the **PaintProc** is simply all of the steps that you have used to create each of the blocks in order. The procedure starts by establishing the form dictionary operand as the current dictionary. This makes all the procedures and definitions in the dictionary available to the **PaintProc**, and also removes the dictionary from the stack, as required by **execform**. Then it executes each of the block procedures that you have seen before in turn, and ends by removing the form dictionary from the dictionary stack. That's all there is to it.

The last task, then, is to place all the blocks that you have worked on up to now into a form dictionary with the correct internal structure and with some external structure as well. Figure 5.27 shows you how this might be done.

```
%%BeginResource: procset OrderForm 1.0 0
/OrderForm 30 dict def
OrderForm begin
%-------------------------Required Entries------------------------
/FormType 1 def
/BBox [ 0 0 612 792 ] def
/Matrix matrix def
/PaintProc
{
        begin   %OrderForm dictionary
        1 setlinewidth
        0 setgray
        %produce logo block
        gsave
                .5 inch 55 line translate
                logo
        grestore
        %produce header block
        gsave
                headTitles
                .5 inch 48 line translate
                2.5 inch 1 inch cornerBox
        grestore
        %produce main text & totals block
        gsave
                .5 inch 4 line translate
                2 setlinewidth
                7.5 inch 43 line screenBox
        grestore
        verticalLines
        dataTitles
        footTitles
        %form page finished
        end             %OrderForm dictionary
}
def

...followed by the procedures and auxiliary definitions required for the

end             %OrderForm
%%EndResource
```

Figure 5.27: The OrderForm procset

This places the new form dictionary into a separate resource procset, which is named OrderForm, and given the version and revision numbers of 1.0 and 0, respectively. The dictionary itself is defined first, with enough entries to hold the entire set of definitions for the form, along with the required entries for the form dictionary. Once the dictionary is defined, it is made the current dictionary, and you can start inserting information into it. You begin with the required entries, as described earlier, and then continue with the remaining procedures and auxiliary definitions for drawing the form. When you're done, you release the new form dictionary and end the resource structure. This entire block can now be used as an independent unit to create the order form, if it is called correctly.

Producing the Form

Now we have the necessary form dictionary, and the associated procedures to make a form. There is, however, one more item that you need in order to generate the final form. This is the mechanism to image the form by calling the form dictionary and executing its **PaintProc**. Remember that you also want this mechanism to work on both Level 1 and Level 2 devices.

The answer to this problem is to create a new procset, distinct from the form dictionary, which will test for the language level and will execute the form in a way that is appropriate for the actual level in the device. To do that, you want to emulate the Level 2 **execform** operator in your new procset. Figure 5.28 shows you how this code might look.

```
%%BeginResource: procset FormDict 1.0 0
/FormDict 10 dict def
FormDict begin
%-----------------------------Level Check-----------------------------
/languagelevel where
        {pop languagelevel}
        {1}
ifelse
2 ge
/LV2 exch def

%----------------------------Emulation Procedures--------------------
LV2
{
        %if Level 2 or greater, use the native execform operator
        /xform /execform load def
}
{
        %if Level 1, emulate execform
        /xform
        {
                gsave
                        newpath
                        dup
                        /PaintProc get
                        exec
                grestore
        }
        def
}
ifelse
end                %FormDict
%%EndResource
```

Figure 5.28: Procset to execute or emulate execform

The procset begins in the standard way, by defining a private dictionary, FormDict, and making that the current dictionary. Then it tests for Level 2 in the same manner that we discussed above, and stores the resulting boolean for later use. Next it looks at the boolean LV2 and defines a new procedure, xform, based on that. If this is a Level 2 device, xform is simply made identical to **execform**; no problem there. If this is a Level 1 device, however, xform is defined to provide the same functions that **execform** does, so far as possible. You begin the emulation with a **gsave** to save the graphics state, so that the form generation does not disturb any previous or subsequent graphic operations. Next you do a **newpath** to remove any previous path segments that might still be around; remember, the **grestore** at the end of this procedure will bring them back. Then you duplicate the form dictionary which is the top operand on the stack, retrieve the **PaintProc** from it, and execute the **PaintProc**. When the **PaintProc** is finished, you perform a **grestore** to return to the previous graphic state. That's all that you have to do at this point to emulate **execform**.

There is one additional thing that you must do to your form procedures to allow them to work with the **execform** operator. As we said above, **execform** requires that the **PaintProc** be self-contained and independent of all outside definitions. It enforces this requirement by changing the form dictionary to read-only status while it is creating the form. As a result, any attempt to define a variable, such as DimX or DimY, within the painting procedures will cause an error. One solution would be to simply use the actual values in the procedures instead of variables. This has the drawback, however, that it would make the procedures unique to this form. Another solution is the technique that you see here. As described earlier, the cornerBox and screenBox procedures that use DimX and DimY don't define these variables directly; instead, they use the store operator to replace an existing definition. Now you simply insert these variables into the standard userdict instead of keeping them in the form dictionary, using the code shown in Figure 5.29. The result is that the form dictionary remains self-contained, and you get your variables anyway. Note, however, that this works only because you do not change these definitions within the context of the form: that is, the screenBox and the cornerBox are always the same size for this form.

Now you need to combine these two segments. The structure is familiar to you by now; it repeats what you have seen in previous examples. The script has the usual **save** and **restore** functions around the page output and then calls the emulation procedure, xform, with the form dictionary Order-Form as an operand. Figure 5.29 shows you the complete form program.

```
%!PS-Adobe-3.0
%%Title: Form Exercise
%%Creator: David Holzgang
%%CreationDate: 1:29:42 PM  1/8/92
%%For: Understanding PostScript Programming (3rd Edition)
%%BoundingBox: 0 0 612 792
%%Orientation: Portrait
%%Pages: 1
%%EndComments
%%BeginProlog
%%BeginResource: procset FormDict 1.0 0
/FormDict 10 dict def
FormDict begin
%----------------------------Level Check----------------------------
/languagelevel where
        {pop languagelevel}
        {1}
ifelse
2 ge
/LV2 exch def


%----------------------------Emulation Procedures--------------------
LV2
{
        %if Level 2 or greater, use the native execform operator
        /xform /execform load def
}
{
        %if Level 1, emulate execform
        /xform
        {
                gsave
                        newpath
                        dup
                        /PaintProc get
                        exec
                grestore
        }
        def
}
ifelse
end             %FormDict
%%EndResource

%%BeginResource: procset OrderForm 1.0 0
/OrderForm 30 dict def
OrderForm begin

%----------------------------Required Entries------------------------
/FormType 1 def
/BBox [ 0 0 612 792 ] def
/Matrix matrix def
/PaintProc
{
        begin   %OrderForm dictionary
        1 setlinewidth
        0 setgray
        %produce logo block
        gsave
                .5 inch 55 line translate
                logo
        grestore
        %produce header block
        gsave
                headTitles
```

Figure 5.29: Completed form program

```
                .5 inch 48 line translate
                2.5 inch 1 inch cornerBox
        grestore
        %produce main text & totals block
        gsave
                .5 inch 4 line translate
                2 setlinewidth
                7.5 inch 43 line screenBox
        grestore
        verticalLines
        dataTitles
        footTitles
        %form page finished
        end             %OrderForm dictionary
}
def

%--------------------------Support Procedures-----------------------
/inch
{
        72 mul
}
def
/line
{
        12 mul
}
def

/centerText
{
        2 index
        stringwidth pop
        2 div
        3 1 roll
        1 index sub
        2 div
        3 -1 roll
        sub
        add
        currentpoint exch pop
        moveto
        show
}
def
/rightJustifyText
{
        2 index
        stringwidth pop
        sub
        exch moveto
        show
}
def

%--------------------------Fonts & Variables-----------------------
/F1
        /Helvetica findfont 10 scalefont
def
/F2
        /Helvetica-Bold findfont 10 scalefont
def
/F3
```

Figure 5.29: Completed form program (continued)

```
             /Helvetica-Bold findfont 15 scalefont
def
/F4
             /Helvetica-Bold findfont 12 scalefont
def
/F5
             /Helvetica-BoldOblique findfont 18 scalefont
def

userdict /DimY 0 put
userdict /DimX 0 put

%---------------------------Main Text & Totals Block-----------------
/screenBox
{
        newpath
   /DimY exch store
   /DimX exch store
   .5 inch 0 moveto
   DimX 0   DimX DimY .25 inch arcto
   4 {pop} repeat
   DimX DimY  0 DimY .25 inch arcto
   4 {pop} repeat
   0 DimY      0 0     .25 inch arcto
   4 {pop} repeat
   0 0      DimX 0   .25 inch arcto
   4 {pop} repeat
   closepath
   stroke
}
def

/verticalLines
{
        newpath
        144 47 line moveto
        144 12.5 line lineto
        317 47 line moveto
        317 12.5 line lineto
        365 47 line moveto
        365 12.5 line lineto
        413 47 line moveto
        413 12.5 line lineto
        467 47 line moveto
        467 12.5 line lineto
        stroke
}
def

 /dataTitles
{
        newpath
        .5 inch 45 line moveto
        7.5 inch 0 rlineto
        stroke
        .5 inch 45.5 line moveto
        F1 setfont
        0 45.5 line moveto
   (ITEM NO.) 72 144 centerText
   (DESCRIPTION    ) 144 317 centerText
   (ORDER) 318 365 centerText
   (SHIP) 366 413 centerText
   (UNIT $) 414 467 centerText
   (EXT. PRICE) 468 540 centerText
```

Figure 5.29: Completed form program (continued)

```
)
def

/footTitles
(
        newpath
    .5 inch 12.5 line moveto
    7.5 inch 0 rlineto
    stroke
    467 12.5 line moveto
    467 4 line lineto
    stroke
    F2 setfont
    (SUBTOTAL) 11 line 463 rightJustifyText
    (SALES TAX) 9 line 463 rightJustifyText
    (SHIPPING)  7 line 463 rightJustifyText
    (TOTAL)     5 line 463 rightJustifyText
)
def

%---------------------------Header Block---------------------------
/headTitles
(
        %first set invoice title
        F3 setfont
        0 52 line moveto
        (ORDER) .5 inch  8 inch   centerText
        %now set number title
        F4 setfont
        (NO. :) 52 line 7 inch rightJustifyText
)
def

/cornerBox
(
        newpath
        /DimY exch store
        /DimX exch store
        %bottom left corner
                0    0   moveto
                0    12  rlineto
                0    0   moveto
                12   0   rlineto
        %bottom right corner
                DimX 0  moveto
                0    12  rlineto
                DimX 0  moveto
                -12  0  rlineto
        %top left corner
                0 DimY  moveto
                0  -12  rlineto
                0 DimY  moveto
                12   0  rlineto
        %top right corner
            DimX DimY moveto
                0  -12  rlineto
            DimX DimY moveto
             -12   0  rlineto
        stroke
)
def

%---------------------------Logo Block---------------------------
```

Figure 5.29: Completed form program (continued)

```
        /sun
        {
                0   0
                3 -1 roll
                0   360
                arc
        }
        def

        /hill
        {
                0 0 moveto
                dup 2 div
                3 -1 roll
                lineto
                0 lineto
                closepath
        }
        def

        /logoGraphic
        {
                newpath
                %begin logo
                %do background mountain
                gsave
                        3   0   translate
                        8   8   hill
                        .3 setgray
                        fill
                grestore

                %do left and right hills
                gsave
                        %left hill
                        5   6   hill
                        .7 setgray
                        fill
                        %right hill
                        7   0   translate
                        5   6   hill
                        fill
                grestore

                %do sun
                gsave
                        14 9 translate
                        1.5 sun
                        stroke
                grestore
                %logo finished
        }
        def

        /logoTitles
        {
                F5 setfont
                0 .75 inch moveto
                (MOUNTAIN SPORTS, LTD.)
                0 8 inch centerText
                F1 setfont
                0 .5 inch moveto
                (123 Mountain Way,   Chatsworth, CA  91311)
                0 8 inch centerText
```

Figure 5.29: Completed form program (continued)

```
            0 .5 inch 12 sub moveto
            ((818) 882-8144                    (213) 555-1212)
            0 8 inch centerText
     )
     def

     /logo
     {
            logoTitles
            gsave
                    9.5 9.5 scale
                    1 9.5 div setlinewidth
                    logoGraphic
            grestore
     )
     def

     end            %OrderForm
     %%EndResource
     %%EndProlog

     %-----------------------------Script------------------------------
     %%BeginSetup
     FormDict begin

     %%EndSetup

     %%Page: i 1
     %-------------------------Setup form-------------------------
     /PgSave save def

     % Execute the desired form procedure
     OrderForm xform

     % Clean up after the form has been completed
     PgSave restore
     showpage

     %%Trailer
     end            %FormDict
     %%EOF
```

Figure 5.29: Completed form program (continued)

Once again, you notice how short and simple the body of the program is compared to the prolog. Properly constructed and defined, the procedures do all the work in PostScript. This exercise produces the page of output in Figure 5.30.

This blank form is a fairly complex page, but it is only half of what we set out to accomplish. Now you must turn your attention to the other half of the desired output, the data that comes from the application.

FILL-IN

Now that the form has been completed, you are ready to begin work on the application information that will provide the data to fill in the blank

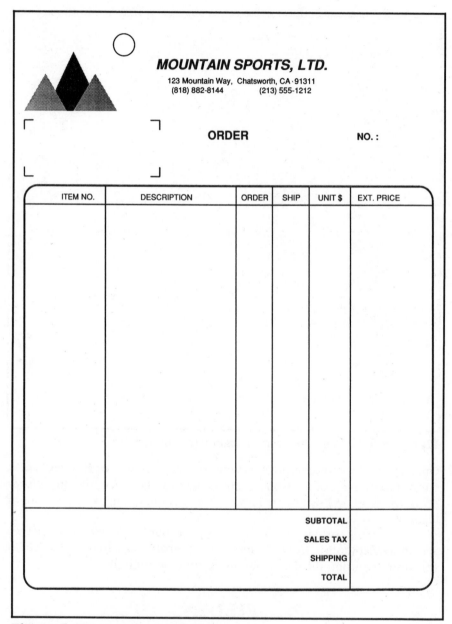

Figure 5.30: Complete blank form

form. You have already done quite a bit of work on the application, so this stage will go quickly.

One of the main issues regarding any form input is the number and size of the data fields that will be required. You established this information earlier in the chapter when you were designing the form. Let's recap here all the data items that need to be on the form and the sizes that were selected for each of them.

DATA ELEMENT	NUMBER OF CHARACTERS	TYPE
name and address (4 lines)	30	alphanumeric characters
order number	6	digits (999999)
date	9	*DD–MMM–YY*
item number	8	alphanumeric characters
	5	spaces
item description	25	alphanumeric characters
	3	spaces
quantity ordered	5	four digits and sign (– 9999)
	3	spaces
quantity shipped	5	four digits and sign (– 9999)
	3	spaces
unit price	6	three digits, decimal, and two digits (999.99)
	3	spaces
	2	spaces
extended price	10	– 99,999.99
items total	11	– 999,999.99
sales tax	9	– 9,999.99

DATA ELEMENT	NUMBER OF CHARACTERS	TYPE
shipping and handling	10	– 99,999.99
order total	11	– 999,999.99

The spacing information for each line item has been retained in this list because it plays an important part in setting up the data.

Output Considerations

You need to set up the output from your application to generate the required data. This can be done directly into PostScript format if you are using an application with a macro or programming language, such as dBase or HyperCard. If you cannot generate the correct PostScript commands for your data output directly from the application, you can also save the application output to a disk file and edit that file into the correct format. In either case, the raw data for this exercise is shown in Figure 5.31.

Interface to the Form

You are now ready to edit or otherwise modify the output data to prepare it for your PostScript device. However, first you must decide what you're going to do. You want to be able to print the data onto a page using PostScript procedures. Now that you have the necessary data, you need the procedures.

The identification of the procedures follows from the work you have already invested in the design of the form and data. Let us assume, for this part of the exercise, that the data has been written to disk as a series of output lines, as shown in Figure 5.31. The alternative would be for the data to be presented in your application as a series of strings for output. You need to take these output strings, make them into PostScript strings, and display them on the page at the correct locations. You will also need to do some further setup work in PostScript before you can display the strings; for example, you need to set the current font, and so on.

The procedures will be concerned primarily with the placement and display of these strings. As you think about this issue, you will see that there

```
      10423

David Holzgang
22621 Penfield Ave.
Chatsworth, CA  91311


   31-Dec-86

Item #           Description         Order    Ship    Unit $     Ext. Price
12-456     Backpack - Blue             1       1      28.95        $28.95
28-145     Wool socks - Size 10        4       4       3.95        $15.80
95-004     Strawberries               10      10       1.45        $14.50
95-010     Apricots                    5       5       1.29         $6.45
96-148     Chicken Cacciatore          4       4       2.95        $11.80
96-104     Beef Stew                   4       3       2.95         $8.85
96-107     Spaghetti with Meat Sauce   2       2       2.95         $5.90
96-242     Trail Mix                   4       4       0.98         $3.92
35-129     First Aid Kit               1       1       9.49         $9.49




                                                                 $105.66

                                                                   $6.87

                                                                   $3.42

                                                                 $115.95
```

Figure 5.31: Application output before editing

are two different approaches that you might take to the problem of displaying the data on the form. The first would be to position and display each element of the data individually. If you did this, you might place and display the name, then the first line of the address, the second, and so on. In particular, if you follow this method, you would place and display each item number, each description, each price, and so on throughout the entire range of data.

Alternatively, you could display the data in groups, with the name and address data in one group and each line of item data as a single string. This is the approach that has been taken here. It is simpler than the first approach, and it involves much less editing or parsing of the output data; however, it has limitations. The first, and most obvious, limitation is that this method depends upon display in a monospaced font. If the display font were not monospaced, you could not be sure that each line was the same length; worse yet, you could not be sure that the data was aligned from one line to the next. That would clearly be unacceptable. Since the display font is monospaced, however, you need have no concern on that score. Another limitation is that the relative positions of the data elements within a group cannot be changed. This is not an issue here, since you are printing on what is, effectively, a pre-printed form; but it might become an issue if you were displaying data on a group of forms, or moving the same data from one type of output to another.

Once you have chosen to display the data as groups, the composition of the groups comes easily. The natural groups follow the blocks that you have already structured and will look like this:

DATA GROUP	COMPOSITION
name and address	all four lines of name and address data (or less if all four lines are not present). Each element will be a separate string.
order number	a single number, treated by itself.
date	the date as a string, positioned by itself.
data item	each data line, treated as an individual string.
totals	all the totals elements, treated as a uniform set; all four must be present, at least as zeros.

With these groups, you can identify the procedures required to create the desired output, as follows:

SYNTAX	FUNCTION
address	takes four strings on the operand stack and places them as the name and address on the output page.
invNumber	sets the order number in the correct font onto the output page.
date	sets the date element in the correct font and positions it onto the page.
totals	sets each of the totals onto the correct line; must right-justify them to match the positioning of the extended price in the data items.
showLine	sets one line of item data at a given location on the page.

These procedures are not difficult; however, they are complex enough to deal with various possibilities in the output data. Let's look at all of them in Figure 5.32 and then discuss each individually. Some of these will probably surprise you a little, but you will quickly see why each step was taken when we discuss each procedure.

```
%-------------------------------Data Procedures----------------------
/address
{
        .6 inch 49 line moveto
        count 3 gt
        {show} if
        .6 inch 50 line moveto
        count 2 gt
        {show} if
        .6 inch 51 line moveto
        count 1 gt
        {show} if
        .6 inch 52 line moveto
        count 0 gt
        {show} if
}
def

/invNumber
{
        52 line 8 inch rightJustifyText
}
def


/date
{
        50 line 8 inch rightJustifyText
}
def

/totals
{
        5 line 7.5 inch rightJustifyText
        7 line 7.5 inch rightJustifyText
        9 line 7.5 inch rightJustifyText
        11 line 7.5 inch rightJustifyText
}
def

/showLine
{
        moveto
        show
}
def
```

Figure 5.32: Fill-in procedures

Let's begin with the first procedure, **address**. This procedure has several qualities that may surprise, and it introduces a new operator, **count**.

The basic issue here is that you want to allow for name and address groups that have less than four lines of data; and you have a related, but distinct, problem in that the data will come to you—as you know from other Post-Script procedures—in the reverse order from the one it had as it went onto the stack. The order onto the stack will normally be the name followed by each address line; so the name will be at the bottom of the stack with the address lines above it. However, you want the name always to appear on the top line provided on the form; and conversely, you want the address lines to appear below the name with blank lines at the bottom when there are less than four lines of data.

How do you tell what line the top string on the stack goes on if it's the last of a variable number of lines? You do what you naturally would do and count the number of lines you have to print. That's where **count** comes in. This oper-ator counts the number of items on the stack and returns that number to the top of the stack, without affecting anything underneath. Now you can count the items on the stack, which will be the number of lines you have to print. If the number is equal to or greater than the relative number of lines remaining to be printed on, then you **show** the string; otherwise, you don't. The **if** operator does this for you. The conditional **gt** tests the current count from the stack against one less than the current line number. If the count is greater than that number, the boolean value **true** is pushed onto the stack; otherwise the value **false** is pushed. The **if** operator tests that value and executes the **show** proce-dure if it is true, but does not execute it if the value is false. The net result is that each line is positioned as you want it to be, and all four lines are used only if there are four lines to be displayed.

The next two procedures, invNumber and date, are virtually identical. They both assume that there is an appropriate string on the stack and display it at the correct line number, right-justified against the 8-inch margin. The margin to be justified against is shown in Figure 5.3, which gives the com-plete form layout. Notice that the order number and date line up against the same margin as the right side of the data box, which is $1/2$ inch from the right edge of the paper, hence 8 inches from the left edge. The correct line num-bers are also shown in Figure 5.3.

The next procedure is totals, which display the totals information on the form. This procedure assumes that there are four strings on the stack and that they have been placed on the stack in order from subtotal to total. As before, this means that you will have to remove them from the stack and place them in reverse order; in other words, the total first, followed by the other items up the page to the subtotal. You already specified that all four items are required, even if they are zero, so you don't need any conditional testing here.

You want to align these totals under the extended prices on the data section of the form. In order to do so, you need to look back at Figures 5.4 and 5.6. Figure 5.6 shows the line numbers for the totals, and it also shows the relation of the totals block to the last data line. You see there that the decimal position of the totals should align with the decimal position for the extended-price column. Figure 5.4 gives detailed spacing information for the data line; in this case, you want to notice the spacing for the extended-price column. This data column ends ½ inch from the right side of the data box, or 1 inch from the right edge of the page. Using the usual PostScript coordinates, that is 7.5 inches from the left edge of the page. Now the totals are larger than the extended price, but they can be lined up using the right margin, since all of these numbers have a decimal point followed by two digits. Therefore, you must right-justify the totals against the 7.5 inch margin to align them under the extended price.

The last procedure, showLine, is the simplest. It displays a line of text at a given position. It requires that the string for display be placed first on the stack, followed by the position in the correct sequence—x-coordinate followed by y-coordinate. The procedure itself simply does a **moveto** to get to the correct position for the display, followed by a **show**. Since each line is displayed as a unit, you don't need to worry any further here about positioning for the item display. Each line of text will be displayed one after another, beginning on line 43, as shown in the layout in Figure 5.3. The right margin for all the displayed items will be 1 inch, based on the layout in Figure 5.4. The assumption here is that the data line is exactly 78 characters wide. No additional placement or spacing of the data is being done.

Finally, notice that there is no font selection or setting within these procedures, unlike some of the procedures used for the form output. These procedures are more like the support procedures you identified before; they have some potential for wider applicability. I don't want to mislead you; these procedures are partially dependent upon the font used to output the strings. In particular, they depend on having a monospaced font to ensure alignment of fields within the strings, as you read earlier. Nevertheless, it improves flexibility, control, and efficiency to keep the setting of fonts outside the procedures themselves.

Draft Page

Now that you have defined your procedures and know what the example data looks like, you should be able to combine the two to create the data for the fill-in part of your output. There is no good way to suggest how you should do this, because each application or editor (if you are working with a disk file) is different.

As you did earlier with the various blocks that made up your form, let's first turn this into a draft page to see how the output looks by itself. To do this, you must first create a small prolog, which will include the required support procedures, the font definitions, and the data procedures that you identified and coded in the previous section. For fonts, you will use 12-point Helvetica-Bold for the order number, to match the literal NO.: in the header block, and 10-point Courier, as discussed earlier, for the remainder of the text. When you have finished with this, the final version of this part of the program should look like Figure 5.33. The page itself is surrounded by the usual **save**, and **restore** to ensure that this page does not cause changes to any previous or subsequent

```
%application output converted to PostScript format
F2 setfont
(10423)
invNumber

F1 setfont
(David Holzgang)
(22621 Penfield Ave.)
(Chatsworth, CA  91311)
address

(20-Feb-91)
date

( 12-456        Backpack - Blue              1        1     28.95
1 inch 43 line showLine
( 28-145        Wool socks - Size 10         4        4      3.95
1 inch 42 line showLine
( 95-004        Strawberries                10       10      1.45
1 inch 41 line showLine
( 95-010        Apricots                     5        5      1.29
1 inch 40 line showLine
( 96-148        Chicken Cacciatore           4        4      2.95
1 inch 39 line showLine
( 96-104        Beef Stew                    4        3      2.95
1 inch 38 line showLine
( 96-107        Spaghetti with Meat Sauce    2        2      2.95
1 inch 37 line showLine
( 96-242        Trail Mix                    4        4      0.98
1 inch 36 line showLine
( 35-129        First Aid Kit                1        1      9.49
1 inch 35 line showLine

($105.66)
($6.87)
($3.42)
($115.95)
totals
```

Figure 5.33: Completed fill-in program

page. These are, as you have read before, an important element in good Post-Script code. There are no surprises in this program, and unsurprisingly, it produces a page of text that looks like Figure 5.34.

This is essentially the output that you would expect to get from any application that was printing onto a pre-printed form using a standard line printer. The fonts may be a bit fancier, and the spacing more accurate than most applications can support; nevertheless, this is generally what application output is supposed to look like.

If you hold your results, shown in Figure 5.34 and 5.27 up to a strong light, you will see that they fit over one another perfectly. You have now created, as individual pages, each of the parts of the completed form that you want to print as a unit. The remaining task is to perform, within the printer, the same action that you just took by holding the two pages together. Essentially, you are going to create each page on the printer, as though they were transparent, and then print the pair together.

Form and Fill-In

The process of printing each of these pages together, one overlaying the other, is easy. You could just take the two finished programs above and

```
   David Holzgang
   22621 Penfield Ave.
   Chatsworth, CA  91311
                                               20-Feb-91


   12-456   Backpack - Blue              1    1    28.95     $28.95
   28-145   Wool socks - Size 10         4    4     3.95     $15.80
   95-004   Strawberries                10   10     1.45     $14.50
   95-010   Apricots                     5    5     1.29      $6.45
   96-148   Chicken Cacciatore           4    4     2.95     $11.80
   96-104   Beef Stew                    4    3     2.95      $8.85
   96-107   Spaghetti with Meat Sauce    2    2     2.95      $5.90
   96-242   Trail Mix                    4    4     0.98      $3.92
   35-129   First Aid Kit                1    1     9.49      $9.49



                                                         $105.66
                                                           $6.87
                                                           $3.42
                                                         $115.95
```

Figure 5.34: PostScript output from the fill-in data file

run them as one job, one after the other, as long as you didn't issue a **show-page** between them. Although this would work, it is hardly a satisfactory solution for a regular, repetitive use of a form; the correct method is to integrate the two pieces into one program.

It may surprise you to learn that you can run either of the two segments of this program first without affecting the other page output. First, the page descriptions for each page are effectively isolated, so that no changes in the graphic state for one piece of the output can interfere with the other—no matter in which order they are produced. In addition, you might expect that printing the strings of data over the form would wipe out the lines on the form. That would happen if you had a graphic element, filled with white, and displayed it over the form. Because PostScript colors are opaque, the white would overlay and obliterate the black lines. With text, however, the situation is different. Text spaces are not graphics, as the letters are, but rather are true spaces. Therefore, they don't affect the black lines printed by the form even if those lines were painted before the **show** command for the text line.

The completed program, with all its support procedures and with the complete PostScript structure, is shown in Figure 5.35. After this, you finally have the two pages combined onto one output page, as in Figure 5.36.

There is nothing new in this program; only the packaging has changed. You are familiar with all the procedures and are accustomed to the structuring conventions as well. As before, the actual program (script) is relatively short, and most of the real work has been done in the design and test of the procedural components. You will note that the only data in the script is the variable data that was supplied by the application. All the other information—the titles, fonts, spacing, and so on—is contained in the procedures themselves.

There are only two important, and related, issues to mention about the marriage of these two previous pieces of code. The first is the issue of where to locate the data procedures, and the second is why do you have the support procedures, inch, line, and rightJustifyText, in the final program twice. In both cases, the answer lies in how the form is built and accessed by your program. When you execute the form's **PaintProc**, you place the Order-Form dictionary onto the dictionary stack and then draw the form. As noted earlier, you must design your **PaintProc** to use only its own data and procedures, and not to rely on anything outside, since the order of execution for the **PaintProc** cannot be predicted. Therefore, the OrderForm must have a copy of all required support procedures. On the other hand, when the data is painted onto the form, the OrderForm dictionary is not on the dictionary

```
%!PS-Adobe-3.0
%%Title: Form Exercise
%%Creator: David Holzgang
%%CreationDate: 3:56:20 PM  1/9/92
%%For: Understanding PostScript Programming (3rd Edition)
%%BoundingBox: 0 0 612 792
%%Orientation: Portrait
%%Pages: 1
%%EndComments
%%BeginProlog
%%BeginResource: procset FormDict 1.0 0
/FormDict 15 dict def
FormDict begin
%------------------------------Level Check-----------------------------
/languagelevel where
        {pop languagelevel}
        {1}
ifelse
2 ge
/LV2 exch def

%----------------------------Emulation Procedures---------------------
LV2
{
        %if Level 2 or greater, use the native execform operator
        /xform /execform load def
}
{
        %if Level 1, emulate execform
        /xform
        {
                gsave
                        newpath
                        dup
                        /PaintProc get
                        exec
                grestore
        }
        def
}
ifelse
%--------------------------Support Procedures------------------
/inch
{
        72 mul
}
def
/line
{
        12 mul
}
def

/rightJustifyText
{
        2 index
        stringwidth pop
        sub
        exch moveto
        show
}
def

%---------------------------Fonts-------------------------------
/F1
        /Courier findfont 10 scalefont
```

Figure 5.35: Program for the completed form with data

```
        def
        /F2
                /Helvetica-Bold findfont 12 scalefont
        def

        %-------------------------Data Procedures--------------------
        /address
        {
                .6 inch 49 line moveto
                count 3 gt
                {show} if
                .6 inch 50 line moveto
                count 2 gt
                {show} if
                .6 inch 51 line moveto
                count 1 gt
                {show} if
                .6 inch 52 line moveto
                count 0 gt
                {show} if
        }
        def

        /invNumber
        {
                52 line 8 inch rightJustifyText
        }
        def


        /date
        {
                50 line 8 inch rightJustifyText
        }
        def

        /totals
        {
                5 line 7.5 inch rightJustifyText
                7 line 7.5 inch rightJustifyText
                9 line 7.5 inch rightJustifyText
                11 line 7.5 inch rightJustifyText
        }
        def

        /showLine
        {
                moveto
                show
        }
        def

        end             %FormDict
        %%EndResource

        %%BeginResource: procset OrderForm 1.0 0
        /OrderForm 30 dict def
        OrderForm begin

        %---------------------------Required Entries-------------------------
        /FormType 1 def
        /BBox [ 0 0 612 792 ] def
        /Matrix matrix def
```

Figure 5.35: Program for the completed form with data (continued)

```
/PaintProc
{
        begin    %OrderForm dictionary
        1 setlinewidth
        0 setgray
        %produce logo block
        gsave
                .5 inch 55 line translate
                logo
        grestore
        %produce header block
        gsave
                headTitles
                .5 inch 48 line translate
                2.5 inch 1 inch cornerBox
        grestore
        %produce main text & totals block
        gsave
                .5 inch 4 line translate
                2 setlinewidth
                7.5 inch 43 line screenBox
        grestore
        verticalLines
        dataTitles
        footTitles
        %form page finished
        end              %OrderForm dictionary
}
def

%----------------------------Support Procedures----------------------
/inch
{
        72 mul
}
def

/line
{
        12 mul
}
def

/centerText
{
        2 index
        stringwidth pop
        2 div
        3 1 roll
        1 index sub
        2 div
        3 -1 roll
        sub
        add
        currentpoint exch pop
        moveto
        show
}
def

/rightJustifyText
{
        2 index
        stringwidth pop
```

Figure 5.35: Program for the completed form with data (continued)

```
        sub
        exch moveto
        show
}
def

%---------------------------Fonts & Variables----------------------
/F1
        /Helvetica findfont 10 scalefont
def
/F2
        /Helvetica-Bold findfont 10 scalefont
def
/F3
        /Helvetica-Bold findfont 15 scalefont
def
/F4
        /Helvetica-Bold findfont 12 scalefont
def
/F5
        /Helvetica-BoldOblique findfont 18 scalefont
def

userdict /DimY 0 put
userdict /DimX 0 put

%---------------------------Main Text & Totals Block---------------
/screenBox
{
        newpath
   /DimY exch store
   /DimX exch store
   .5 inch 0 moveto
   DimX 0   DimX DimY .25 inch arcto
   4 (pop) repeat
   DimX DimY  0 DimY .25 inch arcto
   4 (pop) repeat
   0 DimY     0 0     .25 inch arcto
   4 (pop) repeat
   0 0      DimX 0    .25 inch arcto
   4 (pop) repeat
   closepath
   stroke
}
def

/verticalLines
{
        newpath
        144 47 line moveto
        144 12.5 line lineto
        317 47 line moveto
        317 12.5 line lineto
        365 47 line moveto
        365 12.5 line lineto
        413 47 line moveto
        413 12.5 line lineto
        467 47 line moveto
        467 12.5 line lineto
        stroke
}
def
```

Figure 5.35: Program for the completed form with data (continued)

```
    /dataTitles
    {
            newpath
            .5 inch 45 line moveto
            7.5 inch 0 rlineto
            stroke
            .5 inch 45.5 line moveto
            F1 setfont
            0 45.5 line moveto
       (ITEM NO.) 72 144 centerText
       (DESCRIPTION     ) 144 317 centerText
       (ORDER) 318 365 centerText
       (SHIP) 366 413 centerText
       (UNIT $) 414 467 centerText
       (EXT. PRICE) 468 540 centerText
    }
    def

    /footTitles
    {
            newpath
       .5 inch 12.5 line moveto
       7.5 inch 0 rlineto
       stroke
       467 12.5 line moveto
       467 4 line lineto
       stroke
       F2 setfont
       (SUBTOTAL) 11 line 463 rightJustifyText
       (SALES TAX) 9 line 463 rightJustifyText
       (SHIPPING)  7 line 463 rightJustifyText
       (TOTAL)     5 line 463 rightJustifyText
    }
    def

    %----------------------------Header Block----------------------------
    /headTitles
    {
            %first set invoice title
            F3 setfont
            0 52 line moveto
            (ORDER) .5 inch  8 inch  centerText
            %now set number title
            F4 setfont
            (NO. :) 52 line 7 inch rightJustifyText
    }
    def

    /cornerBox
    {
            newpath
            /DimY exch store
            /DimX exch store
            %bottom left corner
                    0    0    moveto
                    0    12   rlineto
                    0    0    moveto
                    12   0    rlineto
            %bottom right corner
                    DimX 0    moveto
                    0    12   rlineto
                    DimX 0    moveto
                    -12  0    rlineto
            %top left corner
```

Figure 5.35: Program for the completed form with data (continued)

```
                        0 DimY   moveto
                        0  -12   rlineto
                        0 DimY   moveto
                       12    0   rlineto
               %top right corner
                   DimX DimY moveto
                        0  -12   rlineto
                   DimX DimY moveto
                      -12    0   rlineto
               stroke
       )
       def

       %---------------------------Logo Block---------------------------
       /sun
       (
               0   0
               3 -1 roll
               0  360
               arc
       )
       def

       /hill
       (
               0 0 moveto
               dup 2 div
               3 -1 roll
               lineto
               0 lineto
               closepath
       )
       def

       /logoGraphic
       (
               newpath
               %begin logo
               %do background mountain
               gsave
                       3   0   translate
                       8   8   hill
                       .3 setgray
                       fill
               grestore

               %do left and right hills
               gsave
                       %left hill
                       5   6   hill
                       .7 setgray
                       fill
                       %right hill
                       7   0   translate
                       5   6   hill
                       fill
               grestore

               %do sun
               gsave
                       14 9 translate
                       1.5 sun
                       stroke
```

Figure 5.35: Program for the completed form with data (continued)

```
        grestore
        %logo finished
)
def

/logoTitles
(
        F5 setfont
        0 .75 inch moveto
        (MOUNTAIN SPORTS, LTD.)
        0 8 inch centerText
        F1 setfont
        0 .5 inch moveto
        (123 Mountain Way,  Chatsworth, CA  91311)
        0 8 inch centerText
        0 .5 inch 12 sub moveto
        ((818) 882-8144                 (213) 555-1212)
        0 8 inch centerText
)
def

/logo
(
        logoTitles
        gsave
                9.5 9.5 scale
                1 9.5 div setlinewidth
                logoGraphic
        grestore
)
def

end             %OrderForm
%%EndResource
%%EndProlog

%-----------------------------Script----------------------------
%%BeginSetup
FormDict begin

%%EndSetup

%%Page: i 1
%-------------------------Setup form-------------------------
/PgSave save def

% Execute the desired form procedure
OrderForm xform

%application output converted to PostScript format
F2 setfont
(10423)
invNumber

F1 setfont
(David Holzgang)
(22621 Penfield Ave.)
(Chatsworth, CA  91311)
address

(20-Feb-91)
date
```

Figure 5.35: Program for the completed form with data (continued)

```
( 12-456        Backpack - Blue              1       1      28.95
1 inch 43 line showLine
( 28-145        Wool socks - Size 10         4       4       3.95
1 inch 42 line showLine
( 95-004        Strawberries               10      10       1.45
1 inch 41 line showLine
( 95-010        Apricots                     5       5       1.29
1 inch 40 line showLine
( 96-148        Chicken Cacciatore           4       4       2.95
1 inch 39 line showLine
( 96-104        Beef Stew                    4       3       2.95
1 inch 38 line showLine
( 96-107        Spaghetti with Meat Sauce    2       2       2.95
1 inch 37 line showLine
( 96-242        Trail Mix                    4       4       0.98
1 inch 36 line showLine
( 35-129        First Aid Kit                1       1       9.49
1 inch 35 line showLine

($105.66)
($6.87)
($3.42)
($115.95)
totals

% Clean up after the form has been completed
PgSave restore
showpage

%%Trailer
end             %FormDict
%%EOF
```

Figure 5.35: Program for the completed form with data (continued)

stack, and there is no reason why it should be. Instead, the current dictionary is FormDict. To keep the program neat, and to insulate the form generation process from the data, you install the support procedures in both dictionaries, so that both parts of the program can use them with confidence. Notice that this would allow you to change these definitions independently if you needed to do that.

By the same token, you want to define your data procedures in your FormDict. This is the master dictionary for your program, and it is the one that will be current when the data is displayed. Therefore, the data procedures are added there to the level determination and xform procedure that you saw earlier.

Wrap-Up

The entire program is presented in Figure 5.35 as one piece, because that is the best way to read the program and because, if you want to run the

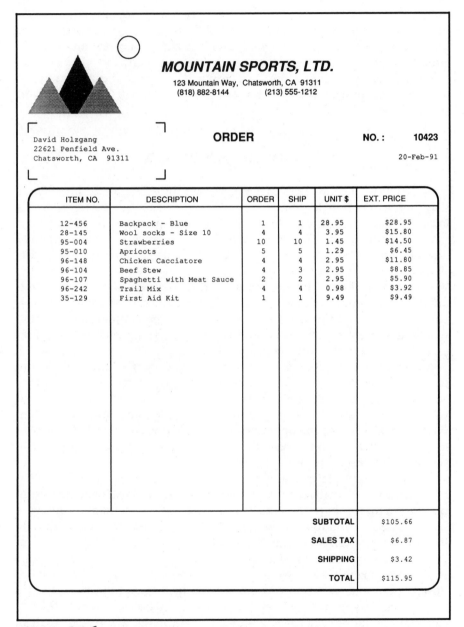

Figure 5.36: Completed form with data

program, you need to present it to the interpreter in more or less that order. In practice, however, you may prefer to split the OrderForm procset into a separate file. In that way, you could send it to the printer first and store it, either in global memory or, perhaps, on a disk, and then send whatever sets of variable data you had for the form. You will then have the ability to send multiple pages of data to the printer. The next section will focus on this and similar topics.

Recap and Review

Before we look at alternative ways to use the skills and the procedures you have worked on so diligently, we should discuss the intention of this exercise. The exercise was done for illustrative purposes to demonstrate what can be done with the PostScript techniques that you now know, and to illustrate how to combine Level 1 and Level 2 code in a correct way. In particular, some of the techniques used here for justification, for example, would normally be moved into the application that was producing the output data. This would be more efficient, in most cases, than doing these calculations in PostScript itself. The result would be simpler code, which would do more **moveto show** operations and less calculation and placement of strings within the PostScript code. In addition, in a real program you would have to make some additions to the **PaintProc** described here to provide additional features to correspond to the complete set of **exec-form** operations. We have not done these here because they were not required for the simple, full-page form that we are using, and they require PostScript procedures and operators that you do not know yet but will meet in later chapters. Nevertheless, the exercise here is important because it shows two points clearly.

First, PostScript is a language of remarkable power and flexibility. Using a relatively small set of the PostScript operators, you have created an order form that looks professionally produced—if not, perhaps, professionally designed. If you look around, you will discover how many corporate logos and forms can be precisely reproduced with basic PostScript operations. Limitations of point size, graphic shape, and so on, which may be imposed for many reasons by applications, even applications that produce PostScript output, are in no way inherent in the language itself.

Along the same lines, I hope you have noticed how efficient PostScript can be at generating such pages. Although we began the chapter calling this a basic document, that does not imply that the final page is simple to produce;

a significant amount of information is on this page. If you were to try to reproduce this page using straight bit-mapped patterns, it would require a large amount of printer memory and transmission time, and you would have lost the flexibility inherent in building common, reusable procedures for handling such documents.

Second, the structure of this exercise begins to show you how application output may be created or modified to generate practical results. The process of producing a form as a dictionary procset, which can be preloaded into the printer, and following that with the actual document data, is precisely the general format followed by most of the applications that produce PostScript output. Once you understand PostScript structure, the process itself becomes more or less transparent.

Adding New Data

You would not have to do anything new or difficult if you wanted to use this form with additional data. You would repeat the same process that you used here; image the form, add the data, and output the page, for as many sets as you wished. With a Level 2 device, you would have the added benefits of form caching and faster processing, but even on a Level 1 device, this process is reasonably fast and quite easy.

Moreover, this approach enables you to do many things that more traditional, pre-printed forms would not allow. For example, you could change the form, if required, without any loss of inventory or waste of paper. You can change from one form to another internally, within the printer, under application control, instead of requiring operator intervention, with its attendant slowness and possibility for error. In all, this approach can be cost-effective and powerful in a wide variety of environments.

Form Sets and Data

Notice also that these procedures have all been debugged and tested. They make up a reliable set of building blocks to use with this form and to create other forms. If you did want to create other forms to use within this same family, there are some issues to consider.

To begin with, the procedures are well designed for this purpose. Procedures like logo, for example, could be transferred to any other form. The procedure has been deliberately constructed to be able to be placed and scaled anywhere onto a page with minimum fuss. Many of the other procedures are equally portable, especially the supporting procedures.

6

Working with Advanced Text

THIS CHAPTER DEALS WITH advanced topics that relate to handling and using text output. These are important issues to understand if you are going to make the best use of your application software, and this chapter will clarify the techniques and procedures that might be used in typical applications to handle text processing. The primary emphasis is to help you understand and be able to read the PostScript code used by applications.

The first section of the chapter deals with advanced text-handling techniques. These are primarily concerned with adjustment of text strings during output for justification and aesthetic reasons. The section begins with some new, advanced techniques for handling strings, which are the basic building blocks of all text output. Then the section continues with a discussion of several operators that can be used in place of the **show** operator to handle special spacing requirements during text output. Finally, you are introduced to a class of operators that allow you to control individual letter placement.

You will learn one technique for setting text that is justified on both the left and right margins using the string-handling operations identified earlier as part of a general text-justification procedure. This procedure is then included in a portion of a previous exercise to show you how easily you can revise most well-structured PostScript code.

The second section of this chapter covers handling text generated by application programs. There are two parts to this section. The first part discusses file transmission and file handling in PostScript; the second deals with understanding and changing output that has been generated by an application program.

The first part of this section examines two specific issues relating to file handling. The first issue is very practical; you may already have been using it. This is a discussion of how to transmit files to your PostScript printer, and how you might use this to send PostScript programs to the printer for execution. The second issue is a brief overview of PostScript file-handling operations and an explanation of PostScript standard files.

The second part of this chapter deals with the use of applications to generate PostScript output and how you can modify that output to change the results, using the knowledge you have developed about the PostScript language. There are two basic methods for altering the PostScript output from an application. One is to add your own procedures to the output; the other is to modify the procedures provided by the application. Both methods are covered at a general level.

The chapter ends with the usual review of the operators that were introduced.

TEXT TECHNIQUES

This section of the chapter discusses techniques for handling text. Text is the most common object of PostScript processing and probably the most important topic for you to handle well. You have worked with basic text in a variety of situations and ways, all using the **show** operator. You have also worked with fonts, using simple font handling at first and then more complex techniques in Chapter 4, where you learned about the font machinery in detail. You now have a working knowledge of PostScript font capabilities.

Now we are going to turn from concentrating on font mechanisms to text processing itself. We touched on these issues in Chapter 4, when we discussed some of the concerns about the interaction of the font machinery and display operations for text via the font cache. The present section emphasises the text handling process that exists in addition to, and separate from, any of the font mechanisms or processes. Here you will learn how to use PostScript text-handling operations effectively.

STRING HANDLING

To learn more about PostScript text processing, first you must learn more about PostScript operations on strings. Strings are the fundamental objects that allow you to store and manipulate text, and PostScript has several operators that can carry out complex and useful actions on strings. Some of these operators are familiar to you, and some are new; but all of them have an important role in helping you work on strings, particularly text strings. This part of the chapter explores both the basic structure of strings and the operators that work on them.

Text as Strings

Strings are the basic components of text in PostScript. Text strings were the first thing you worked with in the exercises and examples, and you have hardly had an exercise that has not included some text output. Like your first font experiences, you have been working with text in a variety of formats but have really not yet examined the operation of strings and text display in any depth. You have created strings and used the **show** operator to paint the strings onto the page, using the information provided by the current font.

There are additional points that have been made implicitly about strings that we will review and make more explicit here. You will remember that a string essentially consists of a series of numbers, each number representing a single character in the current font. This was the essential concept that enabled the reencoding process that you worked through earlier. You know that strings are enclosed in parentheses, ( ), and you have learned that there are a variety of ways of including characters within the string delimiters. The most usual way is to type the required characters within the bounding parentheses, but you can also use the *ddd* notation and other special codes to include characters that are not otherwise readily encodable within the string.

From all of this, you can see that strings and text are inextricably connected within PostScript; and if you want to learn to handle text more accurately, you must first learn some of the more advanced operations that PostScript provides for handling strings.

Operators on Strings

Strings are composite objects, like arrays; and, also like arrays, they can be accessed and worked on by using an index. Consequently, a variety of operators can be used with strings in the same way that they are used with arrays. This concept is important to keep in mind when you are working with strings. Basically, any of the operations that you worked with in the earlier chapters on arrays can be adapted for use on strings. Below is a short list of the string operators that parallel the array operations that you used earlier. Note that, in most cases, the operator is identical to the array operator; only the type of the operand (in this case, a string) determines the behavior of the operator. In the case of the **string** operator, the behavior is identical to the matching **array** operator.

int **string** string

Creates a *string* that initially contains *int* null objects as entries. *int* must be a non- negative integer less than the device-dependent maximum string length.

array index

string index get any

Looks up the *index* in *array* or *string* and returns the element identified by *index* (counting from zero). The *index* must be between 0 and $n - 1$, where n is the number of elements in *array* or *string*.

array index count   subarray

string index count **getinterval** substring

Selects a segment of *array* or *string* and returns the selected segment as *subarray* or *substring*. The segment begins with the element identified by *index* (counting from zero), and extends for *count* elements. There must be enough elements in *array* or *string* for correct operation; that is, the sum of *index* and *count* must be between 0 and $n - 1$, where n is the number of elements in *array* or *string*. The *subarray* or *substring* that is returned shares its values with the original *array* or *string*. Any change to either one will change the other.

array index value

string index value **put** —

Stores *value* into *array* or *string* at the position identified by *index* (counting from zero). *index* must be in the range 0 to $n - 1$, where n is the number of elements in *array* or *string*.

array string **length** int

Returns *int* as the number array of elements that make up the value of *array* or *string*.

array1 array2   subarray2

string1 string2 **copy** substring2

Copies all elements of *array1* or *string1* into *array2* or *string2*. The
types of the two operands must be the same; that is, array or string.
The length of the second operand must be at least the length of the
first; **copy** returns the changed elements of the second operand onto
the stack as *subarray2* or *substring2*. If the second operand is longer
than the first, the remaining values are unaffected by the **copy**.

array proc

string proc **forall** —

Executes procedure *proc* for every element of *array* or *string*. **forall**
pushes each element from the array or string onto the stack, and then
executes the *proc* procedure, which may access the element on the
stack. If the *proc* does not consume the element on the stack, it
should remove it; although **forall** itself does not leave any object on
the stack, if *proc* does not clear the stack before exiting, the elements
of *array* or *string* will remain on the stack. In the case of *string*, the
objects placed on the stack are the codes (numeric values) of the
characters, not one-character strings.

Two additional operators are important in handling strings. These two
operators are quite different, but they each address an important issue in
handling strings.

if found:

string seek **search** post match pre true

if not found:

string seek **search** string false

Looks for the first time that the string *seek* occurs within *string* and
returns the results of the search on the operand stack. The search is

successful if there is any subset of *string* that exactly matches the string *seek*. If there is such a match, **search** divides the *string* into three pieces and pushes them onto the operand stack: *pre*, the portion of *string* preceding the match; *match*, the portion of *string* that is identical to *seek*; and *post*, the remainder of *string*. Each of these is pushed onto the operand stack in the order indicated, followed by the boolean value *true* to indicate that a match was found. If no part of *string* is found to match *seek*, the operator returns the original *string* on the operand stack and pushes the boolean value, *false*.

any string **cvs** substring

Converts object *any* to a string. *any* is changed from its current form to an appropriate string representation, and stored in the first section of *string*, which is overwritten. There must be enough room in *string* to hold the representation of *any*, or you will get an error.

This conversion process depends on a notion of what constitutes an appropriate string representation of each object type. The following table lists what that representation is and how **cvs** uses it.

OBJECT	STRING REPRESENTATION
string	copies the string object over onto the first elements of the receiving string.
numeric	turns the numeric value into a string representation of the number; that is, the number 123 becomes the string (123).
boolean	returns the strings *true* or *false* as appropriate.
name	returns the text representation of the name.
operator	returns the text name for the operator.
any other	returns the string nostringval.

Each of these operators has a specific place in your PostScript repertoire. The **search** operator is used to analyze a string and break it up into appropriate units for processing. Later in the chapter, you will see some examples that make use of this operator.

The **cvs** operator is perhaps more difficult to understand, but its basic function is to turn other objects into strings for display or representation on an output page. For example, you cannot display a numeric object directly on a page; you must turn it into a string for the **show** operator to function correctly. This operator is one of several, all beginning with the character *c* (for convert), that will perform conversions from one type or class of Post-Script object to another. The complete set is presented in the *PostScript Language Reference Manual, Second Edition.* Remember these functions when you need to transform a result from one type of object to another.

String Handling Example

In Chapter 4, you used some advanced techniques to make an outline version of characters for the title of the menu exercise. In that example, we discussed how you cannot make a string for outlining very long, as you risk exceeding the path limits of the interpreter. This happens because letter shapes are quite complex, and so, when you go to outline them, adding a string of letters may cause an error.

You can use some of these new operators to overcome this limitation. The basic approach is to take any arbitrary string and display each letter in the string as an outline, one at a time. Figure 6.1 shows you the same process you did earlier, in Figure 4.8, but now it's been modified to handle any arbitrary string.

The basic change here is to use a **for** loop to access each element of the string individually. Remember that **for** requires four operands: beginning value, increment value, ending value, and a procedure. It creates an index, starting at the given beginning value, which is tested against the ending value. If it does not exceed the ending value, **for** then places the current value of the index onto the operand stack and executes the procedure. After the procedure completes, **for** adds the increment value to the current value of the index and does this again.

This gives you a good method for accessing the string. If you use a beginning value of 0, and an ending value that is the **length** of the string minus 1, then each time the procedure is executed the index will be the current letter in the string. Note that you must use the **length** minus 1 since the index for a string or array begins at 0.

The procedure that you execute must do three things: it has to retrieve each letter in turn, outline it, and draw it onto the page. You retrieve the element with the **getinterval** command. This takes a string, an index value,

```
%------------------------Prolog -------------------------
/inch
{
      72 mul
}
def

/centerText
{
      /Right exch def
      /Left exch def
      dup
      stringwidth pop
      2 div
      Right Left sub 2 div
      exch sub
      Left add
      Line moveto
}
def

%------------------------Script-------------------------
/Times-Italic findfont 36 scalefont setfont
/Line 10 inch def
(DINNER MENU) 1 inch 7.5 inch centerText
0 1 2 index length 1 sub
{
      1 index exch
      1 getinterval
      false charpath
      currentpoint
          stroke
      moveto
}
for
pop

showpage
```

Figure 6.1: Revised method for outline text

and a count. In this case, the string and the index are already on the stack when **for** executes the procedure. However, **getinterval** removes its string operand from the stack when it executes. Since you will be performing this procedure repeatedly, you need to ensure that the string remains on the stack for the whole time. To do this, you copy the string operand to the top of the stack with the **index** operator and then exchange the string and the index value to put them in the correct order. Now you have two copies of the string on the stack, with the index value above them. Since you want to take one character at a time, you push 1 onto the stack as the count and execute the **getinterval**. This returns the selected character, as a 1-character string, to the operand stack. Now you do the same **false char-path** sequence that you saw before to turn the character into an outline. This time, however, you do a **currentpoint** before you **stroke** the path, so that the next character will paint in the correct location. Since **stroke** erases the current path, if you didn't save the location after each letter all the letters would image in the same place. Note that you don't want to do a **gsave**, **grestore** here since the **gsave** would save all of the path, not just the current point; since exceeding path limits is the issue, saving the entire path won't solve the problem. Instead you just save the current point and restore it with a **moveto** when the **stroke** is completed. This images a single character from the string in outline format.

Since you have saved the string each time you executed the procedure, it is still on the stack at the end of the **for** loop. So, when you're done, you **pop** the string off of the stack. That isn't strictly necessary here, since you simply print the page and end the job, but it's good PostScript programming practice to leave the stacks in the same state as you found them at the end of any processing. This illustrates how you can use some of these new operators to handle strings in better ways than you did before.

JUSTIFICATION

This set of string operators is complemented by a set of operators that display strings on the output page. Until now, you have relied on the **show** operator to perform this function. The **show** will probably remain the most-used operator for your text display, but there are a variety of other operators, each of which has a specific focus and can facilitate operations that you will want to perform. The focus of these additional operators is to improve the process of justifying text strings.

What Is Justification?

Justification is the process of lining text up on both the left and right margins of a page or column. This is the process that is generally used in high-quality publications for setting and displaying text. Justification, however, is both laborious and resource-intensive. If a person is doing it, the primary resource consumed is time; if a computer is used, the time required is much less, but a high demand is placed on the computational resources within the computer.

Obviously, each line of text is a different length, both because there are different numbers of characters in each line and because (if you are using proportional fonts) each character has a different width. The process of justification, then, consists of adding additional space to a line of text to make it come out the same length as all the other lines; usually some fixed width. The intention is to add space to the line in such a way that the additional space does not confuse the eye or detract from the legibility of the text.

This process can be accomplished in three ways. In the first method, additional spaces or fixed fractions of spaces are added at specific locations between sentences and words to align the lines. The second method is a refinement of the first, in which a smaller amount of space is added to the all spaces between words and sentences. This process is inherently dependent upon the ability of the text to be adjusted by an arbitrary fractional amount, whereas the first method can be accomplished using whole and half-space increments, for example. The third way of adjusting the length of the text line is the most subtle, but it is also the most difficult. In this case, the necessary space is added between each letter, essentially incrementing the font width for each character on the line by the appropriate width adjustment. Notice that you can combine adjustments of the second and third type to make a line that is exactly justified and yet easy to read. PostScript provides operators for each of these methods: space adjustment, character adjustment, and a combination of both.

Space Adjustment

The first method of justification mentioned above, adding full or fractional spaces at selected positions within the line, is the least desirable (and most obvious) method. The second method, however, is not so obvious and is a marked improvement over the first. PostScript has a specific operator, **widthshow**, that can help you perform this process. A description of the operator follows:

c_x c_y char string **widthshow** —

Prints the characters of *string* but adjusts the width of each occurrence of the character *char* in *string* by adding c_x to its x-dimension and c_y to its y-dimension, thereby adjusting the spacing between this character and the following character.

The **widthshow** operator works like the **show** operator for all characters except the selected character, called *char* above. Each time there is an occurence of *char* in *string*, the operator essentially modifies the width of the bounding box for the selected character by adding c_x and c_y to the box.

The net result is to widen the line of text by the number of occurences of the specified character multiplied by the width adjustment. This process obviously is identical to the second method of justification given above; however, it is more general, since the the **widthshow** operator can be used with any character, while the process outlined above will only add space between words and sentences. If that is what you want (and it usually is), you would call the **widthshow** operator using the space character as the delimiter; in that way, you could add a specific amount to each of the spaces between words or sentences.

Clearly, an additional step must be performed before you can make effective use of **widthshow**. That is, you must know by how much you need to adjust each occurance of *char* in order to make the line the length you want. An exercise later in the chapter will show you how you might go about this process.

Letter Adjustment

The other basic method to justify text, as outlined above, is to add a smaller amount to each character within the text line. PostScript has an operator for this process:

a_x a_y string **ashow** —

Prints the characters of *string* but adjusts the width of each occurrence of every character in *string* by adding a_x to its x-dimension and a_y to its y-dimension, thereby adjusting the spacing between all the characters.

The **ashow** operator behaves very much like the preceding example. The only difference is that here each character in *string* is affected, where before only the specified character was modified. This operator conforms exactly to the third method of justification presented earlier, in which additional space is evenly distributed across a line of type. The requirement to compute the necessary space adjustment has not gone away; the computation still must be done externally to this operation so that you know how much space to add to each character in order to justify the line.

Combined Techniques

Finally, PostScript provides an operator that combines both of the above processes. Not surprisingly, it is the **awidthshow** operator, which combines the two preceding operators. It looks like this:

c_x c_y char a_x a_y string **awidthshow** —

Prints the characters of *string* and performs two adjustments. It adjusts the width of each occurrence of every character in *string* by adding a_x to its x-dimension and a_y to its y-dimension, thereby adjusting the spacing between all the characters; and it adjusts the width of each occurrence of the character *char* in *string* by adding c_x to its x-dimension and c_y to its y-dimension, thereby adjusting the spacing between this character and the following character.

The **awidthshow** operator provides the finest automatic adjustment of the text line, but also requires the most computation for it to operate effectively. It combines the adjustment of a specific character, such as the space, with a uniform adjustment of all characters within the line. To use this operator, additional computation would be required to apportion the total space required for the justification of the line between the two methods of adding space.

Kerning

An additional topic related to justification should be discussed here. This is the process called *kerning,* which consists of adjusting the space between particular letters for aesthetic reasons. In fine typesetting, an adjustment is made to the width between specific letters, based on the fit of the two letters. Consider the letters shown in Figure 6.2.

As you can see, the letter *W* looks further away from the letter *A* than from the letter *H*. This is an optical illusion, created by the fact that the side of the *A* slopes in the same direction as the side of the *W,* whereas the side of the *H* is straight. You can compensate for this effect by moving the *A* and the *W* slightly closer together. This process is called kerning.

PostScript provides an operator, **kshow**, for such fine adjustment. The operator must look at each pair of characters in the string and perform

next character origin

Figure 6.2: Letters for kerning pairs

an appropriate procedure for the ones that require adjustment. The exact format of the operator is as follows:

> proc string **kshow** —
>
> Prints the characters of *string* but allows the user to execute the procedure *proc* between each character of *string*. The operator shows each character of *string* in turn, adding the width of the character to the current point and then executing the procedure *proc*.

The name **kshow** is derived from "kern show," and is intended to provide the facility for user-directed kerning operations. However, the operation is in no way constrained to performing kerning; any operation or procedure may be included. The procedure invoked may have any effects it wishes, including modification of the graphic state. If the procedure does modify the graphics state, those modifications will persist throughout the subsequent operation of **kshow** and afterward also. In other words, it is incumbent upon the procedure to control its effects and the results of its processing; the **kshow** operator will not perform any cleanup operations.

As an example, let us consider the operation of **kshow** on a short string, *(abcd)*. The operation would proceed in the following fashion:

1. The **kshow** operator displays the first character in the string, *a*, and updates the current point by the width of the character.

2. It pushes the character codes for *a* and *b* onto the stack leaving *b* on the top of the stack, and then executes the procedure that has been defined. Typically, this procedure will alter the current point to affect the placement of the next character.

3. When the procedure is done, **kshow** paints the character *b*, beginning at the current point as defined after the execution of *proc*, and updates the current point by the width of the character.

4. The **kshow** operator pushes the character codes for *b* and *c* onto the operand stack, with *c* on the top of the stack this time and *b* underneath, and executes the procedure.

5. The process continues repeatedly until the string is exhausted. The final action is to show the character *d* and terminate the process.

Obviously, if you were going to do kerning, the procedure that you defined would look at each of the two characters on the stack and compare them with a list or table of character pairs. When you found a pair of characters that were in the table, the procedure would then adjust the current point by some amount to adjust the positioning of the two characters relative to one another. Probably the easiest method for doing that task would be to have the desired adjustment for each pair of characters in the table, and simply take it from there. In fact, this is exactly how *kerning tables* work.

The **kshow** operator, however, is not limited in any way. The procedure that you define can do anything that you want. For example, you might use the procedure to insert a particular character between each character of a string, or you might use it to perform tests on the current point to determine your position on the page and take some action. You can use **kshow** in any way that you want; you are not limited by the implications of the name "kern show."

Individual Character Spacing

Although these operators allow you to do every type of justification, they are not equally useful in the real world. In particular, most justified text that is set in PostScript is generated by a word-processing or page-layout application. When such an application displays text on the screen, it very often will calculate the correct position for each character it displays in

order to provide WYSIWYG ("What You See Is What You Get") text placement for the user. Such precision allows the user to adjust kerning and justification on the screen and get output that looks best for the document being
created.

The act of displaying this text on the screen means that the application
has already calculated where the user wants each letter of the display to be
placed. The problem with the PostScript operators above is that they
require different calculations—number of spaces, number of characters,
additional space required, and so on—to produce the same effect. Realizing
this, PostScript Level 2 and Display PostScript have some new operators
that allow an application to place every character in a string at a precise location. These new operators are as follows:

string numarray

string numstring **xyshow** —

Paints each successive character in *string* at the positions specified by
the array *numarray* or the encoded number string *numstring*. Each
character is painted in the same way that the **show** operator would
paint the character. After the character is painted, **xyshow** takes
two successive numbers from the operand, which are the relative
location, in user coordinates, of the position of the next character to
be displayed. The first number is the x-coordinate displacement and
the second number is the y-coordinate displacement for the next
character's origin relative to the current character's origin. The
numarray or *numstring* operand must have at least as many pairs of
values as there are characters in *string*; if there are not enough number pairs for all the characters in *string*, an error will occur.

string numarray

string numstring **xshow** —

Works in a manner similar to **xyshow**, except that only one number
is taken from *numarray* or *numstring*. This number determines the

x-coordinate displacement for the next character, while the y-coordinate displacement is taken as 0.

string numarray

string numstring **yshow** —

Works in a manner similar to **xyshow**, except that only one number is taken from *numarray* or *numstring*. This number determines the y-coordinate displacement for the next character, while the x-coordinate displacement is taken as 0.

As you can easily see, these new operators allow an application to place every character in a string very accurately, without any additional calculations, once the original display has been completed. This can be the most efficient method for displaying kerned and justified text with high-end word-processing or page-layout applications. However, because of the amount of calculation required for correct placement, these operators are not often used for general PostScript programming except in special circumstances.

TEXT HANDLING EXAMPLE

You have been reading about many operators; a little practical example may help show you how you might use these operators. Obviously, not every one of these operators is used in a program; only one of them is primarily used for justification in any program. For this example, you will use the **widthshow** operator to create several lines of justified text.

Analysis

In this example, you will create a procedure, **justifyText**, that will take a string and justify it between preset margins. The example assumes that the string to be adjusted has already been fitted between these margins to the nearest word, or fraction of a word if hypenation is being used. The task is a relatively simple one: to adjust the length of the string to match the line length. You will do this by using the simplest method of justification that we discussed above; namely, to add the required additional space to the existing spaces in the string. Note that there are some potential limitations on this process. If the string has only a few spaces, because it contains long words or is constrained by narrow margins (perhaps it's set in a narrow column) or both, you may find that you have to add a lot of additional space to each space within the string to make the adjustment work. This would be obvious and disruptive; in such a case, you would prefer to use another technique.

The justification process in this example will be less complex than that and will not perform any testing to determine whether to use alternative justification methods. The process at this basic level consists of three steps, as follows:

1. Count the number of spaces in the string.

2. Calculate the difference in length between the string and the line.

3. Adjust each space in the string by the difference in length divided by the number of spaces in the string.

This is the process that you will implement as justifyText. In the preceding steps, you can see where you could increase the sophistication of the process. For example, you could test the number of spaces that you count to determine whether it was greater than some desired amount and then choose the adjustment method based on the results of that test. Or, with more sophistication, you could test the adjustment factor to see if it was greater than some acceptable maximum, and take appropriate action to use alternative methods.

Structure of the Routine

You already know how you are going to implement Step 3, above. You can do this by using the **widthshow** operator on the output string. That leaves Steps 1 and 2 for you to work out in the design of the procedure.

Step 2 is not difficult; you will subtract the length of the output string, which can be determined by the **stringwidth** operator, from the length of the line, which can be determined by subtracting the right margin from the left. This is very similar to the process you used in some of the earliest examples to center text between two margins.

Step 1 is more complex. You need to examine the output string and count the number of spaces that you find in the string. This is a place where you might use the **search** operator, which can do this fairly easily. As is always true in programming, there are alternative ways to achieve the same result. You also might design a loop, using **forall** and an **ifelse** test to tally the space characters. For the sake of instruction, we will use **search** here; but you should always keep in mind that there are often many approachs to a procedure, and that you may need to choose one over another based on speed, efficiency, or some other external consideration.

In either case, the processing loop for counting the blanks will be fairly complex. Let's analyze what you need to do. First, you want to create a procedure that you can call to count blanks in an arbitrary string. You can call this procedure countBlanks. The heart of such a procedure will be the **search** operator, which will take the string and break it up at each blank. That bit of code will look like this:

```
(string) ( ) search
```

This will return the following code onto the stack:

post match pre true *if found*

string false *if not found*

If a blank is found, you want to add 1 to a counter and continue to analyze the remainder of the string; if no blank is found, you're finished. At that point, the counter will contain the number of blanks in the string. This sequence naturally suggests the **ifelse** operator, since you would like to add 1 to the counter *if* there is a blank, or *else* you want to end the process.

The **ifelse** operator requires three operands: a boolean value and two procedures, one to be executed if the boolean value is true, the other to be executed if it is false. In this case, the boolean value will be supplied by the **search** operator, which leaves a boolean result on the stack; and the two procedures are as outlined above. They will look something like this:

TRUE: add one to counter

clean up the stack for next search

FALSE: clean up the stack

end the process

You may wonder why you need to "clean up the stack." Remember that **search** leaves several results on the stack; the **ifelse** operator will remove the boolean result, but it is your responsibility to remove anything else. In the false case, you will need to **pop** the remainder of the string (presumably the final word on the line) before you exit the procedure, and in the true case you will need to do two **pop** operators to get rid of the *pre* and *match* results, and thus leave the remainder of the string on the stack for the next **search**.

The actual **ifelse** operation would then look like this:

```
(string) ( ) search                      % boolean

{

        /BlankCtr BlankCtr 1 add def  % true procedure

        pop pop

}

{

        pop                           % false procedure

        exit

}

ifelse
```

You need to continue this process for the entire string, until the false result is returned by **search**. You can do this with the **loop** operator, which also has a matching **exit** operator to terminate processing. The **loop** operator requires one operand, which is the procedure to be executed repeatedly. The assumption is that there will be an **exit** operator within the procedure to terminate the loop processing; otherwise, it would continue indefinitely in what programmers call "an endless loop." In this case, you have provided the **exit** operator as part of the false procedure within the **ifelse**. The loop process also requires one additonal change from the **ifelse** outlined above. You need to remove the *(string)* reference, since the loop will be called with the string already on the stack.

This revised loop procedure will then form the major part of the countBlanks procedure. In addition to the loop, you will need to initialize the counter within the procedure, to ensure that it starts at zero. The entire procedure will then look like Figure 6.3. With this process now in hand, you can proceed to constructing the full justifyText procedure.

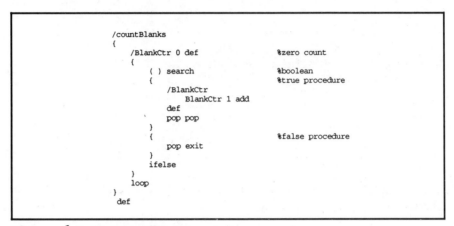

```
/countBlanks
{
    /BlankCtr 0 def                    %zero count
    {
        ( ) search                     %boolean
        {                              %true procedure
            /BlankCtr
                BlankCtr 1 add
            def
            pop pop
        }
        {                              %false procedure
            pop exit
        }
        ifelse
    }
    loop
}
def
```

Figure 6.3: The countBlanks procedure

Code for Justification

The procedure shown in Figure 6.4 will require you to implement the steps outlined earlier for justification. The best way to approach this is to look at the procedure and then discuss it in detail. The justifyText procedure starts out with four comment lines, designed to give you some helpful information about how to call and use it. Notice that these lines don't give you any direct information about how the procedure itself is constructed; they merely remind you how to invoke and use the procedure when you need it. This is the kind of information that really should be kept in comments; otherwise you would have to read the procedure to remind yourself how to use it every time you needed it.

The actual code begins on line %1 with a **dup** command. This command is necessary because you need to save the string on the stack for the **widthshow** on line %12, but you also need to use the string as an input to the countBlanks procedure on line %2. Because we have already analyzed this procedure, there isn't any more to say here except to note that this takes care of the first step in the list of requirements.

```
/justifyText
%procedure to justify a line of text
%   by adding extra space to space characters
%called as:   (string)  justifyText  --
%assumes variables LM (left margin) and RM (right margin)
{
        dup                                     %1
        countBlanks                             %2
        /LS RM LM sub def                       %3
        dup                                     %4
        /SS exch stringwidth pop def            %5
        /Space LS SS sub def                    %6
        /BlankCtr 0 ne                          %7
        {
            /Space
            Space BlankCtr div                  %8
            def
        }
        if                                      %9
        Space 0 8#040                           %10
        4 -1 roll                               %11
        widthshow                               %12
}
def                                             %13
```

Figure 6.4: justifyText procedure

Then you begin the computations to set up for Step 2. This starts in line %3 by computing the variable LS as the difference between the left margin, LM, and the right margin, RM. The next step is to calculate the string length. In the same fashion as before, the **dup** on line %4 provides the operand for the **stringwidth** on line %5. Line %5 contains more than just the **stringwidth**, however. This line defines the string size variable SS, which is determined by the width of the string on the stack. Since the string is on the stack when the definition begins, you have to use the familiar **exch** to get the name and the value into the proper position for the definition. Once the name literal is beneath the string, the **stringwidth** operator is called, and returns the x- and y-widths of the string. Remember that the y-width, which is on top of the stack, is always 0 for English; therefore you issue a **pop** command to throw away the y-width value, leaving the x-width on the stack. This is now defined as SS by the **def** operator. Line %6 then subtracts the SS variable from the LS variable to determine the amount of Space that needs to be added to the string to fit it perfectly within the two margins. This completes the second step.

Line %7 may surprise you until you think about it. It is possible that there were no blanks in the string—improbable, perhaps, but still possible. If there were no blanks, the BlankCtr will be zero, and division by zero is not defined mathematically and will result in a PostScript error. So you only perform the division in line %8 if there are blanks in the string. This is done by the test of BlankCtr for a zero value in line %7, which is matched by the **if** operator in line %9. The net result is that the division in line %8 is performed if the condition in line %7 is true, and not otherwise. Although the procedure will still execute if there are no blanks in the string, you should notice that the effect will be identical to **show**, since there will be no character to which **widthshow** can add the extra space.

Line %8 divides the total space required, which you have stored in the variable Space, by the number of blanks in the line, which was stored in the BlankCtr variable by the procedure **countBlanks**. The result is a real number that is the required adjustment for each space within the string and is stored back into the Space variable.

Line %10 begins the setup for the **widthshow** operator on line %12. This operator requires four operands: the additional x-distance, the additional y-distance, the character to be added to, and the string to be examined. On line %10 you push three of the four required operands in the correct order onto the stack. These are the x-space adjustment, which has been stored in the Space variable, the y-space adjustment, which is 0, and the character that is to be adjusted, in this case the blank, which has character code octal 40, written *8#040* in PostScript. The string, which is the fourth operand, is already on the stack, but it is beneath the other operands and needs to be brought to the top of the stack. The **roll** operator in line %11 does this. This use is similar to the one in the exercise regarding re-encoding fonts; as in that exercise, you have all the required information on the stack, but not in the right order. This time, you have four elements to maneuver instead of three, and you need to move the bottom element of the stack to the top rather than the other way around. The four elements are represented by the 4 as an operand, and – 1 tells the **roll** that you are moving the contents of the stack down one by one, just as the 1 before told it to move one element up at a time. The movement down pushes every item on the stack one level lower, except the string, which is the designated fourth element on the stack and therefore moves to the top. This leaves the top four elements on the stack in the desired order and you now issue the **widthshow** command.

There are two other points to note about this procedure. First, it expects that the margins have already been set into the two variables, LM and RM, which is very important. The second point is that the **widthshow** is really a **show**, and, just like **show**, it requires a current point and a current font to be set before you issue the procedure.

Justification Procedure

The **widthshow** procedure is now in place, and you can use it in any of the text-handling examples that you have already completed. As a short example, Figure 6.5 shows a portion of the text-and-commentary example from Chapter 2. Notice how easily you can integrate this function into the previous work. I won't reproduce all of it here, for space reasons, but you can easily complete the entire exercise if you want. This example is only the first paragraph of the original exercise, and it produces a portion of the original output that looks like Figure 6.6.

Insofar as this example is identical to the earlier exercise, it doesn't need further explanation here. Let's briefly discuss the additional code that was added to provide the justification mechanism. First you had to add the two procedures countBlanks and justifyText to the prolog. Then the show in bodyText was changed to justifyText. That completes all the changes in the prolog. Notice how small a change this really is, and how easily it can be inserted into the program as long as the program is structured into a prolog and script.

In the body of the text, you had to add three statements. The first one sets the variable, LM, to the beginning position for the text column, Second-Column. The second sets the variable, RM, to 7.5 inches. In the original program, since the body text was not justified, there was no reason to set the right margin precisely; now, when you want to justify the right margin as well as the left, that margin needs to be precisely defined. In this case you could have readjusted the variable, RightMargin, to the precise 7.5-inch value after centering the headline; or you could do as here and simply set the RM variable to the precise value. The RightMargin variable had to be 8 inches initially to correctly center the headline between the edges of the paper.

The third additional line is the reset of RM just before output of the last line of the paragraph. This is necessary because this is a deliberately short line, and the right margin for it is not the same as the preceding lines. If you used the same value of RM, you would get too much space between the words because justifyText would space the words over the entire column. Since you don't want that, you set the value of RM to the precise length of the string which will be the last line, using essentially the same technique as you used earlier in the justifyText procedure.

```
%---------------------Prolog----------------------

%---------------------Procedures-----------------
/inch
    {    72 mul }
def

/advanceLine
{
    /NextLine
    NextLine LineSpace sub
    def
}
def

/advancePara
{
    /NextLine
    NextLine ParaSpace sub
    def
}
def

/countBlanks
{
    /BlankCtr 0 def
    {
        ( ) search
        {
            /BlankCtr BlankCtr 1 add def pop pop
        }
        {
            pop exit
        }
        ifelse
    }
    loop
}
 def

/justifyText
{
    dup
    countBlanks
    /LS RM LM sub def
    dup
    /SS exch stringwidth pop def
    /Space LS SS sub def
    /BlankCtr 0 ne
    {
        /Space
        Space BlankCtr div
        def
    }
    if
    Space 0 8#040
    4 -1 roll
        widthshow
}
def

/bodyText
{
```

Figure 6.5: Justified-text example

```
                        SecondColumn NextLine moveto
                        justifyText
            }
            def

            /centerText
            {
                dup
                stringwidth pop
                2 div
                    RightMargin LeftMargin sub 2 div
                exch sub
                LeftMargin add
                NextLine moveto
                show
            }
            def

            /rightJustifyText
            {
                dup
                stringwidth pop
                RightColumn exch sub
                NextLine moveto
                show
            }
            def


            %--------------------Script---------------------
            %set up constants
            %--------------------Named Constants-------------
            /TopStart 9.5 inch def        %vertical start for head
            /BodyStart 8.5 inch def       %vertical start for body

            /LineSpace 14 def         %set line spacing (leading)
            /ParaSpace 28 def         %set paragraph spacing

            /LeftMargin .5 inch def       %set absolute left margin
            /RightMargin 8 inch def       %set absolute right margin
            /RightColumn 2.5 inch def     %set right edge of first column
            /SecondColumn 3 inch def      %set left edge of second column

            %--------------------Program (Title)------------
            %Setup font for Title
            /Times-Bold findfont 16 scalefont setfont

            %Move to selected position
            /NextLine TopStart def
            (ACME WIDGETS INCORPORATED) centerText
            /NextLine NextLine 20 sub def
            (Fiscal Year 1986) centerText


            %-------------------Program (Text Column)------------------
            %Setup new font for Body Text
            /Times-Roman findfont 12 scalefont setfont

            /LM SecondColumn def
            /RM 7.5 inch     def

            /NextLine BodyStart def
            (Acme Widgets was founded in 1958 by Dippy and Daffy Acme) bodyText
            advanceLine
```

Figure 6.5: Justified-text example (continued)

```
(to produce high technology widgets for the booming aerospace) bodyText
advanceLine
(industry. Acme was quickly recognized as being the best) bodyText
advanceLine
(widget works in the country. Continued investment in new) bodyText
advanceLine
(technology and manufacturing methods has kept Acme Widgets) bodyText
advanceLine
(in the forefront of this industry. In the last year alone, Acme) bodyText
advanceLine
(has invested over $10 million in new manufacturing tooling) bodyText
advanceLine
/RM 5.53 inch def
(and computer-aided order processing.) bodyText

%-----------------------Program (Titles)-------------------
%set font for Paragraph Titles
/Times-Bold findfont 12 scalefont setfont

/NextLine BodyStart def
(History:) rightJustifyText

showpage
```

Figure 6.5: Justified-text example (continued)

ACME WIDGETS INCORPORATED
Fiscal Year 1986

History: Acme Widgets was founded in 1952 by Dippy and Daffy Acme
to produce high technology widgets for the growing aerospace
market. Acme was quickly recognized as being the best
widget works in the country. Continued investment in new
technology and manufacturing methods has kept Acme Widgets
in the forefront of this industry.

Figure 6.6: Output from justified-text example

Review and Concerns

The justifyText example gives you a small taste of how you can use the justification operators in actual text processing, and also shows you a new use of the **search** operator. There a one or two points to review and discuss before we leave this topic, however.

The first is that of proper, or perhaps better, appropriate use of Post-Script. PostScript is a page description language; it is not designed or best used for calculation. In particular, justification of large amounts of text requires a fair amount of computation, as was mentioned earlier. Moreover, the presumption that we made, even for the justification above, was that the line of text was already fitted fairly closely to the line length; that is, there was no room for the next word in the text on the line. Neither of these tasks is really appropriate use of PostScript.

The best approach to justification is for the word-processing program, or other application program that creates the text, to perform the necessary calculations before creating the PostScript output. This requires knowledge of the precise measurement of characters, so that the application can perform the equivalent of a **stringwidth**; this information is available in the font metric files provided by Adobe for each font. Using these font metric files (which have the extension .AFM), the application programmer can determine the length of a text string and calculate the adjustment factor required for justification in much the same manner as you did above. With the new **xyshow** and similar operators in Level 2, this becomes even more compelling, as the application can use the font metrics plus user input to place every character precisely on the line and then output it in PostScript with no further changes.

This division of labor between the application and PostScript is more efficient than using PostScript for the entire process. Certainly you can perform all the calculations within PostScript; PostScript is a complete, general-purpose programming language and provides all the capabilities necessary for any processing that you need to do. The issue here is not what can you do in PostScript (since you can do anything that you can in another language), but what is best done in each language, considering efficiency and the intrinsic facilities in each. PostScript is a language designed and best used to drive raster-output devices; it is not designed to compete with C, for example, in computational speed or facilities, just as C is not designed to draw arcs or fill and shade letter shapes.

You should notice two things about inserting this additional code into the previous program. First, it is not difficult to add new features to properly structured PostScript. Although this has been noted before, it bears one more repetition. Besides the added procedures, you only had to change four lines of code to change from unjustified to justified text, and you wouldn't have had to change much more if you had wanted to adjust the entire page. That leads directly to the second point: with some redesigning, you could have eliminated the changes in the script entirely. To do that, you would need to modify the bodyText and advanceLine procedures so that the moveto was done in advance-Line; this would allow you to display the last line of each paragraph using a show operator rather than adjusting the RM variable. You would also need to provide the RM and LM variables in the setup in the same way the other variables are defined. Having done these two things, there would be no need for changes to the script. This type of consideration is of particular interest when you want to add or change PostScript code in applications, which we will discuss in the next section of this chapter.

TEXT APPLICATIONS

This section of the chapter covers two distinct PostScript topics. Both of these topics are related to text handling and processing, but each has a different emphasis. They are presented here in one section, since they both deal with the relationship between PostScript and the programs that generate PostScript code.

You have spent a lot of time and effort working on the various examples and exercises in PostScript. Almost all of this work has been done one-on-one with the machine, using the interactive mode (if you have been following the examples). The single exception was the exercise in Chapter 5 that integrated the application data with a PostScript form.

Obviously, this is not the typical method of dealing with PostScript. As explained when we discussed how to get started in Chapter 1, this is a good method for learning PostScript and an excellent way to analyze and debug PostScript routines, but it is not an efficient way to run in a production mode. Normally, you will be running PostScript files in a batch mode to the printer, and normally those batch files will have been created, either entirely or partially, using an application program. You have now reached the point where you need to find out more about PostScript facilities in such a situation.

FILES AND FILE HANDLING

The first topic for us to examine consists of two separate, but related, issues: the transmission of files to a PostScript device in your present circumstances, and PostScript files and file handling operations. Each of these issues is important for you to be familiar with. The first issue is an extremely practical one, however, while the second is primarily conceptual.

File Transmission

The idea here is simple. Instead of typing every line into the interpreter, you can simply send a completed file. Suppose you have prepared a file containing PostScript commands, using an editor or some other method, and you want to transmit it to the interpreter for execution. The easiest and most effective way is to use the same techniques that you have been using for the interactive mode. Start up PostScript, get the PS> prompt, and then use your communications or terminal software to "upload" the file to the printer. The interpreter will read the lines of data as though they came from the terminal keyboard, and will execute them it the identical fashion. Remember that all of this is still in the interactive mode; the transmitted file here represents the lines of code that you would otherwise have to type, and the PostScript interpreter is processing each line as though it came from your terminal.

There are two potential problems with this method. First, the transmission will tie up the link between the terminal and the printer, and you may not get any error messages back over the link. Second, the transmission may be too long and overrun the printer's buffer. The first problem can be solved in two ways. If you have the option of full duplex communication, that will solve it, since that allows transmission of data in both directions simultaneously. It isn't likely that this option is available, but if it is, it can be an excellent solution. Another way to solve the problem is to wait until you produce an output page. If the output is not what you expected, you can often tell what the error is from looking at the output; at least, it provides a clue. You can also run each of the procedures individually, using **copypage** and **pstack** to help determine what exactly is happening within the procedure.

The second problem is essentially one of how the printer and the computer communicate. This was also discussed briefly in Chapter 1 and more extensively in Appendix C, where specific hardware and software implementations are addressed. The secret here is to use a method that allows the printer to stop the data flow from the computer until the printer has room for more information. Generally, for serial communications PostScript uses the XON/XOFF method of control, so you need to use that as your control. This requires having some resident software that can do XON/XOFF. If your computer doesn't have this feature, it is possible to change PostScript to use the other common method of controlling flow, called DTR. In either case, you should refer to the printer supplement for your printer for advice on handling the data flow parameter. Of course, if you are using a network protocol, like AppleTalk, to communicate, neither of these issues will be a problem since the network protocol handles these automatically.

PostScript File Operations

The second issue is a discussion of PostScript files and file handling. PostScript has a small but useful set of file operators that you may want to know about. A complete discussion of the file operators, including examples and so on, is really an advanced topic and so beyond what we set out to do in this book; but you do want to know that the file operators exist and you want to know something about PostScript standard files.

PostScript provides a basic, but complete, set of file operations for use in programs. PostScript defines a file as a stream of characters terminated by an end-of-file indication. Both input and output files can be used. The input files represent a source of data, or characters; the output files are places for PostScript to write data. Each file is represented within PostScript by a file object. File objects are created by the interpreter upon execution of the **file** operator, which associates a specific file identifier with the new file object.

Once the file object is created, PostScript provides all the expected facilities for reading and writing it. The only point to be aware of here is that most of the PostScript write operations may be buffered; that is, the write operation does not necessarily take place at the moment the command is issued, but instead may send characters to a buffer. However, PostScript does provide operators to deal with the situation when you require that the write operation take place immediately.

File operations follow a normal flow, and all the operations will return a standard end-of-file condition and execute standard error-handling procedures for exceptional conditions. An explicit operation closes a file when the program finishes operation, disassociating the file object created earlier and the external file.

PostScript implements three standard files which have uniform names in all PostScript environments:

- the *standard input file,* which is the source of the input to the interpreter;

- the *standard output file,* which is the place that the interpreter writes error and status messages; and

- the *standard error file,* which receives certain types of low-level error messages and is typically the same as the standard output file.

If the PostScript device has an external storage medium, such as a disk, then you may also have a variety of other files. Generally, these will be used to provide font or procedure storage for the interpreter.

Most of the PostScript file operations on the standard files are transparent to the user. The point here is for you to know that there are standard files and to realize that there is a set of operations and associated operators that you can take advantage of if you need them.

APPLICATION INTERFACE

The second topic in this chapter is a discussion of the relationship between PostScript, particularly the kind of PostScript that you have been doing in your programming exercises, and the "real world" of application output. Most PostScript code, after all, is generated by one or more applications that provide an interface for making the creation of text and graphics much simpler and more intuitive than writing PostScript code directly. As you worked through the examples and exercises, you must have realized how much effort is required to design and lay out even a relatively simple page. The effort that is required should give you some appreciation of the magnitude of the task that your application program must handle.

Precisely because the transformation of pages of text and graphics into PostScript commands is such a large task, there is a place for and a purpose in understanding the underlying principles of PostScript. There will always be times when you want a result that the application either cannot handle or can handle only with difficulty. In addition, there are always those times when your application output will not print because of a problem. Because you have invested the energy in learning PostScript, you will be well-equipped to handle such situations by modifing facilities provided by the application, by debugging the application output, or by writing new code if necessary.

You might use several types of modifications for these purposes. In this portion of the chapter, we will discuss what in my experience are two of the most common modificiations: embedding PostScript code in an existing application and modifying existing PostScript procedures provided by an application. Both of these modifications are highly dependent upon the exact nature of the application program, and it isn't possible or reasonable to provide specific directions here on how to do this for specific applications. Instead, I will discuss the general approach that you should take to each of these kinds of changes, and you will learn some of the potential problems and opportunities—and how to avoid the former and take advantage of the latter. With this information, you should be able to use the application documentation to determine the precise methods for making whatever changes you want.

Embedded PostScript Code

The first type of addition that you should think about is adding PostScript code directly into a file that is otherwise being created by an application program. This is basically done by somehow marking the PostSript code in such a way that the application program doesn't rearrange or process it. Successful embedding depends on the application; some applications that generate PostScript themselves make it quite easy to embed PostScript code, while other applications don't make it easy at all.

The most straightforward applications to work with are straight editor programs. These usually are designed for creation and modification of program text, and will basically allow you to enter anything you want. For creating PostScript programs that you are going to send directly to the printer, these are the best tools. You can also create PostScript files with a word-processing program. Many word processors have a mode or method whereby you can enter simple text without having it edited; such a method is quite acceptable for creating and working with PostScript. In almost every case, you can direct the application output to a disk file, as you did in the exercise in Chapter 5, where it can be edited with either of the above techniques to include PostScript program text and to modify the application output, if necessary.

Some applications allow you to embed PostScript directly into the work that you are doing within the application. Generally, to do this you must create your PostScript program with an editor or another application that will generate output that conforms to the Encapsulated PostScript structuring conventions. These conventions are similar to, but more rigid than, the standard structuring conventions. Once you have prepared your output in this format, you can often import it directly into other applications for output.

Sometimes it is possible to create a segment of PostScript within another text when you are using a word processing program. When this can be done, generally you are flagging the PostScript code in the same fashion that you would flag printer control codes or other nontext material. Some more sophisticated applications understand that this is PostScript code and provide help for creating procedures within the application. For example, in Microsoft Word you can bracket lines of PostScript with a special Post-Script Style that tells the word processor to ignore everything in that Style and transmit it directly to the printer with no changes or formatting. This allows you to write your own procedures and embed them directly into Word's document output. Be sure to read your documentation before you attempt this, as there are special rules and requirements for it to work correctly.

For applications that don't provide such easy access, you can always print the output file to disk and then edit it there in nondocument or program mode, or use a separate editor program on it.

Modification of Prologs and Prep Files

Another method of modification for application output is to modify the prolog for an application. You have been working with prologs and scripts for most all of this book, so you are familiar with the concepts of prologs and scripts in your own programs. This structuring convention is also followed by most of the application programs that produce PostScript output. Typically, such prologs are called header files or *prep files,* probably because the Macintosh version is called "Laser Prep."

The typical application behaves in the following manner. There is a header file that essentially consists of the procset that will be used by the application. This file is downloaded to the printer either at the start of a session, or when you request printing for a specific file. The application output is then coded with procedure calls and data to generate the desired output. This process should certainly be familiar, since it replicates what you have been doing in all the exercises.

This replication is not an accident; nor is it just that the exercises follow the same structural guidelines as the applications (although we have). The basic reason for this compatibility in approach is the native structure of PostScript. You have seen time and again throughout the book how this approach is the only effective and sensible way to make use of PostScript's many facilities. So it is no suprise that the various application programs use the same technique.

This approach also allows you to change and modify the prep file for your application if you want to. This task is not trivial nor to be undertaken lightly. However, it can be done safely if you follow a few rules, and it is a very useful technique. Again, we cannot give you a detailed look here at any specific prep file; but we can discuss some of the practical rules that you should follow to protect yourself (and your output) against errors and provide some tips on how you might take advantage of this approach.

To begin with, the prep files are all quite readable. Like most PostScript code, they are essentially straight ASCII files and can be looked at using any simple text editor. I would strongly recommend that you take two important steps before you do anything else with your prep files. First, make a copy of the file and store it in some safe place with a new (but easily remembered) name. I assume that you already have a backup copy of whatever applicaton software you're using; make sure that you include the new safety copy of the prep file on the backup as well. Second, use an editor to read and review the file, or better yet, print the file out for reference. Note that some prep files, such as Apple's Laser Prep and LaserWriter files, which together make up a complete prep file, may be stored in a compressed, non-ASCII format. In such cases, you will have to generate some output and store it on disk to get a readable version of the file. Then read and study the code used in the prep file. This will be straight PostScript code, and it will provide good exercise for you.

Although the code may be more complicated than what you have worked so far in the book, you will see that it is similar to the exercises and examples that you have been working with. You may find that some of the routines are quite familiar, perhaps even identical to ones that you already know; the reencoding routine that you worked with in an earlier chapter, or some variant of that, is one example of a fairly common routine.

The next thing I would recommend is to take a short, not very complex piece of output from the application and print it to the disk instead of to the PostScript printer. Then look at both the output and the prep file together, either printing both out or having one printed while you reference the other one on the screen with an editor. You will quickly see how the application uses the procedures in the procset to produce its effects.

You should know one or two things about prep files at this point. First of all, when you look at the prep file or files that you may have available, you will notice that they use very short names for procedures and variables, often only one or two letters long. This is a matter of efficiency and space conservation within the interpreter. As stated previously, when you are creating procedures for your own use, it is recommended that you use names that have some relevance and mnemonic value; however, when the application prep file is being used, such names are not beneficial. Instead, the emphasis is on speed and efficient coding, which encourages the use of almost unintelligible names. If you are trying to follow the use of a specific procedure, you can use the global search and replace mechanism in your editor to change the name to something easily recognized; just remember to change the application output at the same time.

The second point to be aware of is that some techniques may be used in the application prologue that you have not been introduced to. Two of the most common are the special techniques used to store a procset permanently in memory and the use of the **bind** operator to speed up the execution of PostScript code. Each of these techniques is quite clear once you understand the requirement that the technique is intended to address; this sort of thing is known generally in data processing as "clear if previously understood." To help you understand, we will examine each of these techniques in turn.

Procset Storage

Many application procsets will begin with one or two lines of code that look something like this:

```
userdict /appldict known {stop} if

serverdict begin 0 exitserver

/appldict 100 dict def

begin
```

This sequence of code is intended to insert the application procset into PostScript memory in such a way that it won't be flushed out at the end of a job. The first line tests whether the name */appldict* is already in **userdict** by explicitly placing **userdict** onto the operand stack and testing to see if the name is present. If so, the **if** operator will execute the **stop** to end the current processing and wait for the next job. The name */appldict* is the name of a private dictionary that will be created in line 3, which will hold all the procedure definitions for the application procset. The intention here is to test, right at the start, whether the application procset has already been loaded into memory. If it has, there is no point in reloading it; to do so would have some negative effects which we will discuss in a moment. If it hasn't been loaded, then the processing continues with line 2.

Line 2 performs a special PostScript function. It allows the application to bypass the normal processing mode of the interpreter and install the code that follows, up to the next end-of-file, into PostScript memory in such a way that the procedures and so on will not be removed until the device is reset or power is turned off. This process is known as loading *outside the server loop,* and is device-dependent; luckily, you don't need to know any more about it than the intention of this piece of code in order to read and use the procset file. Do notice, however, that once your printer is turned on and the procset has been loaded, any changes you might make to the procset will not be loaded until the next power-off. That will happen because the application dictionary, /appldict, is already defined in the system, and therefore the changed dictionary will not be loaded.

Lines 3 and 4 perform a function that you have worked with in the previous exercises. The new dictionary, /appldict, is defined to hold a specific number of items (in this case 100) and then is pushed onto the dictionary stack as the current dictionary. After this action, all the code for the application procset, usually consisting of procedures and perhaps some variables, will be stored into the application dictionary.

There is one issue regarding this type of mechanism that you should be aware of. This is the concern regarding the consumption of PostScript memory by the application procset. Like every PostScript composite object, the application procset takes up memory. However, unlike other programs, this application procset will remain in memory even after the job is finished, until the power to the printer is turned off or the printer is reset. It remains in memory because the procedures were loaded with the special commands that we discussed above, which store the procset outside of the normal processing cycle. That means that the procset doesn't go away at the end of the job, a fact that has both good and bad implications. If you are running multiple jobs, all of which are output from the same application, this feature is good. It means that the procset, which is relatively long and complex, doesn't have to be downloaded every time in order to print, which would be slow and inconvenient. On the other hand, it also means that the procset remains in memory, in a place where you cannot remove it. If you wanted to run some other application, for example, you would get the new application's procset but not lose the old one. The net result is to have less memory for things like fonts and page descriptions of your own. This can be a problem in some circumstances.

If you are going to be running more than one application, or if you have any reason to suspect that you have multiple prep files in your printer, you can clear the memory and restore the maximum available space to the interpreter by shutting off the power to the printer and restarting it. This is the one sure and simple way to recover the memory used by such prep files. You can also see that you may want to run all of one type of application in a group, in so far as possible, to minimize the poor use of memory within the printer; and you may want to shut the printer off when you change to a new application to provide the maximum room for fonts and so on.

Early Binding

Another common technique that you may see in a procset is the use of the **bind** operator. This will catch you by surprise if you don't know what it is used for. A typical line of code that uses this operator might look like this:

```
/avg { add 2 div exch round } bind def
```

This is a simple averaging procedure, like those you have created before in the examples. The new feature is the insertion of the **bind** operator just before the **def**. This operator takes the operator names in the preceding procedure and replaces them with their actual values, so that the interpreter doesn't have to do any additional lookup when it encounters avg in the script. This process is called *early binding,* because it happens before the normal binding process, called *late binding,* which occurs when the interpreter looks up the operator in the dictionary stack at the time it executes the script. Early binding has two important features. First, it greatly improves the speed of execution of the procedures. Second, it ensures that the bound procedure has the actual operator values when it executes. For example, suppose that someone loaded a procset after your procset that defined **add** as some other operation. Without binding, when you execute avg, you will retrieve that definition of **add** and your procedure may not work. With binding, however, avg will use the operator definition of **add** which is loaded into avg by the **bind** operator; it doesn't need to worry about subsequent redefinitions.

You can ignore the **bind** operator whenever you find it, knowing that is intended to accelerate the procedure immediately preceding it, but that it has no other effect.

This use of **bind** is one of a general class of techniques that are used to optimize PostScript performance. The complete range of such techniques falls into the catagory of advanced PostScript and, as such, is more complex than what we intended to discuss in this book. The use of **bind**, however, is important to mention so that, if you come across it in a procset, you will understand that it does not change the overall operation of the procedure being defined.

OPERATOR REVIEW

This section presents all the new operators that were introduced to in this chapter in the standard format. As before, these are presented here as a combination reference and review.

int **string** string

Creates a *string* that initially contains *int* null objects as entries. *int* must be a non- negative integer less than the device-dependent maximum string length.

array index

string index **get** any

Looks up the *index* in *array* or *string* and returns the element identified by *index* (counting from zero). The *index* must be between 0 and *n – 1*, where *n* is the number of elements in *array* or *string*.

array index count   subarray

string index count **getinterval** substring

Selects a segment of *array* or *string* and returns the selected segment as *subarray* or *substring*. The segment begins with the element identified by *index* (counting from zero), and extends for *count* elements. There must be enough elements in *array* or *string* for correct operation; that is, the sum of *index* and *count* must be between 0 and *n – 1*, where *n* is the number of elements in *array* or *string*. The *subarray* or *substring* that is returned shares its values with the original *array* or *string*. Any change to either one will change the other.

array index value

string index value **put** —

Stores *value* into *array* or *string* at the position identified by *index* (counting from zero). *index* must be in the range 0 to *n* – *1*, where *n* is the number of elements in *array* or *string*.

string **length** int

Returns *int* as the number array of elements that make up the value of *array* or *string*.

array1 array2   subarray2

string1 string2 **copy** substring2

Copies all elements of *array1* or *string1* into *array2* or *string2*. The types of the two operands must be the same, that is, array or string. The length of the second operand must be at least the length of the first; **copy** returns the changed elements of the second operand onto the stack as *subarray2* or *substring2*. If the second operand is longer than the first, the remaining values are unaffected by the **copy**.

array proc

string proc **forall** —

Executes procedure *proc* for every element of *array* or *string*. **forall** pushes each element from the array or string onto the stack, and then executes the procedure *proc*, which may access the element on the stack. If the *proc* does not consume the element on the stack, it should remove it; although **forall** itself does not leave any object on the stack, if *proc* does not clear the stack before exiting, the elements of *array* or *string* will remain on the stack. In the case of *string*, the objects placed on the stack are the codes (numeric values) of the characters, not one-character strings.

if found:

string seek **search** post match pre true

if not found:

string seek **search** string false

Looks for the first time that the string *seek* occurs within *string* and returns the results of the search on the operand stack. The search is successful if there is any subset of *string* that exactly matches the string *seek*. If there is such a match, **search** divides the *string* into three pieces and pushes them onto the operand stack: *pre*, the portion of *string* preceding the match; *match*, the portion of *string* that is identical to *seek*; and *post*, the remainder of *string*. Each of these is pushed onto the operand stack in the order indicated, followed by the boolean value *true* to indicate that a match was found. If no part of *string* is found to match *seek*, the operator returns the original *string* on the operand stack and pushes the boolean value, *false*.

any string **cvs** substring

Converts object *any* to a string. *any* is changed from its current form to an appropriate string representation, and stored in the first section of *string*, which is overwritten. There must be enough room in *string* to hold the representation of *any*, or you will get an error.

c_x c_y char string **widthshow** —

Prints the characters of *string* but adjusts the width of each occurrence of the character *char* in *string* by adding c_x to its x-dimension and c_y to its y-dimension, thereby adjusting the spacing between this character and the following character.

a_x a_y string **ashow** —

Prints the characters of *string* but adjusts the width of each occurrence of every character in *string* by adding a_x to its x-dimension and a_y to its y-dimension, thereby adjusting the spacing between all the characters.

c_x c_y char a_x a_y string **awidthshow** —

Prints the characters of *string* and performs two adjustments. It adjusts the width of each occurrence of every character in *string* by adding a_x to its x-dimension and a_y to its y-dimension, thereby adjusting the spacing between all the characters; and it adjusts the width of each occurrence of the character *char* in *string* by adding c_x to its x-dimension and c_y to its y-dimension, thereby adjusting the spacing between this character and the following character.

proc string **kshow** —

Prints the characters of *string* but allows the user to execute the procedure *proc* between each character of *string*. The operator shows each character of *string* in turn, adding the width of the character to the current point and then executing the procedure *proc*.

string numarray

string numstring **xyshow** —

Paints each successive character in *string* at the positions specified by the array *numarray* or the encoded number string *numstring*. Each character is painted in the same way that the **show** operator would paint the character. After the character is painted, **xyshow** takes two successive numbers from the operand, which are the relative location, in user coordinates, of the position of the next character to be displayed. The first number is the x-coordinate displacement and the second number is the y-coordinate displacement for the next character's origin relative to the current character's origin. The *numarray* or *numstring* operand must have at least as many pairs of values as there are characters in *string*; if there are not enough number pairs for all the characters in *string*, an error will occur.

string numarray

string numstring **xshow** —

Works in a manner similar to **xyshow**, except that only one number is taken from *numarray* or *numstring*. This number determines the x-coordinate displacement for the next character, while the y-coordinate displacement is taken as 0.

string numarray

string numstring **yshow** —

Works in a manner similar to **xyshow**, except that only one number is taken from *numarray* or *numstring*. This number determines the y-coordinate displacement for the next character, while the x-coordinate displacement is taken as 0.

7

Working with
Advanced Graphics

THIS CHAPTER COVERS A VARIETY
of advanced graphics operations that are available in PostScript. You will see
very few examples in the chapter because to adequately explore the potential of most of the operations discussed here would require almost a separate
chapter for each operator. The chapter is primarily devoted to letting you
know what these operations are and how they work in general. In any case,
you are now familiar enough with PostScript programs and programming to
be able to work out examples and experiment with these new features on
your own. If one of these operations seems interesting, try to create your
own examples and work out the exact requirements and possibilities. This
chapter will provide you with a basic framework for these operations, and
you can then use the *PostScript Language Reference Manual, Second Edition* to guide you in the detailed requirements.

The first section of the chapter is divided into four subsections that discuss several important graphics processes. The first subsection covers various issues about how a line is displayed on your output device. This covers
controls in the graphics state that set line endings, line corners, and whether
a line is solid or dashed. In addition, you will learn about the issue of stroke
adjustment. This deals with the problem of making a series of horizontal or
vertical lines the exact same width. This is important for several reasons.
First, it represents a type of problem in dealing with an output device that
you might not expect. Second, the solution illustrates a type of control over
the device that you have not yet met. Finally, it is an area where Level 2 provides some special features that you can use to correct the problem.

The second subsection deals with the clipping process, which is both
easy to use and important. This PostScript operation functions in a manner
similar to a common stencil, where you apply paint only where the cutout
is. This is the one section in the chapter that contains several examples for
you to follow. The clipping operation is so straightforward and so useful
that it is important to ensure that you feel fully comfortable with it.

The third subsection deals with the two processes of the creation and
description of arbitrary curved line segments and coordinate transformations.
We covered both of these topics earlier in the book in a more restricted format.
In both cases, the operators that you learned and practiced with represent the
most common and accessible type of each operation. This section introduces
you to the general operators that lie behind the specifics that you have been
using and discusses some of the mathematics that you need to understand in
order to work with the general functions effectively.

The last subsection discusses the manipulation of PostScript graphics. Specifically, it examines the methods that are available to determine the size and shape of a graphics object, such as might be described by the current path, within a PostScript program. Several operators provide this type of information and this section both introduces you to these operators and discusses when you might want to use them.

The second section of the chapter covers processing general images in PostScript. These are the operations that deal with bit-mapped graphics and halftone images. An overview is provided for the concepts that are necessary to use these operations, including image-sampling techniques and control of such images on the output device. This type of work becomes intimately connected with the specific output device, and it is one of PostScript's many strengths in that it provides remarkable control of these processes, including the ability to work at the device level if necessary without sacrificing essential device independence. It is possible to create a PostScript program that will make maximum use of a specific device and yet still run correctly on any PostScript printer.

The chapter ends with the usual summary of PostScript operators. This summary also contains the full definition for some operators that are only described briefly in the chapter; by now, I'm sure that you can read these quite easily by yourself.

ADVANCED GRAPHIC OPERATIONS

This section of the chapter will present several advanced techniques for handling graphics. In many ways, each of these techniques is different, but they all share a common point of reference: they all are extensions of graphics operations that you learned earlier. Each of them depends on one or more basic concepts and operations that thereby form the building blocks to develop progressively more powerful operations.

Other than this common genesis, however, each of these processes is distinct. Each one represents an important additional concept that you will want to understand and use in your PostScript programming; more important, perhaps, they also represent some of the most powerful graphics operators available. You will find that these functions are at the heart of the most powerful and sophisticated graphics software.

ADVANCED LINE HANDLING

One advanced tool that affects the current path is the variety of parameters that PostScript provides to control what happens when you issue a **stroke** command. Until now, you have used the default values for all of the functions that we will discuss below and you have not had any reason to be concerned. This is a good indication of how well the defaults have been chosen. However, now you want to learn how to change these defaults for the occasional special situation that requires it. Please don't worry about remembering all these variations; it will be enough to remember that such controls exist. When you need them, you can look up their exact use and syntax in the *PostScript Language Reference Manual, Second Edition*.

The first thing you need to know about the **stroke** operator is how it paints a line. Generally, since the lines that you use are relatively thin, you don't notice how the line is drawn. However, there are certain situations, such as when you are drawing a thick line, where this will be important to know. The **stroke** operator draws the line evenly on either side of the current path; that is, if you are drawing a line that is 2 units wide, the line will extend 1 unit on either side of the current path. This can be especially important when drawing lines under or over text, where the baseline is the current path. Even though both current paths, the one for the text and the one for the line, may seem to be a sufficient distance apart, you may find that the line and the text run into one another. If so, this will usually be caused by the fact that you have forgotten about the physical width of the line itself.

It is possible to draw a very thin line by using a 0 line width; in this case the line will be one *device* unit (one pixel or dot) wide. However, this is very dangerous, since it is extremely device dependent. For example, a one-dot line on a LaserWriter (at 300 dpi) is quite visible, but a one-dot line on a typesetter (at 1200 dpi or more) is virtually invisible. When the PostScript interpreter goes to paint the line, it determines how many device pixels are required to display the desired line width. For a line width of 0, this will always be one device pixel. As a result, the interpreter paints the line one dot wide. If you want a very thin line, the best method is to use a small positive number for the line width, such as .01.

Stroke Adjustment

The translation of line width into device pixels leads to another issue, called *stroke adjustment*. The idea behind stroke adjustment requires some explanation. When the PostScript interpreter goes to paint a line, it must convert the desired line width into device pixels, as you just read. You can imagine this being done in two steps: first, the interpreter converts the user coordinates into device coordinates, using the current transformation matrix (CTM), and then it converts the device coordinates into pixel values. There is, however, one catch to this process. While PostScript units are real numbers, and therefore can be fractions like .01, device pixels are physical entities and cannot be divided into fractions. In essence, you can't have ½ of a pixel. So when the interpreter makes its conversion to device pixels, it must adjust the result to an integer value. (That's how we got to the 1-pixel line for a line width of 0). This rounding must take into account not only the line width, but also the physical position of the line on the page. The result is that lines with the same width printed at different points on the page may differ by one pixel in displayed width. Figure 7.1 shows you how this works.

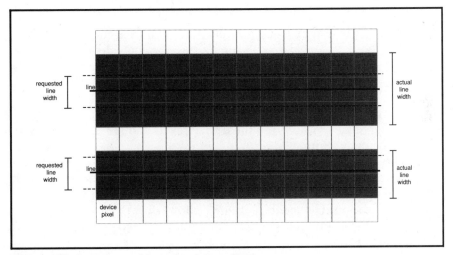

Figure 7.1: Line width and stroke adjustment

As you can see, the problem is caused by the rounding of the device coordinates and the line width into device pixels. If the coordinates of the line fall along a pixel boundary, the line will be two pixels wide; if the line falls in the middle of a pixel, it will come out three pixels wide. On a high-resolution device, like a typesetter, this is not a problem since a difference in line width of one pixel is not visible to the unaided eye. On low- or medium-resolution devices, like a laser printer, this difference is visible.

The solution to this problem is the process known as stroke adjustment. Essentially, this means adjusting your line coordinates so that each line is always in the same position relative to the device pixels. As you can easily see from Figure 7.1, if both lines fall along a pixel boundary, for example, then they will both be the same visible width. The issue, then, is how to adjust your line position so that it always falls at the same position relative to the device pixels.

To make this adjustment, you can use two new operators, **transform** and **itransform**, which allow you to change user coordinates into device (pixel) coordinates and vice-versa. Here they are in the standard format:

SYNTAX	FUNCTION
ux uy **transform** dx dy	transforms the user-space coordinates, *ux* and *uy*, into the equivalent device coordinates, *dx* and *dy*, using the current transformation matrix (CTM).
dx dy **itransform** ux uy	transforms the device coordinates, *dx* and *dy*, into the equivalent user coordinates, *ux* and *uy*, using the inverse of the current transformation matrix.

Using these two operators, you can adjust your lines so that they always fall in the same relative position to the device pixels and are therefore always painted the same width.

The ideal position for a line, relative to the device pixels, is one-quarter pixel up and one-quarter pixel in from the bottom-left corner of the pixel boundary. The one-quarter position is preferable to either the center of the pixel or the pixel boundary, because it allows lines to grow evenly as you make them wider. To adjust your line, therefore, you would use code similar to the one in Figure 7.2.

This short routine takes two operands, an *x* and a *y* position, and adjusts them so that they are positioned at a one-quarter pixel boundary. Let's look at how this works. On line %1, you transform the user coordinates into device coordinates. These will represent coordinates for the device pixels. On line %2, you subtract .25 from the returned device y-coordinate to compensate for the amount you will add to the coordinate after rounding; this keeps you as close to the same pixel as possible. Then you round the result to the nearest integer. This puts you at a pixel boundary. Now you add .25 to that integer value to move into the pixel by the desired distance, one quarter pixel. On line %5,

```
/adjstroke
{
    transform                   %1
    .25 sub                     %2
    round                       %3
    .25 add                     %4
    exch                        %5
    .25 sub round .25 add       %6
    exch                        %7
    itransform                  %8
}
def
```

Figure 7.2: Stroke-adjustment code

you swap the converted y-coordinate for the x-coordinate and perform the same transformation on that value on line %6. Then you return the values to their original order with another **exch** on line %7. Now that the coordinates are adjusted in device units, you change them back into user coordinate units in line %8. By applying this routine to a point, you always position it one-quarter pixel up and in from a pixel boundary. Using this for line definitions will ensure that all lines of the same width come out looking alike.

Stroke Adjustment Example

Let's apply this technique to a simple routine, called horizontalLines, shown in Figure 7.3. True to its name, this procedure generates a series of horizontal lines across a defined portion of the page. Although this is a straightforward procedure, let's look at a few points in it. First, you see from the comments that it is designed to produce rows of horizontal lines spaced 10 units apart with a specified height and width. The procedure starts with the necessary **newpath**, as we explained above. The height and width are on the stack when the procedure is called, and are used directly from the stack in the procedure. The heart of the procedure is a **for** loop, which produces the lines. You remember that **for** performs a procedure for a number of times, determined by incrementing a counter. The operator requires four operands: the initial value of the counter, the increment value, the end value, and finally the procedure to be executed. As **for** executes, the current value of the counter is placed on the operand stack while the procedure is executed, so it is available for the procedure's use. In this case, the counter will represent the y-coordinate for the lines, and it begins at 0, increments by 10 units, and ends when the current value of the counter exceeds the height specified. In order to set up for the **for**, you have to rearrange the operands on the stack by using a **roll**. You have seen this technique several times before and you can easily see here how it is used to move the height value to the top of the stack.

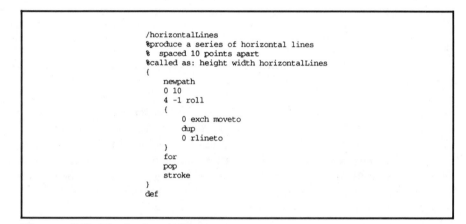

```
/horizontalLines
%produce a series of horizontal lines
%   spaced 10 points apart
%called as: height width horizontalLines
{
    newpath
    0 10
    4 -1 roll
    {
        0 exch moveto
        dup
        0 rlineto
    }
    for
    pop
    stroke
}
def
```

Figure 7.3: The horizontalLine procedure

The procedure being called first does a **moveto** to the point 0 and the current *y* value, as stored on the operand stack by **for**. The **exch** is required to move the y-coordinate into the proper relationship for the **moveto**. Then the procedure makes a line from the current point horizontally for the designated width. To avoid losing the width value on the stack, the procedure duplicates the width before using it. This procedure is done the required number of times by the **for**, and then the resulting lines are filled in by **stroke**. As a last act the width value, which was left on the stack by the **for**, is removed by a **pop** and the horizontalLines procedure is finished.

Let's see how the finished output from horizontalLines looks. Figure 7.4 shows a short program that just uses the procedure alone. The program assumes that you have already defined horizontalLines. It produces the single page of output shown in Figure 7.5. Since you didn't use any stroke adjustment in this version, you can see that the output lines vary slightly in darkness (width); about every third line is actually one pixel larger than the other lines, which makes it darker. This is what happens if you don't have stroke adjustment.

```
%-----------------------Program------------------------.
% example -- horizontal lines
72 288 translate
288 432 horizontalLines

showpage
```

Figure 7.4: Program using horizontalLines

Figure 7.5: Output from unadjusted horizontalLines

Since that's the case, let's add stroke adjustment to this process, as shown in Figure 7.6. As you see, there are a few changes that you have to make to the horizontalLines procedure to use stroke adjustment. First of all, you add the call to adjstroke before both the **moveto** that starts the line and before the **lineto** that draws the line. If you didn't adjust both ends of the line, it would be slightly crooked. Second, the stroke adjustment must be done to the actual coordinates for the line; this means that you have to convert the relative coordinates used in the earlier horizontalLines procedure to absolute coordinates. You do this by changing the **rlineto** operator to a **lineto** and calculating the actual line-ending coordinate within the procedure. To do that, you copy the x- and y-coordinates for the starting point, using the **copy** operator to duplicate the top two items on the stack. Then, after the **moveto** has removed the first set of these coordinates, you add the width—now the third item down on the stack—to the x-coordinate which you left on the top of the stack. Now you have the x- and y-coordinates for the ending point. You place them into the correct order with an **exch**, as before, adjust them, and issue the **lineto**.

```
/adjstroke
{
    transform
    .25 sub round .25 add exch
    .25 sub round .25 add exch
    itransform
}
bind def

/horizontalLines
%produce a series of horizontal lines
%  spaced 10 points apart
%called as: height width horizontalLines
{
    newpath
    0 10
    4 -1 roll
    {
        0
        2 copy
        exch adjstroke moveto
        2 index add
        exch adjstroke
        lineto
    }
    for
    pop
    stroke
}
bind def
```

Figure 7.6: horizontalLines using stroke adjustment

If you load this version into your printer and run the program in Figure 7.4 again, you now get the output shown in Figure 7.7. As you see, the new output has nice, uniform lines all across the page. This is a result of the stroke adjustment that you applied here.

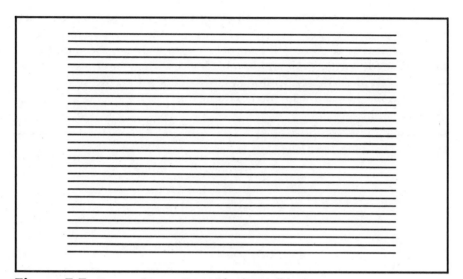

Figure 7.7: Output from adjusted horizontalLines

Level 2 Stroke Adjustment

All of this works the same way whether you have a Level 1 or Level 2 device. On a Level 2 device, however, you can perform stroke adjustment automatically using the **setstrokeadjust** operator, and find out its current setting with the **currentstrokeadjust** operator, which are defined as follows:

SYNTAX	FUNCTION
boolean **setstrokeadjust** —	If *boolean* is *true*, then stroke adjustment is performed automatically whenever any subsequent **stroke** or equivalent operators are executed. If *boolean* is *false*, then stroke adjustment is not performed.
— **currentstrokeadjust** boolean	Returns the current value, *boolean*, of the stroke adjustment parameter in the current graphics state.

These operators allow you to avoid all the computations for each **moveto** or similar operator. However, because this is an automatic function, it does require some different handling to make a procedure that is compatible for both Level 1 and Level 2 devices. The easiest way is to test for the **setstrokeadjust** operator and then define **adjstroke** accordingly. Figure 7.8 shows you one method of doing this.

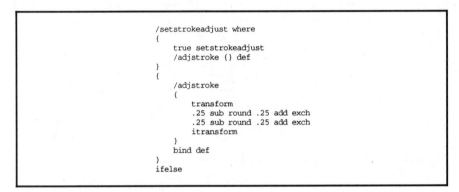

```
/setstrokeadjust where
{
    true setstrokeadjust
    /adjstroke {} def
}
{
    /adjstroke
    {
        transform
        .25 sub round .25 add exch
        .25 sub round .25 add exch
        itransform
    }
    bind def
}
ifelse
```

Figure 7.8: adjstroke redefined to test for and use Level 2

As you see, this code starts with a test for the existence of the **setstrokeadjust** operator. If the operator exists, then **setstrokeadjust** is set to **true** and **adjstroke** is defined as a null procedure. If the operator does not exist, then **adjstroke** is defined as before. In either case, **horizontalLines** works correctly. Note that this approach is preferable to testing for **languagelevel**, since you only need the **setstrokeadjust** operator for this to work. However, if you are defining a lot of Level 2 emulations or procedures, you can easily change this to use a simple boolean, as you saw in Chapter 5.

Line Endings

With PostScript, you can control how the ends of lines are drawn. There are three possible methods of ending lines, as shown in Figure 7.9.

The interpreter uses a *line cap* code, kept in the current graphics state, to determine which of these ends is used when it draws a line segment. The line cap code can be changed by the **setlinecap** operator, which takes the new value from the operand stack and stores it in the current graphics state.

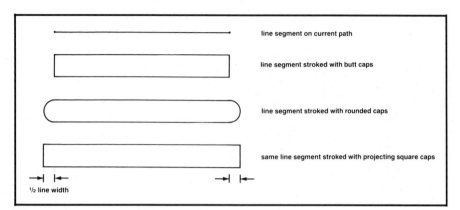

Figure 7.9: Line ending appearance

The possible values of the line cap code are:

VALUE	TYPE OF CAP
0	Butt caps. The line segment has square ends perpendicular to the path and ending at the end of the path. This is the default PostScript line cap.
1	Rounded caps. The line segment ends with semicircular caps that have a diameter of the width of the line.
2	Projecting square caps. These are similar to butt caps in that they are square, perpendicular caps; but they extend out from the end of the line segment by one-half the width of the line.

Line Joining

As you might imagine, if you can control the ending of a line, you can also control the joining of a pair of lines. The *line join* parameter in the current graphics state controls this, and is further affected by the *miter limit* parameter. The line join parameter works in a similar fashion to the line cap parameter: it controls the way PostScript paints the joints between line segments when they meet. If the segments merely cross, both continuing on the other side of one another, then there isn't any problem. The lines are merely drawn over one another, just as you might do with a pen. But if the lines end and join, then you have to decide how to paint the join. The three possible joins are shown in Figure 7.10.

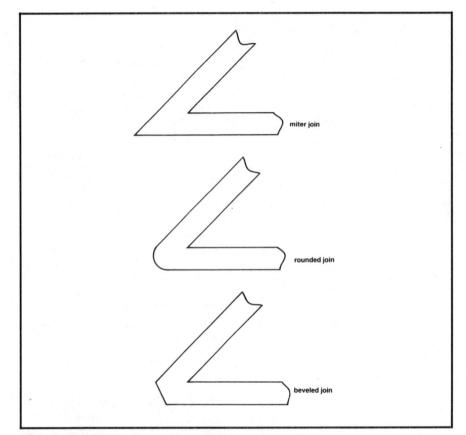

Figure 7.10: Line join appearance

Each of these joins again corresponds to a value of the line join parameter. The value of the line join parameter can be set by the **setlinejoin**
operator. The three values for the line join are as follows:

VALUE	TYPE OF JOIN
0	Mitered join. The edges of the lines are extended until they meet. This is the default line join, and is affected by the current miter limit discussed below.
1	Rounded join. The line segments are connected by a rounded end, formed by a circular arc that has a diameter equal to the line width.

VALUE	TYPE OF JOIN
2	Beveled join. The segments are finished with butt end caps and filled in to form a bevel.

Miter Limit

When you are using a mitered join, which is the default join in Post-Script, it is possible that the point on the join will extend some distance from the actual end of the line. This will happen when the lines meet at very small angles. This can be annoying under some circumstances, and to prevent such occurrences, PostScript changes from a mitered join (line join 0) to a beveled join (line join 3) at small angles. The precise angle at which this change occurs is controlled by the *miter limit* parameter in the current graphics state. This parameter defines the ratio of the line width to the length of the spike: when the ratio of these two for the actual join exceeds the miter limit, the join is turned from a mitered join into a beveled join. The default PostScript value makes this transition at about 11°. Because it is a ratio, the parameter works in a counterintuitive fashion, where smaller numbers for the miter limit make the transition at progressively larger angles. If you need to change it, you will probably have to experiment to discover the correct value for your application.

Solid and Dashed Lines

PostScript normally creates a solid line in the current color when you issue a **stroke** command. However, here again, this is controlled by the *dash pattern* in the current graphics state. This is not quite as simple as the previous controls; PostScript provides a flexible control for the line pattern.

Naturally, the default line is a solid one. The character of the line is set by the **setdash** operator, which takes two operands from the stack: an array and an offset. If the array is empty, the line is solid; if there are elements in the array, they determine the dash pattern of the line. The elements of the array specify alternately the length of the dash and the length of the gap along the line segment. Thus, an array with one element, such as [4], would produce a line composed of a 4-unit dash, followed by a 4-unit space, and so on until the length of the line was reached. Multiple elements in the array are each used in turn to determine the cycle of dashes and spaces along the line. You can generate some interesting patterns by using more complex arrays. It is not necessary for the line to be a multiple of the array factor; the array just stops wherever it is in the cycle when it reaches the end of the line segment.

The offset operand determines when the array pattern starts on the line. The interpreter starts to process the array pattern, but doesn't actually paint anything until the total of the units used in the array equals the offset value. Then the pattern begins, starting at the beginning of the line. Notice that the offset affects the beginning of the pattern, not the beginning of the line. Let's use two examples to illustrate this process.

Suppose that you have an array and offset as follows:

[4] 2 **setdash**

You might think that the pattern should start 2 units into the line; in other words, that the line should start with a 2-unit space. That would be incorrect. When you stroke a line, the interpreter will begin processing the array, which specifies alternating 4-unit dashes with 4-unit spaces. But the actual stroking will not begin until 2 units of the array have been used; hence, the first dash will be only 2-units long, followed by a 4-unit space, then a 4-unit dash, and so on throughout the remainder of the line. The first 2 units of the first dash were used by the offset parameter. The line, however, was stroked from the beginning; that is, the first 2-unit dash begins at the start of the line.

Another example is given by the following:

[4] 6 **setdash**

Here, the pattern defined by the array is the same as before, but the offset produces a slightly different pattern. This line will look the way we said the earlier line would not look; that is, it begins with a 2-unit space. At the beginning of the **stroke**, the array is processed until 6 units are used. In this example, that uses up the first dash and 2 units of the first space, and so the line begins with the remaining space of 2 units, followed by a dash of 4 units, then a 4-unit space, and so on. In each case, you see how the interpreter used the offset against the array, not against the line.

All of these techniques are fairly exotic, and the important point is for you to remember that they exist and that there are controls for you to work with if you ever need to. The default values work satisfactorily and you should change them only for well-planned reasons.

CLIPPING

All of these advanced techniques deal with some feature of the current path. You are certainly familiar by now with the current path and the current graphics state. Up to this point, only the current path has been used to apply paint to the output page; now we are going to discuss a new type of path and an alternative use of the current path.

Clipping Path

This new type of path is the clipping path. The *clipping path* is defined as the path that defines the current boundary that crops, or limits, all output on the current page. This is similar to the idea of a current path, in that it represents a path in the user space that has been created by normal PostScript operations. It differs from the current path in that it is not stroked or filled. Instead, it defines a border that limits where marks can be made on the current page.

The clipping path starts out as the entire imageable portion of the current page, which is effectively the whole page. You may reduce it by means of the **clip** operator, which we will discuss in detail below. The new region defined by the clipping path must lie inside the current clipping region; you cannot expand it outside what is presently defined. The clipping region is automatically reset to the entire page when you perform a **showpage**. You might think of this in the following way: you create an image on a temporary page, trim the page to the shape that you want with electronic scissors, and paste the remaining material down onto the current page to create your output. The clipping path defines the path that the electronic scissors follow to cut, or clip, your temporary page to the shape that you want. This shape can be as arbitrary as you like; obviously, you should keep the path reasonable so that you know what is going to be inside and what outside. In particular, you may find that you want to use the text characters as a clipping path. For example, you might create some outline text and want to fill it with a pattern of lines, other shapes, or even other text. All of these things can be done with the clipping mechanism. Further on in this section you will do an example that uses letters as a clipping path.

Notice one benefit to this model. When you take a pair of scissors and cut something away, there's no way to put it back. The same is generally true with the clipping function: once you have reduced the area on the page, using a new, larger clipping path will not restore the clipping area. However, by using **gsave**, **grestore** to bracket the clipping action, you can restore the clipping region to a larger, previous area. The clipping path is part of the current graphics state; if you save the graphics state with a **gsave**, you also save the current clipping path, and it will be restored when you issue the matching **grestore**. Any changes to the clipping path should be enclosed in the **gsave**, **grestore** pair even if you don't want to restore a larger path for the same reasons that we discussed earlier for all major changes to the graphics state: to insulate the rest of the page from consequences of the changes.

Clip Operations

Here is a complete description of the **clip** operator in the usual format.

SYNTAX   **FUNCTION**

— **clip** —   intersects the inside of the current path with the
                  inside of the current clipping path to produce a new
                  (smaller) current clipping path. Before creating the
                  intersection, **clip** implicitly closes the current path.

When you are using the **clip** operator to generate a clipping region, you should remember that this operator, unlike **fill** and **stroke**, does not erase the current path when it has finished its operation. Therefore, if you want a new path, you will have to generate it by using the **newpath** operator. This is especially important in generating graphics; all procedures that construct graphics should begin with a **newpath** to be sure that no extraneous pieces of the current path are left on the page.

Simple Graphic Examples

Let's illustrate these rather dry, abstract concepts by putting them to use in some examples. A set of simple graphics will demonstrate the use of the **clip** operator in several ways. You will see what a clipping region is and how it appears on the page. In order to illustrate this, you will use several of your previous procedures and the horizontalLines procedure you saw above. The other procedures are screenBox and isoTriangle, which you are familiar with. They can be combined, as shown in Figure 7.11, into a general prolog file for use in all these exercises.

```
%------------------------Prolog for clipping----------------------
/adjstroke
{
    transform
    .25 sub round .25 add exch
    .25 sub round .25 add exch
    itransform
}
bind def

/inch
    {    72 mul }
    def

/screenBox
    {    newpath
        /Dim exch def
        .5 inch 0 moveto
        Dim 0    Dim Dim .25 inch   arcto
        4 {pop} repeat
        Dim Dim   0 Dim .25 inch   arcto
        4 {pop} repeat
        0 Dim      0 0   .25 inch   arcto
        4 {pop} repeat
        0 0       Dim 0  .25 inch   arcto
        4 {pop} repeat
        closepath }
    def

%define graphic procedure for isosceles triangle
/isoTriangle
    %stack: height base
    {    newpath
        /Base exch def
        /Hgt exch def
        /HalfBase Base 2 div def
        0 0 moveto
        HalfBase Hgt rlineto
        HalfBase Hgt neg rlineto
        closepath }
    def

/horizontalLines
%produce a series of horizontal lines
%  spaced 10 points apart
%called as: height width horizontalLines
{
    newpath
    0 10
    4 -1 roll
    {
        0
        2 copy
        exch adjstroke moveto
        2 index add
        exch adjstroke
        lineto
    }
    for
    pop
    stroke
}
    bind def
```

Figure 7.11: Prolog for clipping examples

Now let's add a clipping path to this exercise. This can be done as shown in Figure 7.12. This assumes that the prolog from Figure 7.11 has been loaded into the interpreter. This program produces the page of output shown in Figure 7.13.

This program is quite simple; the only thing to explain is the use of the **clip** operator itself. The program begins with a translation to the same vertical position (5 inches) used earlier for the output from horizontalLines, but moves in to the 3-inch position to center the figure more. Then it produces a current path in the familiar screenBox form, 3 inches on a side. This path is neither stroked nor filled; instead you issue the **clip** operator, which takes the current path and makes it into the clipping path. Now the only portion of the page that

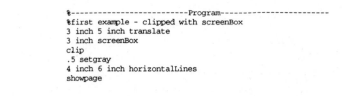

```
%-------------------------Program---------------------
%first example - clipped with screenBox
3 inch 5 inch translate
3 inch screenBox
clip
.5 setgray
4 inch 6 inch horizontalLines
showpage
```

Figure 7.12: Program using clip

Figure 7.13: Output using clip

you can mark is the portion that lies inside the screen box figure. To demonstrate this, the program sets 0.5 gray and, on the next line, again generates a 4-inch by 6-inch set of horizontal lines, as you did in the previous example. This time, however, the output only shows inside the screen box, as demonstrated in Figure 7.5. This shows you the most straightforward use of **clip**.

The next example is more complex graphically, although not much more complex as a program. In this case, you are going to use two clipping paths and then paint the resulting area with horizontal lines. This will demonstrate how the clipping path always getting smaller and never larger.

This example is done in two parts. The first part produces the figures that will be used for the clipping paths, strokes them, and prints them out to show you what they look like. Then the second part uses both of the figures, once to stroke them and again as clipping paths, and then prints a set of horizontal lines to show you what path remains after the two **clip** operators. Both parts of the program are shown in Figure 7.14. The first part produces the page shown in Figure 7.15.

This output is what you might have expected, based on the first half of the program in Figure 7.14. This program creates an overlapping screen box figure and an isosceles triangle. The two figures overlap so that a portion of each is outside the other. Before you go on, try to visualize what portion of this pair of

```
%second example - screenBox and isoTriangle
%first half - line figures only
3 inch 5 inch translate
3 inch screenBox
stroke
5 inch 4 inch isoTriangle
stroke
showpage

%second half - as clipping paths also
3 inch 5 inch translate
3 inch screenBox
stroke
5 inch 4 inch isoTriangle
gsave
     stroke
grestore
clip
3 inch screenBox
clip
.5 setgray
4 inch 6 inch horizontalLines
showpage
```

Figure 7.14: Two figure clipping region procedures

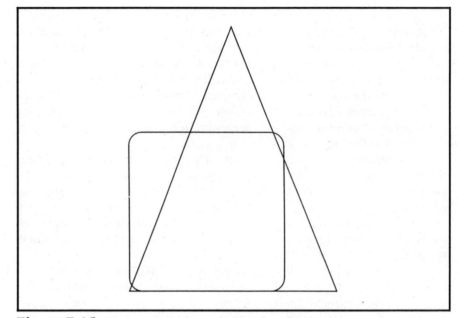

Figure 7.15: Line output of two figures for clipping

figures will be retained by the **clip** operators. The actual result is shown Figure 7.16.

This program is easy to follow, so we won't spend any time in detailed analysis. The output, however, is more complex, and so the example both strokes the paths and uses them as clipping paths. This makes it a bit easier to relate this figure to the preceding one, and allows you to see exactly what the results of the successive application of the **clip** operator are.

Although the screenBox path was the last path used for **clip**, notice that the portions of the screen figure that lay outside of the previous clipping path, which was produced by isoTriangle, do not now become part of the new clipping region. This is also why you had to produce the screen box twice; in order to stroke the entire figure, you had to draw it and stroke it before the triangle was drawn, stroked, and used as a clipping region. Otherwise you would only have been able to stroke the portion of the screen figure that lay within the triangle.

The use of **gsave** and **grestore** around the **stroke** for isoTriangle should be familiar; it is required so that the current path doesn't disappear when you stroke the triangle. An alternative would have been to issue the **clip** first, and

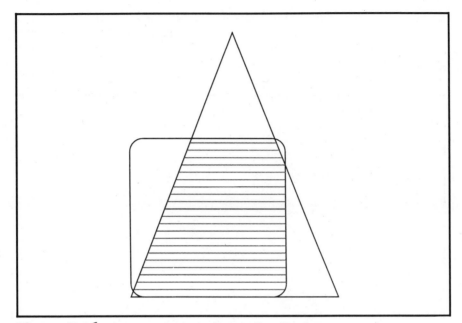

Figure 7.16: Output using two figures for clipping

then **stroke**. Since **clip** leaves the current path in place, that sequence would not have required a **gsave**, **grestore** bracket. The sequence as shown seems more natural and understandable to me, and that's why I used it here. It's just a matter of personal preference.

Text as a Clipping Path

Let's do one more clipping example to illustrate how to use any arbitrary graphic as a clipping region. Text in PostScript, as you are well aware, is a graphic object. Therefore, one of the effects that you can generate with PostScript is to use the text as a clipping path and then show another graphic underneath it. The underlying graphic might be other text or any graphic.

For this example, you will print the word SUN in 3-inch-high outline letters in the Helvetica-BoldOblique font, and then use those letters as a clipping path for an image of the sun with rays radiating from it. This produces a nice graphic image, and one that is beyond the reach of many applications, except as a bit-mapped pattern. There will be two procedures: rays, which draws only the rays, and sunRays, which draws the sun and the rays together. We won't spend much time explaining this; all of the techniques should be familiar to you. The program is shown in Figure 7.17. It generates a complex graphic and uses large type. You can expect it to take a noticeable time, perhaps as much as two minutes, to generate the output which is shown in Figure 7.18.

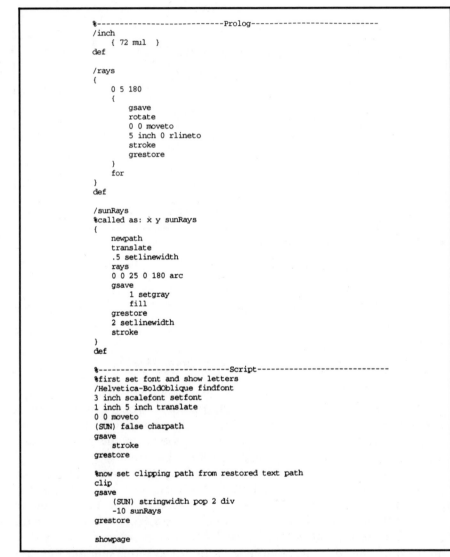

```
%---------------------------Prolog---------------------------
/inch
    { 72 mul  }
def

/rays
{
    0 5 180
    {
        gsave
        rotate
        0 0 moveto
        5 inch 0 rlineto
        stroke
        grestore
    }
    for
}
def

/sunRays
%called as: x y sunRays
{
    newpath
    translate
    .5 setlinewidth
    rays
    0 0 25 0 180 arc
    gsave
        1 setgray
        fill
    grestore
    2 setlinewidth
    stroke
}
def

%----------------------------Script----------------------------
%first set font and show letters
/Helvetica-BoldOblique findfont
3 inch scalefont setfont
1 inch 5 inch translate
0 0 moveto
(SUN) false charpath
gsave
    stroke
grestore

%now set clipping path from restored text path
clip
gsave
    (SUN) stringwidth pop 2 div
    -10 sunRays
grestore

showpage
```

Figure 7.17: Program for text clipping example

Figure 7.18: Output using text clipping

Let's review what you did here. To begin with, let's examine the sun-Rays procedure. This procedure assumes that it will be called with an x- and a y-coordinate as operands. It then translates the origin to this location and uses the rays procedure to draw a set of .5 unit rays around a half-circle, centered at the translated origin. Next it creates a half-circle of 25 units, and both fills it with white (to erase the underlying rays) and strokes it with a 2-unit line. This will create the sun with rays as a graphic image that you want for the program.

The rays procedure also deserves some comment. This is a simple procedure that draws the rays by rotating the coordinates repeatedly and drawing a line directly along the x-axis from the center for 5 inches. The rotation and drawing are enclosed in a **gsave**, **grestore** pair to avoid affecting anything outside the procedure; in particular, to avoid the cumulative effect of the **rotate**. The entire procedure is repeated every 5° around a 180° arc, beginning with 0°; this repetition is performed by a **for** loop.

The body of the program begins by sizing and setting the font. Next the origin is translated to an appropriate point on the page, and a move to the origin is performed to set things up for displaying the string. Then you outline the string, using the techniques you learned in Chapter 4 when we discussed outline fonts. Since you want to use the path in two ways, save it with a **gsave** before you stroke it and then use **grestore** to bring it back for the **clip** operator. This generates the text outline on the page.

Now you need to generate the graphic to underlie the text. You start this with a **gsave**, remembering that these procedures will also modify the current graphics state. You decide to position the graphic in the center of the string just below the baseline for maximum effect. To do this, you calculate the center of the string, using **stringwidth** divided by two, and then call the sunRays procedure with that result on the stack as the x-coordinate and adding a y-displacement of – 10 units. This places the center of the "sun" exactly in the center of the text string and 10 points below the baseline of the text. The procedure does the rest, creating the graphic as you wanted it. Because of the clipping path set earlier, the graphic only shows up inside the outlines of each text letter, as you can see in Figure 7.18.

ARBITRARY CURVES AND TRANSFORMATIONS

In previous chapters, you learned about various graphics operations that allowed you to draw circles and parts of circles, and that allowed you to reshape the user coordinates in various ways. In both of these instances what you learned were special cases of a more general operation that PostScript implements. We covered the special cases first because they are the most common, and most useful, variations of these general operations and because PostScript provides special operators to perform those functions.

However, now we will discuss the two general operators that lie behind building curves and changing the coordinate system. These operators are mathematical because their underlying operations imply some complex calculations in order to generate the desired graphic functions. We are not going to go into much mathematical detail here, but the Bibliography in Appendix D contains references that you can use if you want to know more about how these functions perform mathematically. Based on my own experience, it is almost impossible to use these functions effectively in ordinary PostScript without a good understanding of the mathematics involved. The intention here, again, is to provide you with a knowledge of the existence of these concepts and operators so that, if you do need to use them, you will know that they exist and where to find them.

Curved Paths

PostScript describes all curved paths by using a class of mathematical functions called Bezier cubic sections. The operators that you learned previously, such as **arc** and **arcto**, actually use these functions to calculate the output paths that are drawn on the output page. These functions can be used to produce any arbitrary curve on the output page, and they are invoked by the PostScript operator **curveto**. There is a detailed discussion of the **curveto** operator in the *PostScript Language Reference Manual, Second Edition,* which you should read and understand if you are going to use this operator.

You should be aware of two points regarding these general arcs that PostScript produces. First, the other operators that produce curves use the **curveto** operator internally to generate the required shape. This means that, if you disassemble the path using the techniques we will discuss in the next section, you will get **curveto**s where the program issued operators like **arc**.

The second point is that the shape of the curve generated by **curveto** is a function of four points called *control points*. The first is the current point, where the curve starts. The last point is the end of the curve. The two points in the middle determine the motion and direction of the curve as it proceeds from one end point to the other. Although the first and last points lie on the curve, the two middle points do not; they represent the motion and direction of the curve but are not themselves part of it. If you drew a box connecting all four points, the curve generated by the **curveto** operator would always be inside the walls of the box and connected to only two of the corners. Of course you understand that the "box" may have any arbitrary shape; there is no constraint on the position of the four control points.

This discussion is of most interest in utilizing some of the application software, such as Adobe's Illustrator package, that allow you to manipulate these control points directly to generate curves on the screen and then transfer them to the output page. Frankly, this is the only easy way to use **curveto**; it is extremely difficult to visualize precisely the curve that will result from using any specific set of control points. If you have to use it in ordinary PostScript programming, you will want to experiment to find the exact points that generate the curve you need.

Coordinate Transformation

Just as general curves are an extension of circular arcs, so there is a general coordinate transformation that underlies the more specific operations of scaling, rotating, and translating coordinates that you worked with earlier in the book. This general coordinate transformation is done by the **concat** operator.

In order to understand what **concat** does, it is essential to review and expand the discussion of the PostScript coordinate system that we had earlier. Remember that PostScript transforms the user coordinates into device coordinates using a current transformation matrix, or CTM. This CTM is changed by operators such as **scale** and **rotate** to create the changed coordinates that are used in your programs. We discussed all this in "Measurement and Coordinates" in Chapter 3.

The mathematical operation for transforming one set numbers representing a two-dimensional space into another set of numbers that represents a changed set of two-dimensional coordinates is performed by using a set of numbers called a *matrix*. In PostScript, the matrix for transforming one set of coordinates into another is represented by a set of six numbers in an array, like this:

$$[\, a\ b\ c\ d\ t_x\ t_y\,]$$

Before we explain the purpose of each number, let's define some terms to help us discuss them. These numbers are called *coefficients* and they modify the current x- or y-coordinate values to determine new x and y values. We will denote the current x- and y-coordinate values as x and y respectively, and the new x- and y-coordinates as x' and y'. Then the six coefficients have the following function:

COEFFICIENT	FUNCTION
a	multiplied by x (the original x-coordinate) as part of the determination of the new x' (the new x-coordinate)
c	multiplied by y (the original y-coordinate) and added to the above as part of the determination of the new x'
t_x	added to both of the above as part of the determination of the new x'
b	multiplied by x (the original x-coordinate) as part of the determination of the new y' (the new y-coordinate)
d	multiplied by y (the original y-coordinate) and added to the above as part of the determination of the new y'

COEFFICIENT	FUNCTION
t_y	added to both of the above as part of the determination of the new y'

This is a verbal description of what is represented, in mathematical terms, by the following equations:

$$x' = ax + cy + t_x$$
$$y' = bx + dy + t_y$$

The **concat** operator takes the 6-element array, described above, as an operand and *concatenates* it with the existing CTM to create a new CTM that is placed into operation automatically by the interpreter. The operators that you studied and worked with previously are simply special types of **concat**. As one example, the **scale** operator is identical to a **concat** that changes only the **a** and **d** coefficients of the array. So when you issue the command

    72 108 scale

it is equivalent to the operation

    [72 0 0 108 0 0] concat

However, the former is much easier to understand and remember.

As you may have noticed, this looks similar to the array that you needed to use in the **makefont** operator; they are essentially identical. The **makefont** operator transforms the character-coordinate space in the same way—and using essentially the same mechanism—as **concat** transforms the user coordinate space. You may want review the "Font Metrics" section of Chapter 4 to see some of the transformations that were done there and how these could be applied to the user space with **concat**.

GRAPHICS MANIPULATIONS

As the last part of this section on advanced graphics, we will discuss some of the operators that PostScript provides for determining the size and shape of graphic objects. Again, the intention is not to fully explore the use of these functions, but simply to let you know of their existence and to illustrate some of their possible uses.

Graphic Size and Shape

We will begin with the PostScript **pathbbox** operator. As you might guess from its name, this operator constructs a bounding box for the current path and returns two pairs of coordinates: the x- and y-coordinate values for the lower-left and upper-right corners of the box. The *bounding box* is the smallest rectangle that will completely enclose the points that make up the current path. The concept here is quite similar to the previous bounding boxes that we have discussed in regard to entire pages or groups of pages in the Chapter 2 section called "Program Structure" and in regard to individual characters in the Chapter 4 section called "Font Metrics."

You should note that the bounding box that is returned by **pathbbox** includes control points for any curved-line segments in the current path, as well as the actual lines themselves. If you think about it, this is quite reasonable. As we observed earlier, the control points of a curve form a rectangle that encloses the entire curve. These points, however, may not lie on the curve themselves, as we discussed above. Because the control points for a curved line segment may be distant from the actual line that they define, PostScript provides another operator, **flattenpath**, that changes the curved line segments into a short series of straight lines that closely approximates the curved segment. This is the same process that the interpreter goes through when it actually draws the line on the output page. An example of this process is illustrated in Figure 7.19.

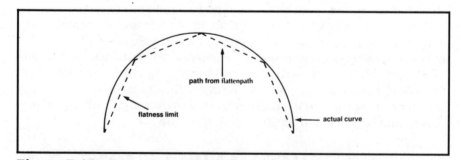

Figure 7.19: Illustration of curve approximation

How close the approximation comes to the actual curve is a function of the *flatness* parameter in the current graphics state. This number varies for each PostScript device and is pre-set in the device set-up routines to a value suitable for most applications using the device. Typically, the standard flatness value is 1, which means that the straight lines cannot deviate from the mathematical curved path by more than one pixel. You can reset this using the **SETFLAT** operator, which is explained in the *PostScript Language Reference Manual, Second Edition.*

Since these are all straight lines and therefore have no control points outside of the line itself, the bounding box that surrounds them will be closer to the actual paths than it will be with a curved segment. If you want a close fit on the bounding box, and the current path includes curved segments, you should use the **flattenpath** operator before you use the **pathbbox** operator.

Common Applications

Not too surprisingly, the most common application of these operators is in determining bounding boxes for text characters. This is especially useful when you wish to scale some other object to the current font. Typically, in such situations, the scaling will be done to a common letter, such as a lower-case *x,* that has no risers or descenders, or to a common capital letter. Once the bounding box is determined, the coordinates provided can be used to calculate the scaling factor to be used. In such a case, it is essential that you use **flattenpath** before you issue the **pathbbox**; otherwise you will get quite different answers from those you anticipate and your scaling will be off.

IMAGE OPERATIONS

This section of the chapter presents the concepts behind PostScript handling of images. PostScript provides very sophisticated processing for transforming and rendering images. There is not room here for detailed examples and explanations of PostScript operations that process images; instead, we will develop and explain the concepts that lie behind these operations so that you can work with them comfortably.

In particular, we are going to explain the nature and representation of images from an internal standpoint and work from that basis to the PostScript operators that are provided to manipulate images. Some of this will repeat, but with more depth, information that was discussed in earlier portions of the book; and some of it may be information that you already know from other sources. In spite of this, the entire process will be presented here as a unit to allow the discussion to flow naturally, to be sure that all the information is covered, and to avoid the need to turn back and forth in the book.

IMAGE PROCESSING

An image is a representation of the outward appearance of something; in other words, an image is a form or shape that represents some object. Obviously, PostScript provides many facilities for creating and manipulating some common types of images, in that sense. Not all representations of forms or shapes can be easily described by the PostScript operators that you have used up to now, however. Complex images, such as photographs or even intricate, shaded line drawings require alternate handling and processing. PostScript provides operators for such processing.

Sampled Data and Images

To understand how PostScript processes such images, we need to discuss how the computer stores and uses them. Image data is stored as an array of sampled data. The image is transformed, by application of a grid, into a series of squares, and then a gray value is determined for each square. (If the image is processed in color, a set of color values is established for each square instead of a gray value. Black-and-white images will be used for our discussion here, since they illustrate all the necessary points without the additional complexity of color; but the discussion applies to color as well.)

At the simplest level, each square can be either black or white, with no intermediate shades. In this case, the color of each square can be represented by a 0 or a 1; if we follow the PostScript conventions, we would use 0 for black and 1 for white (like **setgray**). Each square could also be given some range of gray values to provide additional shading of the image. We will discuss this process in more detail below; for now, let's look at the case where each square is black or white.

It may be helpful, at this point, to look at Figure 7.20, which represents a simple image that is rendered into a grid format. The figure shows the image of the number 1 transformed into a grid. This is a simple image and could easily have been generated with ordinary PostScript operands, but it illustrates the image processing mechanism. In actual practice, images being used might represent the appearance of some natural scene or a complex, generated graphic. The simplicity of our example allows you to focus on the concepts involved.

The entire image is enclosed in a box that is 8 squares wide and 14 squares high. As was said above, you could represent this image as a series of 0's and 1's (where 0 is black and 1 is white); it will look like Figure 7.21. This image is a *bit-mapped* representation of the number 1. Using this figure, we can discuss the PostScript mechanism for processing such images.

Level 2 of the PostScript language provides additional support for sampled images in several areas. The discussion that follows covers Level 1 support in detail and then expands on that to describe the additional features in Level 2. Since the fundamental processing is identical in both levels, this seems like the best way for you to learn these features.

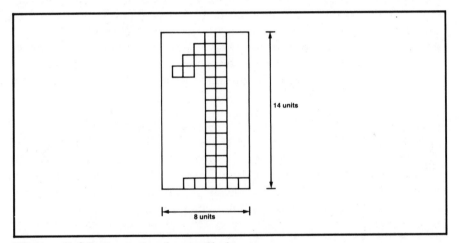

Figure 7.20: Example of a sampled image

```
1 1 1 1 0 0 1 1
1 1 1 0 0 0 1 1
1 1 0 0 0 0 1 1
1 0 0 1 0 0 1 1
1 1 1 1 0 0 1 1
1 1 1 1 0 0 1 1
1 1 1 1 0 0 1 1
1 1 1 1 0 0 1 1
1 1 1 1 0 0 1 1
1 1 1 1 0 0 1 1
1 1 1 1 0 0 1 1
1 1 1 1 0 0 1 1
1 1 1 1 0 0 1 1
1 1 0 0 0 0 0 0
```

Figure 7.21: Bit representation of a sampled image

Image Representation

Each image is defined by three numbers:

- the number of columns in the image,

- the number of rows in the image, and

- the number of bits per sample.

In our example, these are 8, 14, and 1, respectively. The number of rows and columns is easily understood; the number of bits per sample may be less clear. This is a value for the gray level in the square represented by the sample. In the example, you chose to use either black or white; therefore, one bit is all that is required to represent the color value. PostScript allows you to use 1, 2, 4, or 8 bits per sample, giving you up to 256 gray levels for each sample square. Using more bits per sample carries the obvious cost of having to process 2, 4, or 8 times as many bits to generate the image; however, it also gives you a more detailed and more accurate representation of the image being presented.

The sampled data that makes up the image is represented by a stream of characters. PostScript image processing obtains this data by executing a procedure that delivers the data, normally through reading a file that contains the data stream. The data is represented as a stream of characters, which is basically a stream of 8-bit integers in the range of 0 to 255. Each set of 8 bits represents from one to eight sample squares, depending on the number of bits per sample. In this example, each character would represent eight sample squares since each sample is only 1 bit. At the other extreme, if the samples were the maximum of 8 bits, each character would represent 1 sample square. Since the example in Figure 7.21 has 8 columns, each row can be represented by 1 character.

Image data must be presented in a defined order for processing. PostScript considers the image a rectangle, as we have illustrated above, and the coordinates for an image have the same structure as the coordinates on a page. The samples that make up the image are numbered (0,0) from the bottom-left corner, proceed along the bottom row and then move up a row, and so on. In our example, that would make the bottom-left corner square (0,0), and the bottom-right square would be (8,0); the first square in the next row would be (0,1), the top-left corner would be (0,14) and the top-right corner, (8,14). This is also the order that PostScript normally uses to assign values when it reads the data. That is, the first bits are applied to the bottom-left corner of the image, the next are applied to the sample value on the right, and so on up the image until all the data is processed.

One way, and the easiest way, to encode bit-streams like this is to represent them as hexadecimal digits. PostScript provides a convenient notation for writing hexadecimal strings you enclose them in the characters < and > instead of the usual parentheses. In that case, using hexadecimal notation, the rows of Figure 7.21 are equivalent to the hexadecimal values shown in Figure 7.22.

```
1 1 1 1 0 0 1 1 = <f3>
1 1 1 0 0 0 1 1 = <e3>
1 1 0 0 0 0 1 1 = <c3>
1 0 0 1 0 0 1 1 = <93>
1 1 1 1 0 0 1 1 = <f3>
1 1 1 1 0 0 1 1 = <f3>
1 1 1 1 0 0 1 1 = <f3>
1 1 1 1 0 0 1 1 = <f3>
1 1 1 1 0 0 1 1 = <f3>
1 1 1 1 0 0 1 1 = <f3>
1 1 1 1 0 0 1 1 = <f3>
1 1 1 1 0 0 1 1 = <f3>
1 1 1 1 0 0 1 1 = <f3>
1 1 0 0 0 0 0 0 = <c0>
```

Figure 7.22: Sampled image with hexadecimal equivalents

This set of numbers, or characters, would be sent to PostScript as the following hexadecimal string:

<c0f3f3f3f3f3f3f3f3f393c3e3f3>

As you see, it begins with the bottom-most row and proceeds up the image to the top. The only point to watch out for here is that each row of the sample must start with a new character. That means that, if the example were 9 columns wide, you would have to put the ninth bit into a character all alone; the last 7 bits would be thrown out. To illustrate this, let's take the example above and add one column of white space on the right edge—another row of 1's. In that case, each row would have to add an additional character that would be the same for all the rows: an <80>, to set the last bit in the row. A single additional bit would not work. Then the string to represent the image would be changed as follows:

<c080f380f380f380f380f380f380f380f380f3809380c380e380f380>

Image Transformation

The coordinates actually used to generate an image may, of course, be quite different from those the PostScript interpreter uses to generate the image. In particular, the PostScript operators that manage images allow transformations from the actual coordinates used by a device that produces the image into PostScript coordinates. This is done by means of a transformation matrix similar to the one discussed in the previous section of the chapter.

This transformation matrix maps the coordinates used in the source image into the user-coordinate space. The best and easiest method of handling this conversion is to do it in two steps. First, the image is converted into a unit square in the user space by means of the transformation matrix mentioned above. Then that unit square is positioned and scaled on the page in the usual fashion. This process is familiar to you, since you used the same method to work with the logo graphic in the earlier exercises. In that case, the logo was defined in a procedure that was independent of the page itself; then, the entire object was positioned and scaled to fit the space reserved for it on the page. You should use this same technique for processing images.

This transformation matrix is identical in components and operation to the transformation matrix described earlier in the chapter in the discussion of the **concat** operator. Thus, the process of scaling an image that is presented to the interpreter already in the expected sequence, like the string you developed above, would use the following matrix:

[8 0 0 14 0 0]

where the a and d coefficients represent the width and height of the sampled image, respectively. You remember that the a coefficient represents the x-coordinate, which is the width (or number of columns) of the image, and that the d coefficient represents the y-coordinate, which is the height (or number of rows). If you had an image that was scanned left to right, but top to bottom, instead of the bottom-to-top method PostScript expects, the transformation matrix would look like this:

[8 0 0 −14 0 14]

This has the same width, but the y-coordinate is a negative height to indicate that the scan proceeds downward (in the negative direction), and the t_y coefficient is a positive 14 to move the starting point for the scan up to the top of the image. Using similar techniques, any form of scanned image can be converted into a PostScript unit square.

Image Processing Operators

Now that you have been introduced to the image processing mechanism, we can discuss the actual PostScript operators that implement it. This is done by two similar operators, **image** and **imagemask**. These two are sufficiently alike that we will discuss one of them, **image**, first, and then explain the differences that distinguish **imagemask**. These operators are defined as follows:

width height bits/sample matrix dataproc **image** —

Uses the *dataproc* to provide data to paint a sampled image onto the output page. The image is a rectangular array of *width* × *height* cells, where each cell contains *bits/sample* items of data. The sample image is taken to exist in its own coordinate system, with the origin at the lower-left corner of the sample, and the upper-right corner being at the point *(width, height)*. The *matrix* operand defines the transformation from user coordinates to image coordinates.

width height boolean matrix dataproc **imagemask** —

Similar to **image**, except that the data array created by the *dataproc* is used as a mask to apply the current color to the page. If *boolean* is *true*, data values of 1 are painted and values of 0 are ignored; if it is *false*, the reverse happens.

In Level 1, the **image** operator takes five operands: sample width, sample height, number of bits per sample, the transformation matrix, and a procedure. You already understand the function of the first four items; only the procedure is new. This is the procedure that **image** executes, repeatedly if necessary, to get the data to generate the sample image. Typically, the procedure will read the image data from a file, often the current input file—that is, the same file that is supplying the PostScript commands. In that case, the data will be imbedded into the command stream immediately after the **image** operator. In any case, the **image** operator obtains the data by executing the procedure. If the image area defined by the first three operands has not been filled by the end of execution of the procedure, **image** will execute the procedure repeatedly until sufficient data has been obtained.

There are several advantages to this method of producing images on the device. To begin with, there is no need for the entire image to reside in PostScript memory in order for the image to be generated onto the output device. The sample data may also be processed as it is read, allowing various transformations to be done on the file. For example, the data on the file might be compressed by some algorithm to conserve space and then decompressed by the input procedure to generate the final sample image. (In fact, this can be done automatically in Level 2). It is even possible to generate an image entirely internally by using a procedure that calculates the necessary binary pattern instead of reading the data from some source.

The **image** operator produces images by marking the page with an opaque paint, as always. Thus each sample square is painted black, white, or some tone of gray, as selected by the bit/sample value. In this case, the usual PostScript rules apply, and the paint covers every portion of the sampled image, overlaying anything that was on the page previously. This is the effective difference between the two operators, **image** and **imagemask**.

The **imagemask** operator takes the data stream as a series of binary digits, 0 and 1, and uses these as a *mask* to control where the paint is applied. Let's look at Figure 7.21 again. I said earlier that this is a bit-mapped image of the number 1. When we were looking at this in relation to the **image** operator, the 0's represented black paint and the 1's were white paint. Now consider this same data as a mask. In that case, the 0's represent where the **imagemask** operator will apply paint—the current color, as set by **setgray**—and the 1's represent where no color is to be applied. Alternatively, the 0's could be used to represent where no color was applied; and the 1's where the color was applied, which is the reverse of the preceding condition. This is the difference between the two operators: **image** paints the sampled data onto the page, but **imagemask** applies paint in the current color through the sampled data, using it as a mask.

In Level 1, the **imagemask** operator requires five operands, in the same fashion as **image**. The first pair and the last pair of operands are identical: the width and height, and the transformation matrix and the procedure. The difference is in the third operand. Here, **image** had the number of bits per sample; but **imagemask** is a binary mask, so it always has only one bit per position. Instead of bits/sample, **imagemask** has a boolean operand in this position: if the value is true, the 1's are painted and the 0's are blank; if it is false, the reverse occurs. Assuming that you wanted to paint the sample in Figure 7.21 in the current color, you would call the **imagemask** with the operands

    8 14 false [8 0 0 14 0 0] { procedure }

This would paint the 0's in the mask and leave everything else on the current page alone. This is an important point, particularly if you are developing bit-mapped characters. Any marks that are already on the page that lie under the nonpainted part of the mask will not be affected by the operation. This insures that, if you had built your own font, for example, the lines that you painted on the form in Chapter 5 will not be erased by the space character that prints on top of them. If you incorrectly used **image**, instead of **imagemask** with a bit-mapped space character, it would paint white over the line and would not be consistent with the behavior of the internal fonts.

For Level 2, the **image** and **imagemask** operators have some additional capabilities. Most importantly, they can be called with an *image dictionary* as an operand, instead of the standard five operands. The image dictionary contains the following required entries:

KEY	TYPE	DEFINITION
ImageType	integer	must be 1.
Width	integer	the sample width of the source image.
Height	integer	the sample height of the source image.
ImageMatrix	matrix	a transformation matrix that can be combined with the CTM (current transformation matrix) to map from the current user coordinates to the image source coordinates. This is essentially like the *matrix* operand in the standard **image** operator.

KEY	TYPE	DEFINITION
BitsPerComponent	integer	specifies the number of bits per sample. May be 1, 2, 4, 8 or 12. Must be 1 for a dictionary used with **imagemask**.
DataSource	procedure, file or string	the source of the data for the image. Notice that the source may be a file or string; in that case, the interpreter reads the file or string repeatedly until all the data specified by the **Width**, **Height**, and **BitsPerComponent** has been read.
Decode	array	an array of numbers that specifies how to translate image-sample values into device values. The array must have 2 entries for each color component.

As you can see, this provides much the same data that you needed to provide to **image**, except that it is contained in a dictionary. Notice that this provides for up to 12 bits per sample value instead of a maximum of 8 for the Level 1 **image** operator. Also, the **DataSource** allows you to specify a file or string as the data source directly, without setting up your own procedure to read them. This also allows you to use the built-in *filters* in Level 2 to decode compressed image data on the fly, which can be a big help and speeds up processing significantly. The only new item here is the **Decode** entry. This allows you to map sample values into the range of values that are required for your output. This is primarily useful in rendering color images; for a standard black and white (monochrome) image, the suggested value for the **Decode** array is [0 1]. The image dictionary can also contain additional, optional entries that allow you to specify multiple sources for your data and allow you to interpolate data values. Use of image dictionaries definitely falls in the area of advanced PostScript operations, and we will not discuss these further here.

Since Level 2 devices still support the standard format for both the **image** and **imagemask** operators, there is no need to emulate the standard behavior for Level 2 devices. I recommend that you simply use the standard set of five operands in all your code, and only use the new format if you have some special, difficult problem that you need to process.

OPERATOR SUMMARY

As usual, we end this chapter with a brief summary of all the operators that have been introduced. The operators in this chapter have been, in general, more complex than operators that you have met earlier; and we have necessarily gone over them quite rapidly. If you have any questions about these operators, first review the material in the chapter, and then check the operator definitions in the *PostScript Language Reference Manual, Second Edition*.

Advanced Graphics Operations

SYNTAX	FUNCTION
ux uy **transform** dx dy	transforms the user space coordinates, *ux* and *uy*, into the equivalent device coordinates, *dx* and *dy*, using the current transformation matrix (CTM).
dx dy **itransform** ux uy	transforms the device coordinates, *dx* and *dy*, into the equivalent user coordinates, *ux* and *uy*, using the inverse of the current transformation matrix.

SYNTAX	FUNCTION
boolean **setstrokeadjust** —	if *boolean* is *true*, then stroke adjustment is performed automatically whenever any subsequent **stroke** or equivalent operators are executed. If *boolean* is *false*, then stroke adjustment is not performed.
— **currentstrokeadjust** boolean	returns the current value, *boolean*, of the stroke adjustment parameter in the current graphics state.
— **clip** —	intersects the inside of the current path with the inside of the current clipping path to produce a new (smaller) current clipping path. Before creating the intersec- tion, **clip** implicitly closes the current path.

Arbitrary Curves and Transformations

matrix **concat** —	concatenates the *matrix* operand with the current transformation matrix (CTM) to create a new CTM. The new CTM is placed into operation immediately, with the effect that the user coordinate system is transformed by the values in *matrix*.

Graphics Manipulation

SYNTAX	FUNCTION
— **pathbbox** llx lly urx ury	returns the bounding box for the current path in the current user coordinate system. The bounding box

SYNTAX	FUNCTION
	consists of the coordinates for the lower-left and upper-right corners of the box that encloses the path, returned as four numbers: *llx lly urx ury*.
— **flattenpath** —	changes the current path by replacing all curved line segments in the current path into straight line segments that approximate the position of the curves. The closeness of the approximation is governed by the flatness setting in the current graphics state.

Image Processing

dict

width height bits/sample matrix dataproc **image** —

Uses the *dataproc* to provide data to paint a sampled image onto the output page. The image is a rectangular array of *width* × *height* cells, where each cell contains *bits/sample* items of data. The sample image is taken to exist in its own coordinate system, with the origin at the lower-left corner of the sample, and the upper-right corner being at the point *(width, height)*. The *matrix* operand defines the transformation from user coordinates to image coordinates.

dict

width height boolean matrix dataproc **imagemask** —

Similar to **image**, except that the data array created by the *dataproc* is used as a mask to apply the current color to the page. If *boolean* is *true*, data values of 1 are painted and values of 0 are ignored; if it is *false*, the reverse happens.

A

Summary of
PostScript Operators

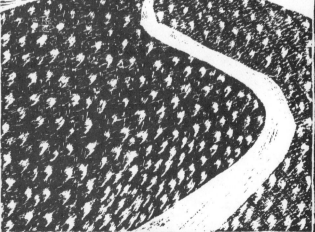

Thisappendix contains a review of the operators that have been presented in this book. It will help you to recall the operators in each chapter and also forms an informal index for review of the topics covered in the book.

Not every PostScript operator is presented in this appendix, but every operator that has been used or discussed in the book is included here. As was noted earlier, the best way to work with a language is to learn its primary functions well and then broaden your scope to include the more specialized operators. That is the rule that has been followed in this book—only the major functions are presented or used. Some related functions or operators have only been noted; others have been omitted altogether. If you want to use these other operators, be sure to consult the *PostScript Language Reference Manual, Second Edition* for full specification of their requirements and results.

This appendix is organized by operator type so you can find related operators quickly. A complete, alphabetical list of all PostScript operators is provided in the *PostScript Language Reference Manual, Second Edition* should you need it.

MATHEMATICAL OPERATORS

num1 num2 **add** sum

Adds *num1* to *num2*.

num1 num2 **sub** result

Subtracts *num2* from *num1*.

num1 num2 **mul** product

Multiplies *num1* by *num2*.

num1 num2 **div** quotient

Divides *num1* by *num2*.

num **neg** – num

Reverses the sign of *num*.

num1 **round** num2

Rounds *num1* to the nearest integer. If num1 is equally close to its two nearest integers, the result is the greater of the two.

int1 int2 **idiv** result

Divides *int1* by *int2* and returns the integer portion of the quotient as *result*; any remainder is discarded. Both operands must be integers, and the result is an integer.

PATH OPERATORS

num1 num2 **moveto** —

Sets the current point to x-coordinate *num1* and y-coordinate *num2*.

num1 num2 **lineto** —

Adds a straight-line segment to the current path. The line segment extends from the current point to the *num1* x-coordinate and the *num2* y-coordinate. The new current point is (*num1, num2*).

num1 num2 **rmoveto** —

(relative lineto) starts a new segment of the current path in the same manner as **moveto**. However, the new current point is defined from the current point (*x,y*) to *x + num1* as an x-coordinate and *y + num2* as a y-coordinate. The new current point is (*x + num1*, y + *num2*).

num1 num2 **rlineto** —

(relative lineto) adds a straight-line segment to the current path in the same manner as **lineto**. However, the line segment extends from the current point *(x,y)* to *x + num1* as an x-coordinate and *y + num2* as a y-coordinate. The new current point is (*x + num1*, y + *num2*).

x y r ang1 ang2 **arc** —

Adds a counterclockwise arc of a circle to the current path, possibly preceded by a straight-line segment. The arc has radius *r* and the point *(x,y)* as a center. *ang1* is the angle of a line from *(x,y)* with length *r* to the beginning of the arc, and *ang2* is the angle of a vector from *(x,y)* with length *r* to the end of the arc. If the current point is defined, the **arc** operator will construct a line from the current point to the beginning of the arc.

x y r ang1 ang2 **arcn** —

Performs the same function as **arc**, except in a clockwise direction.

x1 y1 x2 y2 r **arcto** xt1 yt1 xt2 yt2

Creates a circular arc of radius *r,* tangent to the two lines defined from the current point to *(x1,y1)* and from *(x1,y1)* to *(x2,y2)*. Returns the values of the coordinates of the two tangent points *(xt1,yt1)* and *(xt2,yt2)*. The **arcto** operator also adds a straight-line segment to the current point, if the current point is not the same as the starting point of the arc.

string bool **charpath** —

Makes character path outlines for the characters in *string* as if it were shown at the current point using **show**. These outlines are added to the current path, and form shapes suitable for general filling, stroking or clipping. If *bool* is *true*, the resulting path is suitable for filling or clipping; if *bool* is *false*, the result is suitable for stroking. This distinction only affects stroked fonts (**PaintType** 1); when the current font is an outline font (**PaintType** 0 or 2), the results will be identical. (Nevertheless, as discussed in the book, I recommend that you use *false* for results that you want to **stroke**, and *true* otherwise.)

— clip —

Intersects the inside of the current path with the inside of the current clipping path to produce a new (smaller) current clipping path. Before creating the intersection, **clip** implicitly closes the current path.

— newpath —

Initializes the current path to be empty and causes the current point to be undefined.

— closepath —

Closes the segment of the current path by appending a straight line from the current point to the segment's starting point (generally the point specified in the most recent **moveto** or **rmoveto**).

— pathbbox *llx lly urx ury*

Returns the bounding box for the current path in the current user coordinate system. The bounding box consists of the coordinates for the lower-left and upper-right corners of the box that encloses the path, returned as four numbers: *llx lly urx ury*.

— flattenpath —

Changes the current path by replacing all curved line segments in the current path into straight line segments that approximate the position of the curves. The closeness of the approximation is governed by the flatness setting in the current graphics state.

PAINTING OPERATORS

— stroke —

Paints a line following the current path and using the current color.

— fill —

Paints the area enclosed by the current path with the current color; clears the path.

dict

width height bits/sample matrix dataproc **image** —

Uses the *dataproc* to provide data to paint a sampled image onto the output page. The image is a rectangular array of *width* times *height* cells, where each cell contains *bits/sample* items of data. The sample image is taken to exist in its own coordinate system, with the origin at the lower-left corner of the sample, and the upper-right corner being at the point *(width, height)*. The *matrix* operand defines the transformation from user coordinates to image coordinates. The *dict* operand form is only available in Level 2 devices.

dict

width height boolean matrix dataproc **imagemask** —

Works like **image**, except that the data array created by the *dataproc* is used as a mask to apply the current color to the page. If *boolean* is *true*, data values of 1 are painted and values of 0 are ignored; if it is *false*, the reverse happens. The *dict* operand form is only available in Level 2 devices.

num **setlinewidth** —

Sets the current line width to *num*. This controls the thickness of the lines painted by subsequent **stroke** operators.

num **setgray** —

Sets the current color to a shade of gray corresponding to *num*. num must be between 0, corresponding to black, and 1, corresponding to white, with intermediate values corresponding to intermediate shades of gray.

integer **setlinecap** —

Sets the linecap (line ending) parameter of the current graphics state to *integer*. Possible values for *integer* are

0 for Butt caps (the default)

1 for Rounded caps

2 for Projecting square caps

integer **setlinejoin** —

Sets the line join parameter of the current graphics state to *integer*. Possible values for *integer* are

0 for Mitered join (the default)

1 for Rounded join

2 for Beveled join

array offset **setdash** —

Sets the dash pattern parameter in the current graphics state to *array*. An empty *array* produces a solid line (the default); if *array* is not empty, its elements specify the dash pattern for all subsequent line painting. The *offset* is the amount of the dash pattern that is processed before stoking the line.

boolean **setstrokeadjust** —

Performs stroke adjustment, if *boolean* is *true*, automatically whenever any subsequent **stroke** or equivalent operators are executed. If *boolean* is *false*, then stroke adjustment is not performed. This operator is only available in Level 2 devices.

— **currentstrokeadjust** boolean

Returns the current value, *boolean*, of the stroke adjustment parameter in the current graphics state. This operator is only available in Level 2 devices.

STACK OPERATORS

any1 any2 **exch** any2 any1

Exchanges the top two elements on the stack.

any **pop** —

Discards the top element.

any **dup** any any

Duplicates the top element; adds a copy to the top of the stack.

⊢ ... anyn **clear** ⊢

Empties the stack.

any_1 ... any_n int **copy** any_1 ... any_n any_1 ... any_n

Pops *int* and then duplicates the top int elements of the operand stack when the top element on the operand stack is a non-negative integer *int*.

any_n ... any_0 int **index** any_n ... any_0 any_{int}

Pops *int* and then duplicates the item on the stack that is *int* items from the top of the operand stack. The items on the stack are indexed with 0 as the top item on the stack. The operand *int* must be a non-negative integer between *0* and *n*, and there must be at least *int – 1* elements on the stack.

any_{n-1} ... any_0 n j **roll** $any_{(j-1) \bmod n}$ ... any_0 any_{n-1} ... $any_{j \bmod n}$

Performs a circular shift of the contents of the operand stack. The top *n* objects on the stack are shifted by amount *j*. A positive value of *j* indicates movement up the stack, that is, toward the top of the stack; a negative value indicates movement down the stack. The operand *n* must be a non-negative integer, and there must be at least *n* elements on the stack below the top two operands. The operand *j* must be an integer.

ARRAY AND STRING OPERATORS

int **array** array

Creates an *array* that initially contains *int* null objects as entries. *int* must be a non-negative integer less than the device-dependent maximum array length.

array **aload** $a_0..a_n$ array

Pushes successively all *n* elements of *array* onto the operand stack, where n is the number of elements in *array*, and finally pushes *array* itself.

int **string** string

Creates *string* that initially contains *int* null objects as entries. *int* must be a non-negative integer less than the device-dependent maximum string length.

array index

string index **get** any

Looks up the index in array or string and returns the element identified by index (counting from zero). The *index* must be between 0 and *n – 1*, where *n* is the number of elements in *array* or *string*.

array index count   subarray

string index count **getinterval** substring

Selects a segment of *array* or *string* and returns the selected segment as *subarray* or *substring*. The segment begins with the element identified by *index* (counting from zero), and extends for *count* elements.

There must be enough elements in *array* or *string* for correct operation; that is, the sum of *index* and *count* must be between 0 and *n* − *1*, where *n* is the number of elements in *array* or *string*. The *subarray* or *substring* that is returned shares its values with the original *array* or *string*. Any change to either one will change the other.

array index value

string index value **put** —

Stores *value* into *array* or *string* at the position identified by *index* (counting from zero). *index* must be in the range 0 to *n* − *1*, where *n* is the number of elements in *array* or *string*.

array

string **length** int

Returns *int* as the number array of elements that make up the value of *array* or *string*.

array1 array2   subarray2

string1 string2 **copy** substring2

Copies all elements of *array1* or *string1* into *array2* or *string2*. The types of the two operands must be the same, that is, array or string. The length of the second operand must be at least the length of the first; **copy** returns the changed elements of the second operand onto the stack as *subarray2* or *substring2*. If the second operand is longer than the first, the remaining values are unaffected by the **copy**.

if found:

string seek **search** post match pre true

if not found:

string seek **search** string false

Looks for the first time that the string *seek* occurs within *string* and returns the results of the search on the operand stack. The search is successful if there is any subset of *string* that exactly matches the string *seek*. If there is such a match, **search** divides the *string* into three pieces and pushes them onto the operand stack: *pre*, the portion of *string* preceding the match; *match*, the portion of *string* that is identical to *seek*; and *post*, the remainder of *string*. Each of these is pushed onto the operand stack in the order indicated, followed by the boolean value *true* to indicate that a match was found. If no part of *string* is found to match *seek*, the operator returns the original *string* on the operand stack and pushes the boolean value, *false*.

any string **cvs** substring

Converts object *any* to a string. *any* is changed from its current form to an appropriate string representation, and stored in the first section of *string*, which is overwritten. There must be enough room in *string* to hold the representation of *any*, or you will get an error.

DICTIONARY OPERATORS

int **dict** dict

Creates a dictionary *dict* with the initial capacity for *int* value pairs. In Level 1 devices, this is also the maximum number of pairs that can be contained in the dictionary.

dict **begin** —

Pushes *dict* onto the dictionary stack and makes it the current dictionary.

— **end** —

Pops the current dictionary from the dictionary stack.

key value **def** —

Associates *key* and *value* in the current dictionary.

dict **length** int

Returns *int* as the current number of key-value pairs in *dict*. (See also **maxlength**.)

dict **maxlength** int

Returns *int* as the maximum number of key-value pairs that *dict* can hold using the current amount of memory allocated to it. In Level 2 devices, this can increase as long as additional memory is available; in Level 1 devices, this is the absolute maximum number of entries, as defined by the **dict** operator that created *dict*.

dict key **get** any

Looks up the *key* in *dict* and returns the associated value. If *key* is not defined in *dict*, executes the error procedure **undefined**.

dict key value **put** —

Uses *key* and *value* and stores them as a key-value pair into *dict*. If *key* is already present in *dict*, its associated value is replaced by the new *value*; if it is not present, **put** creates a new entry.

dict1 dict2 **copy** dict2

Copies all elements of *dict1* into *dict2*. The **length** of *dict2* must be 0; that is, *dict2* must be empty when the **copy** takes places; **copy** returns the revised *dict2* onto the stack. *dict2* must have a **maxlength** that is at least as great as the **length** of *dict1*.

RELATIONAL OPERATORS

any1 any2 **eq** bool

Tests whether *any1* is equal to *any2*.

any1 any2 **ne** bool

Tests whether *any1* is not equal to *any2*.

num1   num2

(str1) (str2) **ge** bool

Tests whether *num1* or *str1* is greater than or equal to *num2* or *str2*.

num1   num2

(str1) (str2) **gt** bool

Tests whether *num1* or *str1* is greater than *num2* or *str2*.

num1   num2

(str1) (str2) **le** bool

Tests whether *num1* or *str1* is less than or equal to *num2* or *str2*.

num1   num2

(str1) (str2) **lt** bool

Tests whether *num1* or *str1* is less than *num2* or *str2*.

LOGICAL OPERATORS

int1   int2   int

bool1 bool2 **and** bool

Logical or bitwise *and*.

int1   int2   int

bool1 bool2 **or** bool

Logical or bitwise inclusive *or*.

int1   int2   int

bool1 bool2 **xor** bool

Logical or bitwise exclusive *or*.

int   int

bool **not** bool

Logical or bitwise *not*.

—   **true** bool

Pushes the boolean value *true* onto the stack.

—   **false** bool

Pushes the boolean value *false* onto the stack.

CONTROL OPERATORS

{proc} **exec** —

Executes *proc*.

int {proc} **repeat** —

Executes *proc int* times.

init incr lim {proc} **for** —

Executes *proc* for values from *init* by steps of *incr* until reaching *lim*.

dict

array proc

string proc **forall** —

Executes the *proc* procedure for every element of *dict*, array or *string*.
For *dict*, **forall** pushes the key, then the value for each element of

the dictionary; for other operands, it pushes each element from the array or string onto the stack. It then executes the procedure *proc*, which may access the element or elements on the stack. If the *proc* does not consume the items on the stack, it should remove them; although **forall** itself does not leave any object on the stack, if *proc* does not clear the stack before exiting, the elements of the operand will remain on the stack. In the case of *string*, the objects placed on the stack are the codes (numeric values) of the characters, not one-character strings.

bool {proc} **if** —

Executes *proc* if *bool* is true.

bool {proc1} {proc2} **ifelse** —

Executes *proc1* if *bool* is true; executes *proc2* otherwise.

{proc} **loop** —

Executes *proc* an indefinite number of times.

— **exit** —

Terminates the active loop.

TEXT OPERATORS

string **show** —

Paints the characters of *string* on the page at the current point.

string **stringwidth** wx wy

Calculates the width of *string* in current units in the x- and y-coordinate directions and returns these as *wx* and *wy*.

c_x c_y char string **widthshow** —

Prints the characters of *string* but adjusts the width of each occurrence of the character *char* in *string* by adding c_x to its x-dimension and c_y to its y-dimension, thereby adjusting the spacing between this character and the following character.

a_x a_y string **ashow** —

Prints the characters of *string* but adjusts the width of each occurrence of every character in *string* by adding a_x to its x-dimension and a_y to its y-dimension, thereby adjusting the spacing between all the characters.

c_x c_y char a_x a_y string **awidthshow** —

Prints the characters of *string* and performs two adjustments. It adjusts the width of each occurrence of every character in *string* by adding a_x to its x-dimension and a_y to its y-dimension, thereby adjusting the spacing between all the characters; and it adjusts the width of each occurrence of the character *char* in *string* by adding c_x to its x-dimension and c_y to its y-dimension, thereby adjusting the spacing between this character and the following character.

proc string **kshow** —

Prints the characters of *string* but allows the user to execute the procedure *proc* between each character of *string*. The operator shows each character of *string* in turn, adding the width of the character to the current point and then executing the procedure *proc*.

string numarray

string numstring **xyshow** —

Paints each successive character in *string* at the positions specified by the array *numarray* or the encoded number string *numstring*. Each character is painted in the same way that the **show** operator would paint the character. After the character is painted, **xyshow** takes two successive numbers from the operand, which are the relative location, in user coordinates, of the position of the next character to be displayed. The first number is the x-coordinate displacement and the second number is the y-coordinate displacement for the next character's origin relative to the current character's origin. The *numarray* or *numstring* operand must have at least as many pairs of values as there are characters in *string*; if there are not enough number pairs for all the characters in *string*, an error will occur.

string numarray

string numstring **xshow** —

Works in a manner similar to **xyshow**, except that only one number is taken from *numarray* or *numstring*. This number determines the x-coordinate displacement for the next character, while the y-coordinate displacement is taken as 0.

string numarray

string numstring **yshow** —

Works in a manner similar to **xyshow**, except that only one number is taken from *numarray* or *numstring*. This number determines the y-coordinate displacement for the next character, while the x-coordinate displacement is taken as 0.

FONT OPERATORS

name **findfont** font

Obtains a font dictionary specified by *name* and puts it onto the operand stack.

font scale **scalefont** newfont

Applies *scale* to *font* to create *newfont*, whose characters are enlarged in both the *x* and *y* directions by the given scaling factor when they are printed.

font **setfont** —

Establishes *font* as the font dictionary to be the current font for all subsequent character operators.

name scale **selectfont** —

Obtains a font dictionary specified by *name* and applies *scale* to it to create a new, scaled font dictionary, which is then established as the current font. Only available in Level 2 devices.

key font **definefont** font

Registers *font* as a font dictionary associated with *key*, which is usually a name literal. **definefont** also creates an additional entry in the dictionary, whose key is **FID** and whose value is an object of type fontID; *font* must be large enough to add this entry.

font matrix **makefont** newfont

Applies *matrix* to *font*, and produces *newfont* whose characters are transformed by the values in *matrix* when they are printed. The operator first creates a copy of *font*, then replaces the **FontMatrix** in the copy with the result of combining the original **FontMatrix** and *matrix*. The resulting *newfont* is returned to the stack.

COORDINATE
TRANSFORMATION OPERATORS

tx ty **translate** —

Moves the user-space origin (0,0) to a new position *(tx, ty)* with respect to the current page, while leaving the orientation of the axes and the unit length along each axis unchanged.

any **rotate** —

Turns the user-space axes about the current origin by *ang* degrees, leaving the origin and the unit length along each axis unchanged. Positive values measure counterclockwise.

sx sy **scale** —

Modifies the unit lengths independently along the current x and y axes, leaving the origin and the orientation of the axes unchanged. One new unit is equal to *sx* units in the x direction and *sy* units in the y direction.

matrix **concat** —

Concatenates the *matrix* operand with the current transformation matrix (CTM) to create a new CTM. The new CTM is placed into operation immediately, with the effect that the user coordinate system is transformed by the values in *matrix*.

ux uy **transform** dx dy

Transforms the user space coordinates, *ux* and *uy*, into the equivalent device coordinates, *dx* and *dy*, using the current transformation matrix (CTM).

dx dy **itransform** ux uy

Transforms the device coordinates, *dx* and *dy*, into the equivalent user coordinates, *ux* and *uy*, using the inverse of the current transformation matrix.

MANAGEMENT OPERATORS

— **save** savestate

Saves the current state of PostScript virtual memory as *savestate*.

savestate **restore** —

Restores PostScript virtual memory to the state represented by *savestate*.

dict key **undef** —

Removes *key* and its associated value from the dictionary, *dict*.

key **undefinefont** —

Removes *key*, which is a font name literal, and its associated value, which is a font dictionary, from the font directory.

— **gsave** —

Saves a copy of the current graphics state on the graphics state stack.

— **grestore** —

Resets the graphics state by restoring the state on the top of the graphics state stack.

— **gstate** gstate

Makes a new, empty *gstate* object and saves it on the operand stack.

gstate **currentgstate** gstate

Enters the current graphics state parameters into the *gstate* operand and returns that state.

gstate **setgstate** —

Sets the graphics state to the values contained in the *gstate* operand.

OUTPUT OPERATORS

— copypage —

Prints out the current page onto the output device, and retains a copy of the current page and all current settings.

— showpage —

Prints a copy of the current page onto the output device and clears the page.

INTERACTIVE OPERATORS

any = = —

Shows the top element of the stack and removes it.

⊢ ... anyn **pstack** ⊢ ... anyn

Shows the entire contents of the stack, but does not remove any element.

— quit —

Ends the operation of the PostScript interpreter.

B

Encapsulated PostScript

Encapsulated PostScript is a PostScript file that has a special structure. This structure was designed to allow other programs, particularly application programs that produce PostScript output, to view a PostScript graphic and manipulate it in certain limited ways. This structure is well documented, and a full description is available from Adobe Systems, the creator of PostScript. In the following discussion, let's call the program or person that creates the Encapsulated PostScript file the *source* and the application that uses the file the *destination*; Encapsulated PostScript files are generally abbreviated as EPS files and that shorthand will be used here.

As the name implies, EPS files are intended to be used as separate "capsules" of graphics. They do not interact in most ways with the rest of the destination application's output. The significant deviations from this are the ability of the destination application to position the graphic on a page at any point, and to crop, scale, or rotate the graphic as required for correct placement and viewing on the output page. It is the destination application's responsibility to create the necessary changes in the output environment to insure that this occurs correctly, and to restore the original environment when it's done.

Generally, those file formats that contain preview graphics (EPS files) cannot be edited with a simple text editor the way simple PostScript text files can be. This is because they have the graphic image embedded within them. However, applications that understand the format (such as Lasertalk, which is discussed in Appendix C) can edit the PostScript portion of the EPS file with standard text-editing techniques; that portion of the file is identical in all the output formats.

The destination program cannot redefine any details of the image. It can only transform the image like a distorting mirror in a fun house, expanding or contracting each dimension as requested; or it can crop the image as you might crop a photograph. Destination applications can make these changes because they can interpret certain information about size and shape that is provided by the EPS file format. They don't have to "understand" the PostScript code itself; that is, the destination application does not use the PostScript code to generate the screen image, nor does it interpret the PostScript code that goes with this image. It takes the essential identity of the code and image for granted.

The exchange of graphic information between the source application, like Adobe Illustrator, and the destination application, like PageMaker, is quite simple from the user's point of view. You can easily insert EPS graphics into another application. Furthermore, the placement and transformation of such imported graphics within the destination application are always limited to a fairly basic set of options. Therefore, the role and work of each application is quite well-defined. To get the maximum productivity out of these graphic tools, you need to understand which application performs which functions.

EPS FILE FORMAT

The EPS file format consists of two distinct parts. The first contains the PostScript program created by the source that will generate the desired image on the output device. The second part, which is not required, contains a bit-mapped image of the resulting graphic. The bit-mapped image is used by the destination application for display purposes. The PostScript program follows a rigid structure, which also allows the destination application to translate, rotate and scale the image as required for the new output that it is developing.

This section of the appendix discusses the exact nature of the format of each of these component parts of an EPS file. The PostScript structural requirements are described first, because these are the essential ingredients of an EPS file. The graphic attachment and its relationship to the display is discussed next.

Special PostScript Structure

The EPS file format requires that the PostScript portion of the standard file follow the structuring conventions. However, several of the comments that are part of the 3.0 structure take on new meaning and importance in EPS files. There is also some additional structural information that is very valuable in an EPS file.

Required Header Comments

As is true for all conforming PostScript files, an EPS file must have a correctly formed version comment as the first line of the header. This takes the following form:

```
%!PS–Adobe–3.0 EPSF-3.0
```

where the version numbers may be replaced by any later version number of the EPSF format that is being followed.

This comment indicates to the destination application that the file conforms to both the structuring conventions generally and to the EPSF format conventions in particular. The structure version number is given following the word "Adobe," and the EPSF version number follows "EPSF." This comment also indicates to a destination application that the file is intended for EPSF use; without it, the destination application may reject the file or may not display the graphic information correctly.

Another required comment in the EPS file header specifies the area on the page that is included in the image produced by the PostScript program and represented by the graphic information. It takes the following form:

%%BoundingBox: llx lly urx ury

where the coordinates *llx, lly* are the position of the lower-left corner of the image in the default PostScript coordinates, and *urx, ury* are the position of the upper-right corner. These two corners are sufficient to define the entire box, which, as the name %%**BoundingBox:** implies, completely encloses the graphic image being produced. As you will see later in the Appendix, this bounding box information is the essential ingredient for placement and adjustment of the EPS graphic. If this comment is not present, the destination application may issue an error message and refuse to import the file.

Other Header Information

The following additional comments are not required but are very useful. In particular, if an application cannot access the bit-mapped graphic in an EPS file or does not recognize the precise file format, many destination applications will use the information provided in these comments to produce a text-identification block instead of the bit-mapped graphic.

%%Creator: name

%%Title: file name

%%CreationDate: date and time

These comments provide human-readable character data but should contain the information suggested by the comment name, although there is no specific format requirement for the data.

The following comment explicitly terminates the header comments and is useful for destination applications that are examining the structure of the file:

%%EndComments

Other Optional Comments

The EPS file format may also contain the following types of comments which may help some destination applications provide the required resources for the EPS graphic. We will briefly review each of them and their place in an EPS file.

If the EPS file has any text information, it will require one or more fonts. To enable the destination application to correctly integrate the EPS graphic and control the font handling for the entire output document, the following resource-management comments are useful.

The first comment lists all fonts that are both required and included in the EPS file. It looks like this:

%%DocumentSuppliedResources: font fontname1

The following comment lists all the fonts that are required by the EPS file and are not provided within the EPS file itself:

%%DocumentNeededResources: font fontname2 fontname3 ...

For each font (or other resource) listed in the above comment, there should be one instance of an **%%IncludeResource** comment to indicate that the specified resource must be made available for processing at this point in the file:

%%IncludeResource: font fontname2

The font may be downloaded at this point, or it may be a font that is globally available during the job, for example, because it is a font that is in ROM on the output device.

In addition to fonts, the EPS file may require other resources, such as procedure sets or files.

EPS files that conform to earlier versions of the structuring conventions may use different comments to provide fonts and other resources. In earlier versions, each type of resource had its own comment, so that fonts would be called out with a series of comments like the following:

%%DocumentFonts: fontname1 fontname2

%%DocumentIncludedFont: fontname1

%%DocumentRequiredFont: fontname2

. . . additional header and program data . . .

%%IncludeFont: fontname1

As you can see, these are identical to the resource comments described above, and have the same use. The one difference is the **%%DocumentFonts:** comment, which lists all fonts used in the document whether they are included in the file or not. If you combine the font names from the **%%DocumentIncludedFonts:** comment and those from the **%%DocumentRequired-Fonts:** comment, they will be exactly the same as the list provided for the **%%DocumentFonts:** comment. All of these comments are no longer recommended for use; if you are preparing EPS output, use the newer forms.

In addition, any EPS file that uses extended PostScript operators, such as color or composite font extensions, or uses Level 2 operators without providing emulations for them, should use the two comments **%%Extensions:** and **%%LanguageLevel:** to indicate that fact. This allows an application either to provide its own emulations for the required operators—as you might do for color operators, for example—or to notify the user of this file's special requirements, or to include these requirements in its own header file, or some appropriate combination of these.

Restricted Operators

In addition to having the required structural comments, the EPS format requires that the PostScript code contained within the file follow certain rules and limitations regarding operator usage. The operators in Table B.1 are not to be used within EPS files, and generally should not be used or should be used with care in any PostScript document that conforms to the 3.0 structuring conventions.

Table B.1: Operators Not To Be Used in EPS Files

banddevice	**clear**	**cleardictstack**
copypage	**erasepage**	**exitserver**
framedevice	**grestoreall**	**initclip**
initgraphics	**initmatrix**	**quit**
renderbands	**setglobal** *	**setpagedevice** *
setshared *	**startjob** *	
statusdict *all*	**userdict**	
operators	*imageable area*	
	operators	

* operator only available in Level 2 devices

The **statusdict** is a special, device-dependent dictionary used in Level 1 devices for device-dependent operations. It should generally never be referred to directly by any EPS page description. Also, **userdict** contains several operators that can be used to set page size and other features of the device that affect the actual imageable area that is available on the device. They should never be used in EPS page descriptions.

In addition, the following operators should be used only with great care and under well-defined circumstances.

nulldevice	**setgstate**	**sethalftone**
setmatrix	**setscreen**	**settransfer**
undefinefont		

(The **setgstate**, **sethalftone**, and **undefinefont** operators are only available in Level 2.) Review the operator discussion in "Appendix I: Guidelines for Specific Operators" in the *PostScript Language Reference Manual, Second Edition* for further information.

The restriction on use of most of these operators is quite easy to understand; they either modify the full page image that is being created in raster memory (**erasepage** or **copypage**) or they become device-dependent or they modify the current graphics state in such a way that the effects may prevent inclusion of the graphic within another PostScript page.

The **showpage** operator is also a problem for EPS files. Because it often exists within a file, it is not included in the list above; however, use of **showpage** within an EPS file will certainly cause all the problems that **copypage** or **erasepage** will. In this instance only, it is the destination application's responsibility to disable **showpage** to protect against any surprises, rather than the source application's responsibility to avoid using the operator. In order to do that, the source application must have properly used **showpage** after a **restore** so that the destination application can control the output without damaging the page processing.

Good PostScript Code Practice

In addition to avoiding the operators listed above, and disabling the **showpage** operator, there are some good coding practices that should be maintained by an EPS file. First, all stacks must be returned to their original condition; no new information should be left on any stack after execution of the EPS file. This is essential so that the **save** and **restore** that bracket the EPS file will work correctly. Second, no global string should be changed. Doing so might affect the subsequent processing without warning. The recommended way to ensure against changing a global string is for the EPS file to create and use its own dictionaries, being sure to pop them off the dictionary stack when processing is finished by using the **end** operator. Finally, if any special dictionary is required for processing, or if any fonts require reencoding for the EPS file to execute properly, these resources should be provided for within the EPS file itself, and not presumed to be available.

BIT-MAPPED GRAPHIC FOR SCREEN DISPLAY

In addition to the PostScript code, EPS files may contain a bit-mapped image to be used by the destination application for screen display. The image is stored along with the PostScript file in a format that can be easily used by the destination application.

There are three forms of EPS files because of this potential to provide a bit-mapped image. Since the IBM and the Macintosh have quite different approaches to screen graphics, source applications must provide two separate file types to generate the required screen graphic and link it correctly to the PostScript output. The IBM format of EPS files may use either the Aldus/ Microsoft TIFF graphic format or the MetaFile format for Windows to store the image, and any destination application that wishes to display the image must be able to read these formats. In addition, there is a special, device-independent screen preview mechanism, called EPSI, which is designed to allow EPS files to be interchanged freely among a wide variety of systems.

The Macintosh version of an EPS file contains a standard Macintosh QuickDraw PICT format graphic as the screen display portion of the file that is stored in the resource fork. The PICT resource number must be 256. For the IBM format, the EPS file contains a binary header which specifies the location of the screen data and the location of the PostScript file. The file must begin with the hexadecimal character string 0xC5D0D3C6. This allows an importing application to test the first four characters to determine the nature of the file. If these match the string above, then the file is an EPS file with binary preview data; if the first two are %!, then the EPS file is simple PostScript and does not contain any screen data.

The encapsulated PostScript interchange (EPSI) format is intended to go beyond device- or system-dependent display formats. It is a straight PostScript file with a standard screen representation of the image built into it. In this case, the screen representation is defined by structural comments in the PostScript file itself; as a result, the destination application requires no special code for decompressing or otherwise displaying the image, other than an ability to read and display hexadecimal data. The screen image in an EPSI file is placed within two structural comments, as follows:

```
%%BeginPreview: width height depth lines

. . .hexadecimal screen data goes here . . .

%%EndPreview
```

The data supplied to the %%**BeginPreview:** comment is similar to that used by the **image** operator. The *width* and *height* are the number of pixels that define the image; the *depth* is the number of bits per pixel. The *lines* is the number of actual lines of data that are contained in the preview. This is provided as a convenience for any application that is not prepared to display the screen image, which can simply skip that many lines of input. The data in the screen image is presented in the same coordinate system used by the **image** operator: bottom, left to top, right. The preview section of a document, if present, must appear after the header section, immediately following the %%**EndComments** comment, and before the prolog.

In all formats of EPS files, the bit-mapped images are not intended for final output; they are provided as an aid for page makeup and graphic placement within the destination application. The intention is for the final output to use the PostScript definitions of the graphic while the bit-mapped image is ignored.

The exact format, creation, and use of these bit-mapped images is beyond the scope of this appendix; however, more complete documentation is available from Adobe System developer support at the address given in Appendix D.

Remember that the inclusion of the bit-mapped image is not required for an EPS file. It is quite optional and, as long as you have structured your PostScript correctly, you can create and import EPS graphics without worrying about the bit-mapped image.

DISPLAYING EPS FILES

When you display an EPS file by using the destination application facilities, you should have no problem including the EPS graphic, displaying it on the screen, or printing it. However, you may want to display an EPS file independently of any particular destination application, or, infrequently, the destination application may fail to handle the EPS file correctly. In these cases, you can print an EPS file yourself.

The basic requirements for printing an EPS file are quite straightforward. First of all, if you have an EPSI or IBM-format image, you must remove the screen preview data from the file and reduce it to standard PostScript (this is not necessary in the Macintosh as the screen preview is in the resource fork of the file). Then you must provide three things to display an EPS file: a **showpage** (if one is missing), positioning information for the graphic image, and a proper context for execution. In addition, you may wish to modify the image—by transformation, rotation, or cropping—in some of the same ways that a destination application could.

An EPS file is designed to be included as a unit into a page generated by another PostScript program. That means that the source of the EPS file expects you to take the entire PostScript output from the EPS file and include it with some other PostScript code. In order to do that successfully, or to print the file by itself, you need to define where on the page you want to place the EPS graphic, what coordinates it uses, and what size you want it to be. The first two issues must always be addressed; the second need only be taken care of if you don't want to use your graphic at the same size you created it.

Page Setup

All these issues can be taken care of by two PostScript operators. The first is the **translate**, which can be used to both position the graphic on the new output page and to adjust the coordinates, if required. The second is a **scale** operator, which sets the size of the graphic on the new page. In all cases, you also need to do some housekeeping to insure that the EPS file does not interfere with your work in the process of generating the output to be included on the page. This is done by using paired **save** and **restore** operators.

The first change that you have to make is to correct for the default coordinates used in the EPS file. Without any adjustment, there is a good chance that the EPS graphic will be drawn off of the normal output, and you won't be able to see it. Furthermore, you cannot rely on the fact that the EPS file uses the default page origin. Because the origin of a PostScript page can be moved to any arbitrary location, you need to have an adjustment mechanism that allows you to readjust the coordinates independently of the default settings.

The necessary adjustment can be made by using the information provided by the %%**BoundingBox:** comment. You will remember that this comment is followed by four numbers that represent, in the default user coordinates, the lower-left and upper-right corners, respectively, of the graphic that will actually be created by the EPS file. In particular, the x and y coordinates of each of these corners provides the necessary information for positioning and adjusting the coordinate system on the output page.

The first requirement is to move the graphic origin to the new origin. This can be done most easily, conceptually, by doing a **translate** that adjusts the current origin to the new origin, and then a **translate** again to move the graphic to the new position that you want.

If you want to move the output graphic so that its lower-left corner is at the new position (nx, ny), you would use the following PostScript command:

```
nx ny translate
```

This moves the origin of the page to the point you want.

After you have positioned the origin for the new graphic at (0, 0), it is quite straightforward to make any adjustment to the coordinates that you need to make in order to size or rotate the graphic and then to place it on the new output page by using another **translate**. To do that, you would follow the command above with the command

llx neg lly neg translate

This readjusts the coordinates for the output to a position that is − llx and − lly, since the **neg** operator just reverses the sign of the given number. That will mean that the EPS graphic will begin at the point (llx − llx) and (lly − lly), or (0, 0) since subtracting something from itself will always result in zero. Once the origin of the graphic is translated to (0, 0) the coordinates on the EPS page will map correctly into those of the output page.

Although the order in which you issue **translate** commands is irrelevant to the PostScript interpreter, I would strongly recommend that you do them in the order presented here. If you want to scale or rotate the graphic, you must do that before you move the graphic to the new origin; otherwise, you will not place the image correctly. The order presented here always works, whereas reversing the order does not.

Scaling the Image

Another change that you may want to make to your EPS output is to scale it to fit on a defined space in the new page output. This also can be done with the help of the %%**BoundingBox:** information. In this case, you want to adjust the height and width of the existing output to fit into some new space.

Suppose that the new space to be filled has a width of w and a height of h. Then scaling the EPS graphic to this window means simply that the width of the graphic must be scaled to w and the height, in similar fashion, scaled to h. For example, if the window that you wanted to fit were 1 unit by 1 unit, and the graphic was 2 by 4, you would have to scale the graphic by 1 divided by 2 in width and 1 divided by 4 in height.

This is the general approach for scaling a graphic: the new dimension divided by the old dimension is the scale factor for that coordinate. Thus you see that the width of the graphic is determined by subtracting the two x coordinates from one another, and the height by subtracting the two y coordinates. Therefore, the scale factor for width will be $w / (urx - llx)$ and for height it will be *h / (ury − lly)*. You can use the same method to compute the width and height of the new window as you use to compute the width and height of the EPS graphic: by subtracting the *x* and *y* coordinates of the lower-left and upper-right corners. Using this technique with a new window whose coordinates for those points are given by (nlx, nly) and (nux, nuy), the PostScript commands for the scaling operation are as follows.

```
nux nlx sub     %calculate the width of new window

urx llx sub     %calculate width of graphic

div             %use two results on stack for ratio

                %and leave result on stack

nuy nly sub     %calculate the height of the new window

ury lly sub     %calculate height of graphic

div             %use two results on stack for ratio

                %now both x and y scale are on stack

scale %so issue scale command
```

This can be compressed into one or two lines of PostScript code, but I expanded it here to help you see all the operations and the stack results more clearly.

Execution Context

The last item that you have to set up to display an EPS graphic is a correct execution context. This means setting certain graphics state parameters, protecting against badly behaved EPS files, and inserting the necessary structural comments.

The EPS file has a right to assume that certain graphics state parameters, such as line join, line cap, and so on, are in the default state when it begins processing. Since these items are usually changed only for some specific purpose, making this assumption allows the EPS file to avoid resetting items that usually don't need to be set. If you are providing a context for the EPS file therefore, you should reset these items if they are not still in the default state. For the sake of the example, the code below assumes that all of these parameters need to be reset.

Although an EPS file is supposed to leave all stacks in the same condition that they were when it began execution, some EPS files do not. If you try to display such a file, you will most likely have a PostScript error, unless you protect your code against this possibility. To do so, you can simply use some standard PostScript operators to count the dictionary and operand stacks and clear off any excess items that the EPS file might leave behind. At the same time, you can disable the **showpage** operator, as mentioned earlier, to avoid having the EPS file print the page prematurely.

The following code can be used to start displaying your EPS file within a standard graphics state:

```
/Save_EPS save def          %1 save state before EPS

/DictNum countdictstack def %2 count dictionary elements

count array                 %3 save & clear operand stack

astore /OpStack exch def

userdict begin              %4 place userdict on top

/showpage {} def            %5 redefine showpage to null

                            %6 now set default graphics state
values

0 setgray                   % black

0 setlinecap                % butt caps

0 setlinejoin               % mitered joins

10 setmiterlimit            % standard miter limit

[ ] 0 setdash               % solid lines

/languagelevel where        %7 if this is Level 2

{
        pop
        languagelevel 1 gt
        {
                false setstrokeadjust %no stroke adjustment
                false setoverprint    %no overprinting
```

```
                }
                if
         }
         if

         newpath%8 start a new path
```

Most of this code is quite familiar to you at this point. Let's just look at it and discuss the few new issues that are presented here. Line %1 saves the current state so that the EPS file doesn't alter your own drawing environment. In line %2, you save the count of the dictionary stack so that you can ensure that the EPS file doesn't leave any additional items on that. On line %3, you do something similar for the operand stack. Here, you create a new array object and store all of the items currently on the stack in that array; then you save the array in your current dictionary. This has the effect of clearing the operand stack for the EPS file, which can be important, since the operand stack has a large, but finite, limit. If the EPS file expects to use all of the stack and you have used some of the items, the EPS file may fail unexpectedly. Note that the **count** operator must be executed before you place the name for the variable on the operand stack; otherwise, the count would include the new name literal and be one larger than you want. Line %4 pushes *user-dict* onto the top of the dictionary stack. This is necessary in case the EPS file is ill-behaved and doesn't define its own working dictionary for storing variables. If it tries to store data into your dictionary, it may damage the data there or cause an overflow, which would create a PostScript error. For that reason, you protect your code by putting *userdict* on top of the stack. Line %5 refines **showpage**—in *userdict*—as a null procedure. Now, if the EPS file executes **showpage**, nothing will happen. Beginning with line %6, the next six lines reset graphics state parameters to standard values for the EPS file. As part of this, line %7 tests for Level 2, in the familiar way, and then sets two more graphics state parameters, *stroke adjust* and *overprint*. Finally, line %8 removes any previous path components and starts a new path.

In addition to these steps, the destination application should clip the EPS graphic to the desired window, so that no stray marks extend outside of that area. Since you have to rely on the bounding box, which may not be accurate, it is important to protect your file against any possible errors in the EPS code. Once you have set up the coordinates for the EPS file, you can easily clip to the desired box by using the bounding-box coordinates as the corners of a standard rectangle, and then issuing a **clip** command for that path.

When you are finished processing the EPS file, you have some cleaning up to do if you have used this type of code for setup. That can be done with the following code:

```
count {pop} repeat      %1 clean operand stack

OpStack aload pop       %  and restore old contents

countdictstack DictNum sub

    {end} repeat        %2 clean dict stack

SaveEPS restore         %3 back to original state
```

Line %1 in this code removes any additional operands from the operand stack and restores the previous contents. This means that, if the EPS file is badly-behaved and left items on the stack, you will remove them now to avoid problems when you do the **restore** on line %3. Line %2 does the same thing for the dictionary stack. Note that this line automatically removes the *userdict* that you inserted onto the dictionary stack earlier, since you originally counted the dictionaries on the stack before you pushed *userdict*. Finally, line %3 returns everything else to the original state. This restores all the graphics state parameters to whatever they were—so you don't have to reset anything—and recovers all the virtual memory used by the EPS file.

Demonstration Code for EPS Display

The following code demonstrates the techniques described in this section. It takes a generic EPS file titled (EPSF test art) and rescales, translates, and displays it within a new file titled (EPSF enclosure example). The EPS file is represented by the following code:

```
%!PS–Adobe–3.0 EPSF-3.0

%%Creator: AnyApplication

%%Title: (EPSF test art)

%%CreationDate: 25/01/92 10:14 AM

%%BoundingBox: – 100  – 80 100 120

%%Pages: 1
```

```
%%EndComments
```

. . . rest of the illustration file goes here . . .

```
showpage
%%Trailer
```

. . .any cleanup PostScript code . . .

```
%%EOF
```

The EPS file is to be displayed in the window with a bounding box of (277, 342) to (427 492). Note that this is three-quarters the size of the original artwork. The full display file would then look something like this, using all the techniques that we have already discussed:

```
%!PS–Adobe–3.0
%%Creator: David Holzgang
%%Title: (EPSF enclosure example)
%%CreationDate: 27/01/92 11:42 AM
%%BoundingBox: 0 0 612 792
%%Pages: 1
%%DocumentRequiredResources: font Times-Roman
%% + font Courier
%% + procset MyApp 1.0 0
%%EndComments
%%BeginProlog
%%IncludeResource: procset MyApp 1.0 0
/EPSDict 10 dict def
EPSDict begin
/startEPS
{
        /Save_EPS save def
```

```
/DictNum countdictstack def
count array astore /OpStack exch def
userdict begin
/showpage { } def
        %now set default graphics state values
0 setgray
0 setlinecap
0 setlinejoin
10 setmiterlimit
[ ] 0 setdash
/languagelevel where
    {
        pop
        languagelevel 1 gt
        {
            false setstrokeadjust
            false setoverprint
        }
        if
    }
    if
    newpath
}
bind def
/endEPS
{
    count {pop} repeat
```

```
        OpStack aload pop
        countdictstack DictNum sub
              {end} repeat
        SaveEPS restore
}
bind def
/rectclip
{
        4 2 roll moveto
        1 index 0 rlineto
        0 exch rlineto
        neg 0 rlineto
        closepath
        clip
}
bind def
end    %EPSDict
        %%EndProlog
        %%BeginSetup
        %%IncludeResource: font Times-Roman
        %%IncludeResource: font Courier
        MyAppDict begin
        %%EndSetup
        %%Page: 1 1
        %%BeginPageSetup
/PG_save save def
        %%EndPageSetup
```

```
    . . . code that generates some page output . . .
        %insert an EPS file
EPSDict begin
startEPS
277 342 translate          % reset origin for new graphic
        % now scale graphic to fit new box on page
        %  with coordinates 277 342 427 492
        %  as discussed in the text
277 427 sub                % calculate ratio of new x width
 − 100 100 sub             % to old x width
div
342 492 sub                % and ratio of new y width
 − 80 120 sub              % to old y width
div
scale                      % and scale to those dimensions
 − 100 neg -80 neg translate %move graphic to new origin
 − 100 -80 100 120 rectclip   %clip to window
newpath                    %remove clip path
        %insert actual EPS file (in its entirety) here
%%BeginDocument: (EPSF test art)
%!PS−Adobe−3.0 EPSF-3.0
%%Creator: AnyApplication
%%Title: (EPSF test art)
%%CreationDate: 25/01/92 10:14 AM
%%BoundingBox: − 100 − 80 100 120
%%Pages: 1
```

```
%%EndComments

. . . rest of illustration file goes here . . .

showpage

%%Trailer

. . .any clean up PostScript code . . .

%%EOF

%%EndDocument

endEPS

end        %EPSDict

. . .possibly more code here for additional graphics on this page . . .

PG_save restore

showpage

%%Trailer

end        %MyAppDict

%%EOF
```

This shows you how to turn the code that we discussed earlier into a series of procedures that you use to setup for the EPS display. As you see, the setup is done with the **startEPS** procedure, while the clipping path is set by the **rectclip** procedure. The translation and scaling are handled by inline code; note, however, that you could make this into several procedures if you wanted. I simply think that inline code for this work is clearer than using procedures. In any case, once you are set up, the complete EPS file is inserted between **%%BeginDocument:** and **%%EndDocument** comments. When the EPS file is completely processed, the **endEPS** procedure cleans up the state of the document. The only missing piece here is the procedure set **MyApp**. The code assumes that **MyApp** is an external procset that is either already loaded into the printer or will be included by a document manager into the final file at the **%%IncludeResource: procset** comment. This procset uses a dictionary, **MyAppDict**, which is not otherwise defined in this code. Other than that, this code is very similar to what you have done in the body of the book and should present no problems.

Other Transformations

You can use the same technique that you saw used above for the **scale** operation in order to perform more advanced transformations on EPS graphics. You can rotate the graphic image by using the **rotate** and **translate** operators in sequence, as you did earlier in the book to generate the landscape mode. You can also expand the use of the **clip** operator to crop the image to a particular size if you don't want the entire image to display.

CREATING EPS FILES

Basically, any correctly structured PostScript program can be used as an EPS file. The essential ingredients are, as you have seen, the bounding-box information and the structural comments. It is not essential, although it is useful, to have the bit-mapped image attached to the file.

There is no simple way to include your own bit-mapped image in an EPS file for transfer. If your bounding-box information and other header comments are in place, most destination applications will at least show you the bounding-box rectangle and include within it or next to it the text information from the header comments. This actually works fairly well for many purposes.

This section will briefly review the requirements for an EPS file and provide some general comments and guidance that you can adapt for your programs.

Header Information Example

The required header information is explained above. A good example, in addition to the example above, is a typical header from an Illustrator file, as follows:

```
%!PS–Adobe–3.0 EPSF-3.0

%%Creator: Adobe Illustrator 3.2(TM)

%%For: (David Holzgang) (SYBEX)

%%Title: (EPSF test art2)
```

%%CreationDate: (6/1/92) (6:20 AM)

%%BoundingBox: 103 352 277 608

The easiest way to access and use this information, in my experience, is to create it as a separate file and then just include it, with a program editor, at the beginning of your PostScript program.

Bounding-Box Information

Obviously, the most difficult part of this is the bounding-box information. Unfortunately, there is no easy answer for this. There are several points to mention here. First of all, don't assume that the coordinates of the path that you create are the actual bounding box. Remember that the bounding box includes all marks on the page; that means that you must allow for the width of a line stroke. For example, if you have a rectangle from (100, 100) to (200, 200) and you stroke that path with a line width of two points, then the bounding box will be (99, 99) to (201, 201), since the line will be painted one point on each side of the path. You also probably know the lower-left corner of your image on the page, but getting the upper-right one can be tricky. It is easiest if you have some help, like the Lasertalk programming environment, where you can see the image on the printer along with coordinates. Before I had that facility, I would use both physical rulers (typesetter's rulers are great, because they have point measures that more or less correspond to the PostScript coordinates) and print special index marks on a sample page. Both work but are time-consuming.

However, you want to make your best effort at calculating the bounding-box correctly. If your box is too small, you are likely to lose some of the image, because, as you saw in the code example above, the destination application is likely to clip the actual image to the bounding box. On the other hand, if you are too large, your placement on the output page may be faulty, since the destination application will scale the entire area to the bounding box you define. But if you have to guess, make it too big rather than too small.

C

Configuration Data and Setup

THIS APPENDIX CONTAINS THE
two sample configurations that were used to create and execute the
examples in this book. The purpose of these samples is to provide you with
two working models of actual configurations that can communicate with a
PostScript printer and will run in the interactive mode. These should function as both examples and as a mechanism for you to review in case you have
problems getting your own configuration to run correctly.

There are two example configurations described in this appendix: one
for an IBM-PC, and the other for an Apple Macintosh. Between them, they
represent probably 95 percent of the basic configurations that are likely to
be used by readers of this book. However, this is not a limitation. Any computer that supports communication through an RS-232 port can be used to
communicate with most PostScript devices, certainly with any Apple
LaserWriter or compatible printer.

The selection of hardware and software listed here should not be taken
as a recommendation. The various elements were simply what I had available to do the tasks that needed to be done to communicate between the
computer and the printer and to create and run the exercises.

The configurations that are presented here are by no means unique.
Multiple configurations could be used to achieve the same results. I have
tried to describe the configurations used in some detail, so that they may
provide some guidance for you if you have some problem or difficultly in
making your configuration work. Many specifics of these two
configurations—memory size, features available, and so on—should not be
taken as limitations; they only are presented as examples of working configurations. So if your configuration differs from one or the other of mine,
don't try to match what is listed here; first try out what you have, and only
modify it if it won't work.

Most of the initial development of exercises and examples for the first
edition of this book was done on an IBM-PC clone, and continuing development for the later editions has been done on an Apple Macintosh. All of the
examples have been run in both the IBM and Macintosh systems, and you
should have no trouble with either one you choose.

IBM PERSONAL COMPUTER

I have found an MS-DOS computer to be quite convenient and respon-
sive for performing these tasks. It is not hard to set up, either for interactive

or batch processing. The Apple LaserWriter manual provides some important information on how to connect and run the printer from any MS-DOS or compatible computer in "Appendix C: Connecting to and Printing With an MS-DOS Computer." In addition, the *Apple LaserWriter Reference* contains a long section, titled "Accessing the LaserWriter Directly," which describes in detail how to connect any computer to the various LaserWriter models for interactive processing.

Configuration: Hardware

Hardware in this configuration is as follows:

IBM-PC 386 (clone)

>   40 Megabyte hard disk
>
>   2 Megabyte memory
>
>   1 serial port(COM1:)
>
>   1 parallel port (LPT1:)

>   Apple LaserWriter II
>
>   1 Megabyte RAM

The two devices are connected by a standard 25-pin, RS-232 cable with a "null modem" pin assignment. That means that pins 2 and 3 (at the printer end) are reversed at the computer, so that pin 2 at the printer is connected to pin 3 at the computer, and pin 3 at the printer is connected to pin 2 at the computer. This reverses the data signals, and is required because both devices would otherwise try to send and receive data over the same wire.

The Apple Laserwriter communication switches are set for 9600 baud. Consult Appendix C of your LaserWriter manual for more information on how to use and set this switch.

Configuration: Software

There are two important pieces of software that you will require in order to create and run exercises on the LaserWriter: a communications program and an editor. The communications program makes your PC behave like a terminal, sending data down the communications line to the printer. The editor provides a means to create batch jobs to send to the printer, and may also be necessary to modify disk output from applications into a valid format for the PostScript interpreter.

The communications software that I used was PC-TALK IV. This is an excellent, inexpensive communications program that can be obtained from several bulletin boards and other sources. Since you need only the most rudimentary communications support for this work, you don't need anything more than basic support. Any communications package will allow you to set up communication with your PostScript printer.

The editor that I used was Brief. This is an excellent text editor, primarily intended for programming use. Any editor that you can use to prepare programs will work just as well. Most word-processing programs can also be used for preparing PostScript programs; just be sure that you save the file as simple ASCII text. For some programs, such as WordPerfect, this involves converting your saved file with a second program.

The communications with the LaserWriter are set up as follows:

1. Execute a batch file similar to the following, which sets the mode on the communications port and starts up the communications program.

   ```
   echo off
   mode com1:9600,n,8,1,p
   PC-TALK
   cd c:\
   cls
   ```

2. Enter the communications program dialing menu, and (the first time) create a new entry with the correct communications parameters: 9600 baud, 8 data bits, no parity, 1 stop bit, no echo. Do not enter any telephone number. All other settings were allowed to default.

3. Remove all modem commands from the menu item that you created to access the LaserWriter. These are usually commands that begin with the letters ATDT. Replace them with the "executive" (all lowercase letters) command.

4. "Dial" the entry. I put quotes around that because the communications package doesn't actually issue any dialing commands; it simply opens the COM1: port and sends the string "executive" down the line. This will start the interactive mode on the LaserWriter.

Then you would proceed with the steps outlined in Chapter 1 to complete the connection to the LaserWriter, and begin interactive operations.

APPLE MACINTOSH

There are two ways to send and receive data from a LaserWriter on a Macintosh. One way, which is the one most talked about in the LaserWriter documentation, is through an AppleTalk network. This is fairly straightforward from a user's viewpoint—you just purchase an AppleTalk kit from your Apple dealer, connect the LaserWriter and the Macintosh as instructed, and begin running jobs. That would be all that needed to be said, except that AppleTalk won't allow you to run in the interactive mode without some help.

The AppleTalk connection, by itself, only allows you to prepare PostScript jobs and send them, as batch files, to a LaserWriter using any one of several available downloader programs. You can do the exercises in this book using this method. In fact, if you are on an AppleTalk network with other users, you will probably have to do this. If you are going to do the exercises in here that way, there is software available that provides semi-interactive access to the LaserWriter. Typical examples of such software are Adobe Font Downloader 4.0, LaserWriter Utility 7.1, FileChute 1.0, and many others. If you do use a download program that allows you to load both fonts and PostScript programs, be sure that you use the program download and not the font download. These packages will send your batch job to a LaserWriter over the AppleTalk network and return any errors or output information that belongs to your job back to your terminal. If you are running alone on the network, this is almost the same as interactive use; if more than one person is running, you will have to be careful about mixing up your jobs with other people's.

There is one software package on the market that allows full interactive access to your LaserWriter (or any other PostScript printer) over the AppleTalk network. This is the Lasertalk product, originally created by Emerald City Software and now sold by Adobe Systems. If you have Appletalk, you can save yourself a substantial amount of work and worry by purchasing this software. It will provide immediate interactive access as described in Chapter 1.

Lasertalk provides all the communications and editing facilities that you will want for creation and maintenance of PostScript programs. In fact, Lasertalk provides a complete PostScript programming environment, not just interactive access. This includes an editor with a number of features, a dictionary browser, on-line access to the operator definitions, and a unique, Preview mode that allows you to see what is on the page before printing (thus eliminating the need for frequent use of the **copypage** operator). However, unfortunately, the Preview mode does not work on many of the newer PostScript devices; in particular, it does not work on any image-setter (such as a Linotronic) or on any Level 2 device.

Lasertalk provides the best environment both for learning PostScript and for using it. It is completely compatible with all the exercises and examples in this book. In fact, it comes with the exercises and examples already keyed into an Examples folder.

Configuration: Hardware

Hardware in this configuration is as follows:

Apple Macintosh SE

> 3.5 inch internal disk
>
> 20 Megabyte internal hard disk
>
> 2.5 Megabyte memory
>
> cable M0150 (ImageWriter cable)

Apple LaserWriter IINT

> 2 Megabytes RAM

The cable connects the modem port on the back of the Macintosh to the LaserWriter. The LaserWriter mode switch (or switches if you are using an NTX) are set for 9600 baud on the RS-232 port. Alternatively, as discussed above, you can use a standard AppleTalk connection and Lasertalk to provide interactive access.

Configuration: Software

For serial communications, as in the case of the IBM-PC, you will need two kinds of software to run your PostScript jobs interactively: a communications package and an editor. Any reasonable editor will do; just remember to save your output as Text and not in the word-processor's native format. This can usually be done by making a selection in the Save dialog box.

The software I used to test the programs in this book consisted of the Mac-Terminal communications program and Microsoft Word 4.0 for text editing. Communications are set up with the following sequence of steps:

1. Start up MacTerminal by double-clicking on the MacTerminal icon. This opens a session window.

2. Set the communications parameters in Terminal, Compatibility, and File Transfer as follows:

    > Terminal: Terminal = VT100, Mode = ANSI, Cursor Shape = underline, Character Set = US, LineWidth = 80 column. Select parameters: On-Line, Auto Repeat, Auto Wraparound.

    > Compatibility: Baud Rate = 9600, Bits per Character = 8 bits, Parity = none, Handshake = none, connection = another computer, connection port = modem.

    > File Transfer: Transfer Method = text.

Now you are in communication with the LaserWriter and can begin your interactive PostScript session as described in Chapter 1.

LASERWRITER COMMANDS

There are a small series of commands that you can use to control the LaserWriter while you are in the interactive mode over a serial port. These commands fall into two groups. First are communication functions that are available from the keyboard; the second are some limited editing functions that can be used while you are in the interactive mode. Most of these functions are invoked with the Control key (on the IBM) or the Command key (on the Macintosh) along with the character shown in the tables below. For convenience, IBM

Control and Macintosh Command keys are all designated Ctrl in the tables. You should understand that this means to hold down the Control (or the Command) key and press the designated letter.

Communication Functions

KEY	FUNCTION
Ctrl-C	interrupt; stops the execution of a PostScript program
Ctrl-D	end-of-file
Ctrl-S	stop output (XOFF)
Ctrl-Q	start output (XON)
Ctrl-T	status query; causes the interpreter to respond with a one-line status message
Return	end-of-line; equivalent to a PostScript newline
Linefeed	end-of-line; equivalent to the PostScript newline. When both a Return and Linefeed are received in succession, only one newline is executed.

Editing Functions

KEY	FUNCTION
Ctrl-H	backs up and erases one character
Ctrl-U	erases the current line
Ctrl-R	redisplays the current line
Ctrl-C	aborts the statement and starts over
Backspace	backs up and erases one character
Delete	deletes one character

D

Bibliography

T HIS APPENDIX LISTS BOOKS ON
a variety of topics related, more or less directly, to the subjects of PostScript
and PostScript programming. It also lists some useful PostScript utility programs. The list is neither complete nor authoritative. It represents my own
personal prejudices regarding useful, current, and currently available, materials. There may well be other, perhaps better books on some of these topics;
I just haven't met them.

PostScript References

Adobe Systems. *PostScript Language Reference Manual, Second
Edition*. Reading, MA: Addison-Wesley, 1990. Besides providing a
complete reference for and definition of the PostScript language
itself, this book contains the complete documentation for the 3.0
Structuring Conventions. It also describes using and handling of EPS
files in two of its several appendices.

Adobe Systems and Glenn C. Reid. *PostScript Language Program
Design*. Reading, MA: Addison-Wesley, 1988. This book covers a
series of advanced topics in design and implementation of PostScript
language programs.

Apple Computer. *Apple LaserWriter Reference*. Reading, MA:
Addison-Wesley, 1988. This book provides additional information
on how to maintain and operate the Apple LaserWriter family of
printers. It does not cover the IIf and IIg (Level 2) printers, but much
of its information is still useful even for these printers if you are programming in PostScript. In particular, it includes a thorough discussion of how to set up and use the interactive mode.

Holzgang, David A. *Programming the LaserWriter*. Reading MA:
Addison-Wesley, 1991. This book covers access and use of the
LaserWriter family of printers from within a Macintosh application. If
you are using a Macintosh, it provides additional information about
Toolbox calls and Printing Manager functions that are important to
know when you are programming in PostScript.

Roth, Steven F. *Real World PostScript*. Reading MA: Addison-Wesley,
1988. This is a good collection of articles on advanced PostScript

programming. As the title suggests, the focus of the book is on real-world issues and programming solutions. With the introduction of Level 2, some of the book covering color and halftones is now outdated, but the remainder is still an excellent source of programming techniques and tips.

There are usually additional reference materials, in the form of a *Language Supplement*, available from Adobe Systems regarding almost every kind of PostScript-equipped output device. In addition there are a variety of technical notes and specifications on a wide range of issues, such as composite fonts, Level 2 compatibility strategies, and so on. For a complete, current list, write to

Adobe Systems Incorporated
PostScript Developer Support Group
1585 Charleston Road
Mountain View, CA 94039
(415) 961-4400

Computer Graphics

Although you do not need to know the mathematical and theoretical foundations of PostScript to use the language features effectively, it certainly can't hurt; and it can be of considerable value as you begin to expand your graphics repertoire. The following books give you a good background in computer graphics theory.

Foley, J. D. and A. Van Dam. *Fundamentals of Interactive Computer Graphics*. Reading MA: Addison-Wesley, 1983. A comprehensive introduction to computer graphics, including the mathematics of Bezier cubic functions, which are used to determine curves in the PostScript language.

Newman W. M., and R. F. Sproull. *Principles of Interactive Computer Graphics, 2nd Edition*. New York: McGraw-Hill, 1979. Provides coverage of two-dimensional transformations and raster graphics. The transformation discussions are especially useful for advanced work with the PostScript transformation matrices.

PostScript Utilities

If you are going to do any significant amount of PostScript programming, or even if you are only running a lot of PostScript files, you will find that improving the standard error reporting on your output device provides a lot of help. The PinPoint Error Reporter is an inexpensive commercial error-reporting package that provides a complete description of any error, where it happened in your program, and the state of the printer when the error occured. In my admittedly biased view (since I wrote it) it is the best commercial package for this function. It is available, along with other PostScript utilites and resources—including all the programs in this book on disk in either IBM or Macintosh format—from

Cheshire Group
321 South Main Street, Suite 36
Sebastopol, CA 95472
(707) 887-7510

In addition, if you are working in the Macintosh environment, you should seriously consider purchasing the Lasertalk PostScript programming environment from Adobe Systems. Contact Adobe at the address above for complete pricing and availablity information.

INDEX

Selections from
The SYBEX Library

This engaging, hands-on treatment is for the desktop publisher learning and using the Windows edition of Ventura. It covers everything from working with the Windows interface, to designing and printing sophisticated publications using Ventura's most advanced features. Understand and work with frames, graphics, fonts, tables and columns, and much more.

Mastering Ventura 3.0 Gem Edition
Matthew Holtz
650pp, Ref. 703-7

The complete hands-on guide to desktop publishing with Xerox Ventura Publisher—now in an up-to-date new edition featuring Ventura version 3.0, with the GEM windowing environment. Tutorials cover every aspect of the software, with examples ranging from correspondence and press releases, to newsletters, technical documents, and more.

Understanding Desktop Publishing
Robert W. Harris
300pp. Ref. 789-4

At last, a practical design handbook, written especially for PC users who are not design professionals, but who do have desktop publishing duties. How can publications be made attractive, understandable, persuasive, and memorable? Topics include type, graphics, and page design; technical and physiological aspects of creating and conveying a message.

Understanding PFS: First Publisher
Gerry Litton
463pp. Ref. 712-6

This new edition of the popular guide to First Publisher covers software features in a practical introduction to desktop publishing. Topics include text-handling, working with graphics, effective page design, and optimizing print quality. With examples of flyers, brochures, newsletters, and more.

Understanding PostScript Programming (Second Edition)
David A. Holzgang
472pp. Ref. 566-2

In-depth treatment of PostScript for programmers and advanced users working on custom desktop publishing tasks. Hands-on development of programs for font creation, integrating graphics, printer implementations and more.

Up & Running with CorelDRAW 2
Len Gilbert
140pp; Ref. 887-4

Learn CorelDRAW 2 in record time. This 20-step tutorial is perfect for computer-literate users who are new to CorelDRAW or upgrading from an earlier version. Each concise step takes no more than 15 minutes to an hour to complete, and provides needed skills without unnecessary detail.

Up & Running with PageMaker 4 on the PC
Marvin Bryan
140pp. Ref. 781-9

An overview of PageMaker 4.0 in just 20 steps. Perfect for evaluating the software before purchase—or for newcomers who are impatient to get to work. Topics include installation, adding typefaces, text and drawing tools, graphics, reusing layouts, using layers, working in color, printing, and more.

Your HP LaserJet Handbook
Alan R. Neibauer
564pp. Ref. 618-9

Get the most from your printer with this step-by-step instruction book for using LaserJet text and graphics features such as cartridge and soft fonts, type selection, memory and processor enhancements, PCL programming, and PostScript solutions. This hands-on guide provides specific instructions for working with a variety of software.

DESKTOP PRESENTATION

Harvard Graphics Instant Reference
Gerald E. Jones

154pp. Ref. 726-6

This handy reference is a quick, non-technical answer manual to questions about Harvard's onscreen menus and help displays. Provides specific information on each of the program's major features, including Draw Partner. A must for business professionals and graphic artists who create charts and graphs for presentation.

Harvard Graphics 3 Instant Reference (Second Edition)
Gerald E. Jones

200pp; ref. 871-8

This handy, compact volume is the single complete source for quick answers on all of Harvard's menu options and features. It's small enough to keep on hand while you work—and fast enough to let you keep working while you look up concise explanations and exact instructions for using Harvard commands.

Mastering Animator
Mitch Gould

300pp. Ref.688-X

A hands-on guide to creating dynamic multimedia presentations. From simple animation to Hollywood-style special effects, from planning a presentation to bringing it all to life—it's all you need to know, in straightforward, easy-to-follow terms.

Mastering Harvard Graphics (Second Edition)
Glenn H. Larsen

375pp, Ref. 673-1

"The clearest course to begin mastering Harvard Graphics," according to *Computer Currents*. Readers master essential principles of effective graphic communi-

cation, as they follow step-by-step instructions to create dozens of charts and graphs; automate and customize the charting process; create slide shows, and more.

Mastering Harvard Graphics 3
Glenn Larsen
with Kristopher Larsen

525pp; Ref. 870-X

This highly praised hands-on guide uses engaging tutorials and colorful examples to show exactly how to create effective charts, graphs, presentations, and slide shows. Readers create virtually every kind of chart, including many not covered in Harvard's manual. Companion diskette features over $40 worth of clipart—absolutely free.

Teach Yourself Harvard Graphics 3
Jeff Woodward

450pp; Ref. 801-7

A graphical introduction to the hottest-selling presentation graphics program! This illustrated guide leads newcomers through the exact steps needed to create all kinds of effective charts and graphs. There are no surprises: what you see in the book is what you will see on your screen.

Up & Running with Harvard Graphics
Rebecca Bridges Altman

148pp. Ref. 736-3

Desktop presentation in 20 steps—the perfect way to evaluate Harvard Graphics for purchase, or to get a fast, hands-on overview of the software's capabilities. The book's 20 concise lessons are time-coded (each takes no more than an hour to complete), and cover everything from installation and startup, to creating specific types of charts, graphs, and slide shows.

Up & Running with Harvard Graphics 3
Rebecca Bridges Altman

140pp; Ref. 884-X

Come up to speed with Harvard Graphics 3—fast. If you're a computer-literate user who needs to start producing professional-looking presentation graphics now, this book is for you. In only 20 lessons (each taking just 15 minutes to an hour), you can cover all the essentials of this perennially popular progam.

OPERATING SYSTEMS

The ABC's of DOS 4
Alan R. Miller
275pp. Ref. 583-2

This step-by-step introduction to using DOS 4 is written especially for beginners. Filled with simple examples, *The ABC's of DOS 4* covers the basics of hardware, software, disks, the system editor EDLIN, DOS commands, and more.

The ABC's of DOS 5
Alan Miller
267pp. Ref. 770-3

This straightforward guide will haven even first-time computer users working comfortably with DOS 5 in no time. Step-by-step lessons lead users from switching on the PC, through exploring the DOS Shell, working with directories and files, using essential commands, customizing the system, and trouble shooting. Includes a tear-out quick reference card and function key template.

ABC's of MS-DOS (Second Edition)
Alan R. Miller
233pp. Ref. 493-3

This handy guide to MS-DOS is all many PC users need to manage their computer files, organize floppy and hard disks, use EDLIN, and keep their computers organized. Additional information is given about utilities like Sidekick, and there is a DOS command and program summary. The second edition is fully updated for Version 3.3.

The ABC's of SCO UNIX
Tom Cuthbertson
263pp. Re. 715-0

A guide especially for beginners who want to get to work fast. Includes hands-on tutorials on logging in and out; creating and editing files; using electronic mail; organizing files into directories; printing; text formatting; and more.

The ABC's of Windows 3.0
Kris Jamsa
327pp. Ref. 760-6

A user-friendly introduction to the essentials of Windows 3.0. Presented in 64 short lessons. Beginners start with lesson one, while more advanced readers can skip ahead. Learn to use File Manager, the accessory programs, customization features, Program Manager, and more.

DESQview Instant Reference
Paul J. Perry
175pp. Ref. 809-2

This complete quick-reference command guide covers version 2.3 and DESQview 386, as well as QEMM (for managing expanded memory) and Manifest Memory Analyzer. Concise, alphabetized entries provide exact syntax, options, usage, and brief examples for every command. A handy source for on-the-job reminders and tips.

DOS 3.3 On-Line Advisor Version 1.1
SYBAR, Software Division of SYBEX, Inc.
Ref. 933-1

The answer to all your DOS problems. The DOS On-Line Advisor is an on-screen reference that explains over 200 DOS error messages. 2300 other citations cover all you ever needed to know about DOS. The DOS On-Line Advisor pops up on top of your working program to give you quick, easy help when you need it, and disappears when you don't. Covers thru version 3.3. Software package comes with 3½" and 5¼" disks. **System Requirements: IBM compatible with DOS**

2.0 or higher, runs with Windows 3.0, uses 90K of RAM.

DOS Instant Reference
SYBEX Prompter Series

Greg Harvey
Kay Yarborough Nelson
220pp. Ref. 477-1

A complete fingertip reference for fast, easy on-line help:command summaries, syntax, usage and error messages. Organized by function—system commands, file commands, disk management, directories, batch files, I/O, networking, programming, and more. Through Version 3.3.

DOS 5: A to Z

Gary Masters
900pp; Ref. 805-X

A personal guru for every DOS 5 user! This comprehensive, "all you need to know" guide to DOS 5 provides detailed, A-to-Z coverage of DOS 5 commands, options, error messages, and dialog boxes—with syntax, usage, and plenty of examples and tips. It also includes hundreds of informative, in-depth articles on DOS 5 terminology and concepts.

DOS 5 Instant Reference

Robert M. Thomas
200pp. Ref. 804-1

The comprehensive quick guide to DOS—all its features, commands, options, and versions—now including DOS 5, with the new graphical interface. Concise, alphabetized command entries provide exact syntax, options, usage, brief examples, and applicable version numbers. Fully cross-referenced; ideal for quick review or on-the-job reference.

The DOS 5 User's Handbook

Gary Masters
Richard Allen King
400pp. Ref. 777-0

This is the DOS 5 book for users who are already familiar with an earlier version of DOS. Part I is a quick, friendly guide to new features; topics include the graphical interface, new and enhanced commands, and much more. Part II is a complete DOS 5 quick reference, with command summaries, in-depth explanations, and examples.

Essential OS/2
(Second Edition)

Judd Robbins
445pp. Ref. 609-X

Written by an OS/2 expert, this is the guide to the powerful new resources of the OS/2 operating system standard edition 1.1 with presentation manager. Robbins introduces the standard edition, and details multitasking under OS/2, and the range of commands for installing, starting up, configuring, and running applications. For Version 1.1 Standard Edition.

Essential PC-DOS
(Second Edition)

Myril Clement Shaw
Susan Soltis Shaw
332pp. Ref. 413-5

An authoritative guide to PC-DOS, including version 3.2. Designed to make experts out of beginners, it explores everything from disk management to batch file programming. Includes an 85-page command summary. Through Version 3.2.

SYBEX

FREE BROCHURE!

Complete this form today, and we'll send you a full-color brochure of Sybex bestsellers.

Please supply the name of the Sybex book purchased.

_____

How would you rate it?

_____ Excellent   _____ Very Good   _____ Average   _____ Poor

Why did you select this particular book?

_____ Recommended to me by a friend

_____ Recommended to me by store personnel

_____ Saw an advertisement in _____

_____ Author's reputation

_____ Saw in Sybex catalog

_____ Required textbook

_____ Sybex reputation

_____ Read book review in _____

_____ In-store display

_____ Other _____

Where did you buy it?

_____ Bookstore

_____ Computer Store or Software Store

_____ Catalog (name: _____)

_____ Direct from Sybex

_____ Other: _____

Did you buy this book with your personal funds?

_____ Yes   _____ No

About how many computer books do you buy each year?

_____ 1-3   _____ 3-5   _____ 5-7   _____ 7-9   _____ 10+

About how many Sybex books do you own?

_____ 1-3   _____ 3-5   _____ 5-7   _____ 7-9   _____ 10+

Please indicate your level of experience with the software covered in this book:

_____ Beginner   _____ Intermediate   _____ Advanced

Which types of software packages do you use regularly?

_____ Accounting	_____ Databases	_____ Networks
_____ Amiga	_____ Desktop Publishing	_____ Operating Systems
_____ Apple/Mac	_____ File Utilities	_____ Spreadsheets
_____ CAD	_____ Money Management	_____ Word Processing
_____ Communications	_____ Languages	_____ Other _____ (please specify)

Which of the following best describes your job title?

_____ Administrative/Secretarial _____ President/CEO

_____ Director _____ Manager/Supervisor

_____ Engineer/Technician _____ Other _____
(please specify)

Comments on the weaknesses/strengths of this book: _____

_____

_____

_____

_____

Name _____

Street _____

City/State/Zip _____

Phone _____

PLEASE FOLD, SEAL, AND MAIL TO SYBEX

SYBEX, INC.
Department M
2021 CHALLENGER DR.
ALAMEDA, CALIFORNIA USA
94501

SYBEX

SEAL

COMMON POSTSCRIPT OPERATORS

<table>
<tr><td colspan="2" align="center">Logical Operators</td></tr>
<tr>
<td>int1 int2 int
bool1 bool2 and bool</td>
<td>logical or bitwise and.</td>
</tr>
<tr>
<td>int1 int2 int
bool1 bool2 or bool</td>
<td>logical or bitwise inclusive or.</td>
</tr>
<tr>
<td>int1 int2 int
bool1 bool2 xor bool</td>
<td>logical or bitwise exclusive or.</td>
</tr>
<tr>
<td>int int
bool not bool</td>
<td>logical or bitwise not.</td>
</tr>
<tr>
<td>— true bool</td>
<td>pushes boolean value true onto stack.</td>
</tr>
<tr>
<td>— false bool</td>
<td>pushes boolean value false onto stack.</td>
</tr>
<tr><td colspan="2" align="center">Control Operators</td></tr>
<tr>
<td>{proc} exec —</td>
<td>executes proc.</td>
</tr>
<tr>
<td>int {proc} repeat —</td>
<td>executes proc int times.</td>
</tr>
<tr>
<td>init incr lim {proc} for —</td>
<td>executes proc for values from init by steps of incr until reaching lim.</td>
</tr>
<tr>
<td>dict
array proc
string proc forall —</td>
<td>executes the procedure proc for every element of dict, array or string. For dict, forall pushes the key, then the value for each element of the dictionary; for other operands, it pushes each element from the array or string onto the stack. It then executes the procedure proc.</td>
</tr>
<tr>
<td>bool {proc} if —</td>
<td>executes proc if bool is true.</td>
</tr>
<tr>
<td>bool {proc1} {proc2}
ifelse —</td>
<td>executes proc1 if bool is true, executes proc2 otherwise.</td>
</tr>
<tr>
<td>{proc} loop —</td>
<td>executes proc an indefinite number of times.</td>
</tr>
<tr>
<td>— exit —</td>
<td>terminates active loop.</td>
</tr>
</table>